Cultures and Traditions of Wordplay and Wordplay Research

The Dynamics of Wordplay

Edited by
Esme Winter-Froemel

Editorial Board
Salvatore Attardo, Dirk Delabastita, Dirk Geeraerts, Raymond W. Gibbs,
Alain Rabatel, Monika Schmitz-Emans and Deirdre Wilson

Volume 6

Cultures and Traditions of Wordplay and Wordplay Research

Edited by
Esme Winter-Froemel and Verena Thaler

DE GRUYTER

The conference "The Dynamics of Wordplay / La dynamique du jeu de mots – Interdisciplinary perspectives / perspectives interdisciplinaires" (Universität Trier, 29 September – 1st October 2016) and the publication of the present volume were funded by the German Research Foundation (DFG) and the University of Trier.

Le colloque « The Dynamics of Wordplay / La dynamique du jeu de mots – Interdisciplinary perspectives / perspectives interdisciplinaires » (Universität Trier, 29 septembre – 1er octobre 2016) et la publication de ce volume ont été financés par la Deutsche Forschungsgemeinschaft (DFG) et l'Université de Trèves.

ISBN 978-3-11-070972-8
e-ISBN (PDF) 978-3-11-058637-4
e-ISBN (EPUB) 978-3-11-063087-9

[CC BY-NC-ND]

This work is licensed under the Creative Commons Attribution-NonCommercial-NoDerivs 4.0 License. For details go to http://creativecommons.org/licenses/by-nc-nd/4.0/.

Library of Congress Control Number: 2018955240

Bibliographic information published by the Deutsche Nationalbibliothek
The Deutsche Nationalbibliothek lists this publication in the Deutsche Nationalbibliografie; detailed bibliographic data are available on the Internet at http://dnb.dnb.de.

© 2020 Esme Winter-Froemel and Verena Thaler, published by Walter de Gruyter GmbH, Berlin/Boston
This volume is text- and page-identical with the hardback published in 2018.
Printing and binding: CPI books GmbH, Leck

www.degruyter.com

Contents

Esme Winter-Froemel, Verena Thaler and Alex Demeulenaere
The dynamics of wordplay and wordplay research —— 1

I New perspectives on the dynamics of wordplay

Raymond W. Gibbs, Jr.
Words making love together: Dynamics of metaphoric creativity —— 23

Dirk Delabastita
The dynamics of wordplay and the modern novel: A paired case study —— 47

Astrid Poier-Bernhard
Wor(l)dplay: Reflections on a writing-experience —— 75

II Approaches to wordplay and verbal humor

Salvatore Attardo
Universals in puns and humorous wordplay —— 89

Angelika Braun and Astrid Schmiedel
The phonetics of ambiguity: A study on verbal irony —— 111

Joshua T. Katz
Exercises in wile —— 137

III Traditions of wordplay in different social and cultural settings

Eline Zenner and Dirk Geeraerts
One does not simply process memes: Image macros as multimodal constructions —— 167

Gesa Schole
Wordplay as a means of post-colonial resistance —— 195

Monika Schmitz-Emans
Examples and poetics of wordplay in Han Shaogong's language-reflective novel *A Dictionary of Maqiao* —— 217

Natalia Filatkina and Claudine Moulin
Wordplay and baroque linguistic ideas —— 235

Appendix

List of contributions and abstracts —— 261

Index —— 275

List of contributors —— 279

Esme Winter-Froemel, Verena Thaler and Alex Demeulenaere
The dynamics of wordplay and wordplay research

Approaches, contexts and traditions

1 Discovering the dynamics of wordplay

Wordplay appears in a broad range of situations of communicative exchange, including spontaneous manifestations in everyday communication, strategic uses in advertising messages and argumentative texts as well as literary texts from different authors, cultures and historical periods. In spite of its ubiquity, however, wordplay also appears to be to a certain extent ephemeral: the ludic character of utterances can get lost over time as they become reused in other contexts, and in many instances, ludic language use merely functions as a momentary pause inserted into a communicative exchange that pursues different aims. Wordplay thus appears to be a complex phenomenon which is difficult to grasp, but which at the same time appears to be a highly interesting and relevant one, as it can reveal basic principles of language and communication.

In previous research on wordplay, there has been a strong focus on wordplay in specific authors (e.g. William Shakespeare, James Joyce, Raymond Queneau, see among others Kohl 1966; Mahood 1957; Delabastita 1993, 2011; Heibert 1993; Kemmner 1972) or literary domains such as nonsense literature (see among others Schöne 1951; Sewell 1952; Hildebrand 1970; Petzold 1972; Lecercle 1994; Zirker 2010a, 2010b). A particular interest can be observed in the translation of wordplay, frequently in relation to particular authors (Grassegger 1985; Heibert 1993; Rauch 1982; Delabastita 1994, 1996, 1997; Chiaro 2010a, 2010b; Vandaele 2011). Linguistic approaches have focused on the use of wordplay in particular text types, e.g. newspaper articles (see among others Hausmann 1974; Sullet-Nylander 2005, 2006, 2010; Kerbrat-Orecchioni 2011) and textual elements (e.g. headings, see Dittgen 1989), or in particular domains such as the press, advertising or the media (see among others Carstensen 1971; Vittoz-Canuto 1983; Grunig 1990; Tanaka 1999; Chovanec and Ermida 2012), and in particular contexts of use, e.g. private conversation (e.g. Priego-Valverde 2003).

In addition, previous research has aimed to provide overviews and classifications of wordplay and verbal humor (see e.g. Preisendanz and Warning 1976; Hesbois 1986; Defays 1996; Alexander 1997; Guiraud 1976; Charaudeau 2006; Blake 2010). Raskin (1985) proposed a Semantic Script Theory of Humor (SSTH), which has been expanded into the General Theory of Verbal Humor (GTVH; Attardo and Raskin 1991; see also Attardo 1994, 2001 as well as Attardo 2011 and the contributions of the issue 24(2) of *Humor – International Journal of Humor Research*).

Other works have focused on specific realizations of wordplay, e.g. puns (Culler 1988; Redfern 1985), and on further phenomena related to verbal humor, e.g. verbal irony (see among others Ruiz-Gurillo and Alvarado-Ortega 2013), figurative meaning (e.g. Gibbs and Colston 2012), allusions (Wilss 1989), verbal humor in garden paths (Dynel 2009), comic discourse (Nash 1985), functions of punning in conversation (Kotthoff 1996), or wordplay and the motivation of linguistic signs (Käge 1980; Rettig 1981; see also Partington 2009). Overviews of wordplay research and the state of the art of research on verbal humor are provided among others by Winter-Froemel (2009, 2016) and Attardo (2017).

In addition to the various approaches described above, recent research has aimed to integrate linguistic and literary perspectives as well as approaches from the point of view of rhetoric (see Rabatel 2008, 2012, 2013; Brône and Vandaele 2009; Valero-Garcés 2010), and various authors have argued for interdisciplinary approaches to wordplay, verbal humor and ambiguity (see Winter-Froemel and Zirker 2010; Bauer et al. 2010). In our view, there are indeed lessons to be learnt about language and communication (literary communication as well as everyday communication) by studying wordplay (see also Gauger 1971, 2006, 2014; Goldstein 1990; Koch, Krefeld, and Oesterreicher 1997; Goatly 2012), and this is one of the main motivations of the present volumes as well as of the book series *The Dynamics of Wordplay* in general.

This aim has already been pursued by the first two volumes in the series (Zirker and Winter-Froemel 2015, Winter-Froemel and Zirker 2015) by bringing together linguistic and literary approaches. In addition, the inherently dynamic dimension of wordplay has been put forward in the interdisciplinary project "Dynamik des Wortspiels / The Dynamics of Wordplay / La dynamique du jeu de mots" (funded by the German Research Foundation and directed by Esme Winter-Froemel since 2013). Main aspects which have been explored in this project are the relations between wordplay and language contact, wordplay and linguistic innovation, and wordplay and speaker-hearer interaction.

Phenomena of language contact can give rise to playful language use (see among others the third volume of the book series, Knospe, Onysko, and Goth 2016), and the transitions between wordplay and linguistic innovation in synchrony and diachrony provide important insights into the importance of ludicity in language and language use (see among others Arndt-Lappe et al. 2018 and Full and Lecolle, in press). The interactional dimension of wordplay represents an additional, transversal topic which is addressed in many contributions to these volumes. Another main result of the discussions in the research project was the difficulty of defining wordplay and its limits in an uncontroversial way. We thus set up a discussion forum (see pp. 9–94 in Knospe, Onysko, and Goth 2016, with contributions by Winter-Froemel, Thaler, Lecolle, Onykso and Knospe) aiming to debate the central question which is at the very heart of all analyses of wordplay: how can the phenomenon be defined and approached?

The contributions in the discussion forum were intended to foster further discussion and interdisciplinary explorations of wordplay, as launched in this book series. This was also the central aim of the conference organized in Trier from September 29, 2016 to October 1st, 2016. The topic chosen for the conference, "The Dynamics of Wordplay / La dynamique du jeu de mots – Interdisciplinary perspectives / perspectives interdisciplinaires", was motivated by recent trends in wordplay research: New approaches have been proposed to link the domain of wordplay and verbal humor to Cognitive Linguistics (see e.g. Veale 2009; Brône, Feyaerts, and Veale 2015) and (cognitive) pragmatics (see e.g. Yus 2016). On the whole, it can be observed that recent research stresses the pragmatic and interactional dimension of wordplay and verbal humor (see e.g. Kotthoff 1998; Norrick and Chiaro 2009; Dynel 2011; Charaudeau 2015; Farhat 2015), which opens up new research perspectives, e.g. on humor as a metapragmatic ability (Ruiz-Gurillo 2016) or on the relationship between humor and gender (Chiaro and Baccolini 2014). All these recent approaches point to the dynamic nature of wordplay, which is not only a phenomenon to be described on the basis of its structural features, but also to be analyzed as an element of social interaction and dynamic processes of linguistic and social change. We thus chose the topic of the conference in order to investigate various facets of the dynamics that become apparent in wordplay, revealing basic principles of language and communication.

The high number of international submissions confirmed the interest in and relevance of the topic. In addition to the keynote lectures delivered by Salvatore Attardo, Dirk Delabastita, Dirk Geeraerts and Eline Zenner, Raymond W. Gibbs, Catherine Kerbrat-Orecchioni, Alain Rabatel and Françoise Rubellin, the thirty-six papers selected for the conference dealt with different aspects of the theory and practice of wordplay, studying cases of wordplay from different historical periods, languages and discourse traditions. In addition, the papers brought together research perspectives from fourteen different countries, including approaches from linguistics and literary studies as well as adjacent disciplines such as cultural studies, media studies, comparative literature, theater studies, and phonetics.

Finally, the research project has sought to cooperate with a "panel of practicioners" of authors, artists, and other professional "word players" to exchange on practical perspectives and applications of wordplay. As part of the conference program, the actors Aurélie Rusterholtz and François Chaix brought to life the comedy *L'Amour maître de langue* (1718) in a stage-reading at the Theater Trier. The performance was introduced by the specialist Françoise Rubellin, who not only gave an overview of the play and its historical context, but also motivated the audience to join in and sing the chorus of the final *vaudeville*, thus becoming part of the performance. The author Yoko Tawada, who writes in Japanese and German, presented some of her texts during another – plurilingual – lecture at the theater, and Joshua T. Katz directed a workshop on didactic perspectives of wordplay based on his long teaching experience at Princeton University. Finally, in her closing statement, the author, Oplepo member and specialist on potential literature Astrid Poier-Bernhard shared her reflections on creativity and wordplay with the conference audience, stressing the links between different research perspectives and approaches and stimulating further discussion and exchange.

2 Outline of contents

The two volumes of the conference proceedings bring together a selection of twenty-five research papers presented at the conference, focusing on cultures and traditions of wordplay and wordplay research (*The Dynamics of Wordplay 6*) and on the use of wordplay in different texts and contexts, stressing the social dimension of wordplay (*The Dynamics of Wordplay 7*). In addition, the volumes also include an interview and two papers on practical perspectives and applications of wordplay.

The Dynamics of Wordplay 6 opens with a section introducing new perspectives on the analysis of wordplay and, more precisely, the dynamic aspect of wordplay. The three contributions in this section focus on the question of how the production and the description of wordplay are inherently dynamic and how this dynamicity can be integrated into a descriptive model of wordplay. In his paper "Words making love together: Dynamics of metaphoric creativity", Raymond W. Gibbs outlines a linguistic and psychological model of dynamic wordplay, focusing on metaphorical language use as one of the forms of language use in which people engage in wordplay. He argues that creative metaphor use cannot be reduced to conscious, deliberate acts that are intended to be seen as such by listeners and readers. Creative metaphor use rather emerges from an interaction of social, cognitive and linguistic forces that do not easily fall into a simple division between the conscious and unconscious minds. The paper describes different studies that offer support for such an expanded view of metaphoric creativity and illustrates it with various examples. More generally, the paper aims to provide a more comprehensive, psychologically realistic way of what people are doing when they engage in wordplay.

From a different perspective, Dirk Delabastita's contribution "The dynamics of wordplay and the modern novel: A paired case study" also argues for a dynamic approach to wordplay. Delabastita's argumentation is based on a multi-dimensional definition of wordplay and illustrates the dynamic nature of wordplay by means of an analysis of two recent English-language novels, *A Concise Chinese-English Dictionary for Lovers* (2007) by Xiaolu Guo and *My Sister, My Love* (2008) by Joyce Carol Oates. The former may be described as a "global novel" which turns out to suggest different wordplay readings to different readerships, depending on their cultural background and multilingual literacies. The latter gives an example of a multi-voiced postmodern narrative style in which wordplay is characterized by an elusiveness of a very special kind. Both examples thus illustrate the need for a dynamic approach to wordplay in the analysis of literary texts which can be extended to other forms of communication.

From yet another perspective, Astrid Poier-Bernhard in her essay "Wor(l)d-play: Reflections on a writing-experience" describes her personal writing-experience as a literary author and argues for an integral (or aesthetic) approach to wordplay in the sense that not only the techniques but also the experience of wordplay must be taken into consideration. In this context, she argues that (active) wordplay is always connected with (passive) *worldplay* or *play which happens*. Wordplay lets us experience the playfulness of language, the mind and the world all at once and often provokes a *pleasure of the text* or even an instant of *jouissance* (R. Barthes). At the same time, the aesthetic qualities of wordplay can be described with the help of the values suggested by Italo Calvino in his *Lezioni americane* (lightness, exactitude, rapidity, visibility, multiplicity).

The following section continues these reflections by presenting general thoughts and ideas about wordplay and verbal humor and different ways to approach these phenomena. Salvatore Attardo's paper "Universals in puns and humorous wordplay" is dedicated to an analysis of humorous wordplay and punning as universal phenomena. Building on previous research on puns in different languages, he identifies basic phonological and semantic mechanisms of punning. Moreover, it is argued that different kinds of evidence clearly show that naive speakers hold a Cratylistic view of language, which is at the very heart of the universal mechanism of incongruity resolution in puns.

The paper by Angelika Braun and Astrid Schmiedel "The phonetics of ambiguity: A study on verbal irony", on the other hand, focuses on the phonetic dimension of a special kind of language use where the meaning of the utterance is somehow dissociated from its literal wording. In this sense, verbal irony also exhibits a potential ambiguity, and the basic research question of how the disambiguation of the utterances takes place can be linked to other phenomena of ambiguity and verbal humor. By presenting phonetic analyses of single-word utterances in sincere and ironic settings, the authors investigate how the irony is signaled by the speakers and on what cues its detection by the hearers is based. A basic result which emerges from their paper are the overall recognition rates of about 70 %. At the same time, the authors observe a strong variation between sarcasm and kind irony, which thus need to be distinguished as two basically different subtypes of verbal irony.

With "Exercises in wile", Joshua T. Katz presents another general approach to wordplay: Based on his extensive experience of teaching a freshman seminar on the history and practice of wordplay at Princeton University, the author argues that wordplay can be used in a very seminal way in academic teaching to introduce students to the subject of linguistics. The paper, which was presented in a workshop format at the conference, gives an impression of this interactive potential of wordplay and language play as a means to foster metalinguistic awareness and reflection on orthographic, phonetic and lexical peculiarities of English (and other languages).

The papers in the third section of *The Dynamics of Wordplay 6* then turn to specific traditions of wordplay in different social and cultural settings, showing the social and cultural impact on the forms and functions of wordplay as well as on the ways in which wordplay is conceived in different historical settings and cultures. The four papers follow an inverse chronological order, which corresponds to different aspects of traditions and different degrees of traditionality and conventionalization: The first paper focuses on the rise of a specific subtype of Internet meme involving verbal humor as a new tradition shared by communities of Internet users. The second paper focuses on the role of wordplay in post-colonial spaces in expressing a new, hybrid identity. The third paper shows that new and old traditions are strongly intertwined in the Chinese novel *A Dictionary of Maqiao*, which reuses and reinterprets the Western literary tradition of texts structured as a dictionary or a lexicon in a new way. Finally, the fourth paper presents a historical perspective on wordplay in German baroque.

In "One does not simply process memes: Image macros as multimodal constructions", Eline Zenner and Dirk Geeraerts present a Cognitive Linguistic analysis of the highly popular subgenre of Internet memes that consist of text superimposed on an image. Having observed the importance of variation and modification and the difficulty of providing a straightforward definition of the new tradition of image macros, they characterize them as prototypically structured multimodal constructions sharing basic features with jokes and traditional wordplay. In addition, as many image macros also involve instances of "classic" wordplay, the question arises of what the basic processing difficulties are that can be involved in decoding the image macros. To describe the varying degrees of typicality, the authors propose four dimensions along which the image macros vary – multimodality, multilingualism, intra-genre intertextuality and external referencing included in the construction. This opens up perspectives for further research on the mechanisms involved in the production and processing of image macros along these basic dimensions.

Gesa Schole's paper "Wordplay as a means of post-colonial resistance" describes the use of wordplay in a post-colonial context. More specifically, it analyzes the language use of the Mozambican writer Mia Couto in one of his novels and deals with the question of how wordplay phenomena can act as a means of post-colonial resistance in this context. The use of colloquial Mozambican Portuguese and thus the deliberate deviation from European Portuguese is described as wordplay in a wider sense. It is analyzed as a form of linguistic self-mimicry as opposed to the earlier colonial mimicry. Furthermore, wordplay in a narrow sense is identified in the form of lexical blends which may be seen as metaphors for the hybrid character of post-colonial spaces. We are thus dealing with a specific use of wordplay in the context of post-colonial literature.

The next paper by Monika Schmitz-Emans is dedicated to an analysis of "Examples and poetics of wordplay in Han Shaogong's language-reflective novel *A Dictionary of Maqiao*". The Western tradition of literary texts structured as dictionaries can be traced back to authors such as Rabener and Lichtenberg, followed by other satirical "dictionaries" by rationalist writers, by the literary and artistic works of the surrealists, and finally by the lexicographic novel as a specific novel genre emerging around 1970. Schmitz-Emans then shows how the Chinese author Han Shaogong takes up and uses this tradition. As the dictionary provides a model that points to the use of language itself, this tradition involves a self-referential dimension, and wordplay fulfils a key role within this tradition, creating a playful bridge between documentary and inventive narrative and in this way permitting the expression of political criticism.

The final paper of *The Dynamics of Wordplay 6*, "Wordplay and baroque linguistic ideas" by Natalia Filatkina and Claudine Moulin, takes a historical perspective on traditions of wordplay. It studies wordplay in Early Modern language philosophy, focusing more specifically on one of the language theorists of

17th century Germany, Georg Philipp Harsdörffer (1607–1658). The paper analyzes two of Harsdörffer's works, namely the eight-volume series *Frauenzimmer Gesprächspiele* (1643–1649) and the three-volume scientific work *Delitiae Mathematicae et Physicae* (1651–1653). It describes various subtypes of wordplay with letters and argues that in the context of baroque linguistic ideas wordplay should be defined in a broader sense. They show that wordplay as it is conceived by Harsdörffer is deeply rooted in the concept of language peculiar to European baroque culture. The latter provides a conceptual background not only for theoretical reflection, poetry, education and standards of knowledge, but also for the role and functions of wordplay.

Taken together, the papers collected in the first volume of the conference proceedings thus combine different approaches to wordplay and its dynamics and present different perspectives on universal and historical aspects of wordplay. These reflections are complemented by the papers in the second volume of the proceedings, where different aspects of the social dimension of wordplay, depending on its use in specific texts and contexts, are explored. The first section of the volume focuses on the evaluation and the success of wordplay in different contexts of use, including both everyday language and literary texts.

In her paper "Heurs et malheurs du jeu de mots", Catherine Kerbrat-Orecchioni focuses on wordplay in the narrow sense, defined as a conscious and deliberate production of a *double sens* and thus simultaneously involving the levels of signifier and signified. The author then takes up the challenge of classifying wordplays as "good" or "bad", and proposes three groups of linguistic criteria that are relevant for their evaluation: formal criteria permit us to evaluate different degrees of complexity (paronomasia *in praesentia*, antanaclasis, paronomasia *in absentia*, syllepsis), semantic criteria account for different degrees of motivatedness, and pragmatic criteria provide additional conditions for the success of a particular wordplay (comprehensibility, acceptability, adaptation to the genre). In spite of these criteria being well-defined and straightforwardly analyzable, however, the specific effect of a particular case of wordplay will remain highly unpredictable.

The following paper by Alain Rabatel, "À quelles conditions les lapsus clavis sont-ils des jeux de mots?", analyzes cases of lapsus realized in electronic communication / writing, assuming that in certain circumstances, these unintentional phenomena can be reinterpreted as puns. After distinguishing different subtypes of lapsus and other kinds of errors and mistakes, the author analyzes various cases of lapsus along with the morphological and phonological deviations they exhibit, the semantic criteria which indicate a possible interpretation of the lapsus, and enunciative and interactional criteria, the latter being of key importance for deciding on the communicative value and success of the lapsus. Moreover, it is argued that the conditions of success are co-constructed by the communication partners and that the conceptual conflict on which the lapsus is based can be analyzed in terms of conflicting points of view.

Jean-François Sablayrolles, in "Des innovations lexicales ludiques dans des situations d'énonciation marginales ou spécifiques", focuses on instances of playful innovations which are characterized as taking place in marginal contexts of use. In the specific situation in which the innovations are used, these innovations can serve to amuse the hearers and to create a favorable attitude towards the speaker. Among the forms of lexical innovation analyzed are incorrect flectional forms, portmanteau words and words parodying scientific language use. Another context commented on is first language acquisition, when it can equally be observed that children take pleasure in producing paronyms, thereby exploring the ludic dimension of language.

Finally, the paper by Ilias Yocaris, "'En trou si beau adultère est béni': poétique du jeu de mots dans *Histoire* de Claude Simon", takes as its starting-point Claude Simon's observed predilection for wordplay to argue that wordplay is the most appropriate stylistic device in Simon's poetics which claims to be purely formal. Several analyses of puns in the novel *Histoire* show that the puns form part of a complex relational system, serving a triple textual purpose: they densify the text (organizational purpose), they increase the investigative potential of "ordinary language" (referential purpose), and they draw the reader's attention to the materiality of the text (metadiscursive purpose).

The contributions of the second section adopt a more specific perspective and focus on the social dimension of wordplay in particular historical and social contexts of use. In her paper "Pouvoir du jeu de mots. Dominer par la parole en contexte d'inégalité sociale", Karine Abiven is concerned with the use of wordplay in unequal interactions in French court society of the 17th and 18th centuries. Based on courtesy books, collections of brief forms and memoirs, it is argued that wordplay, which is assimilated to the *bon mot*, functions as a social regulator, as it allows the speaker to save face even in situations of social inferiority, as a weapon of defence or a way to circumvent social domination, allowing the speaker to convey implicit meanings while maintaining the requirements of *decorum*. At the same time, precisely because of its inherently ambiguous and surprising character, the repartee is difficult to refute or reply to. In this way, wordplay exhibits the power to circumvent social domination.

The following contribution by Catherine Ruchon, "Le jeu de mots dans les discours sur le deuil: un jeu discursif offensif", switches to current contexts where the use of wordplay may at first sight appear to be surprising: grief discourse of parents who have lost an unborn child. Yet based on a corpus of works written by bereaved parents, the names of associations and texts provided on their websites, it is shown that wordplay can fulfill an important function in the expression of pain, permitting the parents to circumvent taboos surrounding the expression of grief and pain. The wordplays examined exhibit "classical" techniques such as homophony, paronymy and wordplay on phrasemes. Moreover, the wordplays are linked to Freud's concepts of economy and condensation, as developed in his theory of the dream and then applied to verbal humor.

Another approach to the social dimension of wordplay and to further functions beyond amusing the hearer or reader is offered by Michelle Lecolle's contribution "Enjeu du collectif – noms collectifs en jeux". The paper examines utterances which play with the notions of collectivity and plurality by exploiting the morphosyntactic, semantic and interpretative potential of the linguistic material (e.g. *portrait de groupe avec individus, l'innombrable regard de la salle*). Based on her analyses of examples taken from the French press, and additionally literary and advertising texts, the author argues that wordplay is not necessarily humorous, but can also be characterized by the intellectual pleasure it provides.

The social significance of wordplay is also apparent in the communicative setting treated in Lisa Roques' contribution "Jeux de banquet: mots de poète, mots de stratège". Her analysis is based on the *Epidèmiai* by Ion of Chios, which describe a *symposion* taking place at the house of Hermesilaos and assembling the social, political and intellectual elite of Athens in the fifth century B.C. Examining various examples of Sophocles' use of *paidia* – jokes and puns –, Roques shows that they not only aim to amuse the assembled company, but also serve to make fun of the adversary and attack the strategos Pericles by giving his words a malicious interpretation. Tying in with the contribution by Karine Abiven, this paper thus also points to uses of wordplay as a weapon in socially conflictive contexts.

The first two sections of the volume are followed by an interlude in the form of an interview with Aurélie Rusterholtz and François Chaix. The actors comment on their approach to wordplay and verbal humor in their professional lives in general as well as on their preparation and performance of the reading of the French comedy *L'Amour maître de langue* (1718), which was included in the program of the Trier conference. They talk about specific challenges that need to be met and dealt with when performing the plays, but also stress the overall accessibility of the verbal humor of 17th and 18th century comedies for different audiences.

The contributions in the following third section are dedicated to the use of wordplay in particular authors, literary trends, genres and text types, thus bringing together linguistic and literary perspectives. More specifically, the first two papers focus on French 20th century literary authors, including dramatic (Eugène Ionesco, Jean Tardieu) and narrative texts (Boris Vian). The perspectives provided on the importance of wordplay in these literary contexts are complemented by three linguistic contributions focusing on the role and use of wordplay in newspaper headings, advertising and domain names.

In her contribution "Le jeu de mots dans la dramaturgie d'avant-garde des années 1950", Jiaying Li starts by examining the use of wordplay in comedies in the Aristotelian tradition, where it serves to reinforce illusionist effects. She shows that the avant-garde theatre of the 1950s introduces a fundamentally different value of wordplay which is no longer bound to the requirement of *verisimilitude* and serving the connivance between the author and the audience. Instead, wordplay gains a certain freedom, which is, however, exploited differently by Ionesco and Tardieu, although both authors share the ideal of an abstract theatre. While Ionesco stresses the eventual failure of communication with an anarchic spirit of joking, Tardieu puts forward the musical and aesthetic potential of language, respecting the principle of entertainment. Together both authors illustrate the key role of wordplay in the renewal of dramatic language which is a central preoccupation of post-war authors.

The following paper "La dynamique de la syllepse dans la construction fictionnelle chez Boris Vian" by Cécile Pajona pursues these reflections by analyzing another French post-war author, Boris Vian. Pajona's paper is concerned with syllepsis and the literary effects of this figure of speech in his novels, and more specifically, with the role of syllepsis in the construction of a particular fictional world. After commenting on the relationship of syllepsis to wordplay and the delimitation between syllepsis and puns, Pajona shows that this figure operates a deidiomatization and thus plays a key role in the deconstruction of linguistic norms. Finally, the paper analyzes syllepsis from a pragmatic perspective and argues that syllepsis can be regarded as a privileged fictionalization tool aiming to create a bond with the reader, convincing him / her to adhere to the new norms presented.

The recipient-oriented function of wordplay also becomes very clear in Françoise Sullet-Nylander's paper on "Jeux de mots à la Une d'hier et d'aujourd'hui: dynamique et diversité d'un genre", where the use of wordplay in French newspaper headlines is analyzed. The author first presents the results of various previous studies she conducted on this topic, focusing on the headlines taken alone as autonomous texts, on their relationship with the following newspaper article, and on their intertextual or interdiscursive relationship with other utterances. In a next step, Sullet-Nylander presents the results of a survey on 100 newspaper front pages (ranging from 1631 to 2012) collected by Bourseiller, and a second corpus of 372 headlines of the daily newspaper *Libération* (1972–2015), which are analyzed with respect to the importance of cultural references, phraseological expressions, proper names and paradoxical utterances. Whereas wordplay is shown to play only a minor role in the first corpus, which can be explained by the selection criteria put forward by Bourseiller, the second corpus reveals that over the last 40 years wordplay has been a basic feature of newspaper headlines.

Another domain where the importance of wordplay is generally recognized is advertising. This issue is addressed by Giovanni Tallarico's paper "Créativité lexicale et jeux de mots dans les messages publicitaires: formes et fonctions", which aims to determine basic forms and functions of wordplay in French advertising based on a corpus of the weekly *À nous Paris* (2015–2016). Main categories of wordplay identified by Tallarico are cases of wordplay exploiting language itself (alliteration, onomatopoiea), sound-based puns (homophony, paronymy), semantically based puns (polysemy, antonymy) and wordplay involving allusion (modification of fixed expressions). Tallarico shows that the third category – puns on meaning – accounts for about half of the cases analyzed, whereas neological creations play only a marginal role. Moreover, the author argues that in spite of the important role of the visual dimension in the advertisements, slogans are still a key element. Wordplay appears to be particularly apt in this context, as it is also characterized by concision, originality and efficiency. The originality and creativity of slogans can be seen in lexical blending and playful modifications of phrasemes, which fulfill the function of capturing attention and facilitating the memorization of the slogans. Further functions identified by Tallarico are the creation of effects of complicity and the aim of disguising the commercial dimension of the utterances.

The function of wordplay as an attention-grabbing device and a means of enhancing the memorization of the utterance is also clearly manifest in domain names, as studied by Peter Handler in his contribution "Les noms de domaine – une nouvelle source de créativité langagière". Adopting a broad perspective on wordplay, the author demonstrates the frequent use of various creative techniques in the choice of domain names or web addresses. These techniques include blends, phonetic spelling and phonetic deformation, paronymy, double meanings and permutations. Constraints of technical standardization define a certain morphology of domain names and thus impose certain limits, but also foster additional ways of playing with domain name extensions, which can be reinterpreted (e.g. *.tv* and *.fm*) and / or integrated into other terms or phrases (e.g.

superf.lu, *find.me*). This latter tendency is particularly noticeable in the developments following the introduction of "New generic Top Level Domains", considerably enhancing the possibility of introducing playful domain names.

Taken together, the contributions of the third section thus reveal the key role – but also the internal variety – of wordplay in particular contexts of use. The four papers of the last section of *The Dynamics of Wordplay 7* finally investigate specific scenarios of wordplay use which exhibit an inherent dynamics, as the use of wordplay takes place at the crossroads of different languages, traditions and social discourses. Again, this section brings together approaches from linguistics and literary studies.

The first contribution by Esme Winter-Froemel and Pauline Beaucé, "Contacts linguistiques et humour verbal dans le théâtre comique français au tournant des XVIIe et XVIIIe siècles", combines a linguistic and a literary approach to investigate the importance of plurilingualism in the society of the Ancien Régime for the verbal humor in the comedies of this period. The authors start by giving an overview of the historical conditions that are relevant to the analysis of the comedies, including the most important types of language contact and languages concerned as well as the conditions under which the comedies were performed at the different theaters, and strict constraints imposed on the *théâtre de la Foire*. Then they show that plurilingualism is strongly reflected in the comedies, where different forms of contacts can be observed: code-switching, interference and lexical borrowing, but also more inventive and more radical forms of innovations based on contact phenomena, including parodies of linguistic stereotypes and the invention of new languages. The verbal humor related to language contact phenomena points to specific social values attributed to the languages involved. At the same time, the verbal humor of the comedies partly transgresses linguistic and dramaturgic conventions, thus revealing a creative orchestration of existing linguistic differences and tensions.

Elena Meteva-Rousseva's paper on "Les jeux de mots dans le *nadsat* d'Anthony Burgess – comment ses traducteurs français ont relevé le défi" provides another look at contact phenomena and the challenges imposed by linguistic differences. She studies the translation of wordplay in *nadsat*, the specific slang invented by Burgess for the young thugs of his dystopian novel *A Clockwork Orange*. As the wordplay mostly involves Russian, a language English readers are not familiar with, it can be analyzed as a case of secret wordplay. It thus appears to be fully appropriate to be used in a slang which aims to construct a group identity and which has both playful and cryptic functions. Based on these observations, the author distinguishes between two dominant functions of wordplay in Burgess' *nadsat* – a referential and a qualifying function –, and provides examples for the ways the challenges of translation have been met by the French translators of the book.

The following contribution by Anda Rădulescu, "Du calembour simple au calembour complexe dans le roman *À prendre ou à lécher* de Frédéric Dard", is also dedicated to the analysis of creative language use in a literary context. To study the use of puns in Frédéric Dard / San Antonio, the author selects one of his novels and analyzes the puns used according to the underlying mechanisms and the degree of complexity of the puns, referring to established categories of wordplay. Moreover, she shows that the puns frequently involve languages other than French (mainly English and German). A main aim of the puns identified by Rădulescu is to create a connivance between the writer and the readers.

The use of wordplay in the interaction between speaker and hearer (or between writer and reader) is likewise addressed by Hélène Favreau. In her contribution "'Allumeeez le fun': le jeu de mots comme lieu de croisement des dynamiques linguistique et socio-linguistique dans le discours publicitaire", she emphasizes the intentional deviation from established linguistic norms by the speaker in advertising discourse in order to capture the hearer's attention and make them smile or laugh. Favreau argues that wordplay in advertising, which involves the phonological, lexical and semantic level, thus reflects the dynamics of language itself. At the same time, the decoding of the messages may require a more or less active participation on the part of the hearer, who needs to reconstruct the meaning, taking into account both common cultural knowledge and intertextual allusions and suggested subtexts. Moreover, the paper is also concerned with the further evolution of the deviant items and the sociolinguistic dynamics at work, and the author shows that the advertising discourse not only reflects ongoing developments, but can also create and foster new trends in the evolution of the French language.

In spite of the linear order of presentation of the papers contained in the two volumes of the conference proceedings, the various papers present numerous different links and common interests which the reader is invited to discover. To facilitate access to all of the contributions, each volume of the conference proceedings provides an appendix listing all the contributions contained in both volumes, with additional translations of the abstracts of the other volume, and short profiles of all the contributors to the conference proceedings. In addition, both volumes have an index listing the main key words of the contributions contained in the respective volume.

3 Final remarks and acknowledgments

We would like to express our gratitude to the German Research Foundation (*Deutsche Forschungsgemeinschaft*/DFG) and the University of Trier for the financial support provided for the organization of the conference "The Dynamics of Wordplay/La dynamique du jeu de mots" and the publication of the conference proceedings in both print format and an open access version.

Our sincerest thanks go to an almost unbelievably efficient conference team – the co-organizers of the conference, Carolin Munderich and Gesa Schole, as well as the student assistants Samira Jung, Helin Baglar, Armin Rotzler, Marie Winter and Sarah Repplinger – for their extraordinary engagement and commitment. Our special thanks go to Birgit Imade for her most helpful and reliable assistance both during the conference and with all the pre- and post-conference administrative tasks. Moreover, we would like to thank Mathilde Thomas for bringing in her engagement and enthusiasm, and the University of Trier for hosting the conference and providing outstanding support for the wordplay project. Our special thanks go to Katharina Brodauf.

The conference and the publication of the proceedings were prepared with the help of the members of the network "The Dynamics of Wordplay", the Editorial Board of this book series and a committee of over 70 reviewers with the task of selecting from over 80 submissions the papers to be presented at the conference and to be published in the proceedings. Our thanks also go to those who assisted us in the preparation of the volumes, for their invaluable commitment and reliability: Sophia Fünfgeld, Samira Jung, Helin Baglar, Jeanette Hannibal and Carolin Halcour as well as Michelle Lecolle, Véronique Featherston-Lardeux, Angela Oakeshott and Martina Bross.

In addition, we would like to thank the editorial team at De Gruyter, above all Ulrike Krauß and also Gabrielle Cornefert, Christina Lembrecht, Simone Herbst and Anne Rudolph for their efficient support and assistance in preparing the volumes.

References

Alexander, Richard J. 1997. *Aspects of Verbal Humour in English* (Language in performance 13). Tübingen: Narr.
Arndt-Lappe, Sabine, Angelika Braun, Claudine Moulin & Esme Winter-Froemel (eds.). 2018. *Expanding the Lexicon* (The Dynamics of Wordplay 5). Berlin & Boston: De Gruyter.
Attardo, Salvatore. 1994. *Linguistic Theories of Humor*. New York: De Gruyter Mouton.

Attardo, Salvatore. 2001. *Humorous Texts: A Semantic and Pragmatic Analysis*. Berlin: De Gruyter Mouton.
Attardo, Salvatore. 2011. The General Theory of Verbal Humor, twenty years after. *Humor* 24(2). 123.
Attardo, Salvatore. 2017. *The Routledge Handbook of Language and Humor*. New York & London: Routledge.
Attardo, Salvatore & Victor Raskin. 1991. Script theory revis(it)ed: joke similarity and joke representation model. *Humor* 4(3). 293–347.
Bauer, Matthias, Joachim Knape, Peter Koch & Susanne Winkler. 2010. Dimensionen der Ambiguität. *Zeitschrift für Literaturwissenschaft und Linguistik* 158. 7–75.
Blake, Barry J. 2010. *Playing with Words: Humour in the English Language*. London & Oakville: Equinox Pub.
Brône, Geert, Kurt Feyaerts & Tony Veale (eds.). 2015. *Cognitive Linguistics and Humor Research* (Applications of Cognitive Linguistics 26). Berlin & Boston: De Gruyter Mouton.
Brône, Geert & Jeroen Vandaele (eds.). 2009. *Cognitive Poetics: Goals, Gains and Gaps*. Berlin: De Gruyter Mouton.
Carstensen, Broder. 1971. *Spiegel-Wörter. Spiegel-Worte. Zur Sprache eines deutschen Nachrichtenmagazins*. München: Hueber.
Charaudeau, Patrick. 2006. Des catégories pour l'humour? *Questions de communication* 10. 12–54.
Charaudeau Patrick (ed.) 2015. *Humour et engagement politique*. Limoges: Lambert-Lucas.
Chiaro, Delia (ed.) 2010a. *Translation, Humour and Literature* (Translation and humor 1). London & New York: Continuum.
Chiaro, Delia (ed.) 2010b. *Translation, Humour and the Media* (Translation and humor 2). London & New York: Continuum.
Chiaro, Delia & Raffaela Baccolini (eds). 2014. *Gender and Humor: Interdisciplinary and International Perspectives*. New York: Routledge.
Chovanec, Jan & Isabel Ermida (eds.). 2012. *Language and Humour in the Media*. Newcastle upon Tyne: Cambridge Scholars Publishing.
Culler, Jonathan (ed.). 1988. *On Puns: The Foundation of Letters*. Oxford: Oxford University Press.
Defays, Jean-Marc. 1996. *Le comique*. Paris: Seuil.
Delabastita, Dirk. 1993. *There's a Double Tongue. An Investigation Into the Translation of Shakespeare's Wordplay, with Special Reference to Hamlet*. Amsterdam: Rodopi.
Delabastita, Dirk. 1994. Focus on the Pun: Wordplay as a Special Problem in Translation Studies. *Target* 6(2). 223–243.
Delabastita, Dirk (ed.). 1996. *Wordplay and Translation*. Special Issue of *The Translator* 2(2).
Delabastita, Dirk (ed.). 1997. *Traductio: Essays on Punning and Translation*. Namur: Presses Universitaires de Namur.
Delabastita, Dirk. 2011. Wholes and holes in the study of Shakespeare's wordplay. In Mireille Ravassat & Jonathan Culpeper (eds.), *Stylistics and Shakespeare's Language: Transdisciplinary Approaches*, 139–164. London & New York: Bloomsbury Publishing.
Dittgen, Andrea Maria. 1989. *Regeln für Abweichungen. Funktionale sprachspielerische Abweichungen in Zeitungsüberschriften, Werbeschlagzeilen, Werbeslogans, Wandsprüchen und Titeln*. Frankfurt a. M.: Lang.
Dynel, Marta. 2009. *Humorous Garden-Paths: A Pragmatic-Cognitive Study*. Newcastle: Cambridge Scholars Publishing.

Dynel, Marta (ed.). 2011. *The Pragmatics of Humor across Discourse Domains*. Amsterdam: Benjamins.
Farhat, Mokhtar (ed.). 2015. *Humour et identités dans l'espace public. Nouveaux sentiers*, Gafsa: ISEAH.
Full, Bettina & Michelle Lecolle (eds.). In press. *Jeux de mots et créativité* (The Dynamics of Wordplay 4). Berlin & Boston: De Gruyter.
Gauger, Hans-Martin. 1971. *Durchsichtige Wörter. Zur Theorie der Wortbildung*. Heidelberg: Winter.
Gauger, Hans-Martin. 2006. *Das ist bei uns nicht Ouzo. Sprachwitze*. München: C. H. Beck.
Gauger, Hans-Martin. 2014. *Na also, sprach Zarathustra. Neue Sprachwitze*. München: C. H. Beck.
Gibbs, Raymond W. & Herbert L. Colston. 2012. *Interpreting Figurative Meaning*. Cambridge: Cambridge University Press.
Goatly, Andrew. 2012. *Meaning and Humour. Key Topics in Semantics and Pragmatics*. Cambridge: Cambridge University Press.
Goldstein, Laurence. 1990. The linguistic interest of verbal humor. *Humor* 3(1). 37–52.
Grassegger, Hans. 1985. *Sprachspiel und Übersetzung. Eine Studie anhand der Comic-Serie Asterix*. Tübingen: Stauffenburg.
Grunig, Blanche-Noëlle. 1990. *Les mots de la pub*. Paris: Presse du CNRS.
Guiraud, Pierre. 1976. *Les jeux de mots*. Paris: Presses Universitaires de France.
Hausmann, Franz Josef. 1974. *Studien zu einer Linguistik des Wortspiels. Das Wortspiel im «Canard enchaîné»*. Tübingen: Niemeyer.
Heibert, Frank. 1993. *Das Wortspiel als Stilmittel und seine Übersetzung am Beispiel von sieben Übersetzungen des "Ulysses"*. Tübingen: Narr.
Hesbois, Laure. 1986. *Les jeux de langage*. Ottawa: Éditions de l'Université d'Ottawa.
Hildebrandt, Rolf. 1970. *Nonsense-Aspekte der englischen Kinderliteratur*. Weinheim: Beltz.
Käge, Otmar. 1980. *Motivation. Probleme des persuasiven Sprachgebrauchs, der Metapher und des Wortspiels*. Göppingen: Kümmerle.
Kemmner, Ernst. 1972. *Sprachspiel und Stiltechnik in Raymond Queneaus Romanen*. Tübingen: Tübinger Beiträge zur Linguistik.
Kerbrat-Orecchioni, Catherine. 2011. De la connivence ludique à la connivence critique: jeux de mots et ironie dans les titres de Libération. In Maria Dolores Vivero Garcia (ed.), *Humour et crises sociales. Regards croisés France–Espagne*, 117–150. Paris: L'Harmattan.
Knospe, Sebastian, Alexander Onysko & Maik Goth (eds.). 2016. *Crossing Languages to Play with Words. Multidisciplinary Perspectives* (The Dynamics of Wordplay 3). Berlin & Boston: De Gruyter.
Koch, Peter, Thomas Krefeld & Wulf Oesterreicher. 1997. *Neues aus Sankt Eiermark. Das kleine Buch der Sprachwitze*. München: Beck.
Kohl, Norbert. 1966. *Das Wortspiel in der Shakespeareschen Komödie. Studien zur Interdependenz von verbalem und aktionalem Spiel in den frühen Komödien und den späten Stücken*. Dissertation, University of Frankfurt am Main.
Kotthoff, Helga (ed.). 1996. *Scherzkommunikation. Beiträge aus der empirischen Gesprächsforschung*. Opladen: Westdeutscher Verlag.
Kotthoff, Helga. 1998. *Spaß Verstehen. Zur Pragmatik von konversationellem Humor*. Tübingen: Niemeyer.
Lecercle, Jean-Jacques. 1994. *Philosophy of Nonsense: The Intuitions of Victorian Nonsense Literature*. London: Routledge.

Mahood, Molly M. 1957. *Shakespeare's Wordplay*. London: Methuen.
Nash, Walter. 1985. *The Language of Humor: Style and Technique in Comic Discourse*. London & New York: Longman.
Norrick, Neal R. & Delia Chiaro (eds.). 2009. *Humor in Interaction* (Pragmatics & Beyond New Series 182). Amsterdam: Benjamins.
Partington, Alan. 2009. A linguistic account of wordplay: the lexical grammar of punning. *Journal of Pragmatics* 41(9). 1794–1809.
Petzold, Dieter. 1972. *Formen und Funktionen der englischen Nonsense-Dichtung im 19. Jahrhundert*. Nürnberg: Hans Carl.
Preisendanz, Wolfgang & Rainer Warning (eds.). 1976. *Das Komische*. München: Fink.
Priego-Valverde, Béatrice. 2003. *L'humour dans la conversation familière. Description et analyse linguistique*. Paris: L'Harmattan.
Rabatel Alain. 2008. *Homo narrans. Pour une analyse énonciative et interactionnelle du récit*. Vol. 1: *Les points de vue et la logique de la narration*. Vol. 2: *Dialogisme et polyphonie dans le récit*. Limoges: Lambert-Lucas.
Rabatel, Alain. 2012. Ironie et sur-énonciation. *Vox Romanica* 71. 42–76.
Rabatel, Alain. 2013. Humour et sous-énonciation (vs ironie et sur-énonciation). *L'information grammaticale* 137. 36–42.
Raskin, Victor. 1985. *Semantic Mechanisms of Humor*. Dordrecht: D. Reidel.
Rauch, Bruno. 1982. *Sprachliche Spiele – spielerische Sprache. Sammlung, Erklärung und Vergleich der Wortspiele in vier ausgewählten Romanen von Raymond Queneau und in den entsprechenden Übersetzungen von Eugen Helmlé*. Dissertation, University of Zurich.
Redfern, Walter. 1985. *Puns*. Oxford: Blackwell.
Rettig, Wolfgang. 1981. *Sprachliche Motivation. Zeichenrelationen von Lautform und Bedeutung am Beispiel französischer Lexikoneinheiten*. Frankfurt a. M. & Bern: Lang.
Ruiz-Gurillo, Leonor (ed.). 2016. *Metapragmatics of Humor. Current Research Trends*. Amsterdam: Benjamins.
Ruiz-Gurillo, Leonor & M. Belén Alvarado-Ortega (eds.). 2013. *Irony and Humor. From Pragmatics to Discourse*. Amsterdam: Benjamins.
Schöne, Annemarie. 1951. *Untersuchungen zur englischen Nonsense Literatur unter besonderer Berücksichtigung des Limericks und seines Schöpfers Edward Lear*. Dissertation, University of Bonn.
Sewell, Elizabeth. 1952. *The Field of Nonsense*. London: Chatto & Windus.
Sullet-Nylander, Françoise. 2005. Jeux de mots et défigements à la Une de Libération (1973–2004). *Langage et Société* 112. 111–139.
Sullet-Nylander, Françoise. 2006. Citations et jeux de langage dans la presse satirique : le cas de la « Une » du *Canard Enchaîné* (2004–2005). In Gunnel Engwall (ed.), *Construction, acquisition et communication: études linguistiques de discours contemporains*, 219 –239. Stockholm: Almqvist & Wiksell International.
Sullet-Nylander, Françoise. 2010. Humour satirique et jeux de mots dans les gros titres du *Canard Enchaîné* (2009). In Anders Bengtsson & Victorine Hancock (eds.), *Humour in Language. Linguistic and Textual Aspects*, 223–243. Stockholm: Acta Universitatis Stockholmiensis.
Tanaka, Keiko. 1999. *Advertising Language: A Pragmatic Approach to Advertisements in Britain and Japan*. London: Routledge.
Valero-Garcés, Carmen. 2010. *Dimensions of Humor: Explorations in Linguistics, Literature, Cultural Studies and Translation*. Valencia: University of Valencia.

Vandaele, Jeroen. 2011. Wordplay in translation. In Yves Gambier & Luc van Doorslaer (eds.), *Handbook of Translation Studies*, Vol. 2, 180–183. Amsterdam: Benjamins.
Veale, Tony. 2009. Hiding in plain sight: figure-ground reversals in humour. In Geert Brône & Jeroen Vandaele (eds.), *Cognitive Poetics: Goals, Gains and Gaps*, 279–288. Berlin: De Gruyter Mouton.
Vittoz-Canuto, Marie-B. 1983. *Si vous avez votre jeu de mots à dire. Analyse de jeux de mots dans la presse et dans la publicité*. Paris: A.-G. Nizet.
Wilss, Wolfram. 1989. *Anspielungen. Zur Manifestation von Kreativität und Routine in der Sprachverwendung*. Tübingen: Niemeyer.
Winter-Froemel, Esme. 2009. Wortspiel. In Gert Ueding (ed.), *Historisches Wörterbuch der Rhetorik*, Vol. 9, 1429–1443. Tübingen: Niemeyer.
Winter-Froemel, Esme. 2016. Approaching wordplay. In Sebastian Knospe, Alexander Onysko & Maik Goth (eds.), *Crossing Languages to Play with Words. Multidisciplinary Perspectives* (The Dynamics of Wordplay 3), 11–46. Berlin & Boston: De Gruyter.
Winter-Froemel, Esme & Angelika Zirker. 2010. Ambiguität in der Sprecher-Hörer-Interaktion. Linguistische und literaturwissenschaftliche Perspektiven. *Zeitschrift für Literaturwissenschaft und Linguistik* 158. 76–97.
Winter-Froemel, Esme & Angelika Zirker (eds.). 2015. *Enjeux du jeu de mots: Perspectives linguistiques et littéraires* (The Dynamics of Wordplay 2). Berlin & Boston: De Gruyter.
Yus, Francisco. 2017. *Humour and Relevance* (Topics in Humor Research 4). Amsterdam: Benjamins.
Zirker, Angelika. 2010a. *Der Pilger als Kind: Spiel, Sprache und Erlösung in Lewis Carrolls Alice-Büchern*. Münster: LIT.
Zirker, Angelika. 2010b. Don't play with your food? – Edward Lear's nonsense cookery and limericks. In Marion Gymnich & Norbert Lennartz (eds.), *The Pleasures and Horrors of Eating: The Cultural History of Eating in Anglophone Literature*, 237–253. Göttingen: Bonn UP.
Zirker, Angelika & Esme Winter-Froemel (eds.). 2015. *Wordplay and Metalinguistic / Metadiscursive Reflection: Authors, Contexts, Techniques, and Meta-Reflection* (The Dynamics of Wordplay 1). Berlin & Boston: De Gruyter.

I   **New perspectives on the dynamics of wordplay**

Raymond W. Gibbs, Jr.
Words making love together: Dynamics of metaphoric creativity

Abstract: Metaphor is one form of language in which people engage in significant word play. For the most part, scholars assume that each novel metaphor arises from specific rhetorical and pragmatic goals, such as to be creative, polite, vivid, and memorable. In this way, creative metaphor use is a conscious, deliberate act that is intended to be seen as such by listeners and readers. My claim is that this view of metaphorical creativity is overly simplistic and ignores many of the factors, ranging from cultural to bodily influences, which actually shape the automatic, less conscious creation and use of metaphor. I describe various psycholinguistic, linguistic and literary studies that offer support for this expanded view of metaphoric creativity. From consideration of the interacting constraints that gives rise to novel metaphorical discourse, I outline a model of dynamic word play, more generally. This approach offers a more comprehensive, psychologically realistic view of what people really are doing when both mundane and poetic metaphors burst forth in thought and communication.

Keywords: automatic mind, Bob Dylan, Charlie Sheen, conceptual metaphor, consciousness, deliberate metaphor, Donald Trump, metaphoric creativity, mixed metaphor, Wallace Stevens, word salad

1 Introduction

Bob Dylan, recent Nobel Prize laureate in Literature (2016), splashed on to the music scene in the early 1960s with a long list of beautifully crafted, poetic songs. A documentary film, titled "Don't Look Back", released in 1967, followed Dylan as he embarked on a concert tour in the United Kingdom during 1965. At one point in the film, Dylan was smoking a cigarette with a friend on the street outside a traditional English shop. On either side of the shop's entrance were two long vertical signs. The sign on the left said:

> Animals
> & Birds
> Bought
> Or
> Sold On

> Commission
> The sign on the right said:
> We Will
> Collect
> Clip
> Bath &
> Return
> Your Dog
> ---------
> KNNI 7727
> ----------
> Cigarettes
> And
> Tobacco

Dylan stood looking at the two signs for a few seconds, and then spontaneously started to spit out a creative reading of the words in front of him, as he walked back and forth between the two signs. This is what he said:

> I want a dog that's gonna collect and clean my bath, return my cigarette, and, and give tobacco to my animals, and give my birds a commission. I want – I'm looking for somebody to sell my dog, collect my clip, buy my animal and straighten out my bird. I'm looking for a place to bathe my bird, buy my dog, collect my clip, sell me cigarettes and commission my bath.
> I'm looking for a place that's gonna collect my commission, sell my dog, burn my bird, and sell me to the cigarette. Going to bird my buy, collect my will, and bathe my commission. I'm looking for a place that's going to animal my soul, knit my return, bathe my foot and collect my dog. Commission me to sell my animals to the bird to clip and buy my bath and return me back to the cigarettes.

It is difficult to convey the utter joy that Dylan seemed to have experienced as he engaged in this on-the-spot wordplay. He laughed as he spoke, made highly gestured poses, and even danced at different moments as the words poured out. Some of what Dylan produced seemed creative in the sense of using words in new combinations, some of which convey novel (e.g., "commission my bird", "going to bird my buy"), and possibly metaphorical meanings (e.g., "sell me to the cigarette", "going to animal my soul", "knit my return"). Dylan, by the way, was already known at this time for his uncanny ability to sit down and effortlessly write a song or poem.

How do we experience Dylan's creative wordplay in this case? For example, should we characterize the product of Dylan's wordplay as emerging from his conscious, deliberate mind as if he very self-consciously and purposefully aimed to be creative, even cute, in saying what he did? Or should we alternatively attribute Dylan's wordplay production as arising spontaneously from his unconscious mind without any deliberate forethought, perhaps enhanced by his many years of writing songs and poems? This contrast between creative wordplay as a conscious or unconscious process underlies many debates within cognitive science on both verbal metaphor production and human creativity (Gibbs 2017).

My primary purpose in this chapter is to suggest that creative wordplay always emerges from a constellation of interacting forces that do not easily fall into a simple division between the conscious and unconscious minds. All speech events, even creative, playful ones, are constructed from the interaction of many social, cognitive and linguistic factors, and cannot be reduced to a single part of human minds or brains. At the same time, new metaphoric meanings can sometimes arise, more simply, from playing with words when speakers and writers have no preordained thought or topic in mind. One of the main messages I wish to convey here is that it is often difficult to characterize how people are thinking when they engage in wordplay. Looking at the language alone does not necessarily provide clear insights into the relationship between metaphoric language and metaphoric thinking. For example, cognitive linguistic research through its systematic analyses of linguistic patterns provides key insights into the possible cognitive and experiential motivations for why people speak and write in specific ways. However, more detailed, psychological studies are required to fully understand all the complex unconscious forces that dynamically shape any creative instance of metaphoric wordplay. Similarly, we can try to understand some of the specific literary, historical and biographical circumstances that possibly led to different wordplay productions. Yet even with this additional information, we must be careful not to insist that some instance of wordplay can be directly attributed to one, or just a few, of these circumstances. The dynamics of wordplay, like all human behaviors, emerge from many forces which always include complex conscious and unconscious cognitive processes.

2 Metaphoric creativity in action

Metaphor has long been deemed as a topic of creative wordplay, at least in cases of novel verbal metaphor. Consider one of the most discussed metaphor, namely William Shakespeare's phrase, "Juliet is the sun" uttered by Romeo upon Juliet's appearance on her balcony in Act 2, Scene 2 of the play *Romeo & Juliet* (Shakespeare 2009). This metaphor is wonderfully apt in describing some of the ways that Romeo feels about Juliet. We may ponder upon reading and re-reading this metaphor as to what Shakespeare may have been thinking at the very moment when he first wrote down these words (Gibbs 2011). Did Shakespeare first consider various possibilities, beginning with the words that Juliet is "lovely", beautiful", and "gorgeous", but decided that these adjectives were too bland, and so then imagined Romeo saying that Juliet made him "dizzy", lightheaded", or "swoon"? Rejecting these words as also being inadequate, did Shakespeare consider various metaphors, such as "Juliet is the moon" or "Juliet is the center of the universe", before he suddenly came up with the words "It is the East, and Juliet is the sun"?

It is impossible for us to know with any certainty the mental processes that guided Shakespeare on the particular day and specific time he wrote down "Juliet is the sun". We may assume that Shakespeare was playing with words, to some degree, and may even quite consciously intended what he wrote to be interpreted as conveying metaphorical meanings (e.g., "I will now produce a word string to convey metaphoric meaning"). Many traditional theories of metaphor implicitly assume that creative metaphor use is a conscious rhetorical act (i.e., to be vivid, memorable, concise, polite) (Goatly 1997; Grice 1989). This leads us to ask, more generally, if wordplay is primarily a product of human consciousness. After all, literary scholars, for instance, often advocate for the primacy of human agency, including a writer's deliberate rhetorical intentions, in their explanations of literary meaning and interpretation (for examples of this from the world of metaphor see Fludernik 2011). But the vast literature from cognitive linguistics and psycholinguistics demonstrates that much metaphoric thinking and language use arises automatically within the cognitive unconscious mind (Gibbs 1994, 2017). People often think and speak in metaphoric ways without any awareness of doing so. For this reason, many uses of metaphor, even novel one's such as Shakespeare's "Juliet is the sun", may be created and produced without much, if any, conscious deliberation. This observation does not deny that conscious thoughts can contribute to wordplay in various domains. My point, nonetheless, is to emphasize that unconscious mental processes may drive wordplay and creative metaphor production far more so than is typically acknowledged in the scholarly study of wordplay dynamics.

Still, there are examples of metaphoric language that, on the surface, are difficult to imagine as being anything but deliberately created and articulated (see debate between Gibbs 2011; Gibbs and Chen 2017; Steen 2008, 2017). Consider the single expression "Minimalist artist spills bean".[1] This phrase is a play on the common American idiom "spill the beans" meaning "to reveal a secret." The

---

[1] http://www.nytimes.com/1988/04/03/books/on-being-wrong-convicted-minimalist-spills-beans.html?pagewanted=all (accessed 14 June 2018).

creativity, and humor, in "Minimalist artist spills bean" lies in the way it renovates a common idiom by substituting a singular "bean" for the original plural term "beans", a move that reactivates the more literal reading of the phrase "spill the beans". At the same time, the new phrase highlights the impression that a minimalist artist is one who strives for less (singular) rather than more (plural). Reading this creative idiom variation makes one think "oh, that is clever", and it is hard to imagine that the producer of this phrase was not in some way trying to be clever by playing with the words in a familiar idiomatic phrase.

There are other examples of metaphoric wordplay that also seem to be quite consciously created and produced as metaphors. Consider the following newspaper headlines used to talk about the outcome of sporting events, in this case, American college football games: "Cougars drown Beavers", "Cowboys corral Buffaloes", "Clemson cooks Rice", and "Army torpedoes Navy" (Kövecses 2010). The nicknames of the college teams (e.g., "Cougars" are the mascot for Washington State University, "Beavers" are the mascot for Oregon State University, "Buffaloes" are the mascot for University of Colorado, etc.) are paired with verbs that metaphorically refer to defeat. Thus, beavers live in water and can be defeated when drowned, cowboys corral cattle, and therefore would defeat an opponent like buffaloes by corralling them, rice is considered done or defeated when cooked, and a Navy ship is defeated when torpedoed. Clever headline writers take advantage of people's ability to know what literal actions can be metaphorically used to refer to the idea of defeating, and do so in humorous ways, inviting readers to chuckle at the puns. Writing headlines may possibly involve people deliberately creating metaphors, and other rhetorical devices, which ask readers to draw cross-domain comparisons, and appreciate the aesthetic pleasures of doing so.

I must still urge great caution before attributing significant conscious intent to the production of novel metaphors. These metaphoric expressions really appear to be created in a playful manner, yet their production need not be driven by conscious mental processes alone. A sports headline writer may implicitly understand the requirement that headlines should be short, pithy, and "stand out." But this general requirement may be fulfilled in many ways without a writer having to slowly, deliberately attempt to "be creative" or "playful" or even "metaphoric" (e.g., thinking quite consciously about metaphoric ways of describing how cougars can defeat beavers). We can still comment that a writer was a skilled wordsmith without assuming that this competence is mostly a product of that person's conscious mind. After all, psychological research demonstrates that many expert human behaviors arise from well-practiced, automatic mental and physical processes without any conscious deliberation (see Gibbs 2011).

For example, Shakespeare's writing of "Juliet is the sun" is not simplistically caused by some intentional mental state, or some conscious thought about what to say, nor can the metaphorical statement be reduced to some specific linguistic or conceptual knowledge that Shakespeare possesses in his mind. But the "context" for Shakespeare's specific metaphorical production likely emerges from the interaction of many forces, which may include some of the following:
- Cultural models active at that time about love, sex roles, astrology
- Evolutionary history of "sun" as metaphor
- Contemporary uses of "sun" including Shakespeare's own
- Shakespeare's present imaginings/simulations of Romeo's predicament
- Shakespeare's present physical context and bodily positions/movements
- Shakespeare's immediately preceding speech and future plans for play
- Shakespeare's entrenched neural bindings for people and physical objects

Language scholars from many disciplines often debate which of these above factors best explains why people, including specific individuals like Shakespeare, said or wrote what they did. These same scholars will then often privilege one of these forces in their theoretical accounts of wordplay, including creative metaphoric language use, and even explicitly reject that other possible factors are having any major causal relationship to linguistic behavior (e.g., neuroscientists will argue that language production is all a matter of neural activity and reject cultural/historical accounts of why people said what they did) (Gibbs 2017). But all wordplay emerges from the dynamic interaction of forces operating along many different time scales (e.g., slow moving historical and cultural factors to fast moving cognitive and neural processes). The important point, though, is that these forces are tightly coupled so that it makes no sense to attribute wordplay creativity to any single force alone, such as conscious deliberate intentions.

Let's examine a different case of creative metaphor that also suggests at least some sense of delight in wordplay. The great American poet Wallace Stevens produced a series of novel aphorisms, many of which provided pithy commentary on the art of poetry (Stevens 1957). Presented below are several cases:
- The poet makes silk dresses out of worms.
- The poet is the priest of the invisible.
- Poetry is a pheasant disappearing in the brush.
- Reality is a cliché from which we escape by metaphor.
- Realism is a corruption of reality.
- Sentimentality is a failure of feeling.
- Thought tends to collect in pools.

Stevens' aphorisms capture ideas/beliefs that seem immediately pertinent to people's lives and their understandings of the world, even if these sayings are unfamiliar. We may debate the truthfulness of these novel aphorisms, but their playful twist on accepted truths (e.g., do we typically view sentimentality as a "failure"?) may be relevant to different real-world situations, especially in understanding the role of poetry in human life. Still, Stevens' ability to "make silk dresses out of worms" most likely emerges from unconscious, divergent thinking skills that tacitly discern important connections between diverse kinds of ideas (e.g., relations between "words" and "worms"). Creative individuals can spin out clever linguistic patterns without necessarily being conscious of what they are doing, especially in cases when a speaker or author is a practiced, skilled wordsmith. Skilled writers, like all experts in fact, are notoriously unable to describe exactly how they think when engaged in creative behaviors. Automatic mental processes rule supreme in most of these cases of creative metaphoric wordplay (Gibbs and Chen, in press).

As seen here, much wordplay creates new combinations of familiar ideas and linguistic expressions. To take another example, some literary authors have created novel versions of familiar proverbs to represent unusual (e.g., ironic, satirical, absurdist) perspectives on life's enduring themes. Consider the following statements from the book "Proverbs from Purgatory" (Schwartz 1995; itself an allusion to Blake's "Proverbs from Hell"), along with the original proverbs presented in italics:

> A bird in the hand makes waste. (*A bird in the hand is worth two in the bush.*)
> Two heads are better than none. (*Two heads are better than one.*)
> A stitch in time is only skin deep. (*A stitch in time saves nine.*)
> He's just a chip off the old tooth. (*He's a chip off the old block.*)
> Let's burn that bridge when we come to it. (*Let's cross that bridge when we come to it.*)
> It's like killing one bird with two stones. (*It's like killing two birds with one stone.*)

These twisted proverbs blend together parts of familiar expressions to convey new insights into old "pearls of wisdom". Each phrase expresses a satirical view or the dark side of enduring metaphoric life themes that play such an important role in shaping people's beliefs and actions. Thus, "A stitch in time is only skin deep" provides a rather profound alternative view of the worthy reminder that "A stitch in time saves nine" (i.e., even our most conservative actions taken to protect us from future harm may not guarantee that we always remain safe).

"Proverbs from Purgatory" suggests another important lesson about the dynamics of metaphoric creativity. Just as Bob Dylan spontaneously created several new metaphors from his almost random association of words from two signs, so too do the "Proverbs from Purgatory" arise from the playful combination of different familiar proverbial sayings or simply from changing single words within these figurative expressions. Metaphoric creativity, in this sense, does not begin with a creative idea that is subsequently put into words. Playing with words can result in novel ideas bursting forth as if the words themselves were making love together. Creative individuals, such as Dylan, are capable of spinning out playful, and sometimes meaningful, combinations of words right on the spot. Other writers, such as Stevens, may take more time as they sit there and examine different combinations of words to see which, if any, result in something that presents new poetic insights. As was the case with Shakespeare, we do not typically know the exact conditions that shaped specific literary creations. A recurring theme here is that simply looking at the language alone does not reveal the specific psychological processes which give rise to creative wordplay.

3 Creativity and the automatic mind

Are people really capable of producing playful, novel metaphors without much conscious thought or deliberation? Consider cases where certain poets explicitly aimed to be playful with words automatically without the overt influence of their conscious, deliberative minds. Automatic writing is a practice that first arose in the 19th century, and was most seriously explored during the early 20th century during the rise of Surrealism in Europe. There are various techniques to enable automatic writing, the simplest being to allow one's pen in hand skitter across the page to "scribble without self-consciousness" as one focuses only on the words just produced. The writer aims to record whatever was in mind at that moment so as to compose prose with presumably no forethought or planning.

For example, the French writer André Breton in his "Manifesto of Surrealism" wrote that Surrealism was "Psychic automatism in its pure state, by which one proposes to express - verbally, by means of the written word, or in any other manner – the actual functioning of thought" (Breton 1969: 26). Consider one of Breton's famous poems, from 1931, titled "Free Union", which some scholars attribute to automatic writing. Breton presents a series of image metaphors describing his wife. Presented below are its opening lines, first in the original French and then in translation (Benedikt 1974):

> Ma femme à la chevelure de feu de bois
> Aux pensées d'éclairs de chaleur
> À la taille de sablier
> Ma femme à la taille de loutre entre les dents du tigre
> Ma femme à la bouche de cocarde et de bouquet d'étoiles de dernière grandeur

Aux dents d'empreintes de souris blanche sur la terre blanche
À la langue d'ambre et de verre frottés
Ma femme à la langue d'hostie poignardée
À la langue de poupée qui ouvre et ferme les yeux
À la langue de pierre incroyable

My wife whose hair is a brush fire
Whose thoughts are summer lightning
Whose waist is an hourglass
Whose waist is the waist of an otter caught in the teeth of a tiger
Whose mouth is a bright cockade with the fragrance of a star of the first magnitude
Whose teeth leave prints like the tracks of white mice over snow
Whose tongue is made out of amber and polished glass
Whose tongue is a stabbed wafer
The tongue of a doll with eyes that open and shut
Whose tongue is an incredible stone

The poem, imbued with incongruous images, may seem absurd at first – people do not typically associate feminine beauty with "white mice" or "stone", not to mention using them as vehicles to describe a lover's teeth and tongue. "Free Union", with all its uncanny metaphors, captures our attention, spurs our curiosity, and prompts us to see beauty in these disparate, seemingly abhorrent things, which not only describe the physical attributes of his wife, but more essentially, depict his equally complicated feelings towards her. According to Breton, and others, these different metaphors in all of their playfulness may have emerged automatically without the writer explicitly, consciously aiming to create either metaphors or novel comparisons.

A key source of poetic imagery in automatic writing is the way that words, once written, function to activate, or prime, the emergence of semantically related words. Repetition is frequently observed in automatic writings, especially in exercises in which the writer focuses his or her attention on what was just produced (e.g., the repetition in Gertrude Stein's "a rose is a rose is a rose"). "Free Union" exhibits several of these aspects of word repetition (e.g., "stone", "waist", and "tongue") and semantic priming (e.g., "brush fire" primes "summer lightning", "mouth" primes "teeth", and "polished glass" primes "incredible stone"). These lexical and semantic associations are part of the co-occurrence relationships within French (and English), at least some of which are instantiated within the mental lexicons of individual speakers, such as Breton. Again, the words alone are driving part of the metaphoric creativity seen in "Free Union".

The 20th-century Portuguese author Fernando Pessoa also practiced automatic writing, an experience in which he once reported feeling "owned by something else". In his famous "factless autobiography", titled "The Book of Disquietude", Pessoa wrote of his dreams and consciousness, and offered many philosophical commentaries on life, such as the following (Pessoa 1996: 29–30):

> To live a dispassionate and cultured life in the open air of ideas, reading, dreaming and thinking about writing. A life that's slow enough to be forever on the verge of tedium, but pondered enough so as never to find itself there. To live life far from emotions and thought, living it only in the thought of emotions and in the emotions of thought. To stagnate in the sun goldenly, like a dark pond surrounded by flowers. To possess, in the shade, that nobility of spirit that makes no demands on life. To be in the whirl of the worlds like dust of flowers, sailing through the afternoon air on an unknown wind and falling, in the torpor of dusk, wherever it falls, lost among longer things. To be with a sure understanding, neither happy nor sad, grateful for the sun and for its brilliance and to the stars for their remoteness. To be no more, have no more, want no more … The music of the hungry, the song of the blind, the relic of the unknown wayfarer, the tracks in the desert of the camel without burden or destination.

Pessoa claimed this passage to be an automatic composition. He talks here of different metaphoric possibilities that are rooted in our everyday bodily movements as we take different journeys and experience the "open air of ideas", "stagnate in the sun", "possess… the spirit of nobility", feel the power of the "whirl of the worlds", "sailing through the afternoon", "falling lost among longer things", wanting "no more", and recognizing that some journeys are "without burden or destination." These metaphoric ideas are not completely novel suggestions, but are intimately tied to our ongoing embodied actions in the world that we use to better understand more abstract topics, in this case Pessoa's philosophical speculations about the meaning of his own life (Gibbs 2006, 2017).

Note, however, the ways that the intermingling of different words, and their underlying concepts, provide for novel creations. Consider the sentence "To live life far from emotion and thought, living it only in the thought of emotions and in the emotions of thought". This seemingly contradictory statement (i.e., living far from emotion and thought but living within thought and emotion and emotions of thought), made me as a reader think differently about some of the intricate workings of the poetic mind. Simply twisting the words around in various novel patterns, as Pessoa may have done without conscious deliberation, gives readers new ideas to ponder, some of which occur by discerning analogies to previously stated utterances in the text.

The minimal awareness of some aspects of automatic writing does not provide definitive evidence of a clear dissociation between unconscious and conscious mental processes (Koutstaal 1992). It may be more appropriate to refer to the automatic writing behaviors of famous writers as "flow" states in which "a person performing an activity is fully immersed in a feeling of energized focus, full involvement, and enjoyment in the process of the activity" (Csikszentmihalyi 1990). Bob Dylan's spontaneous wordplay creation, described at the opening of this chapter, is another excellent example of a wordsmith being in a mental state of "flow". Flow is not a special state of the unconscious mind, but one where we seem at one with the world, as we lose self-consciousness and act at optimal levels of our abilities. There is no doubt that writers like Breton and others may have been skilled automatic writers and experienced a certain freedom from some limitations of the conscious mind while in a "flow" state. One can imagine Breton in the very moments of writing "Free Union" having novel metaphors spill forth given his deep-rooted poetic sensibilities, without conscious thoughts driving the creative process. As a skilled poet, Breton was able to produce novel, cross-domain mappings regarding his wife without necessarily having any conscious awareness of this during the writing process.

4 Metaphoric creativity and the disturbed mind

Case study analyses of famous historical artists (e.g., Ludwig van Beethoven, Virginia Woolf, Edward Hopper) suggest that creativity and psychopathology share many common features, including the experience of increased speed of thought, flow of ideas, and the heightened ability to perceive visual, auditory, and somatic states (Santosa et al. 2007). Genius and creativity have been linked to psychopathology both in the individual and in the family history (Eysenck 1995). For example, Lord Byron famously described his understanding of the relation between creative arts and personality disorders in the following manner: "We of the craft are all crazy. Some are affected by gaiety; others by melancholy, but all are more or less touched" (from Jamison 1993: 2).

Let me explore one case of the possible relationship between metaphoric wordplay and the disturbed mind through an examination of one period of time in the life of the American TV and movie actor Charlie Sheen (Gibbs, Okonski, and Hatfield 2013). Sheen is notorious for his chaotic personal life, which has been much documented and discussed within Hollywood circles, and is continually the focus of attention within the broader American entertainment media. Starting in 2001, Sheen was the star of the number one rated show on American television, a comedy titled "Two and a Half Men". In the summer of 2010, Sheen was widely reported to be deeply involved with drugs and alcohol. He was eventually fired from the program and then began a very public attack against the producers of the show, the television network who aired the program, the Hollywood media, and the rehab industry for failing to recognize his unique talents as an actor and his special abilities as a person. These "rants" were notable for their unusual linguistic style and for Sheen's apparent physical and mental disarray when speaking.

I have argued that metaphoric creativity does not necessarily require deliberate psychological processes. People can produce creative wordplay effortlessly without much, if any, deliberate intent. Various psychological conditions, in different context, may lead speakers and writers to creative wordplay. To give one example, consider below a short piece, created and produced by Sheen, which he put on the Internet as an advertisement for a series of one-man concert performances he did in the Fall 2010.[2]

> Dog speed my good soldiers
> I give you my word
> This warlock bats 1000 percent
> You know by now my promises are golden
> Hash tag, fastball.
> I am bringing my violent torpedo of truth
> Defeat is not an option' show out to you in the battlefield
> If you are winning, I'll see you there
> Trolls need not apply
> You all suffer from Sheenis envy
> Buy your ticket, take the ride and the ride will take you
> Surge forward Sheen's cadres.
> Ignition, lift off, bye!

This brief advertisement is clearly intended to be understood by those people who had followed, and appreciated, Sheen's past public verbal "rants". Several of these lines convey metaphoric meaning. For instance, "Dog speed my good soldiers" twists the classic "God speed" (meaning "good wishes for your journey") and then refers to Sheen's loyal fans as "good soldiers", which more generally conceives of Sheen as leading an army against all that was trite and conventional in contemporary America. His statement, "This warlock bats 1000 percent", refers to Sheen's magical powers that make him a warlock who is perfection incarnate, as represented by a perfect batting score of 1000 percent in American baseball. "Fastball" is another reference to American baseball suggesting that Sheen's message, or "pitch", is fast and potentially destructive or, switching his metaphor, a "violent torpedo of truth". The claim that there will be no "defeat" on "the battlefield", given that they are "winning", is a direct instantiation of the common conceptual metaphor ARGUMENT IS WAR, in which

---

[2] http://www.youtube.com/watch?v=ntXGNTrT2zI (accessed 14 June 2018).

Sheen and his followers conceive of themselves as being in battle with enemies (e.g., the producers of "Two and a Half Men" who are "trolls" suffering from "Sheenis" (alluding to "penis") "envy". Finally, fans are urged to go "buy your ticket" to one of the scheduled concerts, and "take the ride", suggesting how the event will be a special journey in which "the ride will take you" as if a rocket ship that engages in "ignition", "lift off" and goes metaphorically upward.

Many people found Sheen's rhetoric to be understandable, humorous, and clever, even if also bizarre. Watching Sheen's interviews, with his constant smoking, fast speech rate, gaunt face, and wild looking eyes, enhanced the impression that Sheen was psychologically disturbed and was experiencing a manic episode tied to some possible bi-polar disease, or the negative physical effects of withdrawing from alcohol and drugs. It is situations like this that reinforce the belief that creativity in language use partly arises from disordered psychological mental states or processes (as defined by the "Diagnostic and Statistical Manual of Mental Disorders" or "DSM-V" 2013).

One mode of thinking that underlies Sheen's speech is the adoption of different metaphoric and allegorical perspectives. Sheen often embraced different personae, such as that of a supernatural being, a great athlete, or rock and roll star and then spoke from these different points of view. Consider how Sheen described his life at one point:

> Guys, it's right there in the thing, duh! We work for the Pope, we murder people. We're Vatican assassins. How complicated can it be? What they're not ready for is guys like you and I and Nails and all the other gnarly gnarlingtons in my life, that we are high priests, Vatican assassin warlocks. Boom. Print that people. See where that goes.

This commentary elaborates on the basic metaphor of Sheen as a supernatural being and does so in concrete detail in regard to the roles that Sheen and his followers adopt. We understand that Sheen does not really work for the Pope as a "Vatican assassin warlock" but that Sheen is asking us to imagine him doing so to express broader allegorical messages about his life and thoughts (e.g., that he is more powerful personally and professionally than many of his critics). Sheen's friends are "gnarly gnarlingtons", which is a playful personification on the term "gnarly" that refers to very difficult, dangerous people or situations. He later adds to this metaphoric vision, with a slight change in his leadership role, when he asserts: "There's a new sheriff in town. And he has an army of assassins."

A different conversation shows Sheen elaborating on the metaphoric idea of his being a special machine, or weapon, when he states:

> I'm sorry, man, but I've got magic. I've got poetry in my fingertips. Most of the time – and this includes naps – I'm an F-18, bro. And I will destroy you in the air. I will deploy my ordinance to the ground.

The specificity of Sheen's elaboration on his self-image, in this case, as a specific powerful machine (i.e., "an F-18" fighter jet) that can defeat his opponents works effectively to communicate Sheen's belief of his personal power, once more, but does so indirectly through this "mini-allegory". Nobody believes that Sheen is a fighter jet, but people can appreciate the complexity of his thinking from the particular concrete implications outlined about the ways in which Sheen is a fighter jet and what he can do in this role. The "poetry" in his "fingertips", which is another reference to his special powers, emerges for the spontaneous articulation of this allegorical vision.

Finally, in another excerpt, Sheen continues this machine or fighter jet theme in more specific detail:

> If you love with violence and you hate with violence, there's nothing that can be questioned. People say, 'Oh, you'd better work through your resentments'. Yeah, no. I'm gonna hang on to them, and they're gonna fuel my attack. Because they're all around you. Sorry, you thought you were just messing with one dude. Winning.

These words or phrases are not particularly creative metaphors in isolation. But the detailed way Sheen articulated his simple metaphoric vision by pressing his claim, and doing so in repetitive and alliterative ways sometimes sounds poetic (e.g., "And they're going to fuel the battle cry of my deadly and dangerous and secret and silent soldiers").

The creativity in Sheen's metaphoric talk makes use of extensive, contextually-driven source domain inferences that are both local and personal. Whenever a metaphoric view of some topic is provided, only some of the word choices may have direct relations to the target domain, with others acting to fill out, often in creative ways, our understanding of the source domain. For example, when Sheen refers to himself as a special machine (e.g., an F-18 fighter jet), he does so through the mention of very specific elements in the source domain of military machines (e.g., "I will destroy you in the air", "I will deploy my ordinance to the ground"). Sheen is essentially engaging in on-the-spot reasoning about the source domain and selectively picking out those parts that best illustrate, in vivid detail, his momentary understanding of who he is and the powers he possesses. We cannot, from a distance, determine the extent to which Sheen may have been aware of his implicit choice of different metaphoric persona when he speaks. But his creative wordplay, his ability to refer to unusual associations of different metaphoric source domains, is most likely rooted in unconscious and automatic thought processes.

Like many famous artists, Sheen may have been suffering from a manic depressive disorder that could easily have fueled his expansive verbal behavior. During these periods a person may feel an elevated or irritable mood state and may also suffer from inflated self-esteem, decreased need for sleep, talkative verbal behavior, racing thought patterns, distractibility, increase in goal directed activity, psychomotor agitation, and excessive involvement in hedonistic behaviors that may be pleasurable in the moment but ultimately lead to dire consequences (DSM-V, 2013). Still, Sheen's creative abilities to play with words through on-the-spot source domain reasoning is something shared with many other great linguistic artists. This kind of expansive metaphoric ability may, nonetheless, be facilitated by different mental states, such as having abnormally fast thought patterns.

Mixed metaphors may be another example of creative wordplay which may arise from a range of possible mental disorders. It is again difficult to know exactly what a person was thinking when he or she produced coherent or mixed metaphors, even when they may appear to be quite creative, playful, or clever. Consider the following list of statements, which are also known as examples of "word salad".[3]

> The sheep languished blue trains suffer
> Run desk making dinner sunglasses menu
> Folders pile swimming red clouds
> Sadness cups coffee printer power outage
> Dogs sleep chicken pencil trees
> E-mail purple orange swims blackened
> Garbage pink composition solely bags speak deodorant
> Horse paper handbags skipping forests play together
> In worlds with pencils, schools page drink slime

Psychologists and psychiatrists often equate unusual, bizarre wordplay, such as seen in these word salad examples, with different thought disorders, including schizophrenia. However, some of these statements may be interpretable given an understanding of some unknown context, one that only the speaker is perhaps aware of. Several of the above expressions convey meaningful metaphoric ideas (e.g., "Garbage pink composition bags speak deodorant"). One possibility is that speakers of word salad are imaging contexts in which the above statement makes

---

[3] http://examples.yourdictionary.com/examples-of-word-salad.html (accessed 14 June 2018).

good sense, but fail to recognize that other people may not share the requisite background knowledge to interpret their pragmatic messages.

Many teachers and language mavens have historically warned against the evils of mixed metaphors precisely because these are considered illogical and reflect word salad-like confusion on the part of speakers and writers. One prominent example of this belief is seen in reactions to the speech of the now President of the United States, Donald Trump. Trump is well-known for his rambling, incoherent talk, which is sometimes also seen as "word salad" (i.e., the seemingly random mixing up of words). Several newspaper headlines have attacked Trump for his rambling speech style (e.g., "Trump Rolls Out Word Salad Economic Policy To Room Full Of Economists", "Trump Caught Knowing Nothing, Mumbles Word Salad"). Consider the following response from Trump to a question about a nuclear arms agreement that President Obama had signed back in 2015:

> Look, having nuclear – my uncle was a great professor and scientist and engineer, Dr. John Trump at MIT; good genes, very good genes, OK, very smart, the Wharton School of Finance, very good, very smart – you know, if you're a conservative Republican, if I were a liberal, if, like, OK, if I ran as a liberal Democrat, they would say I'm one of the smartest people anywhere in the world – it's true! – but when you're a conservative Republican they try – oh, do they do a number—that's why I always start off: Went to Wharton, was a good student, went there, went there, did this, built a fortune but when it was three and even now, I would have said it's all in the messenger; fellas, and it is fellas because, you know, they don't, they haven't figured that the women are smarter right now than the men, so, you know, it's gonna take them about another 150 years – but the Persians are great negotiators, the Iranians are great negotiators, so, and they, they just killed, they just killed us.

This narrative does not feature many striking metaphors, but illustrates the slap-dash manner in which Trump often expresses himself when talking about otherwise serious issues. Many commentators in the US media have widely speculated about Trump's possible psychological disorders to explain his frequent incoherent speech. In support of this claim, observers often note that Trump mixes together different metaphors in his speech. In May 2016, for example, Trump complained about China and its trade imbalance with the US by stating that China is "raping our country", but that "we have the cards, don't forget it". It seems odd, on the surface, to blend the topic of rape with one's card playing skills. Of course, many presidents have in the past mixed their metaphors during important political speeches, yet Trump's critics blast him for his lack of a unifying image to bring together his odd assortment of words and metaphors. Nonetheless, as shown by Trump winning the presidency in the Fall 2016 election, his sometimes chaotic speech is not disturbing to many US voters. Indeed, Trump's odd play with words "helps construct an identity for him as authentic, relatable and trustworthy, which are qualities that voters look for in a presidential candidate".[4]

Even if some people worry about the mental states of individuals with a propensity to mix their metaphors, many others take great pleasure, even humor, in the ways that metaphors can be twisted around in speech and writing. One set of studies examined the mixing of metaphors taken from the "Block That Metaphor!" column in the "New Yorker" magazine (Lonergan and Gibbs 2016). The mixing of metaphors mostly resides in the various combinations between target and source domains. Consider one part of an excerpt in which a critic comments negatively about a column posted on an Internet blog.

> This sort of journalistic tripe is poison, and yet, at the same time, grist for the mill among the twisted jackals who make up Congress and who, it seems, have no qualms about using the Internet as a personal whipping post whenever it suits their fancy.

This long statement refers to the original Internet column, members of Congress who may read columns like this one, and how these individuals may use such columns on the Internet for political purposes. Thus, there are three basic target domains explicitly noted, and each of these is described using different source domains. For example, the column is poison tripe for some people, and grist for the mill for others (2 source domains for this single target), the members of Congress who read the column are twisted jackals (2 source domains for this single target), who use the material on the Internet as a whipping post for political ends. Overall, this one part of the mixed metaphor excerpt employs several different source domains for metaphorically talking about several different topics or target domains. The vividness of this example, however, stems from the diversity of the source domain experiences that are mentioned. These different source domains have little or no pre-existing semantic relations when used to convey either metaphoric or non-metaphoric messages. Many of the mixed metaphor excerpts in the Lonergan and Gibbs (2016) studies reflect this type of diverse mixture of different target and source domains which often go unnoticed by listeners and readers.

A different mixing of metaphors uses a single source domain to talk of several different target domains. Consider the following vignette (Lonergan and Gibbs 2016):

> At last, the lip service that education has been lathered in for the past couple of decades seems to have found the razor's edge among people who are willing to do something

---

[4] http://theconversation.com/donald-trumps-chaotic-use-of-metaphor-is-a-crucial-part-of-his-appeal-61383 (accessed 14 June 2018).

about improving it here, at the elementary level all the way up through public universities. But as budgets continue to be shaved, will the arts once again be trimmed from the programming"

Several target topics are referred to in this example, which include talk about education, people who are willing to do something to improve education, and the education budget, particularly relating to the arts. This interrelated set of targets are all metaphorically described in terms of the source domain of men's faces, as in talk of "lip service", and men's shaving of their faces as in "lathered", "razor's edge", "shaved", and "trimmed". This metaphoric journey through a single source domain is quite similar to the on-the-spot reasoning about a single source domain seen in some of Charlie Sheen's speech. One may generally expect people to have less difficulty interpreting this mixed metaphor excerpt precisely because it employs a single extended metaphor referring to men's shaving, compared to mixed metaphors that shift between different source domains. The humor in this case arises from the way contiguously related elements in a single source domain is applied to several different targets (see Lonergan and Gibbs 2016 for other types of source to target domain relationships in mixed metaphors).

One set of empirical studies gave university students the above, and other, mixed metaphor vignettes and they were asked to write out interpretations of what they read (Lonergan and Gibbs 2016). Several interesting results were shown. First, mixed metaphors are not unusual in discourse. Mixed metaphors are not necessarily difficult to interpret. Readers find it relatively easy to interpret a person's mixing of metaphors partly because these reflect our multiple metaphorical ways of thinking of abstract ideas and events (e.g., love can be characterized as a journey, a manufactured object, a magical process, a plant, a mental disorder, and so on). Coherence of metaphor is not a clue to consciousness or deliberateness of intent. Some speakers may take great delight in playfully spitting out clever mixtures of metaphor, hoping that listeners will take aesthetic pleasure in what the speaker said and how he/she said it. In other cases, speakers may mix their metaphors for a wide variety of reasons, often in complex combinations of diverse cultural, historical, social, cognitive and linguistic forces.

The interesting point about word salad and mixed metaphors is that their existence raises deep questions about whether any example of seemingly creative wordplay is really a product of a consciously creative mind or an automatic, almost thought-less output from a disturbed or disordered-mind. Our interpretation of any sequence of words in speech or writing as being creative or not depends dramatically on our assumptions about the persons producing them and the historical, cultural, social and personal contexts in which specific instances of language are produced. Computer scientists in the field of Artificial Intelligence have even developed programs that create novel metaphors through automatic means ranging from discerning literary patterns from large corpora to making random connections between diverse concepts and words (Veale 2012). Whether people find these meaningful depends on their assumptions on who created the words and for what purpose (e.g., the designers of these programs). Simply looking at the text alone is insufficient to tell us whether some apparent wordplay is conscious, deliberate, playful and creative or just a mix of random associations.

For instance, readers' assumptions about authors determine both the amount of cognitive effort they put into understanding linguistic statements and what meanings they infer. One set of experimental studies presented people with various comparison statements (e.g., "Cigarettes are time bombs") and they were told that these were written either by famous 20th-century poets or randomly constructed by a computer program lacking intentional agency (Gibbs, Kushner, and Mills 1991). The participants' task in one study was to rate the "meaningfulness" of the different comparisons and in another study to simply read and push a button when they had comprehended these statements. Readers rated metaphorical comparisons, such as "Cigarettes are time bombs", to be more meaningful when supposedly written by famous 20th-century poets than when these same metaphors were presumably created through random constructions of a computer program.

People also took much less time to comprehend these comparisons when they were told that the poets wrote the statements. Moreover, they took longer to reject anomalous utterances (e.g., "A scalpel is a horseshoe") as "meaningful" when the poets supposedly wrote these statements. Readers assume that poets have specific communicative intentions in designing their utterances, an assumption that does not hold for the output of an unintelligent computer program. Consequently, people put more effort into trying to understand anomalous phrases when they were supposedly written by poets. They more quickly rejected as "meaningless" these same anomalous expressions when told that an unintelligent computer program wrote them, because computers are assumed to lack communicative intentions. Thus, people's assumptions about the basic fact of human intentionality shape their immediate processing, and even in some cases their ultimate interpretations, of creative metaphoric language.

I can illustrate the pervasiveness of assumptions about intentionality in the interpretation of language as possible wordplay by quoting from a paper by Gerard Steen (2017) over the merits of "deliberate metaphor theory". As may be evident from above, I have many doubts as to whether people are ever really capable of distinguishing between metaphoric language that may, hypothetically, be created deliberately and metaphoric language that only arises automatically (Gibbs 2011, 2015). People create and use metaphors given a variety of personal and situational constraints.

In a recent article, Elaine Chen and I took issue with recent developments with the claim that some metaphors are deliberate and accused Steen of "taking metaphor studies back to the Stone age" in making his arguments on behalf of a theory which has so little evidence to support it. Steen (2017: 15) responded to the Gibbs and Chen (2017) article and in one place wrote the following:

> As for wordplay, Gibbs knows that my last name "Steen" means "stone", which turns Stone Age into a pun that must be appreciated as such by readers who share this knowledge. Wordplay, too, draws attention to the source domain as a separate domain of reference outside the target domain because it hinges on the contrast between two word senses (common noun versus proper name) and arguably has the same effect of inducing deliberateness. Equating DMT's "Steen Age" with "Stone Age" is a brilliant stroke of critical genius that may be appreciated by many.

Unfortunately for me, my good friend Gerard should not credit me, and Chen, for a "brilliant stroke of critical genius" in engaging in wordplay by using "Stone" as a way of referring to "Steen" in the title of the Gibbs and Chen (2017) article. As it turns out, I have no recollection whatsoever of learning that "Steen" means "stone" and had no intention of clever wordplay when coming up with the "Taking metaphor back to the Stone age" title. But Steen, who may indeed have told me that "Steen" means "stone" at one point in our long relationship, assumed playful intent when there was none present. This example illustrates that our assumptions about speakers and writers, both in terms of what they may know and who they may be, sometimes leads us to draw different mistaken interpretations of language, including whether some stretch of discourse was intended as wordplay or not.

No single instance of creative wordplay is necessarily tied to one, and only one, underlying reason or cause, as is sometimes suggested by scholars who argue that creative language use, including metaphor, arises from specific conscious processes while ignoring unconscious influences (Steen 2008). As noted earlier for Shakespeare's production of "Juliet is the sun", many cognitive and linguistic forces, such as people's individual abilities to pick out novel elements within metaphorical source domains, may be driven via multiple cognitive unconscious abilities. For example, research shows that people with larger short-term memory spans are often better able to create and understand novel metaphors than are people with smaller short-term memory spans (Chiappe and Chiappe 2007). Creative metaphor production has also been shown to be linked with fluid thinking abilities as measured by different IQ tests (Silvia and Beaty 2012). More generally, metaphor production is also tied to ongoing bodily actions, especially those related to our differing past and ongoing experiences of the source domains (e.g., the taking of journeys) in enduring conceptual metaphors (e.g., LIFE IS A JOURNEY) (Gibbs 2017). These, and many other, factors that shape wordplay behaviors are very difficult to access through conscious introspection. For this reason, wordplay scholars must be careful to not offer simplistic reasons for why some instance of wordplay exists, and always situate wordplay within the complex dynamics of human psychological experience.

5 Conclusion

Wordplay is one of humankind's most creative activities with linguistic metaphor being one of its finest achievements. As Aristotle once famously wrote, "To be a master of metaphor is the greatest thing by far. It is the one thing that cannot be learnt from others, and it is also a sign of genius" (Aristotle 1997: 122). The act of creativity spinning new metaphors, or slightly novel variations of familiar metaphoric sayings, is closely associated with word-playing skills. The scholarly study of wordplay, most generally, and creative metaphor use, more specifically, often assumes that "play" is a special activity in which people consciously decide to engage in some creative, non-serious action. This assumption is not terribly surprising given the common idea that "play" is a separate, sometimes very organized, type of behavior (e.g., "Let's go outside and play", "I am going to the play tonight"), which may operate according to different rules than other aspects of life. We can easily imagine some talented wordsmith sitting down and thinking "I will now play with words", as a special activity in which the person again aims to be creative with language, including trying to produce novel metaphoric sayings. Wordsmiths may embrace this playful activity with great seriousness, exactly in the ways that great athletes place their entire bodies and souls into their participation in competitive sporting events.

There are, of course, innumerable ways in which words can be played with, and the rise of scholarly interest in wordplay begins with describing, and even cataloging some of the ways that creative wordplay are accomplished (Winter-Froemel and Zirker 2015). My interest as a cognitive scientist is, partly, with what the products of wordplay, particularly in terms of creative metaphoric language use, reveals about the human mind and its splendid capacities and functions. I have great sympathy with Aristotle's famous claim that metaphor may be one of the "greatest things by far" in human life. Still, my work, and those of legions of other scholars over the past several decades has shown that metaphoric thinking and language use is not restricted to a special few people, or geniuses, but is a fundamental part of how all people think, reason and imagine about their lives and the world around them (Gibbs 1994, 2017; Lakoff and Johnson 1999). In line with this grand conclusion about the poetics of everyday minds, my main claim in this chapter is that our judgments of some stretches of language being "wordplay" should not be taken as direct evidence of some strictly conscious, deliberate attempt to "play" with words. "Play" is often an after-the-fact justification of what we have done rather than a distinct mode of deliberative thought that we choose to engage in *before* we act (creatively or otherwise). People can produce wonderful, creative examples of different combinations for many interacting reasons, most of which are based on automatic cognitive and linguistic processes rather than on slow, deliberate, conscious thoughts. These fast-acting processes are part of the cognitive unconscious, and interact with each other in complex, dynamic ways in each moment of linguistic creation.

Most importantly, we may be unable to adequately assess exactly how a person produced a novel metaphor, or any other playful use of language, from simply looking at the language alone without understanding the intricate context, including the psychology of the speaker or writer. From which creative language emerges. Wordplay, in everyday discourse and special literary texts, arises as a complex activity that is shaped by the particular individuals (i.e., including their personal histories, psychological talents and cognitive abilities), working in specific historical, cultural, social, and linguistic contexts, all aiming to achieve a massive variety of personal, pragmatic and aesthetic goals. As wordplay scholars, we can dig into the language produced and the broader cultural and perhaps personal contexts in which these novelties came about. Yet we will always be greatly limited in being able to specify the precise sub-personal mental processes from which individual wordplays arose unless we are able to study in great detail all of the psychology motivating people's particular, in-the-moment linguistic actions.

The good news, however, is that we can study the cognitive unconscious workings of human minds, within different cultural contexts and engaged in different tasks, to at the very least map out a larger set of constraints which very well could be contributing to any specific act of wordplay. Part of my plea, then, is for wordplay scholars to recognize the broader range of cognitive unconscious processes that operate when speakers and writers produce words which seem to be making love together in fabulously exquisite ways. Furthermore, we must study words not simply as linguistic resources that people may use, playfully or otherwise, but acknowledge how words in context may reflect particular modes of thought and primarily come into being because of our deeply-rooted, unconscious conceptual, communicative and aesthetic needs. Examining the dynamic complexities of metaphoric language productions is an excellent arena to uncover the automatic and unconscious human impulse to understand the world and our place in it through the playful use of words.

6 References

Aristotle. 1997. *Poetics*. London: Penguin.
Benedikt, Michael (ed.). 1974. *The poetry of surrealism: An anthology.* Boston & Toronto: Little, Brown and Co.
Breton, Andre. 1969. *Manifesto of surrealism*, Richard Seaver & Helen R. Lane, Trans. Ann Arbor: University of Michigan Press.
Chiappe, Dan & Penny Chiappe. 2007. The role of working memory in metaphor production and comprehension. *Journal of Memory and Language* 56. 172–188.
Csikszentmihalyi, Mihaly. 1990. *Flow: The psychology of optimal experience*. New York: Harper and Row.
Diagnostic and Statistical Manual of Mental Disorders (DSM-5). 2013. Washington, DC: American Psychological Association.
Eysenck, Hans. 1995. *Genius: The natural history of creativity*. Cambridge: Cambridge University Press.
Fludernik, Monica. 2011. The rise of cognitive metaphor theory and its literary repercussions. In Monica Fludernik (ed.), *Beyond conceptual metaphor theory: Perspectives on literary metaphor*, 9–17. London: Routledge.
Gibbs, Raymond. 1994. *The poetics of mind: Figurative thought, language, and understanding*. New York: Cambridge University Press.
Gibbs, Raymond. 2006. *Embodiment and cognitive science*. New York: Cambridge University Press.
Gibbs, Raymond. 2011. Are deliberate metaphors really deliberate? A question of human consciousness and action. *Metaphor and the Social World* 1. 26–52.
Gibbs, Raymond. 2015. Do pragmatic signals affect conventional metaphor understanding? A failed test of deliberate metaphor theory. *Journal of Pragmatics* 90. 77–87.
Gibbs, Raymond. 2017. *Metaphor wars: Conceptual metaphor in human life*. New York: Cambridge University Press.
Gibbs, Raymond & Elaine Chen. 2017. Taking metaphor studies back to the Stone Age: A reply to Xu, Zhang, & Wu (2016). *Intercultural Pragmatics* 14. 117–124.
Gibbs, Raymond & Elaine Chen. In press. Metaphor and the automatic mind. *Metaphor and the Social World*.
Gibbs, Raymond, Julia Kushner & Rob Mills. 1991. Authorial intentions and metaphor comprehension. *Journal of Psycholinguistic Research* 20. 11–30.
Gibbs, Raymond, Lacey Okonski & Miles Hatfield. 2013. Crazy, creative metaphors: Crazy metaphorical minds? *Metaphor and the Social World* 3. 141–159.
Goatly, Andrew. 1997. *The language of metaphors*. New York: Routledge.

Grice, H. Paul. 1989. *Studies in the ways of words*. Cambridge, MA: Harvard University Press.

Jamison, Kay. 1993. *Touched with fire: Manic-depressive illness and the artistic temperament*. New York: Simon & Schuster.

Koutstaal, Wilma. 1992. Skirting the abyss: A history of experimental explorations of automatic writing in psychology. *Journal of the History of the Behavioral Sciences* 28. 5–27.

Kövecses, Zoltan. 2010. *Metaphor: A practical introduction*. New York: Oxford University Press.

Lakoff, George & Mark Johnson. 1999. *Philosophy in the flesh: The embodied mind and its challenge to Western thought*. Chicago: University of Chicago Press.

Lonergan, Julia & Raymond Gibbs. 2016. Tackling mixed metaphor in discourse: Corpus and psychological studies. In Raymond Gibbs (ed.), *Mixing metaphor*. 57–72. Amsterdam: Benjamins.

Pessoa, Fernando. 1996. *The book of disquietude*. Manchester: Carcanet.

Santosa, Claudia, Connie M. Strong, Cecylia Nowakowska, Po W. Wang, Courtney M. Rennicke & Terence A. Ketter. 2007. Enhanced creativity in bipolar disorder patients: A controlled study. *Journal of Affective Disorders* 100. 31–39.

Schwartz, David. 1995. Proverbs from Purgatory. *Paris Review* 48. 33–35.

Shakespeare, William. 2009. *Romeo & Juliet*. New York: Modern Library Classics.

Silvia, Paul & Roger Beaty. 2012. Making creative metaphors: The importance of fluid intelligence for creative thought. *Intelligence* 40. 343–351.

Steen, Gerard. 2008. The paradox of metaphor: Why we need a three-dimensional model of metaphor. *Metaphor & Symbol* 23. 213–241.

Steen, Gerard. 2017. Deliberate metaphor theory: Basic assumptions, main tenets, urgent issues. *Intercultural Pragmatics* 14. 1–24.

Stevens, Wallace. 1957. *Opus posthumous*. London: Penguin.

Veale, Tony. 2012. *Exploding the creativity myth: The computational foundations of linguistic creativity*. London: Bloomsbury Continuum.

Winter-Froemel, Esme & Angelika Zirker (eds.). 2015. *Wordplay and metalinguistic/metadiscursive reflection. Authors, contexts, techniques, and metareflection* (The Dynamics of Wordplay 1). Berlin & Boston: De Gruyter Mouton.

Dirk Delabastita
The dynamics of wordplay and the modern novel: A paired case study

Abstract: The article opens by outlining a multidimensional definition of wordplay, designed to do justice to the "dynamic" nature of this complex field of phenomena. Of these various dimensions, the "communicative significance" of wordplay is the main focus of the present analysis, which investigates the wordplay in two recent English-language novels: *My Sister, My Love* (2008) by Joyce Carol Oates and *A Concise Chinese-English Dictionary for Lovers* (2007) by Xiaolu Guo. The latter may be described as a "global novel". It turns out to offer different wordplay readings to different readerships, depending on their cultural background and multilingual literacies. Like Guo's novel, Oates's *My Sister, My Love* abounds in wordplay, much of it of the malapropian variety, too, and with an equally elusive quality about it. However, Oates's novel, which is more firmly rooted in a single culture, also shows a complex multi-voiced postmodern narrative style which endows its wordplay with an elusiveness of a very different kind. Its readerships are likely to be linguistically and culturally more homogeneous but these readers will not always quite know to which character or narrative voice in this novel with its various levels of discursive embedding the wordplays and malapropisms have to be attributed. The corpus analysed is far too small to permit generalisation but the "global" and the "postmodern" qualities of the respective novels invite extrapolations and comparison with wider corpora. The discussion demonstrates the absolute need for dynamic approaches to wordplay in the novel no less than in other genres or speech situations.

Keywords: *A Concise Chinese-English Dictionary for Lovers*, bilingual pun, elusiveness, global novel, interpretive doubt, Joyce Carol Oates, malapropism, multilingual literacy, *My Sister, My Love*, narratology, postmodern novel, static vs. dynamic approaches to wordplay, modern novel, Xiaolu Guo

1 Introduction

Until some three decades or so ago "linguistic" approaches to the pun were strongly dominated by the structuralist paradigm. While the tide of post-structuralism was rising rapidly, "literary" approaches, too, still showed the influence of structuralism, as well as of the lasting legacy of William Empson and the New Criticism.[1] Moreover, the taxonomies and nomenclatures of traditional rhetoric remained an almost mandatory frame of reference for many students of the pun. For all its merits, this existing work turned out to be far too *static*, in that it tended to understand wordplay in terms of strictly identifiable *intrinsic* features of semantically stable texts merely to be unpacked by perceptive readers / listeners, and to be slotted into the linguist's or the critic's taxonomies. *Dynamic* approaches, on the other hand, are understood here as giving due recognition to the *historicity* of wordplay and to its *pragmatics* and *functions*, to be operationalized in terms of genre, context, situation and interaction.

From a literary studies perspective, relevant challenges and possible alternatives to such static models were provided by reader-oriented literary theories and by the functionalist approaches of the late Russian formalists and the Prague School.[2] Further sources of innovation included the idea of the prototype as a powerful format to conceptualize phenomena such as wordplay, as well as Grice's article on "Logic and Conversation" (1975), which remained untapped by students of the pun for several years. Drawing on all these sources, it became possible to define wordplay as a complex category that is graded and open-ended in at least four distinct ways. The term can thus be said to cover

---

1 Empson's *Seven Types of Ambiguity* (1930) became a foundational text for the New Criticism and contributed to making ambiguity one of the most central concepts of this extremely influential critical school, which produced many perceptive "close readings" of poetry; its strong emphasis on the "words on the page" and on the unique singularity of each text went hand in hand with a limited interest in historical contextualization and with a profound mistrust of general theory-building, linguistically inspired or otherwise.

2 Russian formalism was a critical school in Russia from 1915 until the late 1920s, when it was forcefully suppressed by Soviet totalitarianism. It is often seen as the starting point of modern literary theory. Unlike the New Criticism, its focus was more on the general rules and principles that define verbal art (e.g., defamiliarization) than on individual texts. Representatives such as Roman Jakobson and Y. Tynyanov illustrate the continuity with the Prague school, whose research programme had an intrinsic functional orientation.

the various discursive phenomena in which certain features inherent in the structure of the language(s) used are mobilized to produce a communicatively significant, (near) simultaneous confrontation of at least two linguistic units with more or less dissimilar meanings and more or less similar forms.[3]

The following diagram attempts to visualize the definition's main intuitions:

Fig. 1: Visualisation of definition of wordplay

The definition places wordplay at the intersection of four continua: a) formal similarity, b) semantic dissimilarity, c) dependence on language structure, and d) communicative significance.

Thus, "En attendant dodo" (title of a theatre review by a critic who was bored by the performance of Beckett's *En attendant Godot*) qualifies as a pun because it throws into opposition two verbal sequences *Godot* / dodo which show a) formal similarity and b) semantic difference c) on the basis of language structure [namely, paronymy] and d) in a way which is clearly deliberate, namely, as an overtly

---

3 For a fine-grained discussion of this definition, see Delabastita (1993: 55–151). See, furthermore, Section I (The discussion forum) in *The Dynamics of Wordplay* 3 (Knospe, Onysko, and Goth 2016: 9–78), which illustrates just how much issues of definition and classification remain central to the field.

sarcastic expression of the reviewer's dislike of the show. While this example is a clear-cut one, the point that needs emphasizing is that we have to hypothesize a *graded notion* for *each of the four criteria*. Let us briefly exemplify this:

a) formal similarity: depending on specific context (e.g., through grammatical or prosodic foregrounding), the category of alliteration may, or may not, merge into that of sound-based horizontal wordplays (in other words, rather than being an either/or proposition, distinctions between alliteration and sound-based wordplay should be mapped on a continuum);

b) semantic difference: subtle nuances of meaning may, or may not, suffice for wordplay to spring into effect (here, too, we have a cline rather than clear-cut distinctions);

c) based on language structure: double readings and interpretive ambiguities may, or may not, be sufficiently language-based to count as wordplay (again, we often have a continuum here; witness the gradual nature of the process of lexicalization that allows "unique" or "creative" metaphors to evolve into lexicalized polysemy permitting "real" wordplay);

d) communicatively significant: wordplay somehow has to express a communicative intention or achieve a rhetorical effect to be recognized as such (but here, too, a graded notion is needed, as there are many forms, levels and degrees of intentionality or rhetorical effectiveness).

In other words, along each of these four axes separately, membership to the category of wordplay is to be assessed in gradual rather than binary terms and careful contextualisation is required in each specific case. That is what the dotted lines in the diagram are meant to visualize.

Moreover, and no less crucially, *synchronic variation* and *diachronic shifts* are bound to affect our recognition and understanding of wordplay along each of the four axes. To illustrate the former, witness the verbal jokes that work only in one dialect of the language (e.g., requiring US-English pronunciation) but not in another (e.g., when pronounced in British English). To illustrate the latter, consider the many wordplays in older texts (Ovid, Chaucer, Shakespeare, etc.) that have been obscured by later shifts in the language's sound system which had the effect of reducing or even obliterating the "formal similarity" needed for the pun to work as such. One of the reasons often quoted as justifying performances of Shakespeare in so-called OP[4] is precisely that they bring back to life rhymes and

---

4 OP or "original pronunciation" refers to recordings, readings or performances of Shakespeare making use of a linguistically based reconstruction of what his English would have sounded like

sound-based puns that had been eroded by linguistic change. Thus, the famous lines "From forth the fatal loins of these two foes / A pair of star-cross'd lovers take their life" in the Prologue to Act I of *Romeo and Juliet* show a thematically apt extra level of meaning when we discover that "loins" would have been pronounced the same way as "lines" (line of descent, lineage, ancestry). Conversely, semantic shifts may sometimes have to be suspected of "creating" wordplays that could not have been intended or understood at the time of the text's original composition. The semantics of modern English will highlight the sexual meaning in words such as "gay" or "make love" when they occur in Renaissance literature, while such meanings were absent back then, so that we should mistrust such words as historical false friends liable to lead us astray in the historical interpretation of wordplays.

The fourth axis (communicative significance) specifically introduces the pragmatic and functional dimension of wordplay; it challenges us to take into account the often complex communicative settings in which wordplay is found, to recognize the different possible levels of intentionality and comprehension which these entail, and to acknowledge the difficulty (and, indeed, sometimes the impossibility!) of firmly appraising intentions and effects. The impact of synchronic variation and diachronic shifts is perhaps nowhere clearer than on this level.

My present aim is to contribute to a somewhat less researched subfield of wordplay studies, namely, wordplay in recent narrative fiction. Against the background of the afore-mentioned general principles, I shall look at the wordplay in two recent novels: *My Sister, My Love* (2008) by Joyce Carol Oates and *A Concise Chinese-English Dictionary for Lovers* (2007) by Xiaolu Guo. As any Internet search indicates, readers, bloggers and reviewers have been struck by the wordplay in both novels, but it has never been submitted to a systematic scholarly study. Xiaolu Guo's book is a "global novel"; as we shall see, it offers different wordplay readings to different readerships, depending on their cultural background and multilingual literacies.[5] Oates's *My Sister, My Love* is more firmly rooted in a single culture (the USA); it shows a complex multi-voiced postmodern narrative style which endows the novel's wordplay with an elusiveness of a very different

---

four centuries ago. The well-known linguist David Crystal is one of the most prominent champions of the movement.

5 Many "global novels" differ from *A Concise Chinese-English Dictionary for Lovers* in this particular respect. It has been pointed out that novelists targeting a global readership will tend to deal with linguistic diversity in a very different way to Guo's novel, namely, by writing their books in a "bland" and easily exportable style for the purpose of enhancing readability and translatability and thus permitting a more or less homogeneous response to them.

nature, as even its linguistically and culturally more homogeneous readerships will not always quite know to which of the characters or various embedded narrative voices the wordplays and malapropisms have to be attributed.

2 *A Concise Chinese-English Dictionary for Lovers* (2007) by Xiaolu Guo

2.1 Presentation of the novel

Xiaolu Guo was born in 1973 in a village in south China. She published six books in Chinese before moving to London in 2002. The diary she kept in English during this difficult period of linguistic and cultural adaptation provided the autobiographical inspiration for her *Concise Dictionary*; the story is set in the same timeframe. It was her first original novel in English; several have followed since.

The main character and first-person narrator is Zhuang Xiao Qiao; she starts calling herself Z when she finds that the English cannot properly remember or pronounce her name anyway. She is a young Chinese woman (aged 23) who is sent to England by her entrepreneurial parents in order to learn English as the language of international export and economic success. She arrives in England, settles down, follows English classes, and begins a loving but complicated relationship with an unnamed older bisexual sculptor, who will also help her improve her English. Following his advice to further open her mind by visiting other places on her own, Z travels to Paris, Amsterdam, Berlin, Venice, Tavira and Dublin. Towards the end of the book the couple breaks up and when her visa expires Z travels back home, totally transformed by her stay in the West, but also discovering that China has become a very different country during her absence, having been swept by the global wave of Western-style liberalism and consumerism.

The novel is about contacts, bumps and clashes between languages and cultures, and about their unsettling and alienating impact on individual lives. Having to constantly "translate" herself into another language and culture both literally and figuratively, Z experiences anxiety and feels her former self disintegrating. The character's journey of sexual self-discovery is a related subtheme in the novel. It reflects the emancipation of Z from the constraints of old rural China and the difficult search for a new identity. At the same time, the recourse to the universal language of the body also gives her a welcome respite from English grammar and existential dislocation.

Thematically, the novel is a kind of belated-coming-of-age novel. In narrative terms, it combines two generic templates, namely, the diary novel and the dictionary novel. It is a kind of *journal intime* but the chronologically arranged sections in which Z writes down the day's experiences are not prefaced by a date but by a dictionary definition explaining a word that she has had to look up and which was relevant somehow to the day's events.

Stylistically, the book displays vastly different levels of proficiency in English. The first chapters are written in error-riddled basic English, but we witness the rapid improvement of the narrator's linguistic skills. At the end of the book Z is a confident and articulate user of English, with few remaining "mistakes".

Not surprisingly, it is mainly Z's errors that provide a way into the book's ample wordplay. While being on the whole a "serious" book, *A Concise Chinese-English Dictionary for Lovers* contains a lot of humour, much of which follows from the many cultural and indeed linguistic misunderstandings and errors that it stages. Some of these errors reflect the predictable format of funny foreigner English, as we find out in the first entry after her arrival:

(1) **alien**

> **alien** adj foreign; repugnant (to); from another world n foreigner; being from another world

> Is unbelievable. I arriving London, '**Heathlow**[6] Airport'. Every single name very difficult remembering, because just not 'London Airport' simple way like we simple way call 'Beijing Airport'. Everything very confuse way here, passengers is separating in two queues.
> Sign in front of queue say: ALIEN and NON ALIEN.
> I am **alien**, like Hollywood film *Alien*, I live in another planet, with funny looking and strange language. (p. 9)

We shall come back to the intentional (intended by the narrator) "alien" pun later. As to the "accidental" (but, of course, intended by the author) l-for-r substitution in Heathrow/Heathlow, this phenomenon is well-known and perhaps even overworked as a "Chinese" shibboleth and a source of jokes. Later in the book we also find it in:

(2) In my home town everyone take cheap taxi, but in London is very expensive and taxi is like the **Loyal** family look down to me. [Royal family] (p. 19) (similarly on p. 41)

---

[6] Here and below, bold has been added to highlight the wordplay in the excerpts.

(3) You laughing when you hear the names. 'I never knew **flutes** grew on trees,' you say. It seems I am big comedy to you. I not understand why so funny. 'You can't say your Rs. It's *fruit* not *flute*,' you explain me. 'A *flute* is a musical instrument [...]'. (p. 64)

These excerpts give a first idea of how the novel works. Looking at the few examples of wordplay they contain, we can also see a basic pattern in the use of wordplay beginning to emerge.

2.2 Multiple readers, multiple readings

2.2.1 Levels of linguistic awareness and rhetorical control

A first group of puns in the novel may be exemplified by excerpt (1) above, where we see the narrator deliberately producing a wordplay in English on the double meaning of "alien" in English as referring to either "a non-citizen, a foreigner" or a "strange creature from outer space".

Paradoxically perhaps, it is the speaker's very limited proficiency in English that enables her to make such wordplays. Being a newcomer to English, the language has a novel, unfamiliar and surprising aspect to her, which more seasoned EFL speakers and a fortiori native speakers have lost as the language became a habitual cognitive and communicative tool for them. As a language learner, Z keeps making metalingual comments on the differences between English and Chinese which express her strong linguistic curiosity. Not surprisingly, she is quite perceptive to the "strangeness" of form-meaning relationships in English. Even an ordinary street name attracts her attention and makes her wonder about double meanings and semantic motivations, whether she is naively assuming that street names in English are meant to reflect characteristic features of the street, or actually making a deliberate English joke:

(4) Anyway, *hostel* called 'Nuttington House' in Brown Street, nearby Edward Road and Baker Street. I write all the names careful in notebook. No lost. **Brown** Street seems really **brown** with brick buildings everywhere. Prison looking. (p. 12)

While the semantics of this pun (4) are quite simple, the narrator would perhaps not have managed to foreground the polysemy of the word "alien" in example (1) without the help of her dictionary. This is the second way in which her limited proficiency paradoxically helps her produce these wordplays: her limited vocabulary frequently forces her to have recourse to her dictionary, where she finds definitions that heighten her sensitivity to linguistic meaning.

Here are two more examples, if we accept, as I believe we may, that the following plays on "Confucius"/"confusion" and on "deadly" [lethal/extreme] are deliberate on the part of Z:

(5) English food very confusing. They eating and drinking strange things. I think even **Confucius** have great **confusion** if he studying English. (p. 33)

(6) She always threatens to **die** the next day. Whenever it comes to this **deadly** subject, I can only keep my mouth shut. (p. 351)

Admittedly, instances like these, where we see the narrator being and feeling on top of some of the subtleties of English, remain relatively few. In the following example, we see Z realizing the potential ambiguity of "be my guest" [literal/figurative] but only in retrospect, after the initial misinterpretation has had to be pointed out to her:

(7) 'I want to see where you live,' I say.
   You look in my eyes. '**Be my guest.**' [...]
   That's how all start. From a misunderstanding. When you say 'guest' I think you meaning I can stay in your house. A week later I move out from Chinese landlord. (pp. 53 and 54, respectively, separated by an ellipsis of a week)

The laconic wording conveys a sense of Z's amusement when she becomes metalingually aware of how the "silly" literal understanding of an idiomatic phrase had altered the course of the life.

In a similar way, Z retrospectively corrects her initial mishearing of "fizzy water" as "filthy water" in example (9) (see below), but this correction does not happen until more than 300 pages down the novel, when Z's stay in England is drawing to a close and she finds herself rereading her earlier entries: "I sit down [...] and open my notebook. [...] I look at all the words I learned since the first day I arrived in this country: *Alien, Hostel, Full English Breakfast, Properly, Fog, Filthy Water* (actually *fizzy water*, now I know) ... So many words" (p. 337). Incidentally, the idea of narrator rereading and possibly editing her earlier diary entries creates interesting critical perspectives, to which we shall have to turn later.

2.2.2 Accidental wordplay

In most cases, Z produces semantic misunderstandings or playfully ungrammatical utterances *without* the text indicating any form of metalingual awareness or self-correction either instantly or later. The pun on "loyal"/"royal" given above falls into this category. In such cases, intentionality lies entirely and solely with the author.

In the following example, Z does not bother to check the word "homeless" in her dictionary and assumes it simply means *any* person not having a home or fixed residence:

(8) **hostel**

> **hostel** n building providing accommodation at a low cost for a specific group of people such as students, travellers, **homeless** people, etc.

> First night in 'hostel'. Little *Concise Chinese-English Dictionary* hostel explaining: a place for 'people such as students, travellers and homeless people' to stay. Sometimes my dictionary absolutely right. I am student and I am **homeless** looking for place to stay. How they knowing my situation *precisely*? (p. 11)

In the following instance, the misunderstanding has a phonological rather than semantic basis. Apart from the fact the word "fizzy" does not seem to belong to the lexical repertoire of Z, her ear is not well attuned to the [l] sound or to the phonological distinction in English between [z] and [θ] (unvoiced th-sound):

(9) Waiter asks me: 'What would you like? Still water, or **filthy** water'?
'What? Filthy water?' I am shocked.
'OK, filthy water.' He leave and fetch bottle of water. (p. 34)

In the following two instances, the wordplay is largely based on morphology, as we see Z comically – but also very meaningfully – misconstruing the compositional structure and etymology of the words "illegal" and "demonstrator" respectively:[7]

(10) Walking around like a ghost, I see two rough mans in corner suspicionly smoke and exchange something. **Ill-legal**, I have to run – maybe they desperate drug addictors robbing my money. (p. 14) (similarly on pp. 17 and 187)

(11) People in march seems really happy. [...] Can this kind of **demon-stration** stop war?
From Mao's little red book I learning in school: [...] A revolution is an insurrection, an act of violence with which one class overthrows another. (p. 29) (similarly on pp. 96 and 335)

The idea of "illegality" being a state of moral / legal "illness" that you suffer *from* and / or that the law can make you suffer *for* is a powerful one. So is the clever

---

[7] The cognitive mechanism behind these cases of re-analysis and pseudo-motivation is essentially that of folk etymology or popular etymology.

image of "demonstrators" potentially being "demons" about to break out in "street" (Lat. *strata*) violence.

The following list presents a number of other puns which were similarly intended by the author[8] at the expense of the narrator. For the sake of brevity, and since most of them can speak for themselves, they will be listed with a minimum of context and with brief glosses added for the vertical wordplays only:

(12) I get suitcase from airport's luggage **bell** [belt] (p. 12)

(13) Is cold, late winter. Windy and **chilli** [chilly/chilli peppers (known as a 'hot' spice)] (p. 13)

(14) **Spicy** Girls [Spice Girls/hot, exciting, slightly shocking girls] (p. 14)

(15) Abashed: (meaning to feel **embrassed** or regretful) [embarrassed/brassed (off), ?embraced, ?brazen] (p. 15)

(16) I even **saving bacons** for supper [literal/figurative "save one's bacon"] (p. 17)

(17) And verbs has three types of **mood** too: indicative, imperative, subjunctive. Why so **moody**? (p. 24)

(18) **Weather** it rain or **weather** it sunshine, you just not know. [weather/whether] (p. 32)

(19) Buckingham **Place** [Palace] (p. 41)

(20) You say prefer French **Patisserie**. **'Patty surly'**? (p. 49)

(21) You ask if I want visit **Kew Gardens**. **'Queue Gardens'**? (p. 52)

(22) '*For most of the last twenty years I have* **been out with** *men.*' I think is good try love men. World better place. But go **out** where? (p. 72)

(23) '*When I was a squatter, I made a lot of sculptures.* […].' What **squat**? I take out dictionary. Says 'to sit with the knees bent and the heels close to the bottom or thighs.' Very difficult position, I imagine. (p. 72)

(24) 'I presume you are thinking of the *persistent* **vegetative** *state*,' you say. '**Vegetarian** means you don't eat meat.' (p. 75–76)

(25) cheap **biscakes** [biscuits] (p. 79)

---

8 It is worth noting that the novel contains three errors at least which were surely *not* intended by Guo: "mos<u>e</u> common" (p. 40), "sculp<u>u</u>ture" (p. 264) and "yo<u>u</u>self" (p. 320). These three words are spelled correctly "by the narrator" in all other instances in the book.

(26) It is too **out in blue** for me. [out of the blue] (p. 83)

(27) While I sitting here, many singles, desperately mans coming up saying, 'Hello **darling**'. But I not your **darling**. (p. 86)

(28) Maybe also why newspapers always report cases of **peterfiles** and perverts. [paedophiles] (p. 109)

(29) You want to show me somewhere special called the Burnham **Beach**. 'Is it the British ocean?' I ask, excited to visit sea for first time. You are laughing. '**B-e-e-c-h**, not b-e-a-c-h. In English, a beech is a type of tree, not an ocean.' (p. 110)

(30) I was hungry all the time, because I never can have something I really wanted eat, **like** meat, any **kind** meat. [like: preposition/verb] [kind: adjective/noun] (p. 127)

(31) 'That's your **clitoris**,' you tell me. '**Liquorice**?' (p. 137)

(32) 'This **Anon** very good writer,' I say. 'I think I prefer to Shakespeare, much easier.' (p. 144) [abbreviation for Anonymous/(mistaken for a non-existing) author's name]

(33) **Bees** are **beeing** around the jasmine tree. (p. 155)

(34) You move your body to the bathroom. You **throw** yourself **up**. [vomit] (p. 167)

(35) 'But what's wrong with a bit of **hoover**ing?' 'Because I hate that **woover**'. (p. 174)

(36) I thought English is a strange language. Now I think French is even more strange. In France, their fish is *poisson*, their bread is *pain* and their pancake is *crêpe*. **Pain** and **poison** and **crap**. That's what they have every day. (p. 203)

(37) A man, with a huge suitcase and a big **rocksack**, talk in mobile phone in a strange language. [rucksack/?sack with is heavy as a rock, or used for rambling in rocky landscapes] (p. 208) (similarly on pp. 208, 211, 218, 226, 230, 232, 236, 238, 246, 249, 254, 263, 266)

(38) The speaker on the platform **renounces** something loudly. It is 20.09. The train will leave in four minutes. [announces] (p. 212)

(39) 'I am an **avocado**,' he replies. '**Avocado**?' I am surprised to hear. Is a fruit also a job? [It. avvocato = lawyer] (p. 234–235)

(40) The rocks nearby the shore are dirty, polluted. [...] But some seagulls still **convolute** there. [revolve/make convoluted movements] (p. 246)

(41) The old man has very strong accent, and my English listening comprehension becomes hopeless. '**Turf**' or '**Tofu**'? I don't understand this word. Gosh, why they don't simply call it 'black burning stuffs'? (p. 258)

(42) 'Ah, those are *briquettes*, my dear,' the old man answers proudly. '**Briquettes**?' Why it sounds like a French bread? [baguettes] (p. 258)

While not being exhaustive, this list of inadvertently produced puns or near-puns by Z is definitely a representative sample.

Not surprisingly, looking at the page numbers, we see that the overall number of amusing linguistic accidents appears to decrease as the narrator's linguistic skills get better. Correspondingly, their occurrence is increasingly occasioned by the narrator's contacts with unfamiliar dialects (Dublin, in example (41)) or indeed with other languages than English (French and Italian, in examples (36), (39) and (42)), or by her efforts to raise her stylistic game and use a more sophisticated linguistic register (as in example (40)).

This increasing level of Z's proficiency along the book's chronology prompts us to briefly revisit the novel's narrative structure. As we have seen, all the wordplays, whether they are deliberate or accidental on the narrator's part, can be attributed to the same person. This suggests a very straightforward set-up of the book's situation of discourse and induces us to believe – perhaps too easily – that levels of intentionality can be mapped on a simple unilinear scale, which ranges from Z making deliberate jokes (few cases), to Z being blissfully unaware of the double meanings and verbal associations caused by her linguistic blundering (the majority of cases), with a number of intermediate cases (with Z showing at least *some* degree of metalingual awareness, as in example (4)). However, we should acknowledge the fact that for each story-world event reported by Z an analytical distinction can be made between three different "moments" in the novel's narrative logic:

a) the event itself (involving Z as the "experiencing self");
b) the first-time reporting of the event in Z's diary (involving Z as the "narrating self");
c) the subsequent rereading and the copy-editing of the diary (involving Z as the "editing self").

Let us revisit, for instance, the accidental joke in example (2). One may reasonably assume that some time – in both real and psychological terms – must have elapsed between a) the initial mentally made comparison between the rudeness of the cab driver and the arrogance ascribed to the members of the royal family, b) the actual reporting of the unpleasant taxi-taking experience in the day's entry in her notebook, and c) the rereading and possibly revising of this entry in her notebook towards the end of Z's year in the UK and (one imagines, though no mention of this is made in the book) before handing the manuscript over to whoever has accepted to publish the text. The distance in time between these three consecutive moments is potentially relevant for our understanding of the wordplay in the book inasmuch we know that the book's chronology correlates with the rapid development of Z's linguistic proficiency in English. This gave Xiaolu Guo the possibility of exploiting a double gap – between a) and b), and between b) and c), respectively – thus raising interpretive questions such as the following:

a)–b): Could it be, for instance, that the narrating self has embellished her report of the day's events either by silently correcting "embarrassing" linguistic errors she made as an experiencing self (e.g., after having consulted a dictionary) or by inserting "clever" linguistic errors that actually did not occur in the fictional world?

b)–c): Could it be, for instance, that the editing self has corrected or removed certain errors from the manuscript; or, conversely, that a process of self-fashioning (depicting a progress from linguistic and cultural naïveté to greater maturity) has led the editing self to add "typical" or "amusing" linguistic blunders that never happened to the experiencing self or were never initially reported by the narrating self?

Such questions have to be asked, because the textual exploitation of the distinctions between Z's three "selves" could have added interesting polyphonic resonances to the wordplay in the novel. However, I believe that the questions can all be answered in the negative. Not only are there no textual signals that would support such polyphonic readings of the wordplay in the novel; in addition, one has to reckon with the strength of the conventions of the novelist's main generic template, namely, the diary (or notebook), which emphasize the temporal immediacy and the raw authenticity of the writing, thus dispelling the relevance of potential questions following from the theoretical distinction between a), b) and c).

As already suggested, the errors produced by Z mobilize a range of different *linguistic mechanisms*, including accidental sound similarity, morphological re-motivation, literal/figurative reading of idiomatic expressions, lexical polysemy, and so on. The errors show great variety in other ways too, which space restrictions prevent us from discussing in any detail. Some are made in language *reception*, while others occur in language *production*. Furthermore, the unintended meanings may display various degrees of *contextual aptness*: while several jokes in the corpus are quite clever, others strike us as being rather pointless. The puns also show various degrees of originality, with an example such as (36) clearly appearing at the lower end of this scale.

There is a further possible comparative perspective, which invites us to identify the degree to which the various errors result specifically from *Chinese/English linguistic interference* or have some other source. Phonological interference between English and Chinese is all too evidently the basis for the "loyal"/"royal" joke in example (2) or for the "flute"/"fruit" confusion in (3). By contrast, interference between English and Chinese can definitely be ruled out as the basis for the "weather"/"whether" pun in example (18), as a lot of European EFL learners or indeed native speakers of English would struggle to spell these words correctly. However, as soon as we move beyond these very obvious cases at either end of the spectrum, my inexistent knowledge of Chinese fatally disqualifies me from assessing the extent to which certain features of the language "shine through" in the errors, providing a plausible motivation for *why* our Chinese narrator Z makes *this* particular significant error in English and activating any double meanings in Chinese that may be lurking behind the error.

2.2.3 Bilingual Chinese/English wordplay

This brings me to a third group of wordplays in the novel: the "truly"[9] bilingual Chinese/English puns. Inasmuch as I can see, this set contains only one clear member, which, I think, like those is the previous group, is involuntarily produced by Z:

(43) How I finding important places including Buckingham Palace, or Big **Stupid** Clock? (p. 12)

Z is surely alluding to "Big Ben", which is the only landmark in London that has "big" in its name and that features a "clock". But why is Big Ben called "Big *Stupid* Clock"? As I was lucky enough to find out with the help of a generous Hong Kong-based colleague,[10] "bèn" means "stupid" in Chinese.

The corpus contains some Italian/English (example (39): *avvocato*/avocado) and some French/English bilingual wordplay (example (36): *pain*/pain, *poisson*/poison, *crêpe*/crap). There is also some punning on words such as "briquette" and "baguette" (example (42)) or "patisserie" (example (20)), which

---

9 See Delabastita (2005) for a comparative discussion and classification of various types of bilingual and bilingually motivated monolingual verbal humour. Section II (Multilingual wordplay in different communicative settings) and to a lesser extent Section III (Translation of wordplay) of The Dynamics of Wordplay 3 are devoted to various aspects of the bilingual / multilingual pun (Knospe, Onysko, and Goth 2016: 97–257 and 261–378).
10 Dr Robert J. Neather, personal communication, 29 December 2014.

are French loans in English, usefully reminding us that the distinction between monolingual and bilingual wordplay, a subcategory of the "based on language structure" criterion in our wordplay definition, is ultimately no less gradual and porous than its other criteria. But, to the best of my knowledge, "Big Stupid Clock" is the only bilingual *Chinese/English* pun in the novel, and it is one I could never have worked out on my own. The point that needs to be made is precisely that "the best of my knowledge" is nowhere near good enough. As with other bilingual puns, proficiency in both languages is required to decode it.[11]

This is the right time to recall that *A Concise Chinese-English Dictionary for Lovers* is very much a "global novel" not just because of its themes, or because it has been translated into two dozens of languages so far, but also because it has reached out to a global and linguistically diverse readership from the beginning. The original book was written to appeal to monolingual native speakers of English (many of whom will take an interest in the novel inasmuch as they are losing their sense of "belonging" as they feel that their world is being engulfed by globalisation, migration and multilingualism); to non-Chinese and non-Anglophone readers who have acquired English as a foreign language (and who can therefore, albeit from a different linguistic angle, relate to the interlingual and intercultural struggles of Z); and, last but not least, to readers – both in China and in the Chinese diaspora worldwide – who have a certain degree of Chinese/English bilingualism (Li 2016). Crucially, Chinese/English bilinguals will better than other readers be able to imagine the narrative of Z "from the inside"; only they will show a smile of fond recognition when they see how some of Z's funny errors spring from familiar Chinese idioms and grammar shining through; only they will be able to pick up all of the novel's Chinese/English bilingual wordplay. This gives the wordplay in the book an elusiveness which correlates very specifically with the multilingual literacy of its various groups of readers.

3 *My Sister, My Love* (2008) by Joyce Carol Oates

3.1 Presentation of the novel

It is an indefinability of a very different type that characterizes the wordplay in *My Sister, My Love* (2008), written by Joyce Carol Oates, one of America's finest

---

11 This is a well-documented fact; see, for instance, Nicole Nolette's (2015) book on theatre and heterolingualism in Quebec for an analysis of the inclusionary and exclusionary uses to which the principle can be put.

and most prolific novelists of the past half century.[12] As with our previous novel, *My Sister, My Love* contains a lot of punning of the "involuntary"[13] and often bilingual type, but the differences are more striking than the similarities. For a start, one would not qualify *My Sister, My Love* as a "global novel".[14] It is a profoundly "American" book in terms of language, characters, settings and themes. It offers a mercilessly satirical take on America's upper-middle-class in the 1990s and its obsession with money, conspicuous consumption, status and celebrity; institutions like the healthcare industry, the legal system, religion, and, especially, the media come in for some hard-hitting criticism, too.

The primary narrator and main character is Skyler Rampike, whose little sister Bliss ("my sister, my love") was found dead with a head injury on January 29, 1997, in the family home in Fair Hills, New Jersey. It is only towards the end of the novel that the reader learns for sure that Bliss had been killed by her own mother, Betsey Rampike. Skyler was only nine at the time; Bliss was six. But Betsey suggests to Skyler (and she makes her husband Bix believe) that he was to blame for his little sister's death. Skyler's grief and sense of guilt never go away.

Betsey Rampike, a faded beauty queen, had a failed career as an ice-skater as a young girl. She now projects her dreams and frustrations on her little daughter Edna Louise, who turns out to have a special talent for ice-skating. Betsey renames her as "Bliss" and spares no effort or expense to boost Bliss's career and to sexualize / commercialize the little girl, with herself parading in the media as the all-American "loving" mother. It is when Bliss develops an ankle problem, is no longer winning big competitions, and relapses into night-time incontinence that Betsey half-accidentally kills her daughter in a fit of drunken exasperation. Afterwards she never stops playing the part of the grieving but brave mum finding support in her Christian faith. Betsey is a shrewd rather than really clever person. She suffers from dyslexia, as we can see from the facsimiles of her handwritten notes and letters copied into the novel. At the end she dies of a botched plastic surgery operation.

---

[12] The author does not need introducing, but it is worth noting that she got her inspiration for this book from a historical murder case, namely, the JonBenét Ramsey case (Freeman 2016).

[13] It may be worth noting that the novel contains a number of errors that apparently do not belong to the author's artistic design: "lifted lifted" (p. 26), "of indeterminte sex and age" (p. 104), "devastating" (p. 236), "contemproary American history" (p. 448).

[14] It has been translated into six languages (into Chinese, French, Italian, Polish, Spanish, Swedish), against no fewer than twenty-four for *Concise Dictionary* (Jaggi 2014). Note that the latter book was the author's literary début in English, whereas Oates is a highly acclaimed and indeed fully canonized writer in English; this is her thirty-seventh published novel.

The father, Bix Rampike, is from a wealthy family and was a top-class athlete at university. He is tall, muscular, sexy, gregarious, ultra-Republican and fond of showy big cars. He is also chronically adulterous, arrogant and overbearing, and ruthless in the pursuit of his professional ambitions.

Bix had earlier tried to make Skyler into a gymnast, which only resulted in a bad fall that leaves the boy with a permanent limp. That problem, combined with the guilt and trauma of losing his little sister, not to mention the totally inept parenting of Bix and Betsey, result in Skyler dropping out of school, getting over-diagnosed and over-medicated, moving between special-needs elite schools and treatment centres, and further sliding into isolation, depression, and drug abuse.

Skyler as the narrator of the book is nineteen years old now. He has broken with his parents, and is being looked after by the well-meaning evangelical pastor Bob, who encourages him to come to terms with his troubled childhood and traumas by writing the story in his own words. Skyler is highly gifted. He writes his therapeutic memoirs in the format of a postmodern novel, combining filmic narrative techniques with stream of consciousness, elaborate footnotes, embedded narratives, the use of different typefaces, drawings and other graphic gimmicks, self-referential metanarrative comments, disrupted chronologies, false starts, intertextual nods at other genres such as the teen romance (p. 423) and the dictionary novel (pp. 117, 139). In his retrospective narration, he mostly refers to the younger version of himself in the third person.

Importantly, the book's self-conscious postmodern style is Skyler's rather than Oates's. In the final analysis, the book portrays the un-postmodern search for truth, understanding and peace of mind by a young man who was horribly let down by both his parents and American society. It is an intensely human and moving novel which offers glimmers of hope and redemption in the end, to the point of making readers feel sorry for Bix and Betsey. These few notes do not even begin to do justice to the ambiguities and complexities of this massive novel, but they will have to suffice as background to our discussion of wordplay in the novel.

3.2 Punning names

Not in real life perhaps, but in fictional universes names do not have to be arbitrary and can inform us directly or more indirectly about the bearer's personality.[15] Oates's novel is one such novel that invests heavily in names.

---

15 Name-giving is a traditional and well-documented technique of characterization. In some cases, the character's name sums up the key features of the speaker's personality or role in the

We have already mentioned that Skyler's little sister was "rebranded" as Bliss, which not only has the ring of divine joy and salvation about it (an echo to Betsey's religious fanaticism) but also sounds snappier and more marketable than "Edna Louise" (demonstrating the mercantile undercurrent driving Betsey's choices).

The first name "Skyler" had been chosen by Bix to express the high hopes of an ambitious father for his first-born son: "Sky's the limit" (p. 76). Unfortunately, several people characteristically misremember Skyler's name and start calling him "Skeeler" (from p. 74 onwards) or even "Scooter" (from p. 164 onwards), which is more suggestive of directionless horizontal movement than of a meteoric vertical rise to success, illustrating the boy's status as an anti-hero.

The surname "Rampike" (forceful and unsubtle like a battering "ram"; sharp like a "pike") is evocative in itself. So is the way in which it is frequently mispronounced as either "Ram-Pick" or "Ranpick"; the association with "prick" is never more than a single letter away. Elsewhere the name is deliberately and insultingly transformed into "Rampuke" (pp. 121 and 219).

Betsey's maiden name is "Sckulhorne". Does this name "merely" evoke venerable West-European ancestry, or are we to gather that Betsey is all "bone from the neck upwards"? Or consider the following names of secondary characters: the sports-paediatrician treating Bliss is called Dr Muddick; the specialist in child psychopharmacology treating Bliss has the name Dr. Bohr-Mandrake; the coroner who examines Bliss's dead body is called Dr Virgil Elyse; one of lawyers hired by Bix is named Morris Kruk; the pastor who offers Skyler an escape has the name Bob Fluchaus; the shrinks treating Skyler include Dr Splint and Dr Murdstone; and so on.

The name of Dr Murdstone especially ([capable of] "murd[er]" + [hard like] "stone") is a particularly broad hint urging the reader to read personality and satire into names, inasmuch as Murdstone – the name of a character in *David Copperfield* – is known as a textbook example of Dickensian suggestive name-giving. *My Sister, My Bone* is a treasure-trove of examples of such speaking names with degrees of motivation ranging between strong and vaguely evocative, and with intentionality sometimes operating at the author-level (family names), sometimes at the character-level (first names, nicknames). But, however cleverly used here, the technique as such is a well-established one. The effect of many other puns in the novel is contingent on more recent and specifically postmodern modes of writing. It is those we shall now focus on.

---

story, as in overtly allegorical stories such as *Everyman*. In more modern narratives, the "speaking names" operate in more indirect ways. For more detailed typologies, see Birus (1987).

3.3 Multiple voices, multiple readings

3.3.1 Deliberate: looking for rhetorical effect

There is a group of cases where characters make puns which are undoubtedly deliberate in a manner which highlights their personality and their life's agenda.

For instance, the local ice-skating contests for young children are called "Tots-on Ice Capades", a brand name which puns on "escapades" to make it more memorable and commercially effective. Their habitual presenter is fond of making superlative mots-valises for "humorous" effect:

(44) His voice – gravelly baritone, subtly mocking – scraped against the microphone like fingernails: "*Hel*-lo ladiez 'n' gentz 'n' all the rest of you" – pause for laughs, titters – "I am your 'umble 'ost for this **perspercarious** non-puerile Tots-on-**Ice Capades** 1994 – Jeremiah Jericho!" [perspicuous/perspicacious/precarious/perspire] [ice/escapades] (p. 104) (similarly [perspercacious] on p. 106)

To help her cope with the loss of her daughter and the break-up of her marriage and to perpetuate the memory of Bliss, Betsey launches a line of products, beginning with beauty products, later branching out into other markets (p. 477). The punning name of the line – Heaven Scent – shamelessly cashes in on the tragedy of Bliss and on buyers' spiritual sentiments:

(45) **Heaven Scent** [divine or sacred scent/sent by or from heaven] (p. 330 and ff.)

Bix, too, produces a few intentional wordplays that express his personality, more particularly his crude assertiveness. This is how he berates the Russian coach (named Vassily Andreevich Volokhomsky) who is in vain trying to make a gymnast out of Skyler:

(46) 'Scuse me, Vas'ly Andervitch – **Kolonoskopi** – whatever – I'm not seeing much progress here. I know you're a pro, you're a *bonafid* Olympic medal winner, I know because, comrade, I did a little background check, but at these prices, I have to admit that I am just a little disappointed, *verstayen*? [colonoscopy] (p. 82)

Here is Bix's standard joke about Pittsburgh, the city where his mother hails from:

(47) Skyler laughed when Daddy said how Grandmother Rampike and certain relatives of Daddy's lived in "**Piggsburgh**" which was the "gruntiest, stinkiest" city in the United States. [city of pigs] (p. 57)

This is how Bix speaks about Mr Kissler, who is Betsey's business partner and fiancé at the end of her life:

(48) This 'fiancé' – 'Nathan **Kissler**' – Betsey turned a deaf ear to my investigator, who'd turned up some frank evidence that **Kiss-my-ass** would've been arrested for embezzlement not once not twice but three times. (p. 530)

3.3.2 Accidental' wordplay – but whose linguistic accidents?

As opposed to these examples, most of the wordplays in the novel appear to have an accidental character within the fictional world; they often concern foreign phrases or rare words, so that we can refer to them as malapropisms. I am using the hedge "appear to" for a reason. Let us remind ourselves of the novel's narrative structure. The primary narrator is Skyler, who, at the age of 19 tries to come to terms with the traumas of his youth. Within the fictional universe of the book, he is a dyslexic as well as being an outcast and a junkie with serious mental health issues. No less crucially, he is writing his memoir in a self-consciously postmodern style. We cannot therefore avoid questioning his reliability as a narrator. This complicates the interpretation of the malapropisms that are found in Skyler's discourse. Let us review some of Skyler's self-produced malapropisms:

(49) A religious lunatic like who's it – **"Kirky-gard"**. Bullshit nobody believes except pathetic assholes with I.Q.'s drooping around their ankles. [Kierkegaard / guard = protector of the kirk = church] (p. 28)

(50) For you had only to glance at our pedophile, the pariah of Morris County, all knowledge of Gunther Ruscha's lurid past but a ***tabbouleh rosa***, and a primitive warning signal would detonate in the frontal lobe of your reptile brain: "Sex deviate!" [tabula rasa] (p. 360)

(51) *That this boy who assumes a pose of scowling indifference, picking at his face as the adults discuss his future, is so hesitant to acknowledge what is, by this time, a* **fête accompli** [fait accompli / reference to the divorce of Bix and Betsey, a cause for fête = celebration?] (p. 428)

(52) **POOR SKYLER! THWARTED MIDWAY IN HIS JOURNEY TO SPRING HOLLOW, NEW York, and for all we know, maybe he never arrives there. While Skyler is lost in *medias race*** in Fort Lee, New Jersey, we can use the lull in the narrative to present a miscellany of items too unwieldy to have "worked into" previous chapters. [in medias res] (p. 498)

Skyler – being the dyslexic junkie that he is, writing his memoirs in a frenzy and possibly with irregular access to reference books – may well be the inadvertent author of these misspellings. The use of inverted commas (in example (49)) would then signal his doubts; the use of italics (in examples (50), (51) and (52)) may perhaps not only signal "this is a foreign phrase" but also "I am not too sure about the spelling". The following example with self-referential metalingual comment goes some way towards backing up this hypothesis:

(53) **Sick** *transit gloria* or whatever the (Latin) expression is, maybe my editor will know. [Lat. sic transit gloria (mundi)] (p. 78)

As does this one:

(54) **Tabbouleh rasa**. *Damn "foreign phrase" isn't in my dictionary which is an ominous sign maybe I've misspelled it. No matter: for those of us haphazardly (if expensively) educated and pretentious as hell, dropouts eager to be mistaken as* **O current, O fate,** *and* **O fund,** *of the* cognozenti, polylingual *and* polymorphous *and* non plus ultra, *it means, possibly in Latin, "a smooth or erased tablet": that's to say "the mind in its hypothetical primary blank or empty state". (Sounds good!)* [Lat. tabula rasa] [Fr. au courant] [Fr. au fait] [Fr. au fond] (p. 60)

But then, Skyler's narrative is full of medical jargon and other rare polysyllabic words of foreign origin that he *does* spell correctly. Also, in example (54) the metalingual comment might strike the reader as spinning totally out of control, thus throwing into doubt the most straightforward "realistic" reading (Skyler's linguistic blunders result from his dyslexia and mental ill-health) and raising the suggestion that the malapropisms may be just another playful postmodern strategy. If Skyler is "steeped in irony" (p. 424), one wonders why his self-irony would not extend to his apparent malapropisms. Could they perhaps just be part of the "literary 'unreliable narrator' stuff?" (p. 205)?

(55) Think that I, Skyler Rampike, steeped in irony, *ressentiment*, and chronic **sand fraud** like a squid steeped in ink, can't put aside postmodernist strategies of "storytelling" for the naive, raw, throbbing emotions of mere storytelling? [Fr. sang froid] (p. 424)

Is it Skyler-the-dyslexic-junkie who commits such errors accidentally, or is it Skyler-the-smart-postmodern-narrator who produces them tongue in cheek? The novel offers no way to resolve the question.

The matter becomes much more complicated even when we consider the many malapropisms which were to all appearances initially perpetrated by others – not by Skyler-the-narrator but by the people he quotes. There are many of those. Skyler's narrative is reverberating with the discourses of other people, especially those of his parents, making *My Sister, My Love* into a very Bakhtinian novel.[16]

The narrator's quotees include the younger version of himself. The communicative set-up is perfectly clear in the following instances of this:

---

[16] For another application of Bakhtin's notion of polyphony in connection with wordplay in the novel, see Genz (2015).

(56) When the subject came up one day in the Rampike household, and Skyler happened to overhear, the silly kid piped up fearfully, "'**Headhunters**'? After Daddy's h-head?" and Mummy and Daddy laughed at Skyler, and filed away little Skyler's query to be repeated, for laughs, in subsequent years. (p. 63)

(57) Grimly smiling/carelessly shaved Bix Rampike jet-lagged and cranky from a trip to **Saudi Arabia** (which Skyler misheard as **Sandy Arabia**) on oil business, was late driving Skyler to the Gymnastics Lab on that final Saturday. (p. 81)

Skyler-the-narrator unmistakably distances himself from his own "childish" earlier misunderstandings. The same is true in the following two instances, even if context and plausibility have to be factored in to make up for the absence of metalingual comments:

(58) In Mummy's magazines you can read about what adults do all the time: '**adult'ry**'. It's something nasty called 'adult'ry' because that is what **adults** do. (p. 202)

(59) The throaty voice drops solemnly, as if Zelda were trying to keep from bursting into tears, Skyler has to strain to hear what sounds like *cancer of the service. Cancer of the* **service**? Skyler shudders. [cervix] (p. 511) (see also p. 531)

Similarly, in the realistic terms of the novel, there is no doubting that Betsey has a permanent struggle with difficult words:

(60) scolds me for 'wasting gas'! 'Never staying home'! Next thing, he'll be checking the what-is-it on my car – '**odormeter**'. You know, tells how many miles you've driven? [odometer = milometer/odor = smell] (p. 34)

The following Freudian slip occurs in a verbatim transcript of the ransom note addressed to Bix we know to have been written by Betsey and which contains several other spelling mistakes:

(61) Your daghter is in danger of Hell. Yet we will return her to you if you repent. If you return to your **Martial Vows** to have & to hold until death part. [marital vows] (p. 332)

The most tireless generator of malapropisms, however, is undoubtedly Bix. Having picked up some foreign phrases during his education and his many business trips abroad, and always keen to make an impression on his interlocutors, Bix loves to make the most of his limited stock of French, German and Latin phrases, throwing them in at every half-opportunity. The following examples – the first one a misquotation-cum-mistranslation more than a pun – show that his Latin, let alone his Greek, is really non-existent:

(62) **Homo homin lupus**. My father used to quote, know what it means? Greek for '**wolf is friend to man.**' Meaning you got to be man enough to harness the wolf, son, the wolf-blood coursing through your 'civilized' Rampike veins [Lat. homo homini lupus = man is a wolf to man] (p. 114) (similarly on p. 263)

(63) Daddy had returned to work on the morning following Bliss's funeral for Daddy had needed to throw himself into work at once: "More work, the better! **Sick** *transit mundi*." [Lat. sic transit gloria mundi / ?through sickness the world perishes] (p. 397)

Greek-derived words don't fare any better:

(64) your mother is a woman, and they are born with these extra **chromosomes** – 'sensitivity' – 'intuition' – 'nesting instinct'. The bottom line is, it makes them prone to **monogramy**, as the male of the species is naturally prone to **polygramy**, and we have to understand this distinction. [chromosome ≠ gene] [monogamy / monogram] [polygamy / polygram] (p. 269)

Here is another one:

(65) Must've been crazy for her when he'd married her, a fatal weakness he had for submissive / soft-fleshed females gazing up at him in undisguised adoration. Even when one of them reviled Bix as a selfish prick he found such women irresistible, the **sin** *qua* **none** bottom line is such females adored his prick, and him. [Lat. sine qua non] (p. 337)

It looks as if Bix never stops making a fool of himself trying to overreach himself linguistically. Perhaps he inherited this propensity from his mother (as, possibly, Skyler got it from his father):

(66) I hope to see her crowned – what is it? – your mother has been telling me – 'Little Miss Jersey Ice Princess' – and on TV! – the most beautiful amazing **prodity** in the Rampike family, at last – so emphasizing *prodity* with an excited clack of her formidable gleaming-white dentures, Skyler had to wonder if the mispronunciation was deliberate, as it often seemed her son Bix's mispronouncements / malapropisms must be deliberate. [prodigy] (p. 178–179)

Skyler's hypothesis expressed at the end of the quote is not to be dismissed too lightly. We did point out earlier Bix's talent for sarcastic punning. But the possible complications regarding intentionality in these reported puns go much further than this. Consider the following (and final) four examples, where Bix's apparent poor pronunciation of French produces extreme cases of semantic incongruity:

(67) As Daddy used to say with sheepish-shit-eating-Daddy smile *Forgive me my* **foe paws** *as you'd wish to be forgiven yours, hey?* [Fr. faux pas / enemy + animal's feet] (p. 24)

(68) Son, enough of ruining your eyes with that 'print' crap. We're going out. There's a surprise in store. **Pear** und **feese**, eh? **Veeta**! [Fr. père] [Fr. fils] [Fr. vite] (p. 62)

(69) though it did hurt, have to admit, when Betsey went on those damn TV shows promoting her damn 'memoirs' and spoke of me, her ex-, like I'm the woman's **beet-noir**... as if our marriage ending was my fault alone. [Fr. bête noire] (p. 529)

(70) Your mother prepared it for you 'in case God calls me' and it was her wish that you do with it whatever you want and, son, that includes destroying it which is what your dad recommends **toot sweet**. [Fr. tout de suite] (p. 532)

Skyler-now (the narrating self) is reporting and transcribing how Skyler-in-the-past (the experiencing self) heard what his father was telling him. Taking into account these levels of embedding, as well as the possibility that miscommunication can occur on either the production side or the reception side, a whole paradigm of possible interpretations opens up. Perhaps, the linguistic errors here are accidentally and unconsciously produced by Skyler-now (the narrating self), who is, after all, a dyslectic junkie. Or perhaps *not*: Skyler-the-narrator may be fully aware of them. In the latter case, the flippant misrepresentations of the French are perhaps merely another manifestation of the narrator's self-consciously postmodern and unreliable posture. Or perhaps they are *not*, and they are to be interpreted as having a "psychological" basis within the fiction of the novel. In the latter case, they might, for instance, be seen as a psychologically motivated strategy of Skyler as a narrating self to ridicule his father by ascribing to him in retrospect linguistic blunders that Skyler would not have been aware of at the time as an experiencing self. Or such wilful and antagonistic misquotation does *not* occur, and the experiencing self did hear and register the French phrases in the ridiculous form in which they are being reported here. In the latter case, they might have to be attributed to Bix and/or to Skyler. Indeed, perhaps Skyler committed a receptive error by mishearing/misunderstanding and wrongly registering an utterance that was otherwise unproblematic in itself. Or perhaps Bix did make the mistake, and if he did, it was perhaps out of ignorance – or, who knows, on purpose with a comic intent?

This paradigm of possible interpretations is represented visually in Table 1. Clearly, not all these interpretive options are equally plausible. Every single case would deserve separate examination and assessment with close attention given to context. But no amount of critical scrutiny will completely resolve all the text's ambiguities when it comes to attributing sources and causes to its many malapropisms. This makes the wordplay in Oates's novel hard to pin down on account of its multi-voiced nature and postmodern style rather than of the multilingual literacies of its various readerships, as in *A Concise Chinese-English Dictionary for Lovers*.[17]

Table 1: Paradigm of possible readings

Skyler-narrator misrepresents the "reality" of the quoted speech event	involuntarily	errors are caused by Skyler-narrator's dyslexia and mental confusion at the time of writing the memoir	
	deliberately	*literary motivation:* Skyler-narrator indulges in postmodern rhetorical playfulness	
		psychological motivation: Skyler-narrator wants to ridicule his father through caricature	
Skyler-narrator represents the "reality" of the quoted speech event correctly		the errors are produced by Bix	**deliberately:** Bix is joking
			involuntarily: Bix is blundering
		receptive blundering by Skyler-experiencer	

4 Concluding remark

Needless to say, these two novels constitute a ridiculously small sample of the total literary output in English in the past decade or so. That should prevent us from even raising the question of representativeness. That being said, with one being a "global novel" and the other a "postmodern" one, they may to some extent be assumed to stand for two striking trends in the modern novel and therefore potentially aspire to at least a certain degree of typicality or comparability with many other recent novels. To find out whether the findings of our paired case study can indeed be extended to a wider corpus of modern fiction will need further research (as the hackneyed phrase goes). A no less intriguing question is how translators have responded to the major challenges that our two novels represent.[18] One conclusion stands absolutely firm, however. The study of wordplay in the novel requires a flexible, context-sensitive and dynamic understanding of the phenomenon – no less than in other genres or discursive

---

[17] This is not to deny that the linguistic skills of reader do play a part in the case of Oates's book as well, as several of the puns are bilingual ones.
[18] For an excellent first exploration, see Zoé Denis's (2016) study of the French translation of Guo's novel.

contexts such as joking, comedy, sitcoms, advertising, etc., which perhaps tend to display contextual situatedness and pragmatic interactivity in more conspicuous ways.

Acknowledgement: I would like to thank the editors and the anonymous referees for their stimulating comments and suggestions.

5 References

Birus, Hendrik. 1987. Vorschlag zu einer Typologie literarischer Namen. *Zeitschrift für Literaturwissenschaft und Linguistik* 17(67). 38–51.
Delabastita, Dirk. 1993. *There's a double tongue. An investigation into the translation of Shakespeare's wordplay, with special reference to Hamlet*. Amsterdam & Atlanta: Rodopi.
Delabastita, Dirk. 2005. Cross-language comedy in Shakespeare. *Humor* 18(2). 161–184.
Denis, Zoé. 2016. *A comparative analysis of* A concise Chinese-English dictionary for lovers *and its French translation*. Unpublished bachelor paper, University of Namur.
Empson, William. 1930. *Seven types of ambiguity*. London: Chatto & Windus.
Freeman, Hadley. 2016. *JonBenét Ramsey: the brutal child murder that still haunts America*. https://www.theguardian.com/us-news/2016/dec/11/jonbenet-ramsey-the-brutal-child-that-still-haunts-america (accessed 11 December 2016).
Genz, Julia. 2015. "Il wullte bien, mais il ne puffte pas" – de la polyglossie à la polyphonie dans le roman *Der sechste Himmel* (*Feier a Flam*) de Roger Manderscheid. In Esme Winter-Froemel & Angelika Zirker (eds.), *Enjeux du jeu de mots. Perspectives linguistiques et littéraires* (The Dynamics of Wordplay 3), 115–133. Berlin & Boston: De Gruyter.
Grice, Paul H. 1975. Logic and conversation. In Peter Cole & Jerry L. Morgan (eds.), *Syntax and semantics. Vol. 3*, 41–58. New York: Academic Press.
Guo, Xiaolu. 2007. *A Concise Chinese-English dictionary for lovers*. London: Chatto & Windus.
Jaggi, Maya. 2014. *Interview with Xiaolu Guo*. https://www.theguardian.com/books/2014/may/30/xiaolu-guo-communist-china-interview (accessed 30 May 2014)
Knospe, Sebastian, Alexander Onysko & Maik Goth (eds.). 2016. *Crossing languages to play with words. Multidisciplinary approaches* (The Dynamics of Wordplay 3). Berlin & Boston: De Gruyter.
Li, Wei (ed.). 2016. *Multilingualism in the Chinese diaspora worldwide: Transnational connections and local social realities*. New York: Routledge.
Nolette, Nicole. 2015. *Jouer la traduction. Théâtre et hétérolinguisme au Canada francophone*. Ottawa: les Presses de l'Université d'Ottawa.
Oates, Joyce Carol. 2008. *My sister, my love. The intimate story of Skyler Rampike*. New York: HarperCollins.

Astrid Poier-Bernhard
Wor(l)dplay: Reflections on a writing-experience

Abstract: In my essay, I take a personal writing-experience as the starting point for some general reflections on wordplay. I think that the discussion of wordplay requires an 'aesthetic' or 'integral' approach to the phenomenon. This means that not only the mechanisms but the experience of wordplay must be taken in consideration. Ideally wordplay provokes a 'pleasure of the text' or even an instant of 'jouissance' (R. Barthes), because it makes us experience the playfulness of language, mind and world at once. Intentional wordplay can bring us in touch with another notion of play, the 'play which happens' or 'worldplay' – a notion I use here to describe the vivid experience of a complex and combinatorial interaction of any 'elements', and which is close to the notion of 'creativity' and the experience of a 'freshness of mind'.

Keywords: Barthes, Calvino, creativity, exactitude, Jakobson, jouissance, lightness, multiplicity, playfulness, pleasure of the text, poetic function, rapidity, visibility, worldplay

1 Preliminaries

Bettina Kluge and Esme Winter-Froemel invited me in March 2016 to give a workshop on *Oulipian writing under constraints* for the members of the network *Dynamics of Wordplay*. Bettina Kluge, who was my colleague for six years at Karl-Franzens-Universität in Graz, was inspired to pursue her linguistic research on forms of address by my non-academic book *Viel Spaß mit Haas. Spiel – Regel – Literatur* (2003), a series of essays on or around the themes of play, rules and literature, joyfully written 'under constraint' – as a pastiche of the so-called 'Brenner-novels' of the Austrian writer Wolf Haas. I had never intended to write such a book, and the inspiration to do so came from a rather surprising source. The trigger was a kind of involuntary wordplay. Sitting on a very small chair at a parents' evening, I discovered a very funny word on the blackboard: GEMEINSCHAF. Somebody had written this word incorrectly, without its final *t*, so that the intended word *Gemeinschaft* ('community') was transformed into a 'common sheep' or a 'nasty' sheep, the German adjective *gemein* having both these meanings. It was a real surprise to discover 'two potential sheep' in the very ordinary word *Gemeinschaft*, and I could hardly believe that I had never become aware of them before. And right in front of the sheep, there was also the possessive pronoun *mein* ('my'), within which the indefinite article *ein* ('a') was also contained. The lapsus[1] had revealed the word to be a 'multiple word'. The unexpected discovery struck me like a bolt of lightning and kicked off a creative process: within the space of a single moment my mind was filled with a wealth of ideas for a potential text, a text about the relation of a ('my') sheep to its community etc. When I started to write the next day another surprising thing happened in my head: One of the sentences I had written triggered the whole stylistic paradigm of the Brenner-novels of Wolf Haas, whose novel *Wie die Tiere* (2001) I had read a few weeks before. Would I be able to use that unconventional, deliberately imperfect and elliptic style while developing my own ideas? I decided to give it a try, without knowing where the text would lead me. It would have been difficult to stop me once I had started writing, because, for about six weeks, I found myself carried away by the joyful mood that accompanies a creative flow. It very quickly became obvious that several subjects of my academic research on Oulipian literature which popped up wanted to be told in an unconventional way, interrupted or surrounded by all kinds of improvisation or digression. It felt natural to play with sounds, letters, words and meanings and to reflect for example on the syllable 'au' in the word *Bauch* ('belly') or on French cocks and their *cocorico*...

If I develop, in the following pages, the idea of an 'integral approach' to wor(l)dplay, it is based on this writing-experience and, of course, my general experience of reading and my interest in the 'ludic dimension' of literary texts (Poier-Bernhard 2012).

2 Wor(l)dplay

What are my basic ideas?
- The discussion of wordplay requires an 'aesthetic' or 'integral' approach to the phenomenon.
- Wordplay is a form of play which actualizes 'worldplay'. *Worldplay* means the notion of play 'which happens'.

---

[1] On lapsus see also Rabatel in The Dynamics of Wordplay 7.

- A pun is the smallest quantity of text able to provide a physically noticeable 'pleasure of the text' or provoke an instant of 'jouissance' (Barthes 1973).
- The aesthetic values which Italo Calvino suggests for the next millennium – lightness, exactitude, rapidity, visibility, multiplicity – allow us to highlight several aspects and potential aesthetic qualities of wordplay (Calvino 1998).
- Wordplay in literary texts is less the fruit of deliberate decisions than the traces left by a playful, creative state of mind, in which elements of very diverse categories come together in an unexpected way.
- The understanding of wordplay necessitates a re-creative process.

Between *wordplay* and *worldplay* there is only one difference: a simple *l*. What does this *l* stand for? Of course, it does not stand for anything, but I would suggest that it stands for 'letter' or for 'language' – the fact that signs and sounds have become means of communication between human beings. We *use* language intentionally, but at the same time, as human beings, we live *in* or *through* language which already exists. If we think about the world we live in, our thinking is based on the concepts our language offers us. We can communicate because language has become a conventional code, but, at the same time, we can also use language in an unconventional way – *playing with words*. Language unites the notions of (active) wordplay and (passive) worldplay.

From my point of view, active – 'intentional' – wordplay, is always connected with a dimension of play 'which happens'. It is not by chance that *play* has become a fundamental metaphor for basic processes characterizing our lives: you can look *outside*, at either natural or cultural environments and you'll find movements, interactions and combinatorial processes all around; you can also look *inside*, at what is happening mentally and psychologically, and you'll see how many factors (bodily and [environ-] mental factors, conscious and unconscious factors) interact to constitute a constant – yet constantly changing – stream of experience. Finally, you can look at language itself – which might be seen as an interface between our so-called inner and the outer world – and it will become obvious that language is basically a combinatorial and dynamic process.[2]

In various disciplines in which scientists try to find a metaphor for the basic processes they study, they end up with the notion of *play*, because the 'play

---

[2] On the notion(s) of play and its 'passepartout-effect' cf. Matuschek (1998). For Manfred Eigen and Ruthild Winkler (1990) *play* is the main metaphor for their understanding of nature. Manfred Eigen was awarded the Nobel Prize in Chemistry in 1967 for the description of extremely fast chemical reactions.

which happens' implies 'very quick movements' and dynamic, non-predictable and potentially recursive processes of interaction. The notion of 'play which happens' is very close to the metaphor of 'dance' and it is interesting that one of the first definitions of the Old High German word *spil* ('play') is: 'a quick movement, like in dance'. Convincing wordplay, in which the combinatorial potential of language is not only used but where attention is also drawn to it, can allow us to experience this basic playfulness.

Salvatore Attardo (this volume) emphasizes the fact that there are only four basic mechanisms which can be considered universal mechanisms for the creation of wordplay: addition, deletion, substitution and inversion. He says that this is a disappointing result, because these four mechanisms do not contain anything special and are the same as in common linguistic processes. Hence, so long as one wants to purely objectify the phenomenon and does not try to find a view which includes the 'aesthetics' of wordplay – its creative origin and its (intended) effect on (us) language users –, one doesn't perceive or cannot identify a difference.

In my view, one of the main characteristics of the many varieties of wordplay is making *aesthetically visible/audible* what language generally is. Wordplay works with language on the level of 'material' signs, functioning as a combinatorial machine – based on addition, deletion, substitution and inversion. Normally, when we are not working 'creatively' with language, we fail to see the 'combinatorial play' of language because of its conventional form and our interest in the meaning of an utterance.

Wordplay might be based on the same mechanisms as normal language, but, by breaking up the frozen state of linguistic conventions, it creates something unconventional. Often wordplay does not work only with/on syllable units such as prefixes or suffixes, but freely splits up conventional sequences and forms new 'conglomerates' (that is, if it does not simply play on the homonymy or polysemy of given words and make unconventional use of them, playing with the blending of frames or connecting different mental domains).

Wordplay directs the attention of the hearer/reader to the form of the utterance/text itself. At this moment, wordplay shows its poetic function, urging its recipient, 'Hey, look at me! I am something special...!' In several talks at the conference, the poetic function was mentioned, and several times the question was raised whether one should define the ludic function separately or as a subcategory of the poetic function. I am not a linguist, but I would suggest defining it as a unique category – for two reasons: firstly, we can make a distinction between the impression of 'playfulness' on the one hand and the 'aesthetic beauty' or 'interest' of conscious poetic writing on the other; secondly, Jakobson's (1979) other categories are not mutually exclusive, so there is no problem with cases where both functions obviously interact or fuse. The movement of decomposition and composition, deconstruction and construction, splitting and putting together is a basic feature of our 'playing experience', so that it's natural that we experience the creation of a new word or a new sequence of words on the basis of these processes as 'playful'.

While it is possible that the only consciously intended effect of the form of the wordplay is 'to be unconventional', one is nevertheless very likely to immediately become aware that (and how) some letters or syllables have left their places, that others have appeared – from nowhere or somewhere – and been integrated into the new sequence of letters / syllables / words. In all cases where the four basic mechanisms are involved, the word itself turns into the traces left by a 'dancing' of letters and sounds, and the form takes on an interesting background: space. If there is deletion, some letters or syllables disappear, perhaps to leave space for others; conversely, in the case of addition, one or more letter(s) appear/s to jostle for available space. Substitution and inversion operate within the principle of 'changing places', a permutation of signs we have right in front of our eyes or are confronted with acoustically; in the case of substitution, we experience a simultaneous combination of deletion and addition, so again the memory of language, which must be activated in the process of understanding, appears like an open space in which letters are dancing around. This concept is similar to the dance of the atoms as conceived by Demokrit in *De rerum natura*, an idea which creates, as Italo Calvino pointed out in his Harvard Lectures (Calvino 1998), a taste of 'lightness'. The versatility of the dance of letters provokes or even demands agility of the mind. 'Lightness' is the first value Italo Calvino suggested in 1985 for the literature of the next millennium, and it seems to be a good metaphor for the aesthetic quality of this experience. There can be an effect of 'lightness' even in cases where the wordplay doesn't produce a new meaning. But this is the exception. Often wordplay overflows with meaning.

Let us take a moment to imagine in slow-motion what normally happens very quickly. Wordplay will often create a new sequence of letters or words which will be scrutinized by the eye or the ear: potential 'fault lines' are inspected, the 'intrusion' or the 'borrowing' of letters, sounds, or syllables from another word is detected, a word which could belong to a different semantic field, to a different linguistic category of words, to a different register, to a different language... the list goes on. We have to detect at least two word units in our mind or our linguistic consciousness for us to maybe experience the 'in-between-space' of words.

Considerable neuronal activity is required if we are to understand two things at once: the formal mechanism of the wordplay *and* its meaning. Immediately, the semantic potential of the new word presents itself to the mind. Independent of the quality and the semantic felicity of the wordplay, the moment of discovery itself is often a moment of intensity, in which the activation of 'searching' and the pleasure of 'finding' even evoke physical responses in the form of laughter, a smile or just in a more alert state of mind and feelings of pleasure or surprise. Before the complexity of the new meaning has been fully understood, a new neuronal pathway has to have been activated. Even a quite meaningless play on letters and sounds can be fun, especially if the combinatorial play is repeated or sounds take on some special aesthetic qualities in their new combination. There is no doubt that even completely nonsensical wordplay can have aesthetic qualities and provide ludic and poetic 'pleasure of the text'.

Generally, however, wordplay is convincing if it is also meaningful, for example, if it is a ludic and dense semiotic event at the same time. Michelle Lecolle (in The Dynamics of Wordplay 7) points out that 'the form is crucial', which refers to the aesthetic dimension, while Salvatore Attardo (this volume) focuses on the aspect of 'resolution' – the moment of understanding – which should not be conceived as a complete 'solution', as 'both meanings have to stay'. An incongruity activates certain memories and triggers further associations. Because of the unusual form of the utterance or the unusual combination of the utterance and meaning, the dynamics of semiosis might become apparent; it becomes, in our minds, a somehow 'dramatic' event, for which Roland Barthes' term 'jouissance' is actually quite appropriate: For a moment at least we are so deeply involved in the 'dynamics of wordplay' that we might leave behind our habitual manner of intellectual thought and our concept of being a 'personal subject' in an 'objective' world. Somehow forgetting ourselves and the world, we might be, for an instant, *absorbed in language* – the interface of the self and the world – and might mull over the interesting and joyful experiences of the 'wor(l)dplay', and of the playfulness and the creative potential of the world, language and our mind all at once.

Catherine Kerbrat-Orecchioni (in The Dynamics of Wordplay 7) proposes a very interesting way to analyse the degree of complexity and semantic density of a pun. This analysis permits the evaluation of the interest, the pertinence, the 'quality' of a pun with linguistic means. Among the literary values formulated by Calvino, *multiplicity* and *exactitude* come very close to the criterion of *complexity*, one of the categories suggested by Kerbrat-Orecchioni. But like the two other values Calvino gives us – *visibility* and *rapidity* –, *multiplicity* and *exactitude* are terms from aesthetics which means that they refer not only to the pun itself, in its complex 'material' form of letters and sounds, but also to the experience of the reader/hearer and finally also to the playful, creative state of mind of its author.

One could see during the conference, where these reflections were first presented and a huge number of puns was commented on, that the moment of understanding was usually accompanied by more or less intense physical reactions, such as laughter or movements of the body – a slight shaking of the head or a little nod. A wide range of mimic reactions was also displayed: a variety of smiles, more light in the eyes, maybe a special kind of gaze, maybe a relaxation of the brow or other small signs of both relaxation and activation, of both physical and mental presence, of recreation, refreshment, release, and in the case of a strong humorous effect, mimic reactions of amusement and fun.

The more I think about it, the more the term 'jouissance' as a kind of short and extraordinary moment of *destabilization* seems quite satisfactory. Roland Barthes (1973) conceived and defined the term and the relation between the terms 'plaisir du texte' and 'jouissance' in (at least) two ways, namely that 'jouissance' is either an increased experience of 'pleasure of the text', or the opposite of this. The opposition is that while 'plaisir du texte' confirms the reader's expectations, the 'jouissance' as it were shakes him/her up and causes him/her to transcend his/her comfortable horizon. Barthes (1973) developed his reflections on the basis of real 'texts' and not on small textual units, but both terms are fruitful in our context. As already formulated, I would even go one step further in the interpretation of the 'jouissance-effect' and hypothesise that the reason *why the destabilization is joyful* is the fact that a successful pun can 'catapult' us out of our habitual mental set so that for a brief moment we overcome our dualistic mode of perception.

The use of the prefix *re-* which appeared in the enumeration of the bodily reactions, brings to mind that the 'semantic challenge' of a pun can be seen, compared to the usually (quite) effortless decoding of conventional wording, as the playful 'building up of an obstacle'. This is then followed – in the case of 'successful understanding' – by an experience of mental refreshment or recreation comparable to that in common relaxation techniques involving conscious muscle contraction. It demands much more activity than conventional language decoding – a type of attention which allows bisociation and new cognitive connections. On account of the mental activity required, the semantic decoding itself becomes to a certain degree conscious. Because of the unusual aesthetic form or use of language, we not only resolve a semantic problem, but also experience the complexity and dynamics of the searching process – and might even get a taste of a creative state of mind.

A pun which has been formulated deliberately is in any case evidence of a playful state of mind. Raymond Gibbs (this volume) emphasizes the fact that a large number of factors are involved in the creative process, so that one has finally to call into question the concept of 'intentional wordplay'. Based on my personal experience, I can say that there can be playful moods, playful states of mind and even playful thinking habits, which increase the probability of interesting discoveries. When one uses ludic – often combinatorial – wordplay in a writing process, it is very likely that one will also play with other elements of a (literary) text. Creativity is the result of the experience of the basic playfulness of the entity mind / language / world.

If the link between wordplay and creativity is obvious, it might be less evident where the addressee is concerned. If it is not a simple effect of 'resonance' (Rosa 2016), it has to be the playful, unconventional form and / or the unconventional connection of form and content which puts us in touch with creativity and playfulness. We have to be creative in some way to 'resolve' the semantic challenge of the pun. Understanding a pun necessitates 'playing' oneself, in the sense of a combinatorial activity: one must leave the habitual ways of thinking behind and quickly explore other possibilities. In that sense wordplay is literally 'performative'. Wordplay is often based on semantic incongruities, and the aim is not just to resolve them, but to at the same time call to mind different interactions between signifier-signifier and signifier-signified-relations. The effect of this 'crossing-over-activity' is basically an immediate pleasure, a 'freshness of mind', which has probably to do with a necessary change from an intellectual decoding-process used to the linearity of texts to a mode of 'aesthetic decoding' necessitating and leading to an experience of the space-like nature and the clarity of the mind, where one can feel how words and meanings refer to one another in a playful manner; the experience can be the experience of the playfulness of language, or, more basically, the experience of the playfulness of the mind (experienced through language). One may become conscious not only of the complex interactions of forms and meanings, but also of the dynamic movement of thought itself. On the occasions when one becomes aware of this dynamic, it is generally an unusual or sometimes even uncomfortable experience, such as if one notices for example, that words and thoughts are merely swirling around in one's mind without any meaning or aesthetic significance. In the case of wordplay, it is different, because the interest and the semantic challenge of its form provide a clear focus. Either the multiple facets of the dynamic constitution of meaning based on a surprising sequence of words or sounds or letters manifest themselves and the reader / hearer becomes aware of them without any effort on his / her part, or there will be a certain 'hiatus', experienced as a 'task', as a search, with no knowledge as to where it will lead. This provides excellent conditions for a creative – or re-creative – process: a high degree of mental activity, a 'searching' attitude and an unforeseeable result. Being, as it is, the traces left by a playful state of mind, wordplay 'invites' the addressee to perhaps discover, through language, the basic playfulness of the mind: *worldplay*.

3 References

Barthes, Roland. 1973. *Le plaisir du texte*. Paris: Seuil.
Calvino, Italo. 1998. *Lezioni americane: sei proposte per il prossimo millenio*. Milano: Mondadori.
Eigen, Manfred & Ruthild Winkler. 1990. *Das Spiel. Naturgesetze steuern den Zufall*. München: Piper.
Haas, Wolf. 2001. *Wie die Tiere*. Reinbek: Rowohlt.
Jakobson, Roman. 1979. Linguistik und Poetik. In Elmar Holenstein & Tarcisius Schelbert (eds.), *Roman Jakobson. Poetik. Ausgewählte Aufsätze 1921–1971*, 83–121. Frankfurt am Main: Suhrkamp.
Kerbrat-Orecchioni, Catherine. 2018. Heurs et malheurs du jeu de mots. In Esme Winter-Froemel & Alex Demeulenaere (eds.), *Jeux de mots, textes et contextes* (The Dynamics of Wordplay 7), 25–48. Berlin & Boston: De Gruyter.
Lecolle, Michelle. 2018. Enjeu du collectif – noms collectifs en jeux. In Esme Winter-Froemel & Alex Demeulenaere (eds.), *Jeux de mots, textes et contextes* (The Dynamics of Wordplay 7), 157–174. Berlin & Boston: De Gruyter.
Matuschek, Stefan. 1998. *Literarische Spieltheorie. Von Petrarca bis zu den Brüdern Schlegel*. Heidelberg: Winter.
Poier-Bernhard, Astrid. 2003. *Viel Spaß mit Haas – oder ohne Haas, je nachdem wie du das jetzt sehen willst. Spiel – Regel – Literatur*. Wien: Sonderzahl.
Poier-Bernhard, Astrid. 2012. *Texte nach Bauplan. Studien zur zeitgenössischen ludisch-methodischen Literatur in Frankreich und Italien*. Heidelberg: Winter.
Rabatel, Alain. 2018. À quelles conditions les *lapsus clavis* sont-ils des jeux de mots? In Esme Winter-Froemel & Alex Demeulenaere (eds.), *Jeux de mots, textes et contextes* (The Dynamics of Wordplay 7), 49–76. Berlin & Boston: De Gruyter.
Rosa, Hartmut. 2016. *Resonanz: Eine Soziologie der Weltbeziehung*. Frankfurt am Main: Suhrkamp.

Publications by Astrid Poier-Bernhard

Literary texts

2003. *Viel Spaß mit Haas – oder ohne Haas, je nachdem wie du das jetzt sehen willst. Spiel – Regel – Literatur*. Wien: Sonderzahl.

2004. Salzfass 1, Salzfass 2. In Friedrich Achleitner: *Kopf und Zahl, 20 ... Dramolette, Fragen, Jahre*, 29–30. Wien: Sonderzahl.
2008. Chaque alphabet a son histoire [Texts and photographs for an artist's book on Anna Romanello]. Exposition *lib(e)ro d'arte, libri ogetti* in the museum "Museo Hendrik C. Andersen". 26–30 November 2008. Roma.
2012. leben eben. perecs Leben. es lebe perec. In OPLEPO (ed.), *À Georges Perec*, 30–31. Napoli: Edizioni Oplepo.
2013. 3 Reflex-Ionen zum potentiellen Leben. In Ilse Kilic (ed.), *Werkstatt für potentielles Leben. OUVIEPO. Ouvroir de vie potentielle*, 37–39. Wien: Das fröhliche Wohnzimmer.
2013. [pi:tar]. In Kathrin Ackermann & Susanne Winter (eds.), *Nach allen Regeln der Kunst. Werke und Studien zur Literatur-, Kunst- und Musikproduktion. Für Peter Kuon zum 60. Geburtstag*, 205–207. Wien: LIT.
2015. Per non definire l'Oplepo. In OPLEPO (ed.), *Venticinque anni d'Oplepo*, 51–54. Napoli: Edizioni Oplepo.
2016. Logiche dell'eco. In OPLEPO (ed.), *Passar la lunga sera sulla terra*. 58–59 and 81. Napoli: Edizioni Oplepo.

Academic Texts (Selection)

Books

1996. *Romain Gary – Das brennende Ich. Literaturtheoretische Implikationen eines Pseudonymenspiels* (Mimesis, 26). Tübingen: Niemeyer.
1999. *Romain Gary im Spiegel der Literaturkritik*. Frankfurt am Main & Wien: Lang.
2002 (ed., with Werner Helmich & Hartmut Meter). *Poetologische Umbrüche. Romanistische Studien zu Ehren von Ulrich Schulz-Buschhaus*. München: Fink.
2012. *Texte nach Bauplan. Studien zur zeitgenössischen ludisch-methodischen Literatur in Frankreich und Italien*. Heidelberg: Winter.

Articles

1998. Formen oulipotischer Poesie: Zum literarischen Werk Michelle Grangauds. *Sprachkunst: Beiträge zur Literaturwissenschaft* 29(1). 127–151.
1999. Vergessen – Erinnern – Gedächtnis in Georges Perecs 'Oulibiographie' *W ou le souvenir d'enfance*. *Sprachkunst: Beiträge zur Literaturwissenschaft* 30(2). 321–333.
2002. Raymond Roussels Erbe(n). In Werner Helmich, Hans Helmut Meter & Astrid Poier-Bernhard (eds.), *Poetologische Umbrüche*, 355–374. München: Fink.
2002. 'Oskars Moral' von Ilse Kilic als Beispiel eines Spiel- und Regeltextes. *Sprachkunst: Beiträge zur Literaturwissenschaft* 33(1). 131–138.
2003. Oulipotische Rekurse auf das Sonett. In Gisela Febel & Hans Grote (eds.), *L´Etat de la poésie aujourd´hui*, 151–165. Frankfurt am Main: Lang.
2003. Les sonnets potentiels de Franz Josef Czernin. *Formules* 7. 60–71.
2003. Ilse Kilic: Worte und Spielregeln, das bin ich. In Petra Ganglbauer & Hildegard Kernmayer (eds.), *Schreibweisen. Poetologien, Die Postmoderne in der österreichischen Literatur von Frauen*, 212–232. Wien: Milena.

2004. Littérature à contraintes en Autriche à partir de 1980. In Jan Baetens & Bernardo Schiavetta (eds.), *Le Goût de la forme en littérature. Écritures et lectures à contraintes. Colloque de Cerisy août 2002*, 123–131. Paris: Noésis.

2004. 'Babylonische Kombination' als literarisches Verfahren. 'o du roher iasmin' von Oskar Pastior und 'Raphèl' von Bernardo Schiavetta im Kontext oulipotischer Poetologie. In Rainhard Kacianca & Peter Zima (eds.), *Krise und Kritik der Sprache zwischen Spätmoderne und Postmoderne*, 195–211. Tübingen & Basel: Francke.

2005. Bunte Tuben (Brigitta Falkner) – oder die Neuerfindung des Anagramms. *Manuskripte* 167. 112–114.

2006. Aphorismen in Serie. Zur 'Aphorismenmaschine' von Marcel Bénabou. In Klaus-Dieter Ertler & Siegbert Himmelsbach (eds.), *Pensées – Pensieri – Pensamientos*, 225–243. Wien: LIT.

2009. Ludisch-methodische Rekurse auf Schöpfung und Schöpfungsbericht im Kontext oulipotischer Poetologie. In Manfred Kern & Ludger Lieb (eds.), *Genesis – Poesis. Der biblische Schöpfungsbericht in Literatur und Kunst*, 197–214. Heidelberg: Winter.

2010. Reflexionen zu einem *roman oulipien* und zwei *romans d'oulipien(ne)*: *Sphinx* und *Pas un jour* von Anne F. Garréta. *Lendemains: études comparées sur la France – vergleichende Frankreichforschung* 35(140). 73–93.

2011. Ermanno Cavazzoni: Il gioco con la regola. In Gerhild Fuchs & Angelo Pagliardini (eds.), *Ridere in pianura. Le specie del comico nella letteratura padano-emiliana*, 155–172. Frankfurt am Main: Lang.

2015. « Comme deux gouttes d'eau se ressemblent » – caractéristiques et potentialités d'une forme poétique créée par Jacques Jouet: les « À supposer... ». In Marc Lapprand & Dominique Moncond'huy (eds.), *Jacques Jouet*, 187–199. Rennes: Presses Universitaires de Rennes.

2015. Création, contraintes et expérience(s) de l'espace dans l'architecture de Zaha Hadid. In Peter Kuon, Nicole Pelletier & Pierre Sauvanet (eds.), *Contrainte et création*, 383–396. Bordeaux: Presses Universitaires de Bordeaux.

2015. La letteratura 'à contrainte' in Austria: Ilse Kilic e Brigitta Falkner. In OPLEPO (ed.), *Attenti al potenziale*, 53–69. Naples: Edizioni OPLEPO.

2016. Raumbegriffe und Raumerkundungen in *Still life / Style leaf* von Georges Perec und anderen oulipotischen Texten. In Julia Dettke & Elisabeth Heyne (eds.), *Spielräume und Raumspiele in der Literatur*, 119–137. Würzburg: Königshausen & Neumann.

II Approaches to wordplay and verbal humor

Salvatore Attardo
Universals in puns and humorous wordplay

Abstract: This article reviews some of the universal features of humorous wordplay which include the phonological mechanisms used to manipulate strings, the semantic oppositeness found in incongruity, the pseudo-logical Cratylistic resolution of the incongruity, and the relative distribution of types of wordplay involving different types of ambiguity and alliteration.

Keywords: ambiguity, clang response, Cratylism, folk linguistics, glossolalia, humor, iconicity, paretymology, puns, rhyme, sound symbolism, speech error, taboo word, wordplay

1 On defining a few terms

There is a significant literature on puns and wordplay, reviewed in Attardo (1994), Hempelmann (2003) and Hempelmann and Miller (2017). In fact, for a long time, puns were assumed to be the sole purview of the linguistics of humor. The advent of semantic theories of humor in the 1980s changed the perspective and the study of puns was somewhat marginalized. However, lately a resurgence of interest can be seen, for example in the beginning of the Dynamics of Wordplay book series, in 2015. The purpose of this paper is to present an argument for the universality of the linguistic mechanisms used in puns (humorous wordplay). I will also use "verbal humor" (as opposed to referential humor; see Attardo 1994) as a synonym of humorous wordplay. The following are an example of verbal humor (1) and one of referential humor (2):

(1) In Trinidad and Tobago it will cost you £2.50 for a steak pie, in Jamaica it will cost you £3.00. These are pie rates of the Caribbean.
(https://www.reddit.com/r/dadjokes/comments/7hyxk9/in_trinidad_and_tobago_it_will_cost_you_250_for_a/, accessed 10 July 2018)

(2) Can you take shorthand? Yes, but it takes me longer.

The field of wordplay is beset by terminological problems. It is thus useful to begin by clarifying, as much as possible, the scope of one's investigation. Wordplay may take many forms, including games that are played with reference to the spelling of words (such as Scrabble, crosswords, etc.) but also anagrams (the letters are arranged to form another word), palindromes (the word or phrase is readable from left to right and right to left), acrostics (words or phrases the initials of which form another word), word squares (a type of acrostic on a square grid), etc. Other forms of wordplay consist in the creation of sublanguages, such as the French "verlan" based on syllabic units, as exemplified by the name of the "argot" itself from "l'envers" → "ver-lan" by flipping the order of the two syllables. These types of argotic sublanguages are documented in over 100 languages as varied as Afrikaans and Vietnamese.[1]

Even from this short list we can extrapolate some interesting features. Wordplay may be completely unrelated to humor: players of Scrabble and those who solve crossword puzzles are obviously not engaged in humor appreciation. They may be completely metalinguistic, i.e., performed at a different linguistic level than ordinary linguistic activities, for example, anagrams are performed deliberately, and are a separate skill from ordinary language processing. Here a specification needs to be inserted: in some cases, anagrams (or other wordplay) may acquire[2] an ulterior meaning, as in the following example:

(3)   Salvador Dalì → avida dollars (attributed to André Breton)

Finally, all these types of language play are mostly graphemic, i.e., based on the spelling of the words (with the exception of spoken argotic forms, such as verlan which are based on pronunciation). Here too a distinction needs to be made, because there exist some types of wordplay that are based on the differences between graphemic and phonemic representations of language. Here I will quote the "eye dialect" practice (Bolinger 1946) which has the effect of "trivializing" (Gumperz and Berenz 1993: 96–97) the language of the speaker(s). Example (4) is a sample of eye dialect:

(4)   Ah shore could eat mo' po'k chops, Mammy = I sure could eat more pork chops, Mommy
      (Malin 1965: 230)

Another example, from Queneau's novel *Zazie dans le métro* (1959), is the phonetic "transcription" of an utterance (5), resulting in a mismatch between the expected orthographic / graphemic representation, on the right, and the more accurate quasi-phonetic representation, on the left (cf. Attardo 1994: 123).

---

1 https://en.wikipedia.org/wiki/Language_game (accessed 10 July 2018).
2 The human agency in the process of anagramming is limited to the recognition of the semantic/pragmatic potential of some of the combinations. The process of anagramming itself is a simple permutation of letters.

(5) Lagoçamilébou = La gosse a mis les bouts.

Except in the limited sense that graphemic representation is involved in the semantic phenomena exemplified in the previous paragraph, neither graphemic phenomena, nor metalinguistic processes that do not occur in normal language use[3], nor non-humorous phenomena will be considered in what follows. To put it differently, this paper is concerned with wordplay that occurs naturally in the use of language[4] and that has the purpose (perlocutionary goal or effect) of being perceived as amusing, mirthful, or exhilarating by at least one of the participants in the exchange.[5]

2 Definition of puns

We can now present a definition of humorous puns. A pun is a textual occurrence in which a sequence of sounds must be interpreted with a reference to a second sequence of sounds, which may, but need not, be identical to the first sequence, for the full meaning of the text to be accessed. The perlocutionary goal or effect of the pun is to generate the perception of mirth or of the intention to do so. The latter distinction between perlocutionary goal or effect is necessary to account for the fact that involuntary puns may be perceived as humorous only by a member of the audience and no intention to amuse may be present in the speaker.

This definition generalizes over string-based puns and alliterative ones. Let us address the two questions in that order. Puns are not exclusively word-based. Puns involve the presence of (minimally) two senses, but need not involve two "words", as does example (1) "pie + rates". The two senses can come about via the interpretation of any string, be it related or not to a word. In example (6), the two senses come from the proper name *Indiana Jones* and the idiomatic

---

[3] For example, a friend of mine had trained herself to reverse any string (in Italian) on the fly. This is not an activity that occurs naturally in any spoken language. One can always train oneself to perform arbitrary metalinguistic tasks, such as counting the number of letters required to spell a word, for example. However, these are not activities that occur in normal language use by untrained speakers.
[4] Humorous puns have a metalinguistic component, of course (see Zirker and Winter-Froemel 2015). However, there is a difference between the metalinguistic implicit reference to the form, which characterizes puns, as we will see below, and the artificial construction outside of normal exchanges of practices such as anagrams or cross-word puzzles.
[5] "Mirth" is a technical term used in humor studies (Martin 2007: 8) to describe the emotion elicited by humor. Another term is "exhilaration" (Ruch 1993).

expression "to jones for something" ('to desire something intensely') and neither is a separate word. See also example (11) below, for another case in which a string is manipulated, but in the case of (11), a sub-morphemic one.

(6) JONESING FOR INDIANA (Dave Pell, Nextdraft 14 March 2018; www.nextdraft.com)

Moreover, puns may also come about as a result of syntactic ambiguity, as in example (7) below where the syntactic role of the word "bite" (as the verb of an embedded clause "dog bite victim" or as a modifier of "victim", itself modified by "dog" (not to mention the syntactic role of "dog" demoted from the subject of the subordinate clause to a modifier of "bite")).

(7) Squad helps dog bite victim (Bucaria 2004: 292)

Of course the most common category is morphological ambiguity (lexical ambiguity falls in this last category), as in (8) in which we have two ambiguities (*head* 'boss' vs. 'body part', *arms* 'weapons' vs. 'body part').

(8) Iraqi head seeks arms (Bucaria 2004: 288)

Furthermore, alliterative puns involve the repetition of a given phoneme or group of phonemes and may be scattered along (parts of) the relevant text, as in (9) below:

(9) You remember Sunset Strip – where the unneat meet to bleat! (Attardo et al. 1994: 35)

where the repetition of the [i] sound in the last three syllables is highly noticeable.

The literature on puns is vast, as mentioned above. There are numerous issues, of great interest and significance, but they cannot all be pursued in this context. I will thus list a number of assumptions I will take henceforth for granted, without discussion. The interested reader should consult Attardo (1994), particularly chapters 3 and 4, where some treatment of these matters can be found.

– Puns invoke significantly the surface structure (the signifier) of language, but this claim can be generalized to non-verbal linguistic forms (e.g., signed languages) and in general to semiotic systems (e.g., graphic signs).
– Puns are non-casual (Hymes 1958; Attardo 1994: 110) speech forms; in casual speech the speaker is unaware of the surface structure of the forms he/she is uttering. Insofar as this is the case and the speakers reference implicitly the signifier of the sign, puns have also a metalinguistic component.

- Not any ambiguous string is a pun. Ambiguity is generally eliminated by semantic and pragmatic disambiguation.[6] Puns preserve (at least) two meanings or interpretations. Hence, puns exist only in the context of disambiguation and therefore only in context.
- Once two meanings have been brought together, the two senses may either coexist, or one of the two may win out. There are examples in which the first meaning subsists, and cases in which the second meaning subsists. This should not be taken as psychological activation or access, but merely as the potential for the speaker to access the first / second meaning.
- The (usually lexical) unit that allows the two senses to coexist is called a connector, while the unit that forces the presence of the second sense is called a disjunctor.
- Connector and disjunctor may be distinct (i.e., be manifested in the text as two separate entities) or they may be non-distinct (i.e., be manifested as one entity).

3 The universality of punning mechanisms

In this paper, as stated above, I will argue that the linguistic mechanisms that make puns work are universal. Not only will I argue that the phonological and phonetic constraints on puns are the same across languages, but that the syntactico-lexical constraints, the semantic constraints, and the mechanisms that allow the resolution of the incongruity, i.e., the Cratylistic theory of sound-sense matching are universal.

Let us then start with a pretty stark, and deceptively simple, claim in favor of the universality of puns:

> It seems to me that punning owes its occurrence to the essential nature of language and meaning, and that it must therefore occur in all languages and cultures. (Hill, 1985: 450)

Thus posed, the question is probably too simplistic to be answered meaningfully. To a large extent the truth or falsity of the thesis, as stated by Hill, hinges on the definition of "pun".

For example, consider the argument brought forward against the universality thesis. Sherzer (1996: 134) notes that if by puns we mean textual phenomena that are performed (in a broad sense, including both speakers and hearers) by a

---

6 Unless of course the speaker wants the utterance to be ambiguous. See Empson (1930).

culture in the same way that Western European culture performs puns, then puns are not universal, because of course no culture is the same as any other culture. Puns may have, even in our culture, aesthetic, religious, magical, or medical "meanings" (insofar as they may reveal pathologies), so obviously in other cultures puns may be not associated with humor at all, or only marginally. Sherzer brings the example of the Guna (Kuna), an indigenous people of Panama / Colombia, who do not have the text-type "joke". However, he notes that their "life is punctuated by a great deal of verbal humor and joking" (Sherzer 1990: 205).

So, we can conclude that if by the universality of puns we mean that each culture has a literary/folkloric genre identical or similar to puns in Western culture, that is furthermore associated with humor in the same way that puns are associated with humor in Western culture, then it is pretty much tautological that some culture will not have puns-as-Western-culture-has-them. Conversely, if we understand puns to be multifaceted phenomena that may or may not be connected with humor, and that follow the definition presented at the beginning of section 2, then the question becomes an empirical one.[7]

When I wrote the synthesis of the work on puns for my 1994 book (Attardo 1994) that question was not even part of the discussion for the simple reason that there was no way to provide an empirical answer to the question. The situation changed radically after Guidi's work, first defended as her 2008 dissertation and then published as Guidi (2012a, 2012b), which was designed specifically to attempt a first empirically grounded answer.

Tab. 1: Languages examined in Guidi (2012a, 2012b)

Seneca (Iroquoian)	Navajo (Na-Dene)	Winnebago (Siouan)
Mixtec (Oto-Maguean)	Tzotzil (Mayan)	Balinese (Austronesian)
Korean (Isolate)	Japanese (Japanese)	Rundi (Niger-Congo)
Yoruba (Niger-Congo)	Italian (Indo-European)	Sanskrit (Indo-European)
English (Indo-European)	Vietnamese (Austro-Asiatic)	Chinese (Sino-Tibetan)

Guidi built, through extensive bibliographic research, a corpus of 204 puns from 15 different languages spanning 12 different language families. The idea was to be able to make some first generalizations by widening the scope of the research beyond a single language or language family. Table 1 lists the languages and their

---

[7] The definition is provided for puns that afford mirth, in our culture; in other cultures they may afford other perlocutionary effects.

language families. Obviously, Indo-European is over-represented due to its availability, but otherwise the variety of language families is sufficiently broad to generalize beyond a single family.

Guidi's conclusions are striking in their simplicity: She finds four universal phonetic mechanisms, listed and schematically exemplified below:

Addition: abc → abcd
Deletion: abc → ab
Substitution: abc → abd
Inversion: abc → acb

Not all mechanisms are attested in all languages, but all the puns in all the languages of her corpus are accounted for by these mechanisms. We notice immediately that these processes are not new or unique to puns. Inversion is known as metathesis in phonetics; addition is known as epenthesis; deletion as elision. Substitution occurs obviously in other phonetic phenomena such as assimilation/dissimilation, lenition/fortition, etc. This is the bread and butter of the phonetic processes that govern language change.

Obviously, as Guidi herself is well aware and warns her readers, caution must be used when generalizing from her data. Nonetheless, Guidi's work affords us the first ever empirical glimpse at a cross-linguistic comparison of punning mechanisms general enough to be meaningful. Moreover, other generalizations (which are not universals, obviously) are also possible: for example, Guidi's data are consistent with a 5-phoneme threshold she extrapolated from Hempelmann's (2003) data for phonemic distance, since only 10 instances have a phonetic distance greater than 5, i.e., less than 5 %. The largest phonemic distance Guidi found in her corpus is 8 phonemes.

In the following example, in the Seneca language (Chafe 1998, 188–189) there is a difference of one phoneme (the removal of the lengthening of the /a/ in sha:wi?s) which is obviously the smallest possible distance between two paronymous strings.

(10) target o:nó? sha:wi?s   'you are carrying around the oil'
     pun   o:nó? shawi?s   'sores on the buttocks'

In example (11), in the Rundi language (Niger-Kordofanian family), however, as Guidi (2012a: 99) points out, we have a difference of six phonemes (/fundi/ vs. /sindé/; note in passing that the strings replaced are not words):

(11) target Agafundi gasimba agasindé 'The robin jumps on the clod'
     pun   Agasindé gasimba agafundi 'The clod jumps on the robin'

Further evidence that punning mechanisms are sensitive to phonemic distance can be gathered from the fact that manipulations (changes) to the string tend to occur in the central elements of the string and/or in the nucleus of the syllable. In other words, they tend to occur in less cognitively prominent[8] parts of the string (the cognitive prominence of the beginning and the end of the string is known as the bath-tub effect; see Attardo 1994: 123 for discussion).

Guidi's conclusions about the "ordinariness" of the phonological processes of puns, i.e., all phonological mechanisms that can change a string may be used to generate a pun, match a growing awareness that the linguistic phenomena involved in humor are likewise ordinary. The language of humor is not extraordinary. Humor makes marked uses of unmarked linguistic means (Hempelmann and Attardo 2011: 126).

4 Universals of verbal joke texts

We now turn to a much more tentative discussion of "universal" features of joke texts (the "scare quotes" should also alert the reader to the tentativeness of the discussion). We have four studies that collected significant samples of joke texts and analyzed some of their features, in four languages: English, Italian, German, and (classical) Arabic.[9] The studies are, AlJared (2009; Arabic), Attardo (1989; Italian), Attardo et al. (1994; English), Stelter (2011; English), and (Stelter 2011; German). All these studies are based on corpora of jokes collected for commercial or cultural reasons, by non-humor scholars. Thus they reflect the interests and goals of the joke-collectors/anthologists and not those of humor scholars. For one, they are usually opaque on the criteria for inclusion, beyond platitudes as the desire to amuse or include the "best" jokes.

Obviously, since the data consist of canned jokes, no direct generalization is possible to conversational data. However, it is unlikely that any conclusions valid for canned jokes are completely at odds with conclusions for humor at large, because collections of humor cannot depart too significantly from the tastes and practices of the community they are targeting, for risk of losing sales as a result of alienating their audience. In other words, since the joke collections are com-

---

8 Not to be confused with stress-based prosodic prominence.
9 A forthcoming article by Winter-Froemel compares jokes in French, Italian, Spanish and Portuguese. I became aware of this publication too late to include it in the discussion.

mercially produced, they must reflect to a significant extent the tastes of their audience.

By comparing the data in these studies we can reach some conclusions: as Figure 1 shows clearly, most languages prefer referential jokes. Stelter's outlier data are explained by two of her collections of jokes which skew the data (51.3 % and 47.8 %), while the third one is in line with the other data sets (26.8 %). Note that the charts below report the averaged percentages (41.9 % for the English data, for example).

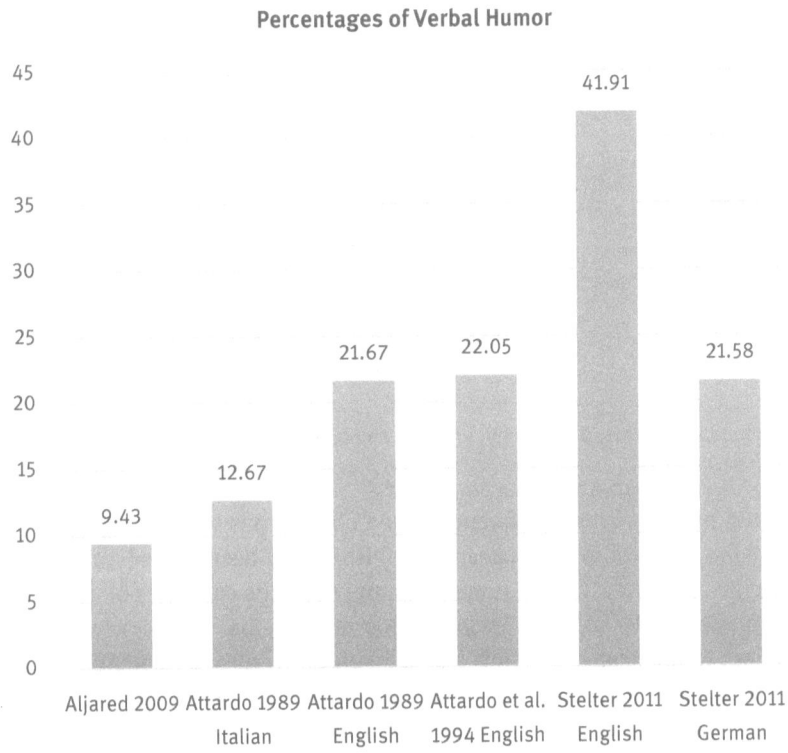

Fig. 1: Percentages of Verbal Jokes in the Corpora

Lexical-ambiguity jokes, i.e., jokes that hinge on the presence of an ambiguous lexical item, such as example (1), are the most frequent type of pun, whereas syntactic ambiguity (such as example (7)) is much less frequent, but nonetheless attested as a humorous mechanism in all corpora. Alliterative jokes, i.e., jokes that involve the unusually frequent repetition of sounds (such as example (9)), are much rarer than either lexical or syntactic ambiguity jokes.[10] The categories are mutually exclusive. See Figure 2 below for the overall percentages.

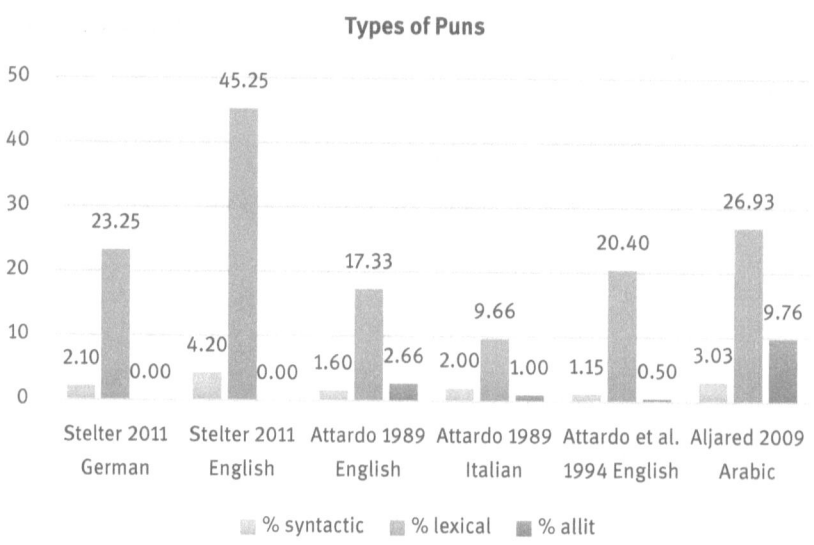

Fig. 2: A comparison of lexical ambiguity, syntactic ambiguity and alliterative jokes

What could motivate these preferences? One obvious answer is that humorous wordplay has, at least in Western culture, historically been looked upon as an inferior type of humor.[11] Hence, it may be simply that the collectors of jokes that appear in print prefer to avoid including too many verbal jokes for fear of appearing less sophisticated and thus lose marketability. Another potential explanation is that verbal humor requires more processing than referential humor and therefore a cost-benefit rationale would guide the choices of the anthologists: Given that a joke delivers amusement, why bother using verbal humor, which requires more processing effort and thus may turn off potential readers.

---

10 One of the anonymous referees suggests that the higher number of alliterative jokes in Arabic may be due to the tri-consonantal roots of the majority of words, with affixes being attached to this consonantal skeleton, which may facilitate the repetition of sounds.

11 The negative attitude toward puns can be summarized by Victor Hugo's famous saying "Le calembour est la fiente de l'esprit qui vole" which compares it to a bird's excrement.

The relative scarcity of syntactic puns compared to lexical ambiguity is clearly due to processing costs: syntactic ambiguity is much harder to perceive and process than lexical ambiguity (MacKay and Bever 1967). It is unclear why alliterative wordplay would also be rare, as there does not seem to be any special cognitive load in processing it. Of course, another hypothesis, probably a null one, is that there simply are more referential jokes than verbal jokes and that therefore the joke collectors merely reflect the way the world is. Needless to say, this only pushes the question back one level: if that is the case, then why is the world that way?

5 Universals of resolution

We now turn to another aspect of puns and humorous wordplay, which is also universal. Namely, we will consider the resolution of the incongruity of puns. Puns have a built-in incongruity: A string activates two unrelated[12] meanings (scripts); by its very presence, the ambiguity between the two activated meanings generates an incongruity (i.e., the presence of two unrelated meanings in the same text string). However, as I pointed out already in Attardo (1994), puns do not consist of incongruity alone but must have a resolution aspect as well, or otherwise they would be indistinguishable from mere incongruous or ambiguous statements, such as the following:

(12) My amoeba thinks I am cool (incongruous)

(13) Flying planes can be dangerous (ambiguous)

(12) is incongruous, but not humorous. (13) is ambiguous and contains the same kinds of ambiguities observed in example (7) above, but is also not humorous.

Let me add that the term "resolution" (inherited from psychology) is unfortunate, as it seems to involve an actual removal of the incongruity, which is not the case: the resolution of the incongruity is partial, playful, or otherwise predicated on "local logic" (Ziv 1984; Hempelmann and Attardo 2011). The term "logical mechanism", introduced for this aspect of jokes in the General Theory of Verbal Humor (Attardo and Raskin 1991), avoids this, but has the drawback of being semantically opaque. Aubouin's (1948) term "justification" never caught on, despite being the most appropriate semantically, since what the resolution

---

[12] Raskin (1985) has "opposed" to be understood as "locally antonymous".

consists of is a partial justification of the presence of the incongruity. Most importantly, the resolution of incongruity in humorous wordplay is non-eliminative, meaning that both senses remain available to the text, unlike in disambiguation, where the "losing" sense becomes suppressed.

Let us consider then a well-worn example:

(14) Why did the cookie cry? Because its mother was a wafer so long.

In (14) we have one signifier, the string [əweifər] and two signifieds, here represented by paraphrases in English orthography: a) "away for" and b) "a wafer". The meanings are incongruous, since an entity cannot uniquely be both at a distance and a cookie simultaneously. An objection might be that an entity may both be a cookie and at a distance (a remote cookie, basically), however, the logical form of the proposition would be different: whereas (14) is P(x), P represents either of the propositions "is a wafer" or "is away", the logical form of the objection is (P)x & Q(x). These are obviously not the same sentences.

Coming now to the resolution, in puns it is provided by a folk-theory of language as a motivated sign (in which sounds correspond to meaning). Speakers assume that same (or similar) sounds should carry the same meanings and that therefore, if two strings sound the same, it is legitimate to bring together their two meanings. This folk-theory is known as Cratylism.[13] Cratylism is the belief that the relationship between the signifier and the signified is motivated naturally; it is true, correct, and universal. Since Saussure's (1916) rebuttal of Cratylism, scholars have a hard time taking Cratylistic beliefs seriously, but they remain deeply entrenched into folk-theory. In section 5.1 we will examine several strands of evidence that support the claim that speakers hold a Cratylistic view of language.

5.1 Evidence for a cratylistic view of language

In this section, we will review some of the evidence that speakers hold Cratylistic sound/sense relationship beliefs: the overall argument follows the one built in

---

[13] Cratylus is a character in the eponymous Platonic dialogue, written in 360 BCE. Hermogenes, Cratylus' opponent in the dialogue, thus summarizes Cratylus position with regard to Socrates: "Hermogenes. I should explain to you, Socrates, that our friend Cratylus has been arguing about names; he says that they are natural (φύσει) and not conventional; not a portion of the human voice which men agree to use; but that there is a truth (ὀρθότητά) or correctness in them, which is the same for Hellenes as for barbarians." (http://classics.mit.edu/Plato/cratylus.html, accessed 30 July 2018).

more detail in Attardo (1994: 149–170) but updates the references to some extent. In particular, we will briefly review the following phenomena: paretymology, taboo words, folk linguistics, sound symbolism, iconicity, and sound-based lexical associations, which include, in order of relevance, rhyme, clang responses, glossolalia, and speech errors. The claim is not that these phenomena are humorous or even related to humor; rather, these phenomena are evidence that speakers hold a Cratylistic view of language.

5.1.1 Paretymology

Paretymology (also known as *Volksetymologie*, folk etymology, para-etymology, popular etymology, and synchronic etymology; see Paul 1880; Baldinger 1973, for example; a fuller set of references is provided in Attardo 1994: 154) defines derivational processes which consist of taking a lexical item, often in another language, and re-analyzing it according to sound/meaning patterns existing in the language, so in the following example:

(15) Ger. *Sauerkraut* → Fr. *choucroute*

The German word *Sauerkraut* (literally 'sour-cabbage') is re-analyzed according to French language patterns in *chou* ('cabbage') and *croute* ('crust').

Recent research on paretymology has occurred mostly in historical linguistics and includes Zuckermann (2003), Rundblad and Kronenfeld (2003), and Fertig (2013: 57–61). Zuckermann proposes to distinguish between Generative Popular Etymology, such as phono-semantic matching, i.e., the camouflaging of a borrowing with a pre-existent native word, as in the English borrowing of French *chaise-longue* (literally 'long chair') which is camouflaged with the lexical item *lounge*,

(16) Fr. *chaise-longue* → Eng. *chaise-lounge*

and Derivational-Only Popular Etymology, which only reinterprets pre-existing items. An example of only derivational reinterpretation is the Mandarin borrowing of English *hacker* as [heike] 'black guest' (Gao 2008: 373).

5.1.2 Taboo words

The phenomenon of taboo words refers to the reluctance of speakers to use a given word, for various reasons, such as respect, fear, or the desire not to convey or offend the bearer of the tabooed name.

A well-known example is the variability of the Indo-European root for 'bear' or 'wolf' due to tabooing: for example, the Indo-European root (*rktho-) that gives *ursus* in Latin and *arktos* in Greek, is replaced in the Slavic languages, with a word derived from 'honey', and in the Germanic languages with a word derived from 'brown'. This avoidance mechanism is born out of the magical fear that by naming an entity one is summoning it. Another example of tabooing is reported among the Faorese fishermen (Lockwood 1955) who, while at sea, used different words to indicate some fish and parts of their fishing equipment to ward off bad luck. More generally, on tabooing, see Allan and Burridge (2006).

5.1.3 Folk linguistics

Linguists call the beliefs that untrained native speakers have about languages "folk linguistics". For example, consider the following quote from Benveniste (1966: 52).

> For the speaker there is a complete identity of language and reality: the sign covers and commands reality; better still, it is reality (nomen omen, verbal taboos, magical power of the word, etc.).

Anderson (1998: 69–70) labels these "Cratyline folk-linguistics". I should point out that Anderson quotes my own work in support of this idea as well, so obviously that introduces a circularity of argumentation.

5.1.4 Sound symbolism

Sound symbolism is the widespread belief that there is a connection between individual sounds or clusters of sounds and meaning. There has always been, within linguistics, despite Saussure's (1916) exclusion of sound symbolism from the core of the linguistic system, a trend to associate sounds and meanings. Hinton, Nicholas and Ohala (1994) state that "sound symbolism plays a considerably larger role in language than scholarship has hitherto recognized" (Hinton, Nicholas and Ohala 1994: 1) and provide a good example of the kind of generalizations they mean: "segments such as palatal consonants and high vowels are frequently used for diminutive forms and other words representing small objects" (1994: 4). This is not the place to provide a review of the vast literature on sound symbolism. The references in Attardo (1994: 157) and Genette's work (1995) provide a general overview.

5.1.5 Iconicity

The idea of iconicity is broader than sound symbolism, but closely related to it. The basic idea is that the sign bears some kind of relationship, not necessarily a sound-based one, with the reality it represents. Or, as Dingemanse et al. (2015) put it "aspects of form resemble aspects of meaning".

An example of iconicity is the scalar progression in (17):

(17) Big [bɪg]; bigger [bɪgə]; biggest [bɪgɪst]

where we go from 3 phonemes, to 4 and then to 6, so that the growth of the signifier matches the "growth" of the meaning.[14] Another example is the widely documented association between reduplication and repetition and/or distribution:

(18) goro: gorogoro, 'one: multiple heavy objects rolling' (Japanese)
wùrùfùù: wùrùfù-wùrùfù, 'fluffy: fluffy here and there' (Siwu)
curuk-nu: curukcuruk-nu, 'a sharp prick: many sharp pricks' (Tamil)
kpata: kpata kpata, 'drop: scattered drops' (Ewe)
(Dingemanse et al. 2015: 606)

Besides the references provided in Attardo (1994: 158), recent work includes Fay, Ellison and Garrod (2014), Schmidtke, Conrad and Jacobs (2014), and the already mentioned Dingemanse et al. (2015).

5.1.6 Sound-based lexical associations

This section reviews the evidence for sound-based relations in the lexicon which have partially semantic values, in some cases.

---

[14] One of the anonymous referees cleverly notes that "small-smaller-smallest" shows the same growth of the signifier with a blatant mismatch of the signified, which grows smaller. There is a reason why Saussure (1916) rejected Cratylism and iconicity: while they offer captivating local examples, they do not work system-wide.

- Rhyme
  It is a well-known fact that rhyming has a semantic counterpart. The greater the semantic distance between rhyming words, the greater the effect. For example, a word does not rhyme with itself (e.g., "peach" does not rhyme with "peach"). Words that have very close meanings rhyme very weakly (e.g., Essex-Wessex, both regions in East England, have a very weak rhyme). On the contrary, rhyming widely different words has a strong effect (e.g., "potato" and "chateau"). In Attardo (1994: 161) I stated the argument thus: "Linking the forcefulness of rhyming effect to semantic distance implies that an inversely proportional relationship exists between sounds and senses and that, the closer the meaning of two words is, the less their rhyming potential."
  Rhyming has another effect that is semantic, but not related to lexical meaning. Rhyme has an asseverative effect, i.e., it reinforces the truth of what is being said. Interesting recent research has examined this phenomenon. McGlone and Tofighbakhsh (1999) investigated aphorisms and call this the "Keats' heuristic": "the aesthetic qualities of a message are equated with its truth" (McGlone and Tofighbakhsh 1999: 240). The phenomenon is not limited to aphorisms: "The rhyme-as-reason effect occurs not only in evaluation of existing aphorisms, but applies also to perception and evaluation of advertising slogans" (Filkuková and Klempe, 2013).
- Clang responses
  In word association tasks, there is also a part, albeit a small one, of responses that are based on assonance. These are called "clang responses". As Fitzpatrick (2013) notes "clang responses, [...] share phonological or orthographic features with the cue, but are otherwise not related". Clang responses are closely related to rhyming phenomena: "Rhyming responses, assonance, responses with the same initial sounds as the stimulus, or a similar prominent consonant cluster are common types of clang associates" (Meara 2009: 13).
- Glossolalia
  Under the broad label of "glossolalia", I mean all phenomena which make use of sounds and syllables from languages known to the speaker to create a language "lookalike" which is devoid of meaning but is structured like a language phonologically. Phenomena like "speaking in tongues" are forms of glossolalia. Both phenomena exhibit frequent repetition, alliteration and assonance, which shows again that sound-based relations are used to "mimic" semantic ones (since the glossolalic utterances "appear" to be meaningful, i.e., are perceived as such by those who produce them). There is also a ludic aspect of glossolalia (for example, in its sounds-based repetitions) that has

been neglected given the different framing of the religious experience as meaningful and even mystical. Classical works on glossolalia include Samarin (1972), Goodman (1972), Courtine (1988a, 1988b), and recently Cartledge (2012).
– Speech errors
  Speech errors are commonly used to investigate the underlying linguistic system (Fromkin 1973, 1980), even though the idea is not universally accepted (Meyer 1992). Recent work includes Shattuck-Hufnagel (1983, 1986), Berg (1997), Dell (2014), Nooteboom and Quené (2015). Significantly, speech errors identify the same four phonological processes found in puns. Finally, it is worth noting that Aarons (2012) uses jokes to argue for the psycholinguistic reality of the system.

5.2 The argument on the cratylistic view of language

The review of the evidence for the psychological reality of the Cratylistic view of language, i.e., a view of language as a motivated, system, in which similarity of sound entails similarity of meaning, and vice-versa, should be convincing enough to show that naive speakers (i.e., those who have not been subjected to extensive training in linguistics) hold a fairly well-documented Cratylistic view of language. I must stress however that this does not mean that they are right. Science is not a democracy. The fact that something is psychologically real to the speakers at the metalinguistic level is not evidence of the correctness of that view. Language remains fundamentally arbitrary and non-motivated, even though speakers like to play with the idea that it may not be.

The Cratylism of naive speakers is the source of the resolution of puns based on the identity or similarity of phonological, morphological, syntactical, and lexical forms. Because this inclination to Cratylism is universal, then the Cratylistic resolution of the incongruity in puns is also a universal.

6 Conclusions

We can now conclude our brief review of the evidence on the universal nature of humorous wordplay. Puns and wordplay are universal, in the sense that they exploit universal structural features of language, as described by Guidi (2012a, 2012b). Humorous wordplay is also universal in the sense that the same mechanisms of incongruity/script opposition occur in all languages and likewise, the

Cratylistic pseudo-resolution of puns is also found in all languages. As for the trends observed in corpora of jokes, it is too early to say if they really are universal, but until further research can shed some light on the problem, we must be satisfied with saying that the evidence seems to be pointing in the direction of universality there as well.

7 References

Aarons, Debra. 2012. *Jokes and the linguistic mind*. London & New York: Taylor & Francis.
Allan, Keith & Kate Burridge. 2006. *Forbidden words: Taboo and the censoring of language*. Cambridge: Cambridge University Press.
AlJared, Amal Abdullah. 2009. *Linguistic analysis of humor on classical Arabic: An application of the isotopy disjunction model*. Jeddah: King Abdulaziz University MA thesis.
AlJared, Amal Abdullah. 2017. The isotopy-disjunction model. In Salvatore Attardo (ed.), *Handbook of language and humor*, 64–79. New York: Routledge.
Anderson, Earl R. 1998. *A grammar of iconism*. Madison (NJ): Fairleigh Dickinson University Press.
Attardo, Salvatore. 1989. A multiple-level analysis of jokes. Contributed section in newsletter. *HUMOR: International Journal of Human Research* 2(4). 438–439.
Attardo, Salvatore. 1994. *Linguistic theories of humor*. Berlin: Mouton De Gruyter.
Attardo, Salvatore & Victor Raskin. 1991. Script theory revis(it)ed: Joke similarity and joke representation model. *HUMOR: International Journal of Humor Research* 4(3–4). 293–347.
Attardo, Salvatore, Donalee H. Attardo, Paul Baltes & Marnie J. Petray. 1994. The linear organization of jokes: Statistical analysis of two thousands texts. *HUMOR: International Journal of Humor Research* 7(1). 27–54.
Aubouin, Elie. 1948. *Technique et psychologie du comique*. Marseille: OFEP.
Baldinger, Kurt. 1973. A propos de l'influence de la langue sur la pensée. Etymologie populaire et changement sémantique parallèle. *Revue de Linguistique Romane* 37. 241–273.
Benveniste, Émile. 1966. *Problèmes de linguistique générale*. Paris: Gallimard.
Berg, Thomas. 1997. The modality-specificity of linguistic representations: Evidence from slips of the tongue and the pen. *Journal of Pragmatics* 27(5). 671–697.
Bolinger, Dwight L. 1946. Visual morphemes. *Language* 22(4). 333–340.
Bucaria, Chiara. 2004. Lexical and syntactic ambiguity as a source of humor: The case of newspaper headlines. *HUMOR: International Journal of Humor Research* 17(3). 279–310.
Cartledge, Mark J. (ed.). 2012. *Speaking in tongues: Multi-disciplinary perspectives*. Eugene (OR): Wipf and Stock Publishers.
Chafe, Wallace. 1998. Polysynthetic puns. In Leanne Hinton & Pamela Munro (eds.), *Studies in American Indian languages: description and theory*. Berkeley & Los Angeles: University of California Press. 187–189.
Courtine, Jean-Jacques. 1988a. Avant-Propos. Pour introduire aux glossolalies: Un hommage à Michel de Certeau. *Langages* 23(91). 4–5.
Courtine, Jean-Jacques. 1988b. Les silences de la voix. *Langages* 23(91). 7–25.
Dell, Gary S. 2014. Phonemes and production. *Language and Cognitive Processes* 29(1). 30–32.

Dingemanse, Mark, Damián E. Blasi, Gary Lupyan, Morten H. Christiansen & Padraic Monaghan. 2015. Arbitrariness, iconicity, and systematicity in language. *Trends in Cognitive Sciences* 19(10). 603–615.

Empson, William. 1930. *Seven Types of Ambiguity*. US edition 1947. New York: New Direction.

Fay, Nicolas, Mark Ellison & Simon Garrod. 2014. Iconicity: From sign to system in human communication and language. *Pragmatics & Cognition* 22(2). 244–263.

Fertig, David L. 2013. *Analogy and morphological change*. Edinburgh: Edinburgh University Press.

Filkuková, Petra & Sven Hroar Klempe. 2013. Rhyme as reason in commercial and social advertising. *Scandinavian Journal of Psychology* 54(5). 423–431.

Fill, Alwin 1992. Joking in English and German: A contrastive study. In Christian Mair & Manfred Markus (eds.), *New departures in contrastive linguistics: Neue Ansätze in der Kontrastiven Linguistik: Proceedings of the Conference held at the Leopold-Franzens-University of Innsbruck, Austria*. 21–30, Vol. 2. Innsbruck: Institut für Anglistik.

Fitzpatrick, Tess. 2013. Word associations. In Carol A. Chapelle (ed.), *Encyclopedia of applied linguistics*, 6193–6199. Oxford: Wiley-Blackwell.

Fromkin, Victoria A. (ed.). 1973. *Speech errors as linguistic evidence*. The Hague & Paris: Mouton.

Fromkin, Victoria A. (ed.). 1980. *Errors in linguistic performance: Slips of the tongue, ear, pen, and hand*. New York & London: Academic.

Gao, Liwei. 2008. Language Change in Progress: Evidence from Computer-Mediated Communication. In Marjorie K.M. Chan & Hana Kang (eds.), *Proceedings of the 20th North American Conference on Chinese Linguistics* (NACCL-20), Vol. 1., 361–377. Columbus (OH): Ohio State University Press.

Genette, Gerard. 1995. *Mimologics*, Vol. 2. Nebraska: University of Nebraska Press.

Goodman, Felicitas D. 1972. *Speaking in tongues: A cross-cultural study in glossolalia*. Chicago: University of Chicago Press.

Guidi, Annarita. 2012a. *Il gioco di parole e le lingue: Dalla semantica alla pragmatica*. Perugia: Guerra.

Guidi, Annarita. 2012b. Are pun mechanisms universal? A comparative analysis across language families. *HUMOR: International Journal of Humor Research* 25. 339–366.

Gumperz, John J. & Norine Berenz. 1993. Transcribing conversational exchanges. In Jane A. Edwards & Martin D. Lampert (eds.), *Talking data: Transcription and coding in discourse research*, 91–122. Hillsdale (NJ): Lawrence Erlbaum.

Hempelmann, Christian F. 2003. *Paronomasic puns: Target recoverability towards automatic generation*. Purdue: Purdue University PhD dissertation.

Hempelmann, Christian F. & Salvatore Attardo. 2011. Resolutions and their incongruities: Further thoughts on logical mechanisms. *HUMOR: International Journal of Humor Research* 24(2). 125–149.

Hempelmann, Christian F. & Tristan Miller. 2017. Puns: Taxonomy and Phonology. In Salvatore Attardo (ed.), *The Routledge Handbook of Language and Humor*, 95–108. New York: Taylor & Francis.

Hill, Archibald A. 1985. Puns: Their reality and their uses. *International Journal of American Linguistics* 51(4). 449–450.

Hinton, Leanne, Johana Nichols & John J. Ohala (eds.). 1994. *Sound Symbolism*. Cambridge: Cambridge University Press.

Hymes, Dell H. 1958. Linguistic Features Peculiar to Chinookan Myths. *International Journal of American Linguistics* 24(4). 253–257.

Lockwood, William Burley. 1955. Word taboo in the language of the Faroese fishermen. *Transactions of the Philological Society* 54(1). 1–24.

Malin, Stephen D. 1965. Eye Dialect in "Li'l Abner". *American Speech* 40(3). 229–232.

Martin, Rod A. 2007. *The psychology of humor: An integrative approach*. Boston (MA): Elsevier Academic Press.

MacKay, Donald G. & Thomas G. Bever. 1967. In search of ambiguity. *Perception & Psychophysics* 2(5). 193–200.

McGlone, Matthew S. & Jessica Tofighbakhsh. 1999. The Keats heuristic: Rhyme as reason in aphorism interpretation. *Poetics* 26(4). 235–244.

McGlone, Matthew S. & Jessica Tofighbakhsh. 2000. Birds of a feather flock conjointly (?): Rhyme as reason in aphorisms. *Psychological Science* 11(5). 424–428.

Meara, Paul. 2009. *Connected words: Word associations and second language vocabulary acquisition*. New York: Benjamins.

Meyer, Antje S. 1992. Investigation of phonological encoding through speech error analyses: Achievements, limitations, and alternatives. *Cognition* 42. 181–211.

Nooteboom, Sieb & Hugo Quené. 2015. Word onsets and speech errors. Explaining relative frequencies of segmental substitutions. *Journal of Memory and Language* 78. 33–46.

Paul, Hermann. 1880. *Prinzipien der Sprachgeschichte*. Halle: Niemeyer.

Ruch, Willibald. 1993. Exhilaration and Humor. In Jeannette M. Haviland & Michael Lewis (eds.), *The Handbook of Emotion*. Chapter 42, 605–616. New York (NY): Guilford Publications.

Rundblad, Gabriella & David B. Kronenfeld. 2003. The inevitability of folk etymology: A case of collective reality and invisible hands. *Journal of Pragmatics* 35(1). 119–138.

Samarin, William J. 1972. *Tongues of men and angels: The religious language of Pentecostalism*. New York: Macmillan.

Saussure, Ferdinand de. 1916. *Cours de linguistique générale. Publié par Charles Bally et Albert Sechehaye*. Paris: Payot.

Schmidtke, David S., Markus Conrad & Arthur M. Jacobs. 2014. Phonological iconicity. *Frontiers in Psychology* 5(80). https://www.ncbi.nlm.nih.gov/pmc/articles/PMC3921575/ (accessed 28 July 2018).

Shattuck-Hufnagel, Stefanie. 1983. Sublexical units and suprasegmental structure in speech production planning. In Peter F. MacNeilage (ed.), *The production of speech*, 109–136. New York: Springer.

Shattuck-Hufnagel, Stefanie. 1986. The representation of phonological information during speech production planning: Evidence from vowel errors in spontaneous speech. *Phonology* 3(1). 117–149.

Sherzer, Joel. 1990. *Verbal art in San Blas. Kuna culture through its discourse*. Cambridge: Cambridge University Press.

Sherzer, Joel. 1996. Review of Attardo (1994). *Language* 72(1). 132–136.

Stelter, Julia. 2011. To pun or not to pun? A contrastive study of paronomastic jokes in English and German. *Language in Contrast* 11(1). 23–39.

Winter-Froemel, Esme. Forthcoming. Traditions discursives et variantes du jeu: La dynamique des blagues en comble dans les langues romanes. To be published in Bettina Full & Michelle Lecolle (eds), *Jeux de mots et créativité. Langue(s), discours et littérature* (The Dynamics of Wordplay 4). Berlin & Boston: De Gruyter.

Zirker, Angelika & Esme Winter-Froemel (eds.). 2015. *Wordplay and metalinguistic/metadiscursive reflection: Authors, contexts, techniques, and meta-reflection* (The Dynamics of Wordplay 1). Berlin: De Gruyter.

Ziv, Avner. 1984. *Personality and Sense of Humor*. New York: Springer.

Zuckermann, Ghil'ad. 2003. *Language contact and lexical enrichment in Israeli Hebrew*. New York: Palgrave Macmillan.

Angelika Braun and Astrid Schmiedel
The phonetics of ambiguity: A study on verbal irony

Abstract: Wordplay and verbal irony are not as different as they might seem at first glance. In fact, they share the property of being *uneigentlich* ('non-actual'), i.e., the meaning of an utterance is somehow dissociated from its wording. Thus the question arises whether this kind of speech is signaled in the production process, and whether the cues thus created can be detected by naive listeners. This contribution presents an overview of the various means by which verbal irony may be conveyed to the listener. This is followed by an empirical study which demonstrates that verbal irony is indeed inherently ambiguous and that the underlying message is phonetically coded. The question addressed is how disambiguation takes place on the phonetic level. In other words – how does a speaker signal the intended meaning and how are listeners able to get the underlying message. The study deals with single-word utterances in sincere and ironic settings. Parameters considered include average voice fundamental frequency (F0) and related measures, intensity of the voice signal, and duration. The results of the acoustic measurements show that production results vary with type of irony (sarcasm vs. kind irony). It is argued that the underlying emotional states have to be taken into account for the interpretation of the measurement results. The perception study yields overall recognition rates of about 70 %, the sincere utterances being identified significantly better than the sarcastic ones in the positive stimulus set (sarcasm) and the ironic ones better than the sincere ones in the negative stimulus set (kind irony).

Keywords: articulatory precision, emotions, formants, intensity, kind irony, loudness, paralinguistic cues, perception of verbal irony, phonetics, sarcasm, sincerity, speaking tempo, (verbal) irony, (voice) pitch, voice quality

1 Introduction

At first glance, verbal irony and wordplay do not seem to have much in common. However, in rare cases like the following one, they may actually coincide:

> *Mein Trumpf* (banner at an anti-Trump demonstration; seen in the German TV-program *ZDF Morgenmagazin* on 11 November 2016)

This example may be interpreted in two different ways: If one focuses on the graphemic level, the German *Trumpf* [tʁʊmpf] 'trump (card)' can be regarded as playing on the name of *Trump* in a sarcastic manner. The personal possessive *mein* 'my', however, suggests a different interpretation: If *Trumpf* is pronounced [tɹʌmpf], *mein Trumpf* will rhyme – at least to German ears – with Hitler's *Mein Kampf*. This would mean to draw an analogy between the two men. Thus, wordplay may in rare instances be sarcastic, but verbal irony normally will not take on the form of wordplay.

However, both wordplay and verbal irony share the property of being non-actual speech (*uneigentliches Sprechen*; cf. Berg 1978), i.e., the meaning is somehow dissociated from the wording of an utterance.[1] Just how this dissociation is implemented forms a question which is for phoneticians to answer.

Irony can be conceived as an extreme case of (pragmatic) ambiguity, as there are (usually two) potential interpretations of an identical wording which are mutually incompatible, and it is up to the listener[2] to disambiguate the utterance and choose the interpretation which is contextually appropriate. From a pragmatic perspective, the concept of irony relies on the listener being able to detect this divergence – otherwise its purpose would be lost. Verbal irony thus creates a kind of camaraderie between speaker and (part of the) listeners.[3]

Even though the above definition of verbal irony seems pretty straightforward at first glance, it is by no means as clear if one takes a closer look. For example, it may prove to be difficult to separate verbal irony from joking or figures of speech like metaphors (*Donald Trump really hit the spot with Kim Yong Un*) or litotes (*not bad* meaning 'very good'). On a more principal strand, Gibbs and O'Brien (1991) point out that (a) verbal irony does not necessarily involve a difference between what is said and what is meant and that (b) verbal irony does not necessarily constitute an intentional speech act. An example for (a) would be as follows: Assume that someone broke a window in the Browns' kitchen by kicking a football right into it. Mrs. Brown asks the neighbors' son James whether he did it. He, who was actually the one who broke the window replies: "Sure I did!"

---

[1] There are exceptions to this rule; cf. the observations on fake irony and unintentional irony below.

[2] Since this paper is dealing primarily with verbal irony, it is mainly concerned with spoken utterances as opposed to written ones. That is why the term "listener" is used to denote the recipient of a message.

[3] Instances of verbal irony at the expense of a person present but not aware of the ambiguity are conceivable. For example, if there are three people playing a card game and one plays the wrong card, one of the other two may say "great play", with only the third player getting the irony and the one having played the card feeling flattered.

Objectively speaking, he is telling the truth, but by his tone of voice he may indicate that he is being sarcastic and therefore trying to convince Mrs. Brown that he does not mean what he is saying. This process could be termed *fake irony*. An example for (b) would be someone who has just been hit by a pigeon's droppings on his shoulder without being aware of it, saying: "I really don't see why people dislike the pigeons so much. They don't do any harm." In this case, everybody but the speaker is aware of the ironic nature of the utterance. It can therefore be called *unintentional irony*.

In view of examples like the above, it is hard to disagree with Haverkate (1990: 106), who concludes that "[...] it is difficult, if not impossible, to register, describe and explain in an exhaustive manner all aspects of that fascinating phenomenon that we call 'irony'".

There is a broad consensus in the literature that ironic speech is signaled by some kind of "tone of voice" (cf. e.g. Gibbs and Colston 2007; Cheang and Pell 2008). On the other hand, there are authors who argue "that there is no particular ironic tone of voice" (Bryant and Fox Tree 2005: 257; similarly Gibbs and O'Brien 1991; Winner et al. 1987). One of their arguments is that readers are able to detect irony in written language, which obviously does not contain any intonational cues. This can be countered by the fact that extensive context information was available to the readers. The experiment described in the present contribution, on the other hand, deals with very short utterances which are presented devoid of context. It therefore seems legitimate to study the influence of vocal factors contributing to the decoding of verbal irony nonetheless. Furthermore, frequently there is no visual channel available to aid with disambiguation, e.g. when talking over the telephone. In these cases, the oral channel is the only one by which to convey the relevant paralinguistic[4] information.

In a study on speech production, Rockwell (2000) described a very clear pattern of signaling irony as being "Lower, slower, louder". Subsequent studies showed that things may not be quite so simple. One reason is that in early studies on verbal irony (cf. e.g. Schaffer 1982; Rockwell 2000; Bryant and Fox Tree 2002) so-called sincere utterances, which could also be called affirmative, were compared to ironic ones. Yet, Anolli, Ciceri, and Infantino (2000, 2001, 2002) were able to show that a third category should be introduced in order to serve as a valid reference, i.e. neutral utterances which are neither actively affirmative nor ironic.

---

4 By paralinguistic we understand information which is conveyed by „tone of voice". This comprises the classical features of voice fundamental frequency and related parameters, intensity, and duration, as well as laryngeal and supralaryngeal voice quality features.

On a different strand, two kinds of verbal irony need to be distinguished: the "genuine" sarcastic irony which can be characterized as using "blame by praise" (*great* to express disapproval) on the one hand and the so-called "kind irony" which can be characterized as using "praise by blame" (*terrible* to express admiration) on the other. It can by no means be taken for granted that those two follow the same pattern.

Relatively little attention has been given to sociolinguistic properties of speaker and listener groups. A few studies focus on intercultural differences (Cheang and Pell 2009, 2011; Adachi 1996 for Japanese), demonstrating difficulties in identifying verbal irony in a different linguistic or cultural context. However, there are hardly any studies focusing on age effects in the encoding or decoding phase.[5] Schmiedel (2017: 122) describes some difficulties on the part of her older listeners in particular, but cannot draw conclusions owing to the small number of subjects. Very few researchers have studied gender effects with respect to either production or perception. Chen and Boves (2018) observe gender effects on various pitch and duration parameters on the production side.

The difference between what is meant and what is said may be looked at from the perspective of the speaker as well as the listener. On the part of the speaker, the ironic, neutral or sincere character of an utterance is cued primarily through context, but also by way of extralinguistic[6] signaling. This may occur in various ways: the literal "tongue in cheek" or a wink being examples on a visual strand.

So far, studies on verbal irony have focused on the distinction between sincere (and, possibly, neutral) stimuli as opposed to sarcastic ones ("blame by praise"). Listeners were asked to classify utterances as either ironic or sincere and have proven to be quite successful at that task. The so-called kind irony ("praise by blame") has not nearly received as much attention.

2 Phonetic means of coding non-actual speech

The relationship between literal and actual meaning of an utterance in ironic speech needs to be communicated to the listener. This applies to "normal"

---

5 In the context of this contribution, "age effects" refer to an adult population. There are quite a few studies on developmental aspects of the decoding of irony in particular (e.g. Creusere 2000; Laval and Bert-Erboul 2005; Wilson 2013) but this aspect is beyond the scope of the present study.
6 By extralinguistic we understand non-verbal, non-vocal means of communication, i.e. facial expression and gestures.

instances of irony, in which there is a discrepancy between the two, as well as to fake irony and unintentional irony. In fake irony it is absolutely essential to use an ironic tone of voice because otherwise the utterance would be interpreted as what it is, i.e. truthful. Unintentional irony, on the other hand, is characterized by precisely the absence of cues to ironic speech.

If all interlocutors are physically present during the exchange, irony is often signaled by nonverbal means ("tongue in cheek", winking, a shrewd smile, etc.). If, however, the exchange takes place without the visual channel being available, e.g. over the telephone, the signaling has to be achieved by vocal and / or verbal means alone. There is quite a range of phonetic mechanisms which may be utilized to signal non-actual speech. They will be discussed in the following sections. So far, not all of them have been studied in conjunction with verbal irony. Whenever findings are available from the literature on the subject, they will be cited.

2.1 Speaking fundamental frequency ('pitch') and related measures

The probably single most important measure in determining physiological stress (Hansen and Patil 2007), affective states (e.g. Banse and Scherer 1996; Braun and Heilmann 2012), deception (Anolli and Ciceri 1997), but also verbal irony is the average *speaking fundamental frequency* (F0) with *pitch* as its perceptual correlate.[7] It describes the number of vocal fold vibrations in the larynx per time unit and is usually measured in Hertz (Hz).[8] Fundamental frequency is generally averaged over an utterance, and its mean or median is established. Deviations from neutral speech are considered to be the consequence of a change in laryngeal muscle tone as a physiological correlate of the emotional state or stress condition.

---

7 The correlation between the acoustic and the perceptual parameters is fairly good but far from perfect. The main reason for this is that the human perceptual organ does not operate in a linear way either with respect to frequency or intensity (see 2.2 below). For instance, the sensitivity of the human ear is much higher in the low frequency range, which also contains the main area of speech, than in the high frequency range. In order to compensate for this it has become good practice to use the semitone scale as opposed to the Hertz scale in order to perceptually reflect voice pitch and its derivatives like standard deviation and range. A similar principle applies to intensity.
8 Especially if male and female speakers are to be compared, it may be useful to express the results in semitones rather than Hz, thus eliminating the effect of the physiological difference between male and female voices and facilitating a comparison between male and female voices.

Besides the *mean F0*, various distributional measures have been introduced in order to capture intonational detail. The most common ones are *standard deviation* and *range*, the former reflecting the degree of monotony or melodiousness, the latter representing the highest and the lowest note produced. Some studies focus on more elaborate prosodic cues like the pitch contour or the timing of the final fall (Chen and Boves 2018).

With respect to verbal irony, previous studies have rendered varying results. Whereas some researchers find a generally lower mean F0 in sarcastic stimuli as opposed to sincere ones (cf. Fónagy 1971; Rockwell 2000; Anolli, Infantino, and Ciceri 2002; Cheang and Pell 2008; Nauke and Braun 2011; Scharrer, Christmann, and Knoll 2011), others (Schaffer 1981; Anolli, Ciceri, and Infantino 2000[9]; Bryant and Fox Tree 2005) establish higher values. When looking at the standard deviations, a similar picture arises: Schaffer (1981) describes higher values for the sarcastic stimuli, whereas the majority of studies report monotony in sarcastic as opposed to sincere speech (Fónagy 1971; Anolli, Infantino, and Ciceri 2002, Attardo et al. 2003, Cheang and Pell 2008; Nauke and Braun 2011; Chen and Boves 2018). Schaffer (1981) and Bryant and Fox Tree (2005) present opposite or inconclusive results. The findings for F0 range are just as contradictory: an increase in F0 range in sarcastic utterances was found by Schaffer (1981) and – to a limited extent – Bryant and Fox Tree (2005); a decrease by Anolli, Infantino, and Ciceri (2002), Cheang and Pell (2008) and Nauke and Braun (2011).

One can speculate about the reasons for these discrepancies. Scharrer, Christmann, and Knoll (2011: 3–4) largely attribute them to different languages being studied. However, it also seems worth considering that methodological issues may have played a role (e.g. the inclusion of different kinds of irony; length of stimuli; inclusion of neutral stimuli).

2.2 Vocal intensity ('loudness')

The sound pressure level or intensity of speech sounds with *loudness* as its auditory correlate[10] is largely caused by an increase in subglottal pressure which is in turn influenced by the respiratory musculature. It can be measured in terms of RMS (root mean square) including standard deviation and range and is expressed in decibels (dB).

---

9 Experiment 1.
10 It should be kept in mind that the human ear is most sensitive to intensity differences within the frequency range of speech sounds.

Studies looking at verbal irony have come to different conclusions regarding the intensity measures. Rockwell (2000) finds an increase in average intensity in sarcastic stimuli, whereas Nauke and Braun (2011) come to the opposite conclusion. The latter finding corresponds to the results reported by Bryant and Fox Tree (2005), who established a lower intensity standard deviation in their sarcastic stimuli as opposed to sincere ones.

Probably it may prove worthwhile to look at the intensity dynamics of the stressed vowel in greater detail in the future. It is of interest whether the timing of the maximum intensity within the stressed vowel differs between ironic and sincere or neutral conditions or will even vary with type of irony. Schmiedel (2017) finds a highly significant delay of the intensity maxima in sarcastic, kindly ironic and sincerely negative stimuli as opposed to neutral utterances. No difference can be established between sincere praise and neutral utterances. This preliminary result demonstrates that this parameter deserves more attention.

2.3 Spectral tilt / center of gravity

The measurement of spectral tilt or the spectral center of gravity can be considered as an indication of the distribution of intensity over the range of frequencies across the spectrum. A predominance of lower frequencies corresponds to a muffled, soft voice, an emphasis of higher frequencies will result in what is perceived as an inherently loud, strong voice. The spectral composition of harmonics reflects the shape of the glottal impulse – the longer the closing phase of the vocal folds, the more harmonics will be visible in the spectrogram, the higher is the center of gravity, and the smaller is the spectral tilt. The present authors are not aware of any studies on verbal irony up to now which have used this parameter.

2.4 Tempo and pausing

Speaking tempo and *pausing* can be considered as interrelated to some extent, because the more pauses occur, the slower the tempo will be. It is advisable, though, to keep those two factors separate by differentiating between syllable rate and articulation rate. The former includes pauses whereas the latter does not, thus taking only net speech into account. Both syllable and articulation rate can be measured in different ways, depending on the linguistic unit per time unit calculated. The linguistic units most commonly used are sounds, syllables or words; the time units are seconds or minutes. The most widespread units are syllables per second – this will, however, become problematic when comparing languages with largely different phonotactics. In those cases, the use of sounds per second may be more advisable.

A follow-up decision concerns the choice between phonetic and linguistic syllables. As an example, the realization of the German lexeme *haben* 'to have' as [ham] contains two linguistic syllables as opposed to one phonetic syllable. Calculating speaking tempo in terms of phonetic syllables will thus provide a close approximation of actual articulator movement whereas linguistic syllables will reflect the degree of articulatory precision (see 2.6 below). In short utterances, sounds per second may be the method of choice in studying speaking tempo.

There is a rare degree of consensus in previous studies in citing a decrease in speaking tempo in sarcastic stimuli as opposed to sincere ones (Fónagy 1971; Schaffer 1982; Rockwell 2000, Anolli, Infantino, and Ciceri 2002; Cheang and Pell 2008; Scharrer, Christmann, and Knoll 2011; Rao 2013; Chen and Boves 2018).

Pauses may take on both the form of filled and unfilled pauses. Fillers have been found to be a stable speaker specific feature (Braun and Rosin 2015). However, studying pauses only makes sense in longer utterances.

Studies which examine the number of pauses and pause length are very rare. Anolli, Infantino, and Ciceri (2002) report a larger number of pauses and at the same time significantly shorter pauses in ironic as compared to normal speech.

2.5 Articulatory precision

Articulatory Precision denotes the degree to which articulatory targets are reached. This presupposes that speaking entails constant movement of articulators from one target point to the next as opposed to producing a sequence of stationary segments as is suggested by alphabetical renditions of speech. In other words, the speech organs are in motion most of the time, whereas the stationary phases are practically non-existent. However, there are differences between various speaking styles with respect to articulatory precision. In careful speech, the targets are generally reached, whereas this is the case to a much lesser degree in everyday speech.[11] For instance, a plosive like /b/ may be pronounced as a fricative [β] in a word like *habe* 'have'. In vowels, lack of articulatory precision means centralization, which implies a movement of the articulators towards the central vowel *schwa* [ə]. An example is the pronunciation of German *gut* 'good' as [gʊtʰ] as opposed to [guːtʰ]. One way of determining the degree of articulatory precision

---

[11] Speaking while intoxicated will, however, dramatically reduce articulatory precision.

is to measure vowel formants. The more "peripheral" the formants are within the vowel trapezoid, the more precisely those vowels are realized. Precise articulation takes more time than sloppy one (Hildebrandt 1961). This is exemplified by the above *gut* example, where the more centralized vowel is also shorter than the more peripheral one. This is part of a general tendency: slower speaking tempo and higher articulatory precision will often co-occur.[12]

Different procedures have been put forward to measure articulatory precision. One of them is the *Lautminderungsquotient* 'sound elision quotient' (Hildebrandt 1961) where

$$LMQ = 10 - \frac{10 \times n_{marked}}{n_{unmarked}}$$

n_{marked} represents the number of phones realized in the marked condition (sample under investigation); $n_{unmarked}$ represents the number of phones realized in the unmarked condition (reference / standard).

Positive values represent elisions (*wir ham* [ham] as opposed to *wir haben* ['haːbən] 'we have'); negative values represent epenthesis (German *faul* [fɐʊl] 'lazy' being pronounced as ['fɐʊəl]).

On a different strand, Low and Grabe (1995) developed the Paired Variability Index (PVI), which was originally intended to provide a tool which would allow to gradually distinguish between so-called syllable-timed and stress-timed languages. This measure might also be used to distinguish ludic from "unmarked" speech. Neither LMQ nor PVI seem to have been applied as yet in studies on verbal irony.

Scharrer, Christmann, and Knoll (2011) approach the issue of articulatory precision from an acoustic point of view. They measure formant frequencies and find a larger vowel space in ironic speech than in literal utterances. They take this to imply that there is vowel hyperarticulation in sarcastic speech (Scharrer, Christmann, and Knoll 2011: 19).

---

12 This, once again, only holds true for "normal" speech. On the other hand, a reduction of speaking tempo may well be accompanied by lack of articulatory precision if the speaker is inebriated, whereas in emotional speech (specifically: anger), high articulatory precision may be accompanied by high tempo (cf. Kienast 2002: 81, 105).

2.6 Voice quality

The term "voice quality" refers to a number of laryngeal as well as supralaryngeal settings which contribute to the individual sound of a particular voice. Examples are the former US Secretary of State Henry Kissinger, who constantly used what is called *creaky voice* or the CNN anchor Richard Quest who frequently uses so-called *ventricular voice*, i.e. phonation of the false vocal folds in addition to or instead of the real ones. The former results in a very low pitch; consequently the individual vibrations of the vocal cords can be perceived. The latter causes a raspy, strained sounding voice. An example of supralaryngeal settings can be observed in the current US-President Donald Trump, who regularly articulates with protruded lips.

While the use of a certain voice quality may have become associated with certain speakers, this does not mean to imply that voice quality will not change with communicative setting. For instance, certain voice qualities have been found to be associated with different emotions, e.g. breathy voice is frequently observed in sad and fearful utterances (Braun and Heilmann 2012; Probst and Braun 2016).

Cutler (1974: 117) and Haverkate (1990: 80) describe ironic speech as nasalized. Fónagy (1971) and Schaffer (1981) find a high proportion of creaky voice in ironic speech. There is certainly much room for further systematic research beyond these isolated observations.

Cheang and Pell (2008) study voice quality from a strictly acoustic perspective and observe a lowered harmonics-to-noise ratio[13] in their sarcastic stimuli.

3 A study on short utterances

While the phonetic dimensions of verbal irony are generally fairly well researched (see section 2 above), there are two main shortcomings which need to be addressed. Firstly, in most studies on verbal irony so-called sincere utterances, which have also been called affirmative or literal, are compared to ironic ones (e.g. Cutler 1974; Schaffer 1982; Rockwell 2000). Yet, Anolli, Ciceri, and Infantino (2000, 2001, 2002) are able to show that a third category should be introduced in order to serve as a valid reference, i.e. neutral utterances which are

---

[13] Harmonics-to-noise ratio (HNR) describes the difference in energy between harmonic and noisy components of speech. Low HNR levels are perceived as rough or raspy; high HNR levels are perceived as clear (Baken and Orlikoff 2000: 282).

neither actively affirmative nor sarcastic. These authors find both types of irony to deviate from neutral stimuli in the same direction. For instance, mean F0 as well as its range and standard deviation are higher in their ironic stimuli than in the neutral ones. The same applies to speech intensity. Finally, while the number of pauses in ironic speech exceeds that in neutral speech, pause length is shorter and articulation rate slower.

Secondly, most previous work on ironic speech is focused on sarcasm, i.e. blame by praise. Kind irony has not nearly received a comparable amount of attention. Furthermore, research has so far relied on utterances of sentence or phraselength (cf. e.g. Rockwell 2000; Anolli, Ciceri, and Infantino 2000; Cheang and Pell 2008; Scharrer, Christmann, and Knoll 2011).

The experiment presented in this contribution[14] pursues a different path: It seeks the ultimate challenge in that it aims to determine whether speakers are able to signal sarcasm and kind irony in single-word utterances consisting of a maximum of two syllables in such a way that listeners can reliably decode them. This experimental approach was chosen with a forensic perspective in mind. In the forensic context, a defendant might argue that the *great* which he or she uttered in reply to a proposal by a hired killer to do away with his/her spouse on that same day was not sincere and therefore cannot be used as proof of guilt. In cases like that, a phonetician may be asked to testify in court whether a judgement on the sincere or sarcastic nature of an utterance is at all possible if it is based on a single syllable only.

This study furthermore draws a distinction between sarcasm ("blame by praise") and kind irony ("praise by blame") and includes neutral utterances as a baseline. The following research questions are asked:

- Do even very short sincere and ironic utterances differ with respect to their phonetic properties?
- Are there differences with respect to the type of irony (sarcasm vs. kind irony)?
- Are there gender differences in the production of irony in such very short utterances?
- Are listeners able to distinguish between very short sincere and ironic utterances?
- Are there gender differences in the perception of irony?

---

[14] The results reported here consist in a subset of those contained in Schmiedel (2017). They are interpreted in a wider context here.

3.1 Materials and methods

When describing the experiment, we adopt the following terminological conventions: "Irony" is used as a cover term for both *sarcasm* and *kind irony*. "Sarcasm" denotes the *blame by praise* type of irony, i.e. *great* as a reaction to a missed train connection. "Kind irony" is used as a realization of irony through *praise by blame*, i.e. *terrible* as a reaction to a very good but less than perfect grade. The terms "sincere" or "affirmative" refer to the opposite of either sarcasm or kind irony, denoting praise in the former and blame in the latter case. They are distinct from "neutral" utterances which are unmarked.

3.1.1 Production experiment

A total of 20 speakers were recorded. They were balanced for sex (10 men, 10 women) with an average age of 27 years. Based on short scripted scenarios, they each produced 20 utterances consisting of monosyllabic (N = 7) or disyllabic (N = 13) words both in a sincere and an ironic context, 10 of which fell into the category of sarcasm ("blame by praise") and 10 into the category of kind irony ("praise by blame"). In addition, the stimuli were recorded in a neutral setting, i.e. in read speech. In order to do that, the utterances were randomized with three repetitions each and then turned into a PowerPoint presentation where each stimulus appeared for three seconds. This was presented to the speakers without context. This procedure was chosen in order to avoid the typical "list intonation". Table 1 shows the lexemes and their translation into English, Table 2 contains examples of scenarios.

Tab. 1: Positive (sarcasm) and negative (kind irony) stimulus sets (Translation: AB)

positive	*danke* 'thanks'	*klar* 'course'	*klasse* 'great'	*lecker* 'tasty'	*nett* 'nice'
	schön 'good'	*Spitze* 'excellent'	*super* 'super'	*toll* 'awesome'	*Wahnsinn* 'phenomenal'
negative	*Blödmann* 'dumbass'	*mies* 'lousy'	*Mist* 'shoot'	*schade* 'too bad'	*Schande* 'shame on you'
	schlimm 'bad'	*schrecklich* 'terrible'	*Streber* 'smart-ass'	*übel* 'nasty'	*Verdammt* 'damn it'

Tab. 2: Sample scenarios for sarcasm and kind irony (translation: AB)

Utterance	Scenario sincere	Scenario ironic
	Paul and Paula are going out to dinner. They are looking at the menu.	Paul and Paula are going out to dinner. They are looking at the menu.
lecker 'tasty'	Paul: Look, they've got your favorite pasta!	Paul: Look, they've got frog's legs and snails. How does that sound?
	Paula: Tasty!	Paula: Tasty!
Blödmann 'dumbass'	It is Paula's birthday, and so far, her boyfriend Paul has neither congratulated her nor given her a present. He calls in the evening.	It is Paula's birthday, and so far, her boyfriend Paul has neither congratulated her nor given her a present. She comes home disappointed. When she enters the apartment, she finds that Paul and their friends have prepared a surprise party.
	Paul: Hi, I'm sorry. I've gotta work late. Don't wait for me.	
	Paula: You do know what day it is today?	
	Paul: Yes, it's Wednesday, why?	Paul (smiling): I'm sure you thought I'd forgotten!
	Paula: Dumbass!	Paula: Dumbass!

Measurements were carried out using the *praat* software package, version 5.3.04 (Boersma and Weenink 2012) with respect to duration, fundamental frequency, and intensity of the stimuli. The SPSS software package version 20.0 was used for the statistical analyses. These included *t*-tests and one-way repeated measures ANOVA, depending on the nature of the hypothesis to be tested.

3.1.2 Perception experiment

In order to test whether listeners are able to detect irony from short speech stimuli alone, a total of 44 listeners were studied. 23 of them women, 21 men. They were 28 years old on average. Thus, speakers and listeners were almost exactly of the same age.[15] Only ironic and sincere utterances were used in the listening experiment. The neutral stimuli were not included in order to limit the duration of the experiment.

---

15 This is worth mentioning because it has been shown in relation to other perceptual tasks like age estimation that listener performance varies with the difference in age between speakers and listeners (Shipp and Hollien 1969).

Listeners were presented with a total of 800 stimuli (20 speakers x 20 words x 2 conditions (sincere and ironic)). Each stimulus was presented twice, separated by a 500 ms pause. The pause between different stimuli was set to 2 seconds. After every tenth stimulus, a 250-Hz tone was inserted in order to enable listeners to keep track of the utterances.

Samples were presented in isolation, i.e., listeners did not receive the scenarios. They had to tick one of two boxes labelled *ironic* or *sincere*. The duration of the listening experiment amounted to 50 minutes in total, which was judged to be too demanding to be carried out in one session. It was therefore split up into three chunks of two times 300 and once 200 stimuli which were judged in separate sessions. The pause between sessions lasted five minutes. Six utterances which were not part of the experiment were used for training purposes.

3.2 Results

When reporting the results, we adopt the following terminological conventions: "irony" is used as a cover term for both sarcasm and kind irony. The terms "sincere" or "affirmative" refer to the opposite of either sarcasm or kind irony, denoting praise in the former and blame in the latter case. They are distinct from "neutral" utterances which are unmarked. We furthermore distinguish between the "positive" and the "negative" stimulus sets. The former refers to the semantically positive lexemes, i.e. *toll* 'great' or *nett* 'nice'. When used in a sincere manner, these utterances constitute praise, when they are used ironically, they constitute sarcasm. The latter, on the other hand, comprises semantically negative lexemes like *Mist* 'shoot' or *verdammt* 'damn', thus denoting either kind irony or blame.

3.2.1 Production experiment

3.2.1.1 Duration

Figure 1 shows the results for the timing parameters in the different scenarios as well as the neutral condition. In single-syllable utterances, there is no point in computing syllable rate or articulation rate. Measurements are thus confined to utterance length. Due to the difference in length between the sarcastic and kindly ironic stimuli, the absolute durations of both cannot be compared. Instead, the differences within each stimulus set will be looked at. As far as the positive stimulus set is concerned, it emerges that the sarcastic utterances are considerably longer than those expressing praise, the latter being only marginally longer than the neutral stimuli. The same is true in principle for the negative stimulus set, but the difference between kind irony and blame is much smaller in this case. Both are markedly faster than the neutral stimuli. Statistical analyses were carried out in order to test the significance of these results. The difference in duration is significant for both types of irony (Wilcoxon two-tailed *t*-Test), however, results are much clearer for sarcasm than for kind irony. This is consistent with most previous research which was carried out on longer utterances. Specifically, Anolli, Ciceri, and Infantino (2000: 287) report a higher rate of articulation for praise as opposed to sarcastic irony and for blame as compared with kind irony. Their "normal speech" is fastest in both cases (cf. also section 2.4 above for further findings by previous authors).

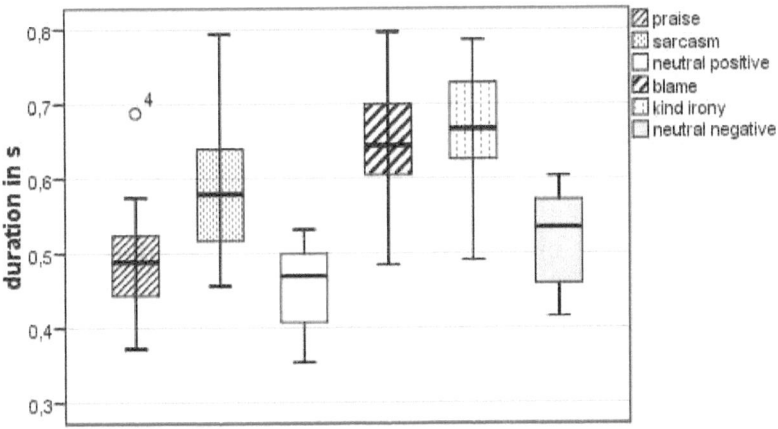

Fig. 1: Utterance duration in the various scenarios as well as the neutral condition

3.2.1.2 Fundamental frequency

The results on fundamental frequency parameters are summarized in Table 3. They include the mean as an indication of voice pitch and the standard deviation and range as indicators of melodiousness. Both standard deviation and range are expressed in terms of semitones in order to keep the absolute values for male and female voices comparable.

Tab. 3: Fundamental frequency: Mean, standard deviation, and range

Speakers	Stimulus set	Stimulus type	F0 mean (Hz)	SD (ST)	range (ST)
Female Ss.	positive set	praise	247	3.89	10.95
		sarcasm	194	2.45	7.54
		neutral	209	1.65	5.40
Female Ss.	negative set	blame	206	2.84	8.71
		kind irony	210	3.34	10.39
		neutral	209	1.54	5.36
Male Ss.	positive set	praise	149	3.65	11.31
		sarcasm	127	2.44	8.20
		neutral	125	1.70	5.85
Male Ss.	negative set	blame	130	2.49	8.31
		kind irony	137	3.20	9.86
		neutral	125	1.55	5.57

What has to be noted first of all is that there is a striking similarity between the neutral stimuli in both conditions. In fact, the difference between the two proved not to be significant for any of the F0 parameters. We thus join Anolli, Ciceri, and Infantino (2000: 290) in taking this as "an important indicator that confirms the internal validity of the experiment". It also underlines the necessity for neutral stimuli to be included as a baseline in contradistinction to "sincere" ones, and it confirms that our subjects did very well at keeping those utterances neutral indeed.

In the positive stimulus set, the sarcastic utterances show a markedly lower mean fundamental frequency than do the sincere ones. This applies to male and female speakers alike. Both differences are highly significant (p = .000). The neutral renditions are closer to the sarcastic ones with a tendency to be slightly higher, though, for the female speakers, whereas they do not seem to follow a clear pattern in our male speakers.

Kind irony is much less clearly marked by mean fundamental frequency than sarcasm. In most male and female speakers alike, however, ironic stimuli are higher in mean F0 than the sincere ones, but the difference is much smaller than it is in the positive stimulus set and fails to reach significance. The deviations from neutral are also fairly small.

The two stimulus sets also differ with respect to *standard deviation*. Whereas F0$_{SD}$ is much lower in sarcasm than for praise, it is considerably higher for kind irony as compared to blame. Only the differences in the positive stimulus sets are significant, though (p = .005 for female speakers and p = .002 for male speakers). Both the sincere and ironic stimuli show a much larger standard deviation than the neutral utterances (sign. p = .000).

When it comes to fundamental frequency *range*, the sarcastic stimuli in the positive stimulus set show a much smaller span than the sincere ones. This is true for male and female speakers alike (sign. p = .000 for both). The values for the neutral stimuli are still more monotonous in 14 out of 20 cases and about equal to the sarcastic ones in four.

Quite the opposite results are to be found in kind irony. Here, ironic utterances show a range equal to or larger than that of sincere samples (sign. p = .023 for the female speakers and p = .037 for the male speakers). The neutral stimuli display the smallest F0 range.

It emerges that all three F0 parameters considered here show opposing results depending on the kind of irony studied. Thus they seem to be less of a marker of "ironic speech" as such but rather one of attitude, a positive attitude being expressed by a higher mean and a larger degree of melodiousness. This applies to both female and male speakers, although is it more marked in the former group.

3.2.1.3 Intensity

Once again, the neutral stimuli are very similar for both stimulus sets and for male and female speakers alike. Neither difference was found to be significant (Schmiedel 2017: 88). Differences emerge, however, when irony comes into play: positive wordings, whether sarcastic or sincere, tend to be louder than the neutral renditions, whereas negative wordings, whether kindly ironic or sincere, tend to be softer than the neutral stimuli. In other words, there is no clear distinction between "ironic" and "sincere" stimuli as such, but instead semantically positive utterances are louder than semantically negative ones.

As far as the positive stimulus set is concerned, there is a clear distinction between ironic and sincere utterances in that the former show a much lesser intensity as compared to the latter. The opposite is true for the n: In this case the sincere stimuli are softer than the ironic ones, albeit to a lesser degree.

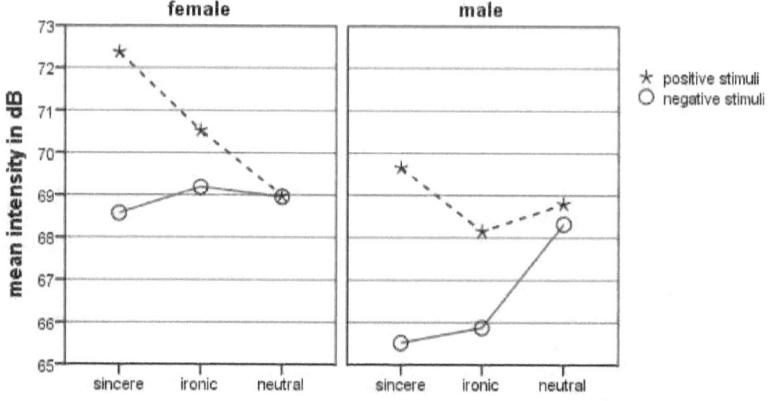

Fig. 2: Mean intensity in sincere, ironic, and neutral stimuli

Gender differences emerge with respect to intensity, not in kind, but in degree: female speakers tend to mark both kinds of irony by a greater intensity as compared to neutral utterances, whereas male speakers show a lower intensity.

These results are in keeping with those reported by Anolli, Infantino, and Ciceri (2002) with respect to the female speakers only; results for the male speakers point to the opposite direction. It seems that many of our male speakers are in the group which Anolli, Infantino, and Ciceri (2002) classify as group (4), for whom sarcasm is similar to cold anger and thus low in intensity.

Table 4 summarizes the findings on the production side including the significance levels established.

Tab. 4: Summary of findings – production

Feature	Type of irony	Relation	Sincere speech	Probability
Duration				
Mean	kind irony	>	blame	p = .035[c]
	sarcasm	>	praise	p = .000
F0 women				
Mean	sarcasm	<	praise	p = .000[a]
Mean	kind irony	>	praise	n.s.
SD	sarcasm	<	praise	p = .005[b]
SD	kind irony	>	blame	n.s.
Range	sarcasm	<	praise	p = .000[a]
Range	kind irony	>	blame	p = .023[a]
F0 men				
Mean	sarcasm	<	praise	p = .003[a]
Mean	kind irony	>	blame	n.s.
SD	sarcasm	<	praise	p = .002[a]
SD	kind irony	>	blame	n.s.
Range	sarcasm	<	praise	p = .000[a]
Range	kind irony	>	blame	p = .037[a]
Intensity				
Mean	sarcasm	<	praise	p = .002[a]
	kind irony	>	blame	n.s.

[a] t-test paired; [b] Wilcoxon; [c] female speakers only (t-test paired)

3.2.2 Perception experiment

In the perception experiment, listeners had to decide in a forced-choice design whether a certain utterance was sincere or ironic. Given that the utterances they heard were disyllabic at the most, the task is much more difficult than in most, if not all, previous research. In view of this, recognition rates could be expected to be lower than those for longer utterances, where the paralinguistic information can be exploited to a much greater extent.

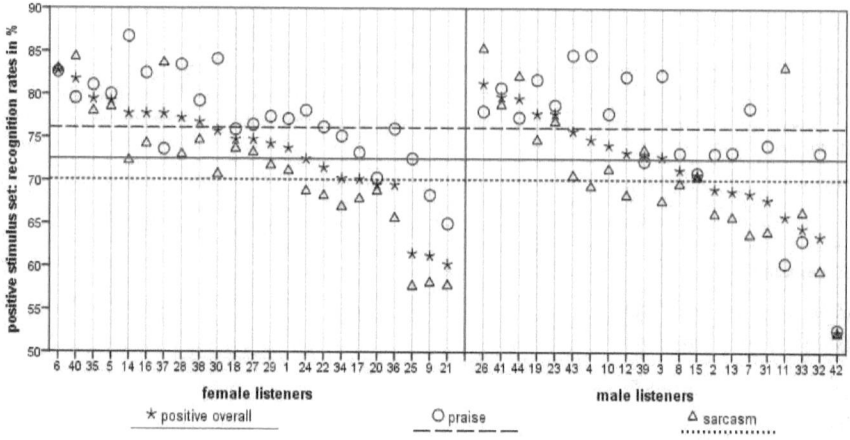

Fig. 3: Recognition rates for the "positive" stimulus set (sarcasm)

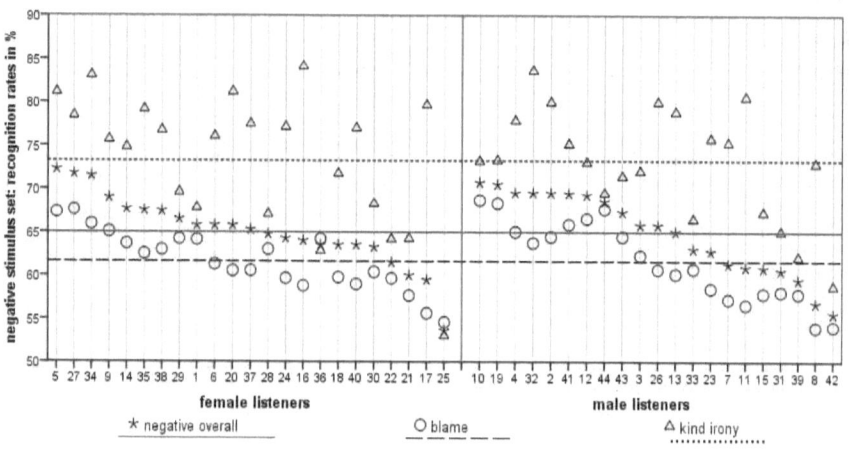

Fig. 4: Recognition rates for the "negative" stimulus set (kind irony)

The results are shown in Figures 3 and 4. When looking at them, it is immediately evident that the overall recognition rate for the positive (sarcastic) stimulus set is much higher than that for the kindly ironic stimulus set (72 % vs. 65 %). This, however, cannot be taken to imply that the kindly ironic utterances as such are identified less frequently than the sarcastic ones. On the contrary, the stimuli exhibiting kind irony were the ones which were recognized correctly more often

(73 %; cf. Figure 4) than the latter (70 %, cf. Figure 3). In fact, the overall recognition rate was best for praise (77 %), followed by kind irony and sarcasm, while blame was recognized only 62 % of the time. This means that the two kinds of irony are handled quite differently by the listeners: whereas the "praise by blame" type of irony is detected slightly better than the corresponding sincere utterances, the opposite is true for the "blame by praise" type of stimuli.

Female speakers' utterances are recognized significantly (t-test paired; cf. Table 5) better than those produced by male speakers with the exception of blame. Listener sex, on the other hand, did not constitute a significant factor in the recognition rates.

Tab. 5: Summary of results of the perception experiment

Stimulus set			
positive (sarcasm)	>	negative (kind irony)	p = .000[a]
Utterance type			
praise	>	sarcasm	p = .000[a]
blame	<	kind irony	p = .000[a]
Speaker sex			
praise / sarcasm / kind irony: female Ss	>	male Ss	p = .000[a]
blame: female Ss	<	male Ss	p = .000[a]

[a] t-test paired

4 Discussion

It is not easy to compare the present findings to previous ones because of essential differences in the language studied and/or the experimental set-up. The latter concerns stimulus duration as well as the (lack of) inclusion of different kinds of irony and of neutral stimuli.

Firstly and most importantly, our results show that there evidently is a way of paralinguistic signaling of irony, which allows listeners to classify even very short context-free utterances as ironic or sincere at a level much beyond chance. It is, in fact, remarkable how well listeners are able to distinguish sincere from ironic monosyllabic words. From a forensic point of view, it is quite likely that listeners can reliably infer irony based on a single syllable even if no context information is available. A major task for future work is thus to determine which of the acoustic parameters will best explain the perception results.

As far as production is concerned, the results for our positive stimulus set (a longer duration and a lower F0 in sarcasm than in sincere praise) are in good agreement with most previous studies which cover sarcasm only (cf. Cheang and Pell 2008; Rockwell 2000; Pexman and Olineck 2002; Scharrer, Christmann, and Knoll 2011; Rao 2013, to name only a few). They are clearly at variance, however, with Anolli, Ciceri, and Infantino's (2000) findings on fundamental frequency and also with other studies which cover languages other than German (Lœvenbruck et al. 2013; Laval and Bert-Eboul 2005; Adachi 1996; Cheang and Pell 2009). This difference finds a plausible explanation in the fact that different languages were involved. Stimulus duration (monosyllables vs. full utterances) may also have played a role.

Our findings for the negative stimulus set (kind irony), particularly those with respect to F0 and intensity, form a mirror image those for the positive one, making it very clear that the two kinds of irony should not be confounded. With respect to the variables analyzed here, men and women pursue similar strategies in encoding the two kinds of irony. There are, however, differences in degree. This may have had consequences for their recognizability (see below).

Despite the clear distinction between sarcasm and kind irony, we do not unequivocally share Bryant and Fox Tree's (2005) conclusion that there is "very little support for the notion of an ironic tone of voice; that is, prosodic consistency across verbal irony utterances" (2005: 273). With respect to sarcasm, at least, typical patterns can be observed.

Whether these paralinguistic cues are exclusive to irony, however, remains open to question. One clear indication against a general classification of utterances as either "ironic" or "sincere" is the fact that the distinction between sarcasm and kind irony which has been pointed out by Anolli, Ciceri, and Infantino (2000) is supported by our results. All production parameters were found to be opposite for sarcasm and kind irony as compared to their sincere counterparts. This means that at least those two variants of irony should be taken into consideration in future research, because only the comparison between ironic and sincere stimuli of different sorts will reveal the different patterns. The same applies to the introduction of the "neutral" category, which may serve as some kind of a baseline.

Secondly, the markers of verbal irony as established in the present study do not seem to be confined to ironic use. As an example, we propose that for the F0 parameters it is the "underlying sentiment" that determines their relationship between the members of a stimulus pair as opposed to the "face value" of the lexemes. We argue that this is the main reason why sarcasm and kind irony behave so differently in many respects while both are distinct from "neutral". For instance, utterances like the sarcastic *toll* 'great' are longer, lower-pitched, and lower in intensity than the sincere *toll*, whereas the kindly ironic *super* 'super' is longer, higher pitched, and higher in intensity than the corresponding sincere token.

In fact, the findings for our positive stimulus set closely resemble the results reported by Braun and Heilmann (2012) on cold anger. Those authors found cold anger to exhibit a lower mean F0 and a smaller standard deviation and range than emotionally neutral utterances. At the same time, the patterns established for praise in the present study are very similar to those for joy as observed in Braun and Heilmann (2012). Our results strongly suggest a closer look at the relationship between emotional speech and ironic speech. This view corresponds perfectly with Anolli, Infantino, and Ciceri's (2002) description of what they call a "family of ironic voices" (2002: 374). Our data for kind irony match their pattern 1a, which they characterize as "bantering joy", and our sarcastic data clearly correspond to their pattern 2b ("cold anger"; Anolli, Infantino, and Ciceri 2002: 374). Bryant and Fox Tree (2005) argue along that same line when they conclude: "Speakers are communicating multiple messages by layering propositional and non-propositional information, and providing prosodic cues in contextually dependent ways that map differentially onto the simultaneously presented information [...]" (2005: 272). It will be a prime task for future research to separate and identify those layers of information and their phonetic correlates.

Thirdly, as far as perception is concerned, there are clearly individual speakers whose ironic signals are more easily decoded than those of others. Generally speaking, female speakers' cues to irony were identified significantly better than those uttered by male speakers. This once again has a parallel in the processing of emotional speech. Braun and Heilmann (2012) found female listeners to be highly significantly better at recognizing emotions than male listeners.

On the other hand, there are listeners who are better at decoding speaker intent than others. This time, however, there was no clear distinction along gender lines. It would be of future interest to establish whether there is a correlation between the ability of a given listener to spot irony and his or her ability to show empathy. If those two abilities are found to be related, further studies on patients who are unable to express empathy or detect emotions, who e.g. have been diagnosed with Asperger autism, would have to constitute the next step.

5 References

Adachi, Takanori. 1996. Sarcasm in Japanese. *Studies in Language* 20(1). 1–36.
Anolli, Luigi & Rita Ciceri. 1997. The Voice of Deception: Vocal Strategies of Naïve and Able Liars. *Journal of Nonverbal Behavior* 21(4). 259–284.
Anolli, Luigi, Rita Ciceri & Maria Giaele Infantino. 2000. Irony as a Game of Implicitness: Acoustic Profiles of Ironic Communication. *Journal of Psycholinguistic Research* 29(3). 275–311.
Anolli, Luigi, Maria Giaele Infantino & Rita Ciceri. 2001. "You're a Real Genius!": Irony as a Miscommunication Design. In Luigi Anolli, Rita Ciceri & Giuseppe Riva (eds.), *Say not to Say: New perspectives on miscommunication. Bd. 3. Emerging Communication: Studies in New Technologies and Practices in Communication*. IOS Press, 141–164.
Anolli, Luigi, Maria Giaele Infantino & Rita Ciceri. 2002. From "blame by praise" to "praise by blame": Analysis of vocal patterns in ironic communication. *International Journal of Psychology* 37. 266–276.
Attardo, Salvatore, Jodi Eisterhold, Jennifer Hay & Isabella Poggi. 2003. Multimodal Markers of irony and sarcasm. *Humor – International Journal of Humor Research* 16(2). 243–260.
Baken, Ronald J. & Robert F. Orlikoff. [1987] 2000 *Clinical Measurement of Speech and Voice*, 2nd edn. San Diego: Singular.
Banse, Rainer & Klaus R. Scherer. 1996. Acoustic Profiles in Vocal Emotion Expression. *Journal of Personality and Social Psychology* 70(3). 614–636.
Berg, Wolfgang. 1978. *Uneigentliches Sprechen: zur Pragmatik u. Semantik von Metapher, Metonymie, Ironie, Litotes und rhetorischer Frage*. Tübingen: Narr.
Boersma, Paul & David Weenink. 2012. Praat. Doing phonetics by computer (version 5.3.04; 3 March 2014). http://www.praat.org (accessed 5 July 2018).
Braun, Angelika & Christa M. Heilmann. 2012. *SynchronEmotion* (Hallesche Schriften zur Sprechwissenschaft und Phonetik 41). Frankfurt am Main: Peter Lang.
Braun, Angelika & Annabelle Rosin. 2015. On the speaker-specificity of hesitation markers. *Proceedings XVIII ICPhS, Glasgow*. 10–14. https://www.internationalphoneticassociation.org/icphs-proceedings/ICPhS2015/Papers/ICPHS0731.pdf (accessed 5 July 2018).
Bryant, Gregory A. & Jean E. Fox Tree. 2002. Recognizing Verbal Irony in Spontaneous Speech. *Metaphor and Symbol* 17(2). 99–117.
Bryant, Gregory A. & Jean E. Fox Tree. 2005. Is there an ironic Tone of Voice? *Language and Speech* 48(3). 257–277.
Cheang, Henry S. & Marc D. Pell. 2008. The sound of sarcasm. *Speech Communication* 50(5). 366–381.
Cheang, Henry S. & Marc D. Pell. 2009. Acoustic markers of sarcasm in Cantonese and English. *The Journal of the Acoustical Society of America* 126(3). 1394–1405.
Cheang, Henry S. & Marc D. Pell. 2011. Recognizing sarcasm without language: A cross-linguistic study of English and Cantonese. *Pragmatics & Cognition* 19. 203–223.
Chen, Aoju & Lou Boves. 2018. What's in a word: Sounding sarcastic in British English. *Journal of the International Phonetic Association* 48(1). 57–76.
Creusere, Marlena A. 2000. A Developmental Test of Theoretical Perspectives on the Understanding of Verbal Irony: Children's Recognition of Allusion and Pragmatic Insincerity. *Metaphor and Symbol* 15. 29–45.

Cutler, Anne. 1974. On saying what you mean without meaning what you say. In La Galy, Michael W., Robert A. Fox & Anthony Bruck (eds.), *Papers from the Tenth Regional Meeting of the Chicago Linguistic Society*, 117–127. Chicago, IL: Chicago Linguistic Society.
Fónagy, Ivan. 1971. The functions of vocal style. In Chatman, Seymour B. (ed.), *The functions of vocal style*. 159–176. London: Oxford University Press.
Gibbs, Raymond & Jennifer O'Brien. 1991. Psychological aspects of irony understanding. *Journal of Pragmatics* 16. 523–530.
Gibbs, Raymond W. & Herbert Colston. 2007. *Irony in Language and Thought: A Cognitive Science Reader*. New York: Erlbaum.
Hansen, John H.L. & Sanjay A. Patil (2007). Speech under Stress: Analysis, Modeling and Recognition. In Christian Müller (ed.), *Speaker Classification I: Fundamentals, Features, and Methods*, 108–137. Springer: Berlin & Heidelberg.
Haverkate, Henk (1990). A speech act analysis of irony. *Journal of Pragmatics* 14. 77–109.
Hildebrandt, Bruno. 1961. Die arithmetische Bestimmung der durativen Funktion. Eine neue Methode der Lautdauerbewertung. *Zeitschrift für Sprachwissenschaft, Phonetik und Kommunikationsforschung* 14. 328–336.
Kienast, Miriam 2002. *Phonetische Veränderungen in emotionaler Sprechweise*. Berlin: Shaker.
Laval, Virginie & Alain Bert-Erboul. 2005. French-Speaking Children's Understanding of Sarcasm: The Role of Intonation and Context. *Journal of Speech, Language and Hearing Research* 48. 610–620.
Lœvenbruck, Hélène, Mohamed Ameur Ben Jannet, Mariapaola D'Imperio, Mathilde Spini, Maud Champagne-Lavau. 2013. Prosodic cues of sarcastic speech in French: slower, higher, wider. In Bimbot, Frédéric, Christophe Cerisara, Cécile Fougeron, Guillaume Gravier, Lori Lamel, François Pellegrino & Pascal Perrier (eds.), *Proceedings of the 14th Annual Conference of the International Speech Communication Association (Interspeech 2013), Lyon, France*, 3537–3541. https://hal.archives-ouvertes.fr/hal-00931864 (accessed 5 July 2018).
Low, Ee Ling & Esther Grabe. 1995. Prosodic patterns in Singapore English. In Elenius, Kjell & Peter Branderud (eds.), *Proceedings of the XIIIth International Congress of Phonetic Sciences (ICPhS), Stockholm, Sweden*, Vol. 3, 636–639.
Nauke, Astrid & Angelika Braun. 2011. The production and perception of irony in short context-free utterances. In *Proceedings XVIIth International Congress of Phonetic Sciences (ICPhS), Hongkong*, 1450–1453.
Pexman, Penny M. & Kara M. Olineck. 2002. Does Sarcasm Always Sting? Investigating the Impact of Ironic Insults and Ironic Compliments. *Discourse Processes* 33(3). 199–217.
Probst, Louise & Angelika Braun. 2016. Geflüsterte Angst und behauchte Trauer – Stimmqualität und Emotionen. Paper presented at P&P Munich, October 13–14.
Rao, Rajiv. 2013. Prosodic Consequences of Sarcasm Versus Sincerety in Mexican Spanish. *Concentric: Studies in Linguistics* 39(2). 33–59.
Rockwell, Patricia. 2000. Lower, Slower, Louder: Vocal Cues of Sarcasm. *Journal of Psycholinguistic Research* 29(5). 483–495.
Schaffer, Rachel. 1981. Are there consistent vocal cues for irony? In C. S. Masek, R. A. Hendrick & M. F. Miller (eds.), *Papers from the Parasession on Language and Behavior*, 204–210. Chicago: Chicago University Press.
Schaffer, Rachel. 1982. *Vocal cues for irony in English*. PhD dissertation Ohio State University.

Scharrer, Lisa, Ursula Christmann & Maja Knoll. 2011. Voice Modulations in German Ironic Speech. *Language and Speech* 54(4). 435-465. DOI: 10.1177/0023830911402608.
Schmiedel, Astrid. 2017. Phonetik ironischer Sprechweise. Produktion und Perzeption sarkastisch-ironischer und freundlich ironischer Äußerungen. Berlin: Frank & Timme.
Shipp, Thomas & Harry Hollien. 1969. Perception of the aging male voice. *Journal of Speech and Hearing Research* 12. 703–710.
Wilson, Deirdre. 2013. Irony comprehension: A developmental perspective. *Journal of Pragmatics* 59. 40–56.
Winner, Ellen, Gail Windmueller, Elizabeth Rosenblatt, Laurie Bosco, Edella Best & Howard Gardner. 1987. Making Sense of Literal and Nonliteral Falsehood. *Metaphor and Symbol* 2(1). 13–32.

Joshua T. Katz
Exercises in wile

Abstract: At Princeton University, I have for the past decade occasionally taught a course – a so-called freshman seminar – on the history and practice of wordplay: "Wordplay: A wry plod from Babel to Scrabble". Zany, rigorous, and popular, the class gives students with interests from literature to mathematics the opportunity to explore the ludic side of language through a combination of three sorts of activities: the reading of primary literature, the consideration of secondary scholarship, and the regular and active creation of new instances of wordplay. The subject is not frivolous. With all due respect to colleagues who study "core" phenomena, I contend that pushing against what one might think of as the margins of language is fascinating in itself as well as an under-utilized but effective way to introduce people to the subject of linguistics. This paper attempts to give the flavor of this offbeat seminar, among other things by describing series of exercises designed to highlight some of the more simultaneously striking and easily exploitable orthographic, phonological, and lexical peculiarities of English. My hope is that this will be seen as a practical contribution to what the call for papers for the conference in Trier referred to as "systematic and analytical approaches to wordplay, its forms and functions".

Keywords: alphabet, Christian Bök, Doug Nufer, emoji, frequency effects, Georges Perec, linguistic exercises, lipograms, marginal phenomena, Oulipo, pedagogy, Scrabble, sounds, wordplay, Zipf's law

1 Introduction: From Babel to Scrabble

About a decade ago, one of my extracurricular pursuits since childhood, playing around with words, became an adult academic interest as well. While writing a couple of papers on elaborate verbal games in the works of the Roman poet Vergil (70–19 BC) – one that involves reading a word backwards at the start of the *Georgics* (Katz 2008) and another, more speculative, on a would-be acrostic in Book 4 of the *Aeneid* (Katz 2007) – I realized that it would be helpful to have a broader and deeper view of wordplay: what the general designation "wordplay" encompasses in Latin, in English, and in language in general; what forms of wordplay have existed, flourished, and been celebrated across time and space; and how puns, palindromes, word squares, and the like can be and have been devised, interpreted, and used for very different reasons and with very different effects, a matter that called for perspectives beyond my accustomed historical, literary, and linguistic ambit, namely anthropological, psychological, sociological, religious, mathematical, and visually artistic. The problem was that there did – and still does – not appear to be a good general introduction to wordplay[1], though bookstores sell innumerable puzzle books of all sorts and library shelves and online repositories hold plenty of specialized studies on topics from autograms to tautograms and from Ancient Near Eastern oneirocritical wordplay to teenagers' ludic uses of the latest electronic devices.[2] As every teacher knows, one of the best ways to learn about a subject is to give a course, and so in the fall of 2009, I decided to offer a so-called freshman seminar, one of a significant number of typically quirky classes, capped at fifteen students apiece, that Princeton University encourages first-year undergraduates to apply to take so that they begin their collegiate career by learning about something interesting and offbeat in an intimate setting under the tutelage of a professor they get to know well. The final sentence of the final footnote of a programmatic paper published just as the term was beginning – it is titled simply "Wordplay" (Katz 2009)[3] – reads as follows: "My goal is to come out of the class knowing much more than when I went in" (105, n. 90).

---

1 In my experience (in the class described below), linguist David Crystal's book *Language Play* (Crystal 1998b) does not fit the bill; Augarde (2011) presents many nice facts about subjects from "spurious words" to contronyms but could not be used as a textbook. Cook (2000), which concentrates on (but goes well beyond) the role of play in language pedagogy, remains a standout. Borgmann (1965) and Eckler (1996) provide unparalleled entertainment.
2 Hofstadter (1985: 64–65, 68–69, and 391–392) gives the classic, albeit brief account of what the English engineer and recreational mathematician Lee Sallows has called an autogram (see http://www.leesallows.com/index.php?page_menu=Self-referential%20stuff&pagename=In%20Quest%20of%20a%20Pangram, accessed 29 July 2018, with Sallows 1985), a self-referential text that enumerates its own letters and/or other characters; I do not know of any special scholarly literature on tautograms, but they are the visual analogue of alliteration, on which there is no shortage of research (see, briefly, Adams and Cable 2012). For ludic oneirocriticism, see Noegel (2007). Unsurprisingly, traditional published books cannot keep up with technological changes, to the point that my eighteen-year-old students in 2009 deemed *Txtng: The Gr8 Db8* (Crystal 2008) embarrassingly out-of-date; the value of this work to their counterparts now, who use iPhones rather than flip phones and emoji rather than emoticons, lies largely in its documentation of a lost world.
3 Katz (2009: 79–84) provides a brief account of another newly spotted instance of Latin wordplay, this time in Cicero, to add to the ones described in the papers cited above in the text. For further accounts of wordplay in the ancient world, see Katz (2013b) on, *inter alia*, a new acrostic in Vergil and Katz (2016a) on a new acronym (see also, briefly, Katz 2014a and 2014d); Katz (2013c and 2015) on Ferdinand de Saussure's "anagram notebooks"; and Katz (2013a) on

I achieved this goal, and I hope, too, that I can accurately claim that the students learned a lot in "Wordplay: A wry plod from Babel to Scrabble", as I called our joint sallies into the history and practice of sometimes quite remarkable verbal gymnastics. The title, besides containing an ironic anagram (*wordplay ~ a wry plod*)[4], is meant to point simultaneously, in part through an oblique nod to the homophony of the words *Babel* and *babble*, to the role of less-than-straightforward linguistic undertakings both across the sweep of human history (from the story in *Genesis* 11:1–9 to a modern board game) and in the history of each individual human (from the babbling of infancy to a world in which winners and losers are decided through the casting of lots marked with numerically assigned letters).[5] By this point, I have taught the class four times (2009, 2011, 2012, and 2015), and on each occasion it has been a happy success, drawing a substantially larger number of applications from incoming freshmen than there were places available. Furthermore, the "plodders" who end up enrolling have tended to be just the extraordinarily bright and extraordinarily zany sorts I want: humanists who are not scared of formal systems and mathematicians who are interested in language and literature. The course has attracted local and national attention: in 2010, the *Princeton Alumni Weekly* ran a story ("Word freaks") about the initial offering; in 2011, it was ranked #2 on *Mental Floss*'s list of "22 fascinating and bizarre classes offered this semester" (the top spot went to a class on Lady Gaga at the University of South Carolina) and #7 on *The Daily Beast*'s list of the eighteen "Hottest college courses"; and *Time* magazine in 2015 profiled it among the "11 bizarre college courses we actually want to take".[6]

---

various *jeux*, in Greece and elsewhere, that involve both sounds and script. Katz (2014b and 2014c) gives quick accounts of Greek puns and riddles.

4 I am indebted to Liesl Yamaguchi for the delightful French translation "Jeu de mots : mode juste de Babel au Scrabble". For German, I propose "Wortspiel: List Power von Babel zu Scrabble".

5 In my dialect of English, *Babel* and *babble* are homophonous: [ˈbæbl̩]. However, many speakers pronounce the former rather as [ˈbeɪbl̩]. In any case, while the ultimate derivation of *Babel/Babylon* is unknown, folk etymology – for whose status as an intermediary between scientific etymology and wordplay I have argued in Katz (2010a, 2010b, and 2016b) – gives it the Akkadian interpretation *bāb ili* 'gate of God' and (of particular relevance here) accounts for the biblical story, in which what happens at Babel is explained through the Hebrew verb *balal* 'mix, confuse, confound'. In a brief paper titled "From Scrabble to babble: Reflections on language attitudes and language play", Crystal (1998a) argues for the social utility of studying wordplay.

6 See respectively Noden (2010) and the follow-up piece "Wordplay winners" (2010); Conradt (2011); "Hottest college courses" (2011); and Waxman (2015).

Those who have taken the course, the most recent catalogue description of which may be found at https://www.princeton.edu/pub/frs/ay201516/fall-courses/index.xml#compfrs123 (accessed 29 July 2018), have engaged in rigorous explorations of ludic language through a combination of three sorts of activities: (1) the reading of primary literature (e.g., poems, stories, and novels by Raymond Queneau, Vladimir Nabokov, Georges Perec, Walter Abish, Paul Muldoon, Christian Bök, and Mark Dunn); (2) the consideration of secondary scholarship on Oulipo, spelling bees, the art of the crossword, graphic wordplay in languages with non-alphabetic writing, and much more; and (3) the regular and active creation by all participants, followed by group discussion, of new and often delightfully inventive instances of wordplay.[7] Of course, in order to be able to discuss properly the aesthetic pleasures and societal roles of wordplay, one needs – or should ideally wish – to have a definition of the term, to be able to enumerate its formal features.

2 What is wordplay?

Defining our term turns out to be difficult, and not merely because it is hard to give a precise account of either "word" or "play".[8] For one thing, if there is a

---

[7] There is a "Princeton dimension" to the course. Paul Muldoon, whose 1990 poem "Capercaillies" (see, conveniently, Muldoon 2001: 198–199) I assign for the first class (along with Nabokov's classic 1951/1959 short story "The Vane sisters") has come to talk to the students, and we also generally consider works by at least two other colleagues of mine: David Bellos's English translations of and scholarship on Perec (e.g., Bellos 1995) and biophysicist Bill Bialek's foray into alphabetic entropy, which he illustrates in part through the totality of four-letter words present in the corpus of Jane Austen (Stephens and Bialek 2010; see also Bialek's chagrined comment re paper #127 at http://www.princeton.edu/~wbialek/publications_wbialek.html, accessed 29 July 2018). Trophy-winning spellers in the student body and a Scrabble champion on the staff also come by to lend their perspectives and challenge us with a smile to best them, which few can do.

[8] For attempts to come to terms with the essence of wordplay, see the volumes already published in the series in which the current collection appears, "The Dynamics of Wordplay": Zirker and Winter-Froemel (eds.) (2015), Winter-Froemel and Zirker (eds.) (2015), and Knospe, Onysko, and Goth (eds.) (2016); Winter-Froemel (2016, esp. 37–42) and Thaler (2016) are especially valuable. The definition of "word" need not overly trouble us (though see sections 5 and 6, especially fn. 53): "language play" would be a better designation of the phenomenon under discussion than "wordplay". As for play, Johan Huizinga in his classic account "[s]um[s] up the formal characteristics of play" as follows: "[W]e might call it a free activity standing quite consciously outside 'ordinary' life as being 'not serious', but at the same time absorbing

sentence, or some other utterance, in English – or, as far as I know, in any other language – that is *not* an example of wordplay, I have yet to imagine it. Or perhaps I should say that *could not* be an example, for wordplay is in part a matter of context. Take, for instance, the sentence *The cat is on the table*. As such, nothing suggests that this is anything other than an ordinary utterance, with no ludic dimension. But it would be easy to take it and add a rhyme, thereby injecting a clear element of play – and easy, too, to continue to a full-blown poem: *The cat is on the table;/Her fur resembles sable./Majestic, she rules –/With gules*. (The fact that this is *bad* poetry is beside the point.) Alternatively, one could play with *The cat is on the table* by highlighting that all the words but the last are monosyllabic (*The cat is on the table; a ball lies in the gutter; no girl sings at John's party*); or that the second word begins with the letter *c* (*The cat is on the table; so are the cod, the cleat, the cereal, and the chasuble*) or the sound [k] (*The cat is on the table; so are the kit, the khat, the qanun, and the chemical*); or that the first and fifth words are identical (*The cat is on the table; fish that like other fish swim; I am happy because I eat*); etc. etc. etc. What makes all of these cases of wordplay – and what makes puns, autograms, and games of Scrabble cases as well – is that each of them not only involves some degree of self-reflexivity, pointing in its very form to its status as language, but elevates form to the point of content and sometimes even beyond.[9] The element of play here is clear enough – play is deliberately self-conscious, "standing", as Huizinga (1949: 13) puts it, "quite consciously outside 'ordinary life'" (see fn. 8 above) – but a bit more time should be spent on the meaning of "language".

Suppose we imagine language as a ball. Most linguists are interested principally in "core" phenomena, that is to say, in what lies at and near the center of the ball; a few, however, find it interesting to consider more "marginal" material, what in German are called *Randphänomene*, figuring that any good theory has to account for everything that counts as language, not just what is usual.[10] This leads to an obvious question: what does *not* count as lan-

---

the player intensely and utterly. It is an activity connected with no material interest, and no profit can be gained by it. It proceeds within its own proper boundaries of time and space according to fixed rules and in an orderly manner. It promotes the formation of social groupings which tend to surround themselves with secrecy and to stress their difference from the common world by disguise or other means" (Huizinga 1949: 13); see also, e.g., Cook (2000: 97–120 and *passim*).

9 I repeat this definition of wordplay – or, perhaps better put, description of the essential character of the phenomenon – nearly verbatim from Katz (2009: 100–101 and 2013b: 3).

10 Gordin and Katz (forthcoming) discuss what we term "non-intrinsic philological isolates", i.e., unique – and hence marginal – forms of language, some of them involving significant guage? Whereas in the last paragraph I endeavored to show that it is essentially impossible to give a good answer to the question, "What does *not* count as wordplay?", there is, I believe, a useful way in the present context to say what is not language: it is what lies outside the ball. To take an infamous example from Chomsky (1957: 15): while *Colorless green ideas sleep furiously* (sometimes called the "Chomsky sentence") is certainly a curious example of English, nowhere near the core from a semantic and pragmatic point of view, it is in fact – and undeniably – English; by contrast, its inverse, *Furiously sleep ideas green colorless*, though it contains the very same five words and thus appears to be language, is "word salad". In the second "sentence", the five words are given in an order that not only makes them (arguably) not an example of English but from some perspectives, including (arguably) the playful one, places their collocation outside the ball of language entirely.[11]

The relevance of this to the present paper is that the instances of wordplay I go on to highlight are extreme in the sense that they toy – and not merely in passing – with the ball's boundary without, crucially, going beyond (compare Katz 2013b: 3: wordplay as "*extreme language*"). Whenever I teach the seminar on wordplay, I start by getting my students to see how difficult the term is to define and then move straight to what I sometimes call "language on the verge", that is to say, to *Randphänomene*, coaching them how to skate along the edge by putting them through series of exercises that revolve around the evaluation and production of original examples of verbal art that are at the same time especially peculiar and – because they adhere to a single unusual but easy-to-articulate principle, or to a small set of them – in one way really quite simple to understand. To quote the Oulipian Georges Perec (1936–1982), arguably the greatest literary producer of work based on unusual principles that are at least

---

wordplay, that could be used outside the confines of the literary works in which they made their debut but generally are not.

11 Recognizing that I am probably pushing the idea too hard, I have included two parenthetical "arguably"-s. To be sure, there are perspectives, especially neurological and psychiatric ones, in which word salad – a subject Ray Gibbs treated with verve in his talk at the conference in Trier – may still be inside the ball: a patient who produces the string *Furiously sleep ideas green colorless* will be treated as having a language disorder, not as not having language. As for the considered use of *Furiously sleep ideas green colorless*, I remain doubtful that this has much of anything to tell us about the ludic function of language, but see Erard (2010, esp. 424–425), who prints one of two poems by the Anglo-Scottish linguist and philologist Angus McIntosh that include it. The literature on Chomsky's two sentences from everything from a literary to a statistical point of view is large: in addition to Erard's essay, see also, e.g., Jahn 2002 (as well as Katz 2013b: 4, n. 10 and the works cited there).

sometimes easy to articulate, "Au fond je me donne des règles pour être totalement libre" (Perec 1977).[12] Huizinga (1949: 13) has called play "a free activity [...] [that] proceeds [...] according to fixed rules" (see fn. 8 above), and one of the leading lessons of my seminar on specifically verbal play is that strict adherence to rules or principles – or, as they are often called, constraints – is, paradoxically, often liberating, with the surprising sense of freedom yielding, in the best cases, extraordinary effects.

The "exercises in wile"[13] that follow are of three kinds: alphabetic, phonological, and lexical.[14] Though based on English, many are adaptable to other languages (some more easily than others);[15] I have selected these specific ones for inclusion because they work neatly together, as I hope will become clear. It should go without saying that alphabetic exercises do not apply to languages that lack a written tradition or make standard use of an orthographic practice very different from the ABCs; other forms of writing – abugidas, syllabaries, logographic systems, etc. – engender further, often wonderful forms of wordplay, discussion of which, however, goes beyond the confines of this paper.

---

12 Levin Becker (2012: 13) writes that Perec's comment "has come to epigrammatize the Oulipo as a whole".
13 An homage, of course, to *Exercises in Style*, Barbara Wright's 1958 English translation of the 1947 collection of stories *Exercices de style* by Raymond Queneau, who would go on to co-found Oulipo in 1960. Only after submitting my abstract for the conference in Trier did I discover that Stump (2003) had anticipated me in the title "Exercises in wile".
14 I start with alphabetic exercises rather than ones concerned with sound because most people in a highly literate society are far more attuned to the nurtured behavior that is spelling than to the subtleties of the natural sonic environment; compare fn. 47 below.
15 I cannot resist pointing out a peculiarity that manifested itself in the multilingual environment of Trier, where the talks at a conference at a German university were in English and French. Because the point values of Scrabble tiles depend on letter frequency (a subject I discuss in section 3) and because languages do not by any means have the same distribution of letters, one cannot reasonably play Scrabble with a set designed for the wrong language. The poster for the conference featured a photograph of a Scrabble rack with the word *words* spelled out as follows: $W_4O_1R_1D_2S_1$. This is English (French has W_{10} and German has W_3, O_2, and D_1). The inside of the program, however, had a photograph of $W_2O_2R_1D_1P_4L_2A_1Y_{10}$ and $J_6E_1U_1X_8D_1E_1M_3O_1T_2S_1$. Amusingly, both the English and the French here are spelled with German tiles – and not just any German tiles but ones from a set that predates 1989/90, after which W_2 was replaced by W_3!

3 The alphabet

Consider the following lipogrammatic exercise:

(1) a. Choose one of the five vowels in our alphabet (*a, e, i, o,* or *u*) and compose an English sentence of at least seven words in which the only vowel used is that one. (You may use any consonants you wish.)[16]

At the conference in Trier, two colleagues in the audience responded quickly, and from my perspective most satisfyingly, to the challenge: Dirk Delabastita produced *A bat has had a bad fall* and Eline Zenner *Ernest the ewe gets the best bet yet* – the latter after first having come up with *The earnest ewe gets the best bet yet*, which contains the disallowed word *earnest*. (This sort of mistake is interesting in its unsurprisingness: experience shows that even highly educated people of exquisite linguistic sensibility frequently make basic errors, a sign that the task they are asked to perform falls well away from the center of the ball of language.) After years of recording how students and colleagues respond to the exercise, I can state unhesitatingly that answers with <a>'s or <e>'s abound, sometimes there are <i>'s or <o>'s, but nearly no one has led off with <u>'s;[17] the reasons for this surely have to do with the strong tendency of people to begin with an article – *a(n)* or *the* – and the fact, not unconnected, that <e> and <a> are especially frequent letters but <u> substantially less so.[18] When one considers the most frequently used letters in any large corpus of English – the conventional order begins with the happily pronounceable ETAOIN SHRDLU – one immediately notices the extraordinary fact that four of the five vowels are among the five most common letters and that even the outlier, <u>, ranked

---

[16] Aside from being the "magical number", there is nothing special about seven; anyone wishing to produce answers to this and other exercises with only five or six words is perfectly welcome to do so. Readers may also wish to attempt the exercise using none of the five vowels and only *y*'s. As for employing *y*'s in addition to one of the standard five vowels, I suggest doing the exercise first without and then with them – and concentrating on what difference this makes.

[17] A standard linguistic convention is to use angled brackets to indicate letters of the alphabet; by contrast, square brackets, which we will see in section 4, indicate pronunciation.

[18] It is also the case that people tend to think of short words with <u> as vulgar: *cum, cunt, fuck, slut,* etc. Reading Bök (2005: 79) will reinforce this impression (see fn. 29 below), though the poem "Stuck-up gulls must trust dumb ducks" in JonArno Lawson's wonderful collection for children *A Voweller's Bestiary from Aardvark to Guineafowl (and H)* (Lawson 2008: 16) belies it (it does, however, contain the naughty phrase *thumps gull's rump*).

twelfth, is in the top half of the alphabet.[19] No wonder, then, that while it is not that hard to produce sentences that use only <e>, <a>, <o>, or <i>, precisely because they are all so ordinary, the devilish catch is that the exercise at the same time eliminates most of the other letters that one would normally employ.

To return to the answers I am used to receiving: most are made up largely of vocabulary items that are monosyllabic, semantically basic, or both (in the Trier sentences, all but *Ernest*, which as a name falls into rather a special category); noteworthy (though, as I have just indicated, not at all peculiar) is that Dirk and Eline, besides attempting in the first place to begin with *a* and *the*, respectively, each made double use of an article. Furthermore, responses very often have an animal as their subject (*bat* and *ewe*, but also *cat*, *rat*, *elk*, *pig*, *ox*, etc.)[20], which suggests that the exercise triggers a desire on the part of adults to return to the state of *1 Corinthians* 13 ("When I was a child, I spake as a child,...") and, indeed, to revel in ludic activities associated with primary school.[21]

There is also the matter of meaning. I applauded Eline's switch from the adjective *earnest* to the proper name *Ernest*, but because the exercise takes our attention away from what most of us use language for most of the time, namely communicating sense, it was a minute or so before some of us, including me, realized that there was something absurd about *Ernest the ewe* or, as Eline then wryly put it, *Ernest the genderbender ewe*.... There are pragmatic issues with Dirk's sentence as well, though they are more subtle: both the indefiniteness of

---

19 Letter frequency used to be a matter of importance to more than wordplayers and specialists in cryptography: when manual typesetting was still the way in which most books were made, type was metal and cumbersome, and it would have been absurd for anyone who was producing texts in English to have to hand anything like as many <z>'s as <a>'s. David Loeb Weiss's short documentary film "Farewell, etaoin shrdlu" (available at, e.g., https://www.nytimes.com/video/insider/100000004687429/farewell-etaoin-shrdlu.html, accessed 29 July 2018) records the night of 1 July 1978, when the *New York Times* was set for the last time in hot type, largely on Linotype machines. There is a considerable body of secondary literature on alphabetic statistics in English and elsewhere; Norvig (2012), using data from Google Books to build on Mayzner and Tresselt (1965), one of a number of classic papers by Mayzner et al. that report data gathered by means of IBM punch cards, is an excellent place to start – for letter frequency in general, the relationship between letter frequency and position in a word, and much else besides, including word frequency, a topic I consider at some length in section 5. Unfortunately (?), Norvig reports that the correct order is actually ETAOIN SRHLDCU, with <u> ranked thirteen.
20 See Lawson (2008), with fn. 18 above.
21 The word *ludic* comes from *ludus*, the Latin word for both 'game, sport, play' and 'place of instruction or training, school'; for the connection between the two senses, see Katz (2013b: 24–25).

the subject and the present perfect tense make *A bat has had a bad fall* odd, whether decontextualized or as the opener of a (children's) tale.[22] We might expect *The bat had a bad fall*[23] – but this is not licit in an environment in which a sentence or story with *a*'s cannot have definite articles, just as one with *e*'s cannot have indefinite articles and one with *i*'s, *o*'s, or *u*'s cannot have any articles at all.

Lipograms are thus not so easy to produce, and all who try their hand at them will do well to ponder the following question:

(1) b. What problems do you encounter?

Above all, exercise (1a) forces highly competent speakers, writers, and readers to come to terms with the different and sometimes dramatic domino effects that result from cleaving to one or another seemingly innocent constraint. For example, no story can talk about *you*, though an *i*-story can talk about *I* (and *him* and *it*), an *e*-story about *me* (and *he*, *she*, *her*, *we*, *they*, and *them* – and, if one wishes, *thee*), and a *u*-story about *us*; past tenses are easiest in an *e*-story, thanks to the ending *-ed*, while present participles (in *-ing*) are possible only in an *i*-story; a story that asks *who* cannot also ask *what* or *where*; no story can give an explanation with *because* or *since*; the conjunctions *and*, *or*, and *but* are impossible except in *a*-, *o*-, and *u*-stories, respectively, only the middle of which can have *no* and *not*; and the preposition *by* can appear anywhere, *near* and *out* can appear nowhere, and *at*, *between* (and *except*), *in* (and *with*), *for* (and *down*, *of*, *on*, *onto*, and *to*), and *up* cannot be intermingled.

I have been talking about stories rather than simple sentences because even more serious problems with exercise (1a) arise when one takes things a step further:

(1) c. Now try to write a follow-up sentence.

A follow-up sentence has to follow up, that is to say, has to continue the theme established by the initial one. But because people rarely respond to the first exercise by producing a sentence in which semantics is paramount, they are

---

[22] It would work with an elaborate set-up: a passerby stumbles on an unknown chiropter with broken bones and calls emergency services, saying, "A bat has had a bad fall. Send an ambulance immediately!" (This is to say nothing of the interpretation in which *fall* is synonymous rather with *autumn*.)

[23] The sentence *A bat had a bad fall* has only six words, which is why Dirk felt he had to add the extra *has*.

usually thoroughly flummoxed by this additional instruction – and even more so when one gently suggests that they might continue for a whole paragraph, or more. The most famous example of a composition along these lines is Perec's novel *La Disparition* (Perec 1969), though rather than use just one vowel, the author of this work of ludic art eliminates the letter <e> – the most common letter in French as well as in English[24] – in an astonishingly coherent 300-odd-page tale of the search for a missing man named Anton Voyl. Translated into languages from German to Turkish to Japanese, the likewise *e*-less English version of novelist and wordsmith Gilbert Adair (1944–2011), cleverly titled *A Void* (Perec 1994)[25], is well worth reading both as a virtuosic example of how to render wordplay in a foreign tongue and, indeed, in its own right.[26] In the words of one critic, "[i]t is almost unbelievable (yet true) that some of *La Disparition*'s first readers didn't notice the disappearance in *The Disappearance*" (Suleiman 1990: 3).

This leads to one more question:

(1) d. How hard is it to keep producing lipogrammatic text that looks and sounds normal enough that no one immediately notices the constraint, i.e., to produce a ludic work that does not appear to be ludic?

---

24 It is generally said to make up 14–15 % of any normal French text and (see, e.g., Lewand 2000: 36 and Norvig 2012) 12.49–12.70 % of any normal English one.

25 Not only is <e> avoided, but, if one allows <v> to stand in for <u>, the title contains all four other vowels in a row – A VOI – and with a void where, in a sequence that begins A, one might have expected the E. The title *A Void* (four vowels plus one consonant) is effectively the *e*-less equivalent of another title, *Eunoia* (all five vowels plus one consonant), to which I turn below in the text. By the way, Perec took all the <e>'s and used them in his 1972 novella "Les Revenentes", whose very title – the "correct" spelling of the French noun is *revenantes* – suggests, correctly, that there will be a massive amount of "cheating". *Vive la différance*, Derridians may say, but while Perec's aim is to mirror the unraveling of the plot in increasingly garbled language, neither "Les Revenentes" nor the 1996 English translation of Perec's fellow Oulipian Ian Monk (a.k.a. "E. N. Menk"), "The Exeter Text: Jewels, Secrets, Sex", has the luminous quality of *La Disparition/A Void*.

26 An entirely *e*-less novel (or theoretically so: there are occasional slips) written originally in English is Ernest Vincent Wright's *Gadsby* of 1939, which carries the unsubtle subtitle *A Story of Over 50,000 Words Without Using the Letter "E"*. It influenced Perec (see, e.g., Bellos 1995: 395, 399, and 402, n. 1) and has a following among wordplay fanatics; though sometimes regarded as a fine piece of literature, in my opinion it may as well be called *The Not-so-great Gadsby*. Hofstadter (1997: 103–139) offers an appreciation of *Gadsby*, *La Disparition*, *A Void*, and the art of translating lipogrammatic text and other forms of elaborate wordplay.

The answer, of course, is that it is all but impossible to manage this for more than a few sentences, especially for <u>. But there are many pleasures to be had in giving oneself over completely to alphabetic revelry. My favorite example from the current century comes from the pen of the Canadian poet Christian Bök (1966–). Directly inspired by Perec and such earlier French examples of the avant-garde as the poem "Voyelles" by Arthur Rimbaud (1854–1891) and works like *Ubu Roi* by Alfred Jarry (1873–1907), Bök wrote the brilliant *Eunoia* (Bök 2005; 1st edn. 2001), a collection whose title poem consists of five univocalic chapters, each dedicated to another experimental artist (Hans Arp, René Crevel, Dick Higgins, Yoko Ono, and Zhu Yu).[27] The first sentence of each chapter gives the flavor of the enterprise: *Awkward grammar appalls a craftsman*; *Enfettered, these sentences repress free speech*; *Writing is inhibiting*; *Loops on bold fonts now form lots of words for books*; and *"Kultur" spurns Ubu — thus Ubu pulls stunts*.[28] If it is in fact true that each vowel has a "personality", it is hard to imagine a better way to discover it.[29] The titular word *eunoia* is iconic: both "the shortest word in English to contain all five vowels" and one whose meaning the poetry instantiates, for "the word quite literally means 'beautiful thinking'" (Bök 2005: 111).[30] There are "many subsidiary rules" (Bök 2005: 111) aside from the obvious one, but to talk much more about Bök here – or to consider in any depth the

---

27 Rimbaud's poem is the inspiration for the cover of the 2005 "upgraded edition" of *Eunoia*, and Bök prints it on p. 84 together with an English translation of his own on p. 85, as part of the section of the book titled "Oiseau"; Ubu is the protagonist of the *u*-chapter, whose first sentence is given immediately below in the text. It is worth pointing out, of Arp, who was born in Alsace and moved to Switzerland, that the *a*-chapter could not have been dedicated to Arp in his Francophone avatar, Jean. While I note, too, the different tones in the name Zhū Yù (朱昱), the infamous poem "Lion-eating poet in the stone den" by the Chinese linguist Yuen Ren Chao (e.g., https://www.youtube.com/watch?v=vExjnn_3ep4, accessed 29 July 2018) will suffice to demonstrate that tonal play in Mandarin Chinese is a fair analogue of Bök's ludic letters.

28 The quotation marks around the first (!) word of the *u*-chapter, *Kultur*, is my way of indicating that Bök italicizes it (because it is German and not really English), unlike the rest of the sentence, which is in regular font. The relative infrequency of <u> as compared to the other vowels (see above in the text) explains why this chapter is far shorter than the other four.

29 The back cover of *Eunoia* makes the following claim: "A unique personality for each vowel soon emerges: A is courtly, E is elegiac, I is lyrical, O is jocular, U is obscene." I find the claim annoying, both because I am not convinced that it is true and, more, because it influences readers rather than allowing them to decide for themselves whether vowels have individual personalities and, if so, what they might be. Most of my students agree that <u> has unusual potential to be obscene (compare fn. 18 above); they tend, however, to disagree, often sharply, about what the other vowels might indicate.

30 If, that is, *eunoia* (from Classical Greek εὔνοια 'goodwill, favor') is an English word. It has not yet made it into the *Oxford English Dictionary*.

literary qualities of either *La Disparition*/*A Void* or *Eunoia* – would take us too far afield.[31] My recommendation: read the books!

4 Sounds

How should one read them? Perec's book is a novel, but Bök's is poetry and hence, one might think, possessing more than passing lyricism. At heart, though, *Eunoia* is indubitably about the alphabet, about writing, about books;[32] anyone who picks up Bök's book[33] will note the special care that both author and publisher (Coach House Books in Toronto) took to make the poetry look good, from the layout of each page to the laid paper.[34] Nonetheless, part of the genius of *Eunoia* lies in the complex interplay between writing and sound, between how words look and what music they make. Bök, whose reading of Kurt Schwitters's "Ursonate" is available on YouTube[35], has made a purchasable CD-recording of *Eunoia* (Bök 2003, also from Coach House)[36], and one of the delights of teaching the text is getting students to read it aloud. The main

---

[31] Still, I cannot resist pointing out one of these rules (another, especially important one is given in the following footnote): "All chapters must describe a culinary banquet, a prurient debauch, a pastoral tableau and a nautical voyage" (Bök 2005: 111). In some sense, then, *Eunoia* is a rendering of the *Odyssey*, and it should be noted – as none other than Perec (1998: 101) himself does in his "History of the lipogram" – that one Tryphiodorus around the third (?) century A.D. produced a lipogrammatic *Odyssey* (no alphas in Book 1, no betas in Book 2, etc.), a work that was explicitly derided by Joseph Addison in a 1711 essay in the *Spectator* that introduced the word *lipogram* into English (see *OED* s.v.).
[32] As Bök (2005: 111) writes, "All chapters must allude to the art of writing." This is pretty clear just from the five initial sentences, reproduced above in the text.
[33] Born Christian Book, he changed his name to Bök (still pronounced [bʊk]) in an effort to "downplay [...] the 'embarrassment' of being an English professor and writer with the last name Book. And not just any book. 'I used to get a lot of Bible jokes when I was a kid,' he says" (Tamburri 2013). Bök's *o*-chapter contains no instances of <ö>, but forms of the word *book* are prominent on the first and last pages (Bök 2005: 59 and 76).
[34] Part of the final step of Bök's short and sardonic essay "How to write Eunoia" (Bök 2002) reads as follows: "Do not bother submitting [the completed manuscript] to any publisher whose editor is not already your closest, dearest friend. Do not let the publisher do any of the design. Do it all yourself. Be a pain in the ass. Go to the publisher and commandeer a computer. Be sure take [*sic*] at least six weeks doing all the typesetting and copyediting".
[35] https://www.youtube.com/watch?v=VCgzRxM5010 (accessed 29 July 2018). One of the most famous instances of "sound poetry", the piece begins thus: "Fümms bö wö tää zää Uu,/pögiff,/kwii Ee."
[36] At the time of writing, YouTube has a few recordings of Bök reading parts of the work.

difficulty comes from the fact that the constant repetition of a given vowel on the page sometimes but by no means always – and in a way that is entirely unpredictable – corresponds to the repetition of this vowel in sound. Take, for example, the phrase *as a papal cabal blackballs*, which appears on the first page of the *a*-chapter (Bök 2005: 12) and whose <a>'s are pronounced sequentially thus: [æ], [ə], [eɪ], ∅³⁷, [ə], [æ], [æ], [ɔ].³⁸ In short, *Eunoia* is a type of extended tongue twister, one in which reader-*cum*-speakers are always in danger of losing their linguistic balance as they struggle to keep their brain and their mouth in sync.

At issue, of course, is that English spelling is an extraordinarily poor synchronic representation of the spoken language. Consider only the seven words *tough* [tʰʌf], *though* [ðoʊ], *thought* [θɔt], *through* [θɹu], *thorough* [ˈθɜɹoʊ] (American) or [ˈθɜɹə] (British), *trough* [tʃɹɔf], and *thou* [ðaʊ]: the digraph <th>, which begins five of them, is pronounced in two different ways; <ou> is pronounced in five or six different ways; and <gh> is never pronounced [g] or [h] but instead either represents [f] or is silent.³⁹ All people who know English and are literate are aware that there are precisely twenty-six letters in the alphabet, but if one asks how many sounds the language has, one receives two kinds of answers: some say twenty-six, because they confuse sounds (which are rarely taught as such) with letters (which are pedagogically fetishized from at least kindergarten), while others make wild guesses from seventy (I have almost never heard a lower number, aside from twenty-six) to 150–200 (the mode) to one or two thousand (a surprisingly common response). The correct answer depends on one's dialect, but the most common count of English phonemes is forty-four (see, e.g., Cruttenden 2014: 159 and 235). A far more interesting number than this, though, is how many representations involving the twenty-six letters there are of these forty-four sounds. By one count, the number is 1120, which means

---

37 The second <a> in *papal* is in some sense not pronounced (hence "∅"): the final <l> is syllabic, [l̩].

38 For the angled and square brackets, see fn. 17 above; the latter are used in connection with the symbols of the International Phonetic Alphabet, a system that, at least in principle, allows anyone to sound out any sequence in any language (https://www.internationalphonetic association.org/content/full-ipa-chart, accessed 29 July 2018). Different people will have different pronunciations of some of these and many other words, which in some sense adds to the fun: in some dialects, for instance, the second <a> in *cabal* is pronounced [ɑ]. More generally, while most will say the indefinite article *a* as [ə] in this context, [eɪ] is also possible.

39 A native of New York City who was not well acquainted with farms, I knew the word *trough* only from reading and was a teenager before I learned that it was not pronounced [tʃɹaʊ]. This appears to be a common error.

that there are, on average, more than twenty-five ways of spelling each sound.⁴⁰ Yes, this includes outliers, both those that are immediately recognizable as odd – e.g., the occasional spelling *hiccough*, with <gh> = [p] – and also *women*, a common word that happens to contain the only instance of the correspondence <o> = [ɪ].⁴¹ Nonetheless, the consequences of having even a 1:10 ratio of sounds to spellings, not to mention a 1:25.5 ratio, are considerable: on the one hand, such a mismatch gives rise to spelling bees and other ludic exercises; on the other, it is a terrible burden for dyslexics, who are blessed when they grow up rather with Italian (see, e.g., Paulesu et al. 2001), in which the ratio is close to 1:1 (in fact something like 1:1.3).

In view of the discrepancy between sounds and letters, it would be surprising if the relative frequency of English sounds looked a whole lot like ETAOIN SHRDLU (or <etaoinshrdlu>). The exact order depends on dialect (and different sources report slightly different things), but a standard up-to-date reference work reports the top twelve sounds in "General British" as [əɪntsdlrðkem], where [ə], [ɪ], [n], and [t] make up respectively 10.72 %, 8.29 %, 7.62 %, and 6.95 % of spoken text.⁴² Among the things to note are that the two most common sounds are vowels but eight consonants are more frequent than the third-most common vowel; that the symbol for the most common sound in the language, schwa, has no correspondent in the standard alphabet; and that there is also no correspondent in the standard alphabet for the seventh-most common consonant (3.47 % of all sounds; see Cruttenden 2014: 235), the voiced dental fricative [ð], on whose distribution see below. At the other end, things are clearer: the sound in English with the lowest functional load is the voiced palato-alveolar fricative [ʒ] (0.07 %; see Cruttenden 2014: 235)⁴³, whose rarity

---

40 For the figure 1120, see Helmuth (2001: 2064).

41 The word *women* is the source of the first vowel of the infamous spelling of *fish* as "*ghoti*" (on <gh> = [f], see immediately above in the text), often incorrectly attributed to G. B. Shaw but in fact predating his birth. See among much else Zimmer (2008).

42 See Cruttenden (2014: 158–159 and 235). (Cruttenden uses slashes for phonemes rather than phonetic square brackets, but the difference is immaterial here.) A mid-twentieth-century report for "General-American English" gives [əɪntrslðdæk] (Hayden 1950: 220), where the only striking differences are (i) the near-flipping of the relative frequency of [d] and [r] (actually [ɹ]), on the second of which see Cruttenden (2014: 158); and (ii) the fact that the third-most common vowel and eleventh-most common sound in British is [e] but in American is [æ] (I note that Cruttenden 2014 makes the "substantial transcriptional alteration[]" (xvii) of changing conventional /æ/ to /a/; I have not followed him).

43 Even rarer, according to Cruttenden (2014: 159) is the diphthong [ʊə] (0.04 %), as in the Received Pronunciation of *cure*; I ignore it, however, since it is not phonemic in American English and is receding in British (see, e.g., Cruttenden 2014: 155–156).

has the evident historical explanation that it first entered English in French borrowings and is synchronically "limited to loanwords, except across word-boundaries" (Minkova 2014: 141).[44] But from the point of view of the lexicon rather than a large corpus of actual usage, the rarest sound in English is almost certainly [ð], which is found in very few discrete words, that is to say, in not more than a few handfuls of separate lemmata in a dictionary.

How can this be? Although the soothing sound that [ð] represents flows rather commonly from all speakers' mouths, those who bother to think about the distribution of words with it should, then, find worthy of attention the way that they gather together semantically. Consider the many examples of [ð] in this last, admittedly awkward sentence: *the* (3x), *that* (2x), *those*, *they*, *then*, *although*, *rather*, *together*, *bother*, *gather*, *mouths*, *soothing*, *worthy*, and for some people *with*, which different people in different contexts can say as [wɪð] or otherwise as [wɪθ].[45] Eleven of the sixteen words (I include *with* and also, *now*, *this* and *otherwise*) are function words, including the two that are repeated, and there is in fact a notable paucity of content words that contain this sound. While the percentage of [ð]'s in standard discourse is quite respectable, the statistic is skewed by the extraordinary frequency of the definite article, *the*, which has the remarkable property – this is perhaps my favorite fact about English – of being by far the most common word in the language (I return to this fact in section 5) and yet consisting, in its pronunciation [ðə][46], of nothing other than the juxtaposition of the sound that is at some level the rarest, [ð], and the one that is by no small margin the most common, [ə].

Consider now the following exercise:

(2) a. Compose an English sentence of at least seven words in which every word has the sound [ð].

---

44 Minkova (2014: 141–143) summarizes the (modest) rise of [ʒ] in English from the Middle Ages to the present. Interestingly, some speakers today have no word-initial examples of the sound at all: the only common nativized word in which I have it is *genre* (which some speakers pronounce with an initial [dʒ]), though note also *gigue* and (as Byron Ahn has impressed on me) the more recent *zhoosh*; see Minkova (2014: 142–143) for these and further examples and the speculation that "[i]t is likely that the globalisation of English will bring in more /ʒ/-initial words, as suggested by a long list of <zh>-initial words on the (unmonitored) online *Urban Dictionary*" (compare also Cruttenden 2014: 84).
45 But not *think*!
46 A modest curiosity of the word *the* is that it has two normal pronunciations, [ðə] and [ði]; compare the two pronunciations of the indefinite article (see fn. 38 above). For phonemic variation in common monosyllables, see Cruttenden (2014: 321).

Most wordplayers who have done this in my presence lead off with the article *the* – hardly surprising given that this is how most people begin when asked to produce a sentence about anything at all, with no constraint (compare what I wrote above in section 3 about Dirk Delabastita's sentence). Those who have not started thus have tended instead to choose the pronoun/pronominal adjective *this* or *these* (which belong to the same dictionary lemma and are etymologically extensions of *the*), the pronoun/pronominal adjective *that* or *those* (ditto), the pronoun *they* or pronominal adjective *their*, or some other "little" word like *then*, *there*, *thus*, *(al)though*, *either*, or *neither*. "Correct" sentences that I have heard[47] include *The other loathsome heathens gather, breathe, bathe* and *Smothering wethers, the mothers tethered their fathers' feathers*; neither can be called semantically normal, and the former is possible only because of the suppression of the conjunction *and* before *bathe*.

What makes the exercise interesting is precisely the fact that so few words contain the sound [ð], coupled with the tendency for these words to be grammatical building blocks. The answer to the question,

(2) b. What problems do you encounter?,

is thus: many! As it happens, the previous two paragraphs contain a not negligible percentage of the small inventory of words in the language that can be used in exercise (2a), and this means that the suggestion,

(2) c. Now try to write a follow-up sentence,

is unusually difficult to fulfill, especially if the goal is to produce something that resembles a narrative. (Still unused words include *heather*, *lathe*, *northern* and *southern*, *paths*, *rhythm*, and *thou*, though by wickedly giving just these few more I leave my readers with an even harder task of coming up with original ideas.) As for this –

(2) d. How hard is it to keep producing text that looks and sounds normal enough that no one immediately notices the constraint, i.e., to produce a ludic work that does not appear to be ludic?

---

47 I stress "correct" since many people's initial attempts have instances of [θ]: even those with linguistic training fall back under pressure on words with the voiceless counterpart of [ð], of which there are far more, though none of them is anywhere near as common (as I note briefly in section 5).

– I submit that it is impossible. But here's a bonus exercise:

(2) e. Compose an English sentence of any length in which every word *begins* with the sound [ð].

Readers who spend some time thinking about this should come up with both the problem and the solution, which in an effort not to spoil the fun I put into two[48] footnotes.[49]

5 Words

One of the most exciting facts about language is that it obeys Zipf's law. Noted before Harvard linguist George Kingsley Zipf (1902–1950) first popularized it in 1935 but rightly associated with him and with the mathematician Benoît Mandelbrot (1924–2010), who provided necessary modification, this power law is easy to state: the frequency of any word in a corpus of natural language (e.g., a novel, every article in the *New York Times* from 2017, the entirety of wikipédia.fr, etc.) is inversely proportional to its rank in the frequency table.[50] Put otherwise, the most common word in the language in question (ranked #1) is twice as common as the second-most common word (ranked #2), three times as common as the third-most common word (ranked #3), and so on. It does not require mathematical sophistication to spot a logarithmic curve: a very few words, like

---

[48] The problem: the only words in English that begin with the sound are *the, this, these, that, those, there, thence, thither, they, them, their, theirs, thou, thee, thy, thine, than, then, though,* and *thus* – plus *themselves, thyself,* and various more or less common forms based on *there* (e.g., *thereabout(s), thereafter, thereby, therefore, therein, thereof, thereon, thereunder, thereupon, thereto, theretofore,* and *therewith*). Not one of them is a verb.

[49] The solution: on the assumption that we disallow verbless "sentences" like *There, there!* (said in a soothing voice, with a pat on the head, to someone who is upset), the only way I know around the problem is to allow contractions: e.g., *That's that, then!* and *They're those.* Some will reasonably object that this is not really a solution because it stretches the definition of "word" past the breaking point.

[50] See above all Zipf (1935: 39–48) but also, e.g., Zipf (1932 and 1949: 19–55 and *passim*). George A. Miller's "Introduction" to a later printing of Zipf's 1935 book offers a delightful look at the man and his work, which begins thus: "*The Psycho-Biology of Language* is not calculated to please every taste. Zipf was the kind of man who would take roses apart to count their petals [...]. However, for those who do not flinch to see beauty murdered in a good cause, Zipf's scientific exertions yielded some wonderfully unexpected results to boggle the mind and tease the imagination" (Miller 1965: v).

the, are extraordinarily common; only a few hundred or a few thousand show up with any regularity at all (*family, high, help, today*, etc.); and the vast bulk of the lexicon shows up so infrequently as to be barely audible statistical background noise (*candelabra, onyx, sled, umbilical*, etc.). There is a quickly growing body of secondary literature on the Zipf-Mandelbrot law: whether it really does apply to all languages; how similar the curve for lexical frequency is to those for alphabetic and phonetic frequencies (as discussed in sections 3 and 4, respectively), which seem rather to follow the Yule-Simon distribution (see Martindale et al. 1996); what other social phenomena aside from language it applies to (e.g., the distribution of wealth (the Pareto distribution) and the population of the world's cities); how it relates to other power laws (e.g., Benford's law, which describes the frequency distribution of leading digits in numerical data sets); and – of particular interest – why it works.[51] Relevant at the moment is how one can harness the statistical facts for ludic purposes.

A few years ago, computer scientist Peter Norvig, spurred on by Mark Mayzner (see fn. 19 above), made use of the Google Books NGram Viewer[52] in order to arrive at a "distillation of the Google books data [for English that] gives us 97,565 distinct words, which were mentioned 743,842,922,321 times" (Norvig 2012). As expected, the top fifty words in English have a Zipfian distribution, with #1 *the* making up 7.14 % of the corpus, #2 *of* 4.16 %, #3 *and* 3.04 %, #4 *to* 2.60 %, etc. – down to #50 *no* 0.19 %. Here is the list:

1. *the*	11. *as*	21. *are*	31. *they*	41. *there*
2. *of*	12. *was*	22. *or*	32. *you*	42. *been*
3. *and*	13. *with*	23. *his*	33. *were*	43. *if*
4. *to*	14. *be*	24. *from*	34. *their*	44. *more*
5. *in*	15. *by*	25. *at*	35. *one*	45. *when*
6. *a*	16. *on*	26. *which*	36. *all*	46. *will*
7. *is*	17. *not*	27. *but*	37. *we*	47. *would*
8. *that*	18. *he*	28. *have*	38. *can*	48. *who*
9. *for*	19. *I*	29. *an*	39. *her*	49. *so*
10. *it*	20. *this*	30. *had*	40. *has*	50. *no*

---

51 On the Zipf-Mandelbrot law, see recently Piantadosi (2015), Sorrell (2015), Williams et al. (2015), and Lestrade (2017). For a quirky application of the methodology of complex adaptive systems to the language (and culture) of furniture (!), see Burkette (2015: 55–57 and *passim*).
52 http://storage.googleapis.com/books/ngrams/books/datasetsv2.html (accessed 29 July 2018).

These fifty vocabulary items account for about 40.5 % of the material in a given text![53] Furthermore, the list has all sorts of properties that are for the most part as obvious as they are remarkable: for example, every single word is monosyllabic (and none has more than five letters)[54] and, indeed, a proverbial "Anglo-Saxon monosyllable" since the only ones that are not quite native are *they* and *their*, which are shallow early borrowings into English from the closely related North Germanic languages; every single word is a function word (whether article, conjunction, preposition, pronoun, copula, basic (always potentially auxiliary) verb – plus a few other forms like *all*, *more*, *no*, and *not*); seven of the words have (or can have) the sound [ð] (*the*, *this*, *that*, *they*, *their*, *there*, and sometimes *with*; see section 4), while its voiceless counterpart, which is found in far more individual words of, however, far lower functional load (*think*, *thorax*, *pathological*, *myth*, etc.), is absent; and the least-common vowel, *u*, is

---

[53] Note that Norvig's list relies on the idea that one word is distinguished from another purely through external form. It would take us too far afield to consider in detail the vexed question of what exactly the definition is of the term "word" (see now Wray 2015), but among the things to think about are: whether *he* and *his* count as different words, and the same for *they* and *their*; whether *a* and *an* count as different words; whether *is*, *are*, *was*, *were*, *be*, and *been* count as six different words (or whether the pair *be*/*been* is one word and/or the synchronically connected but irregular and yet diachronically explicable pair *was*/*were* and/or the synchronically connected but irregular and yet diachronically unconnected (!) pair *is*/*are*), and the same for *have* and *had* and even, perhaps, for *will* and *would*; whether it is reasonable to lump all instances of *to* together, and the same for some other forms, such as *for* and *that*; and whether we should care that some instances of *can* in the corpus are containers rather than modal verbs and some instances of *will* a noun with one or another meaning. Three contributions to *The Oxford Companion of the Word* (Taylor (ed.) 2015) aside from Wray (2015) are of particular relevance to this paper: Sorrell (2015) on "Word frequencies", Grzybek (2015) on "Word length", and Verkuyl (2015) on "Word puzzles".

Many scholars work with the data found at https://www.wordfrequency.info (accessed 29 July 2018), which is based on the 450 million-word Corpus of Contemporary American English. Some differences with Norvig's list are clear just from the top twenty: 1. *the*, 2. *be*, 3. *and*, 4. *of*, 5. *a*, 6. *in*, 7. *to*, 8. *have*, 9. *to*, 10. *it*, 11. *I*, 12. *that*, 13. *for*, 14. *you*, 15. *he*, 16. *with*, 17. *on*, 18. *do*, 19. *say*, and 20. *this*. Here all synchronically allied forms of *be* are lumped together, as are all forms of *have*, and *a* includes also *an*; by contrast, two meanings of *to* are distinguished, as are two of *that* (the other one is #27). The appearance of the verbs *do* and *say* is interesting (as are *n't* at #29 (compare fn. 49 above); the North Germanic loanword *get* at #39 (on *they* and *their*, see immediately below in the text); and a lone disyllable, *about*, at #46 – historically a prefixed form of obsolete *bout* and a word whose first syllable can be omitted in colloquial speech ('*bout*)).

[54] The relationship between brevity of form and frequency of use is well known: see, e.g., Zipf (1935: 20–39) and Grzybek (2015: 107, with references).

found only three times (*but*, *would*, and *you*)⁵⁵, with just the one having it as its only vowel (and thereby usable by Bök in *Eunoia*; see section 3).⁵⁶

There is great potential here for play:

(3) a. Compose an English sentence of at least seven words that does not use any of the ten most-frequent words in the language.

No one finds this difficult: examples that have come my way include *Because bananas smell sweet, rascally monkeys love them* and *She sells seashells by seaweedy, sushi-laden seashores*.⁵⁷ But because this is so easy, the matter of the coherent follow-up is, I believe, especially interesting:

(3) b. Now try to write a follow-up sentence, perhaps one that uses none of the twenty most-frequent words. (Then try to write a third sentence without using any of the thirty most-frequent words. Etc.)

Readers are encouraged to try their hand at this exercise and to pay attention to the point at which it starts to become really tough – and why this is. As always, the question looms:

(3) c. How hard is it to keep producing text that looks and sounds normal enough that no one immediately notices the constraint, i.e., to produce a ludic work that does not appear to be ludic?

The most astonishing creative work I know that wreaks havoc on the fact that words are not distributed at all evenly is Seattle-based Doug Nufer's novel *Never Again* (Nufer 2004). Two hundred pages and about 40,000 words long, it has a perfectly level lexical distribution since no word – by which is meant set of characters set off by a space on either side – is ever repeated (!). The novel's first sentence is perfectly ordinary: *When the racetrack closed forever I had to get a job*. Of these eleven words, six are in the top fifty – *the* (#1), *to* (#4), *a* (#6), *I* (#19), *had* (#30), and *when* (#45) – and only one, *racetrack*, is not especially common. Not one of these words can be used ever again. Here is the first paragraph in its entirety (Nufer 2004: 3):

---

55 By contrast, there are eighteen *e*'s, fourteen *o*'s, thirteen *a*'s, and eleven *i*'s.
56 Another thing to note: the pronouns *I*, *you*, *he*, *it*, *we*, and *they*, all of which are (or can be) conventionally used as subjects, are all more common than *she*, which is not in the top fifty (in fact, it is #51); the conventional objective form *her*, however, is there, though ranked below all the others.
57 Readers who grew up with English will recognize this as a variation on the well-known tongue twister *She sells seashells by the seashore*, which contains the illicit word *the*.

> When the racetrack closed forever I had to get a job. Want ads made wonderlands, founding systems barely imagined. Adventure's imperative ruled nothing could repeat. Redirections dictated rigorously, freely. Go anywhere new: telephone boiler-rooms, midnight grocery shooting galleries, prosthetic limb assembly plants, hazardous waste-removal sites; flower delivery, flour milling, million-dollar bunko schemes. Do anything once; then, best of all, never again.

Two other words in the top fifty show up here – *of* (#2) and *all* (#36) – and the circumstances render thrilling the rhetorical interplay between the ordinary yet iconic (*Do anything once*) and the wacky (*prosthetic limb assembly plants*). In short, the relationship between content and form is palpable, as is Nufer's evident delight in low-level wordplay (*Want ads made wonderlands* and *flower delivery, flour milling, million-dollar*). And how does the work close? Here is the last paragraph (Nufer 2004: 202):

> Worldly bookmaker soulmates rectify unfair circumstance's recurred tragedies, ever-moving, ever-hedging shifty playabilities since chances say someone will be for ever closing racetracks.

In addition to making a ring between initial *When the racetrack closed forever* and final *for ever closing racetracks*, playing with compounded forms of *ever-*, and bringing his linguistic train to an iconic halt, Nufer unveils in his final seven-word clause three of the top fifty words, which, astonishingly, he has saved until the very end: *for* (#9), *be* (#14), and *will* (#46) — plus, just before this, the very common verb *say* (see fn. 53 above) and the conjunction *since*. Truly a virtuoso work in the Oulipian spirit!

6 The future: After Scrabble

Humans are creative, and we can be confident that the generations ahead will produce new and unexpected forms of wordplay. There is, however, one aspect of play with words that I expect to see actively highlighted in the coming years, and it involves paying close attention to what exactly speakers and readers of English count as a word. Every January, the members of the American Dialect Society vote on the "Word of the Year" for the previous twelve months. In 2017, the winner was *fake news*; in 2016 it was *dumpster fire* (a poor choice, in my view); and in 2015 it was singular *they*.[58] We may ask whether *fake news* and *dumpster fire* are actually each an individual word, but a more interesting question concerns the Word of the Year for 2014: #blacklivesmatter. Are this and #metoo really "words"? How do we know? Do they belong in a dictionary? If so, how are they to be alphabetized?

And yet even these questions pale, I believe, next to the challenge to the idea of the word posed by the team at the Oxford Dictionaries, which at the end of each calendar year announces *its* Word of the Year. In 2017, the winner was *youthquake* (another poor choice); in 2016 it was *post-truth*; and in 2014 it was *vape*. But what about in 2015? In that year, the people who might be said to hold the greatest authority over the English lexicon informed the world that the Word of the Year was ... 😂 ("face with tears of joy").[59] The rise of emoji is socio-culturally fascinating for reasons that go well beyond the ludic, but in a brave new world in which 😂 may count as a word and in which it is possible to purchase *Emoji Dick*, a "crowd sourced and crowd funded translation" of *Moby-Dick* (http://www.emojidick.com, accessed 29 July 2018), future students in "Wordplay: A wry plod from Babel to Scrabble" and similar classes will have much to think about and much to look forward to.

In his definition of "play" quoted in fn. 8 above, Huizinga claims that wordplay is "an activity connected with no material interest, and no profit can be gained by it". There is truth to this, but at the same time a significant benefit of actively engaging in verbal games is that one gains an appreciation of just what language can do, of how far it can be bent without snapping. Furthermore, actively engaging with and pushing against the boundaries of the ball of language – of paying attention, e.g., to what Dr. Seuss's *One Fish, Two Fish, Red Fish, Blue Fish* and James Joyce's *Finnegans Wake* do and do not have in common – is, I contend, an outstanding way of getting students interested in linguistics, a subject that vanishingly few encounter even in high school, never mind earlier still. Perec has said that constraints offer freedom, and to this I would add another paradox: marginal phenomena shed significant light on the core.

Acknowledgment: My thanks go to Esme Winter-Froemel for suggesting that I lead a workshop on the teaching of wordplay at the conference in Trier whose

---

[58] See https://www.americandialect.org/fake-news-is-2017-american-dialect-society-word-of-the-year and https://www.americandialect.org/woty/all-of-the-words-of-the-year-1990-to-present (both accessed 29 July 2018).
[59] See https://en.oxforddictionaries.com/word-of-the-year (accessed 29 July 2018).

proceedings are collected here and to the many participants, especially Dirk Delabastita, Ray Gibbs, Cécile Poix, and Eline Zenner. I first read "The Vane sisters" in the summer of 1986 under the brilliant tutelage of Lawrence Raab and the late Lawrence Graver, whose Telluride Association Summer Program seminar "Art and mystery" at Williams College was life-changing. I also thank my own students, above all the sixty once-freshmen whose enthusiastic contributions to my seminar on wordplay at Princeton have taught me so much and brought such joy. I dedicate this paper to "the Larrys" and all my fellow TASPers and to the members of the 2009 inaugural class at Princeton, one of whom, the ever-laughing Emilly Zhu '13, whose photograph and one of whose specific contributions appear in Noden (2010), died on 12 June 2015 after having been hit by a car.

7 References

Adams, P. G. & T. Cable. 2012. Alliteration. In Roland Greene (ed.), *The Princeton Encyclopedia of Poetry and Poetics*, 4th edn., 40–42. Princeton: Princeton University Press.
Augarde, Tony. 2011. *Wordplay: The Weird and Wonderful World of Words*. Charlbury: Carpenter.
Bellos, David. 1995. *Georges Perec: A Life in Words*, rev. edn. London: Harvill.
Bök, Christian. 2002. How to write Eunoia. *Broken Pencil* 19. 72.[60]
Bök, Christian. 2003. *Eunoia*, CD version. Toronto: Coach House.
Bök, Christian. 2005. *Eunoia*, "upgraded edn." from 2001 original. Toronto: Coach House.
Borgmann, Dmitri A. 1965. *Language on Vacation: An Olio of Orthographical Oddities*. New York: Scribner's.
Burkette, Allison Paige. 2015. *Language and Material Culture*. Amsterdam: Benjamins.
Chomsky, Noam. 1957. *Syntactic Structures*. The Hague: Mouton.
Conradt, Stacy. 2011. 22 fascinating and bizarre courses offered this semester. *Mental Floss* (28 August 2011). http://mentalfloss.com/article/28626/22-fascinating-and-bizarre-classes-offered-semester (accessed 29 July 2018).
Cook, Guy. 2000. *Language Play, Language Learning*. Oxford: Oxford University Press.
Cruttenden, Alan. 2014. *Gimson's Pronunciation of English*, 8th edn. Abingdon: Routledge.
Crystal, David. 1998a. From Scrabble to babble: Reflections on language attitudes and language play. In Wolfgang Kühlwein (ed.), *Language as Structure and Language as Process: In Honour of Gerhard Nickel on the Occasion of His 70th Birthday*, 33–45. Trier: Wissenschaftlicher Verlag.
Crystal, David. 1998b. *Language Play*. London: Penguin.
Crystal, David. 2008. *Txtng: The Gr8 Db8*. Oxford: Oxford University Press.

---

[60] The author of Bök (2002) is mistakenly named "Bok", which is amusing in view of the material in fn. 33 above.

Eckler, Ross. 1996. *Making the Alphabet Dance: Recreational Wordplay*. New York: St. Martin's.
Erard, Michael. 2010. The life and times of "Colorless green ideas sleep furiously". *Southwest Review* 95(3). 418–425.
Gordin, Michael D. & Joshua T. Katz. Forthcoming. The walker and the wake: Analysis of non-intrinsic philological isolates. In Sean Gurd & Vincent W. J. van Gerven Oei (eds.), *'Pataphilology: An Irreader*. N.p.: punctum.
Grzybek, Peter. 2015. Word length. In Taylor (2015), 89–119.
Hayden, Rebecca E. 1950. The relative frequency of phonemes in General-American English. *Word* 6(3). 217–223.
Helmuth, Laura. 2001. Dyslexia: Same brains, different languages. *Science* 291, no. 5511 (16 March 2001). 2064–2065.
Hofstadter, Douglas R. 1985. *Metamagical Themas: Questing for the Essence of Mind and Pattern*. New York: Basic Books.
Hofstadter, Douglas R. 1997. *Le Ton beau de Marot: In Praise of the Music of Language*. New York: Basic Books.
"Hottest college courses". 2011. *The Daily Beast* (6 October 2011). http://www.thedailybeast.com/galleries/2011/10/06/hot-college-courses-mad-men-south-park-and-more-unique-classes.html (accessed 29 July 2018).
Huizinga, J. 1949. *Homo ludens: A Study of the Play-element in Culture*. London: Routledge & Kegan Paul.
Jahn, Manfred. 2002. "Colorless green ideas sleep furiously": A linguistic test case and its appropriations. In Marion Gymnich, Ansgar Nünning & Vera Nünning (eds.), *Literature and Linguistics: Approaches, Models, and Applications. Studies in Honour of Jon Erickson*, 47–60. Trier: Wissenschaftlicher Verlag.
Katz, Joshua T. 2007 [publ. 2008]. An acrostic ant road in *Aeneid* 4. *Materiali e discussioni per l'analisi dei testi classici* 59. 77–86.
Katz, Joshua T. 2008. Vergil translates Aratus: *Phaenomena* 1–2 and *Georgics* 1.1–2. *Materiali e discussioni per l'analisi dei testi classici* 60. 105–123.
Katz, Joshua T. 2009. Wordplay. In Stephanie W. Jamison, H. Craig Melchert & Brent Vine (eds.), *Proceedings of the 20th Annual UCLA Indo-European Conference, Los Angeles, October 31–November 1, 2008*, 79–114. Bremen: Hempen.
Katz, Joshua T. 2010a. Etymology. In Anthony Grafton, Glenn W. Most & Salvatore Settis (eds.), *The Classical Tradition*, 342–345. Cambridge, MA: Harvard University Press.
Katz, Joshua T. 2010b. *Nonne lexica etymologica multiplicanda sunt?*. In Christopher Stray (ed.), *Classical Dictionaries: Past, Present and Future*, 25–48. London: Duckworth.
Katz, Joshua T. 2013a. Gods and vowels. In J. Virgilio García & Angel Ruiz (eds.), *Poetic Language and Religion in Greece and Rome*, 2–28. Newcastle upon Tyne: Cambridge Scholars Publishing.
Katz, Joshua T. 2013b. The Muse at play: An introduction. In Jan Kwapisz, David Petrain & Mikołaj Szymański (eds.), *The Muse at Play: Riddles and Wordplay in Greek and Latin Poetry*, 1–30. Berlin: De Gruyter.
Katz, Joshua T. 2013c. Saussure's *anaphonie* : Sounds asunder. In Shane Butler & Alex Purves (eds.), *Synaesthesia and the Ancient Senses*, 167–184. Durham: Acumen.
Katz, Joshua T. 2014a. Acrostic. In Richard F. Thomas & Jan M. Ziolkowski (eds.), *The Virgil Encyclopedia*, [1.] 8. Malden, MA: Wiley-Blackwell.
Katz, Joshua T. 2014b. Puns. In Georgios K. Giannakis (ed.), *Encyclopedia of Ancient Greek Language and Linguistics*, 3. 193–194. Leiden: Brill.

Katz, Joshua T. 2014c. Riddles. In Georgios K. Giannakis (ed.), *Encyclopedia of Ancient Greek Language and Linguistics*, 3. 244–245. Leiden: Brill.
Katz, Joshua T. 2014d. Wordplay. In Richard F. Thomas & Jan M. Ziolkowski (eds.), *The Virgil Encyclopedia*, [3.] 1396–1397. Malden, MA: Wiley-Blackwell.
Katz, Joshua T. 2015. Saussure at play and his structuralist and post-structuralist interpreters. *Cahiers Ferdinand de Saussure* 68. 113–32.
Katz, Joshua T. 2016a. Another Vergilian signature in the *Georgics*?. In Phillip Mitsis & Ioannis Ziogas (eds.), *Wordplay and Powerplay in Latin Poetry*, 69–85. Berlin: De Gruyter.
Katz, Joshua T. 2016b. Etymological 'alterity': Depths and heights. In Shane Butler (ed.), *Deep Classics: Rethinking Classical Reception*, 107–126. London: Bloomsbury.
Knospe, Sebastian, Alexander Onysko & Maik Goth (eds.). 2016. *Crossing Languages to Play with Words: Multidisciplinary Perspectives* (The Dynamics of Wordplay 3). Berlin & Boston: De Gruyter.
Lawson, JonArno. 2008. *A Voweller's Bestiary from Aardvark to Guineafowl (and H)*. Erin, ON: Porcupine's Quill.
Lestrade, Sander. 2017. Unzipping Zipf's law. *PlosOne* (9 August 2017). http://journals.plos.org/plosone/article?id=10.1371/journal.pone.0181987 (accessed 29 July 2018).
Lewand, Robert Edward. 2000. *Cryptological Mathematics*. Washington, D.C.: Mathematical Association of America.
Levin Becker, Daniel. 2012. *Many Subtle Channels: In Praise of Potential Literature*. Cambridge, MA: Harvard University Press.
Martindale, Colin, S. M. Gusein-Zade, Dean McKenzie & Mark Yu. Borodovsky. 1996. Comparison of equations describing the ranked frequency distributions of graphemes and phonemes. *Journal of Quantitative Linguistics* 3(2). 106–112.
Mayzner, M. S. & M. E. Tresselt. 1965. *Tables of Single-letter and Digram Frequency Counts for Various Word-length and Letter-position Combinations. Psychonomic Monograph Supplements* 1(2) = pp. 13–32.
Miller, George A. 1965. Introduction. In George Kingsley Zipf, *The Psycho-biology of Language: An Introduction to Dynamic Philology* [new edn. of Zipf (1935)], v–x. Cambridge, MA: MIT Press.
Minkova, Donka. 2014. *A Historical Phonology of English*. Edinburgh: Edinburgh University Press.
Muldoon, Paul. 2001. *Poems, 1968–1998*. New York: Farrar, Straus & Giroux.
Noden, Merrell. 2010. Word freaks. *Princeton Alumni Weekly* 110(8) (3 February 2010). 24–26.
Noegel, Scott. 2007. *Nocturnal Ciphers: The Allusive Language of Dreams in the Ancient Near East*. New Haven: American Oriental Society.
Norvig, Peter. 2012. English letter frequency counts: Mayzner revisited, or ETAOIN SRHLDCU. http://norvig.com/mayzner.html (accessed 29 July 2018).
Nufer, Doug. 2004. *Never Again*. New York: Black Square.
Paulesu, E., J. F. Démonet, F. Fazio, E. McCrory, V. Chanoine, N. Brunswick, S. F. Cappa, G. Cossu, M. Habib, C. D. Frith & U. Frith. 2001. Dyslexia: Cultural diversity and biological unity. *Science* 291, no. 5511 (16 March 2001). 2165–2167.
Perec, Georges. 1969. *La Disparition*. Paris: Denoël.
Perec, Georges. 1977. "Des Règles pour être libre" [interview with Claude Bonnefoy]. *Les Nouvelles littéraires* 2575 (10 March 1977). 21.
Perec, Georges. 1994. *A Void*, trans. of Perec (1969) by Gilbert Adair. London: Harvill.

Perec, Georges. [1969] 1998. History of the lipogram. In Warren F. Motte, Jr. (trans. and ed.), *Oulipo: A Primer of Potential Literature*, rev. edn., 97–108. Normal, IL: Dalkey Archive.
Piantadosi, Steven T. 2015. Zipf's word frequency law in natural language: A critical review and future directions. *Psychonomic Bulletin & Review* 21(5). 1112–1130.
Sallows, Lee C. F. 1985. In quest of a pangram. *Abacus* 2(3). 22–40.
Sorrell, Joseph. 2015. Word frequencies. In Taylor (2015), 68–88.
Stephens, Greg J. & William Bialek. 2010. Statistical mechanics of letters in words. *Physical Review E* 81, no. 066119.
Stump, Jordan. 2003. Exercises in wile: Raymond Queneau, the novelist as trickster. *Bookforum* 10(3). 12–14.
Suleiman, Susan Rubin. 1990. *Subversive Intent: Gender, Politics, and the Avant-garde*. Cambridge, MA: Harvard University Press.
Tamburri, Rosanna. 2013. The incredibly original pursuits of Christian Bök. *University Affairs / Affaires universitaires* (6 November 2013). https://www.universityaffairs.ca/features/feature-article/incredibly-original-pursuits-of-christian-bok/ (accessed 29 July 2018).
Taylor, John R. (ed.). 2015. *The Oxford Handbook of the Word*. Oxford: Oxford University Press.
Thaler, Verena. 2016. Varieties of wordplay. In Knospe, Onysko & Goth (2016), 47–62.
Verkuyl, Henk J. 2015. Word puzzles. In Taylor (2015), 702–722.
Waxman, Olivia B. 2015. 11 bizarre college courses we actually want to take. *Time* (26 August 2015). http://time.com/4006878/unusual-college-university-courses/ (accessed 29 July 2018).
Williams, Jake Ryland, Paul R. Lessard, Suma Desu, Eric M. Clark, James P. Bagrow, Christopher M. Danforth & Peter Sheridan Dodds. 2015. Zipf's law holds for phrases, not words. *Scientific Reports* 5, no. 12209.
Winter-Froemel, Esme. 2016. Approaching wordplay. In Knospe, Onysko & Goth (2016), 11–46.
Winter-Froemel, Esme & Angelika Zirker (eds.). 2015. *Enjeux du jeu de mots. Perspectives linguistiques et littéraires* (The Dynamics of Wordplay 2). Berlin & Boston: De Gruyter.
"Wordplay winners". 2010. *Princeton Alumni Weekly* 110(11) (7 April 2010). 30–31.
Wray, Alison. 2015. Why are we so sure we know what a word is? In Taylor (2015), 725–750.
Zimmer, Ben. 2008. "Ghoti" before Shaw. *Language Log* (23 April 2008). http://languagelog.ldc.upenn.edu/nll/?p=81 (accessed 29 July 2018).
Zipf, George Kingsley. 1932. *Selected Studies of the Principle of Relative Frequency in Language*. Cambridge, MA: Harvard University Press.
Zipf, George Kingsley. 1935. *The Psycho-biology of Language: An Introduction to Dynamic Philology*. Boston: Houghton Mifflin.
Zipf, George Kingsley. 1949. *Human Behavior and the Principle of Least Effort: An Introduction to Human Ecology*. Cambridge, MA: Addison-Wesley.
Zirker, Angelika & Esme Winter-Froemel (eds.). 2015. *Wordplay and Metalinguistic/Metadiscursive Reflection: Authors, Contexts, Techniques, and Meta-reflection* (The Dynamics of Wordplay 1). Berlin & Boston: De Gruyter.

III Traditions of wordplay in different social and cultural settings

Eline Zenner and Dirk Geeraerts
One does not simply process memes: Image macros as multimodal constructions

Abstract: This paper presents a Cognitive Linguistic analysis of image macros, a subgenre of Internet memes. Internet memes encompass all kinds of online objects that are copied and imitated, altered and modified, propagated and diffused by participants on the web. Image macros are a specific example of such online content, consisting of text superimposed on an image. Whereas the image and discursive theme of image macros are typically fairly consistent in the replication process, the text is particularly open to the online "remix culture" that characterizes Internet memes. Given this pivotal role of variation and modification, it is not straightforward to define the ultimate set of characteristic features of an image macro. The first goal of this paper is to define image macros in a way that captures precisely this interplay between conventionality and creativity. To this end, we will combine insights from Construction Grammar and prototype theory, presenting image macros as multimodal constructions that share characteristics with jokes and traditional wordplay. Moreover, the verbal elements in the memes often also include such instances of traditional wordplay. A second goal of our paper is to explore the processing difficulties involved in these occurrences of traditional wordplay in image macros. Specifically, we present four dimensions that together indicate how the image macros vary along a typicality cline with regard to the degree of multimodality, multilingualism, intra-genre intertextuality and external referencing included in the construction. As such, we open up promising research avenues for the study of this often banalized, but highly popular subgenre of Internet memes.

Keywords: Construction Grammar, constructions, image macros, Internet memes, intertextuality, monolingualism, multilingualism, multimodality, processing wordplay, prototypes

1 Introduction: Genes, memes and the world-wide web

In 1976 Richard Dawkins coined the term *meme* (a portmanteau of *mimesis* and *gene*), by analogy with the biological notion of a gene, to refer to any unit of cultural transmission (Dawkins 1976; and see Blackmore 1999 as important but disputed landmark). Although the memetic approach is often (justly) criticized for taking the biological analogy too far and for underestimating the role of the human being as agent in memetic evolution, several parallels between biological and cultural transmission are at the very least noteworthy: both genes and memes are characterized by (i) gradual propagation from individual to society; (ii) reproduction via copying and imitation; and (iii) diffusion through competition and selection. Leaving the debate on the precise nature of the link between genetics and memetics to one side, it is not very difficult to identify a wide variety of examples of cultural transmission that follow these three parameters, such as the spread of specific architectural styles (e.g. art deco, postmodern architecture), types of clothing (e.g. the advent of "hipsters") and ways of teaching (e.g. naturalistic versus constructivist teaching). A less functional but famous example is "Kilroy was here". This multimodal meme, consisting of a cartoon-like face peeping over a straight line representing a wall accompanied by the phrase "Kilroy was here", finds its origin in World War II, and popped up in all sorts of places during and after the war. Bjarneskans, Gronnevik, and Sandberg (1999) describe several factors that have contributed to the success of "Kilroy was here": the artefact is easy to reproduce, but it is at the same time sensitive to mutation and creative input; it lacks univocal meaning; it does not require direct host-to-host contact for reproduction, though users still experience a sense of "belonging to" when sharing the meme. Shifman (2014) considers precisely these characteristics as the pivotal elements in the rapid emergence of a new and highly popular subbranch of memes, namely Internet memes.

Indeed, the advent of the Internet, and of Web 2.0 and its social networks in particular, gave rise to a large number of artefacts that we can easily classify as memes in the Dawkins sense of the word (Milner 2013, 2016; Nooney and Portwood-Stacer 2014). These so-called Internet memes encompass all kinds of online objects that are mixed and remixed, copied and imitated, propagated and diffused by participants on the web. The principle of imitation and selection is clearly visible in the online evaluation systems for these types of Internet content, such as the "like"-thumb on Facebook or the up- and downvoting system on Reddit. Additionally, Shifman (2014: 41) identifies three core elements that define Internet memes: they should be conceived of as

> (a) a group of digital items sharing common characteristics of form, and/or stance, which (b) where created with awareness of each other, and (c) were circulated, imitated, and/or transformed via the Internet by many users.

In practice, Internet memes can take the form of purely visual, purely verbal or explicitly multimodal items (Dagsson Moskopp and Heller 2013: 73–186). The

Pepperspray Cop (Milner 2013; Huntington 2016) is a prime example of a purely visual meme. It concerns the spread of a central image from the Occupy Wallstreet movement[1], in which we see a campus police officer use pepper spray on protestors who were (at least in the image) peacefully sitting on the ground (Figure 1). The spraying action hence seemed uncalled for. The image itself went viral, but the truly memetic content only emerged as Internet users started remixing the original image with all sorts of other (both trivial and iconic) images: the Pepper Spray Cop was for instance photoshopped onto the original Beatles album cover, on Michelangelo's Sistine Chapel (Figure 2), on scenes from Star Wars and likewise on images of bathrooms and restaurants. Although we will not elaborate on ways to differentiate between virals and memes (see Shifman 2014), it is crucial to appreciate that whereas the former are characterized only by imitation, the latter always also include a component of alteration and modification. The video "Gangnam Style", an example of a multimodal Internet meme, can help further illustrate this point. The original video of the Korean singer PSY reached a record number of views on Youtube within days and was shared all over the world. For a long time, it was the most viewed video on YouTube. As the video grew more popular, people started making their own versions of the song, altering the lyrics, the visuals or both: YouTube now also contains videos such as Kim Jong Style or videos with English translations of the original Korean text. A meme was born.

Often intertextuality plays a pivotal role in the modifications made to original posts. Not surprisingly then, this is one of the key topics studied so far in research on Internet memes (Huntington 2016). Other topics include the verbal and visual rhetorical techniques used in creating a meme (e.g. synecdoche, metaphor, pastiche, and so-called "irritating" juxtapositions; Stroupe 2004; Jenkins 2014; Lou 2017), (critical) discourse analysis of the socio-political messages they communicate (Milner 2013; Nakamura 2014; Vickery 2014), marketing opportunities presented in memes and virals (Woerndl 2008) and methodological explorations of algorithms that can trace the propagation, longevity and peak circulation of memes (Bauckhage 2011; Leskovec, Backstrom, and Kleinberg 2009; Paradowski and Jonak 2012).

---

1 Occupy Wallstreet is the name of a 2011 movement that protested against economic inequality.

Fig. 1: The original Pepper Spray Cop

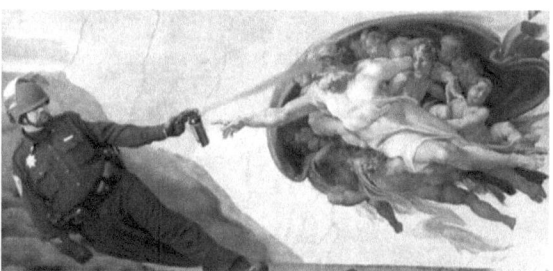

Fig. 2: The Pepper Spray Cop in the Sistine Chapel

In this paper, we want to complement these perspectives with a Cognitive Linguistic analysis of wordplay in image macros, a specific form of Internet memes. Below, we firstly lay the necessary groundwork: Section 2 provides a working definition of image macros and discusses the reasons why these image macros form a prime locus for (multimodal) wordplay and punning. Additionally, we present the main objectives of this paper, viz. to define image macros in a way that adequately captures their potential for creative modulation, and to analyze the specific role of wordplay in image macros. We then round off the section with a brief presentation of the data collected for this study. Section 3 turns to an introduction of the Cognitive Linguistic framework as a suitable tool for defining image macros (see also Brône, Feyaerts, and Veale 2006 on the general applicability of the Cognitive Linguistic framework for humor research): similar to but expanding on Dancygier and Vandelanotte (2017), we show how we can conceive of these digital items as multimodal constructions. Section 4 then focuses on instances of wordplay in these image macros, presenting four dimensions along which to place them in terms of processing and complexity. The final section distils the most pertinent – if preliminary – insights that can be derived from the proof of concept presented in this paper.

2 Image macros and wordplay: A match made in heaven

This paper focuses on one notable subcategory of Internet memes, so-called image macros. An image macro consists of text superimposed on an image. Whereas the image and discursive theme are typically fairly consistent in the replication process, the text of image macros is particularly open to the online "remix culture" that characterizes Internet memes (see Vickery 2014: 312). Figure 3 provides a good illustration of this working definition of image macros[2], presenting an instance of the meme known as Advice Dog. This meme, which shows an image of a dog against a rainbow-like background, rests on irony, presenting something that is quite obviously poor advice as good advice. After the first Advice Dog meme appeared online many more instances were shared on the Internet (see Davison 2012 and Vickery 2014 for the history of the meme), sometimes with a different dog (or occasionally even a different animal), but always with modifications of the text: Internet users shared their own bits of "good" advice through Advice Dog. The surge of online platforms that allow users to easily and quickly generate their own versions of popular image macros such as Advice Dog has rapidly increased the popularity of image macros, leaving us with a massive inventory of image macros to analyze (see below).

As the example illustrates, it is not straightforward to isolate the ultimate set of characteristic features of an image macro: each individual element of the meme is open to modification, with some elements being more stable than others. The first goal of this paper is to define image macros in a way that captures precisely this interplay between conventionality and creativity, between fixedness and adaptation.

---

2 See knowyourmeme.com, accessed 11 July 2017.

Fig. 3: Example 1 of Advice Dog

As has already been noted by Dancygier and Vandelanotte (2017), Cognitive Linguistics provides us with a convenient theoretical framework to undertake this task: combining insights from prototype theory and Construction Grammar (Langacker 1987; Goldberg 1995; Croft 2001) will allow us to come up with a multimodal template that contains the necessary form-meaning ingredients that image macros consist of.

In a next step, we focus our attention on image macros that contain wordplay. Both communalities and differences can be identified between jokes and Internet memes (see Section 4 for a more detailed approach). As Davison (2012: 122) notes, the main differences between jokes in the new and traditional communication forms pertain to the way they are transmitted: not only can jokes be shared faster via the Internet, they are also more susceptible to variation than traditional "offline" jokes. Concerning the communalities, then, besides the obvious point that both share humorous purposes (Dagsson Moskopp and Heller 2013; Lou 2017) the importance of intertextuality and of "networked individualism" specifically stand out. As will become obvious throughout the remainder of this paper, "understanding memes requires sophisticated 'meme literacy'" (Milner 2013): many memes only make sense when the recipient has sufficient experience with Internet memes. As such, analogous to parlour games, "enjoying the genre involves the sweet scent of an inside joke, understood by those who are immersed in the digital cultural landscape" (Shifman 2014). Any individual can make contributions to the stock of image macros, but only those that are sufficiently creative and networked to produce original, funny and / or surprising modulations of existing image macros will be shared, liked, upvoted and spread.

This idea of networked individualism is also prevalent in traditional humor research: "Speakers in running (humorous) discourse often [...] proceed on a humorous topic in collaboration with other participants, or counter another participant's utterance by means of adversarial humor strategies" (Brône, Feyaerts, and Veale 2006 discussing Davies 1984). As such, memes to some extent seem to function as the ingroup code of the digitally literate.

From a practical perspective, these underlying links between traditional jokes and image macros entail that we might expect a fair amount of wordplay in the verbal part of image macros (Dagsson Moskopp and Heller 2013). Although the interaction between humor and wordplay interact in rather complex ways, with humor in memes often being achieved without wordplay and wordplay equally occurring without humorous effects (Winter-Froemel 2016a), we do attest an openness of the image macro genre for wordplay. Our second objective in this paper is thus to describe variation in the processing complexity of wordplay in image macros: four dimensions will be introduced along which individual memes can vary.

In short, this paper sets out two objectives: (1) to propose a definition of an image macro that is sufficiently precise but at the same time accommodates the variations and modulations typically attested in the genre; (2) to propose a model that describes the variation in the processing complexity of wordplay in memes. To attain these goals, we have collected a large number of image macros via some of the most popular platforms for Internet memes, with KnowYourMeme.com, Reddit.com, MakeaMeme.org, Imgur.com and MemeGenerator.net as most important sources.[3] Whenever necessary, the detailed background information logged on KnowYourMeme.com was consulted for better understanding of individual memes. Second, we tagged and stored those image macros that contained instances of wordplay. This initial database was complemented with searches via Google Images based on queries including "meme" or "image macro" combined with "wordplay" or "pun". This approach requires a highly inclusive definition of "wordplay" (see Zirker and Winter-Froemel 2015: 2–3, and see Winter-Froemel 2016a). The information retrieved this way was fed back into the broader search on the meme platforms. For example, we encountered the image macro series "animal puns" through a Google Image search. More instances of the series were then tracked through the online platforms designed specifically for image macros. In all, our analysis of wordplay in image macros is based on over one hundred unique image macros containing wordplay.

---

[3] Consulted between 15 August 2016 and 30 September 2016.

3 A Construction Grammatical approach to image macros

In its intertwining of creativity and stability, the image macro is naturally related to the Cognitive Linguistic notion of construction (Langacker 1987; Goldberg 1995; Croft 2001). Constructions are "form and function pairings" that are characterized by variation in fixedness and conventionality, and that can be expressed across different degrees of schematicity. The resultative construction in English serves as a prime example: at the most schematic level, this construction concerns any form that indicates that something or someone has undergone a change in state as the result of the completion of an event, such as "paint the shed green". One schematic level lower we find a specific grammatical pattern that communicates this meaning, such as the body part-*off* construction ([Vi_{ntr} POSS $N_{inalienable}$ OFF]). This construction is constituted of slots that are more or less fixed (the bodypart is more required than the personal pronoun) and more or less schematic (from the syntactic slot of the verb over the semantically defined body parts to the proposition *off*). Additionally, the construction is characterized by uncompositionality due to the figurative dimension at play (see Section 3). At the lowest level of schematicity we find specific instantiations of this pattern, such as *she yells her head off* (see e.g. Cappelle 2014).

What is particularly interesting for our analysis is the fact that specific linguistic expressions (*she yells her head off, I work my butt off*) share an underlying schematic structure with varying degrees of fixedness paired up with a specific meaning. Admittedly, though, we have to relax the definition of constructions to include the visual information presented in the image macros under scrutiny here, i.e. image macros have to be seen as multimodal constructions. An interpretation of image macros as multimodal constructions has also been put forward by Dancygier and Vandelanotte (2017), but where they focus on selected meme series and discuss these relying on Discourse Viewpoint Spaces, we adopt a more general approach that aims to identify the cornerstones and building blocks of all image macros. As Dancygier and Vandelanotte (2017) point out, "multimodal constructions show prototype structure too, with core examples that are more characteristic and recognizable and more peripheral examples deviating from the prototypes in some respects" (see also Douglas 2014: 331 for short notes on the standardization process of image macros). It is our objective to reveal the characteristics of such core examples, aiming to uncover the prototypical image macro. Given the flexibility assumed by prototype-theoretical definitions of categories, the identification of an image macro prototype at the same time serves the purpose of pinpointing the features that structure the creative variability of image macros.

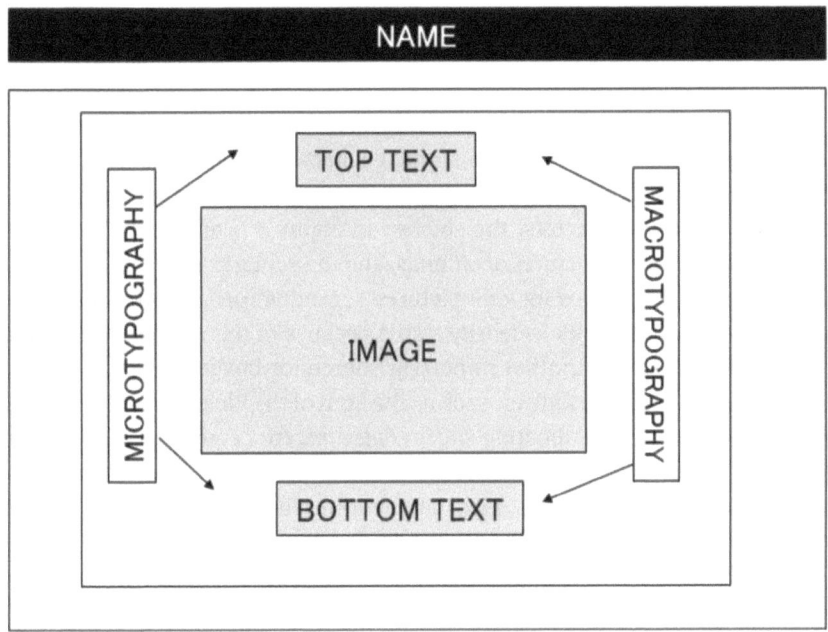

Fig. 4: The prototypical image macro as multimodal construction

Figure 4 presents the proposed structure for such a multimodal Construction Grammatical analysis. The grey boxes in the figure represent directly visible parts of the meme. The black box is used for an implicit element, not visible in the image macro. White is used for analytic categories. The proposal is based on a detailed analysis of the image macros that we consulted through the various platforms mentioned above. Below, we briefly present each constitutive part of the construction. Of course, further empirical analyses are needed to validate the status of Figure 4 as prototype: both frequency-based corpus analysis (see Geeraerts, Grondelaers, and Bakema 1994; and see Schmidt 2007 on the link between frequency and entrenchment) and psycholinguistic studies are needed. Additionally, future research should pay more detailed attention to the multimodal mechanisms at play in image macros, which are only briefly touched upon in our analyses.

Starting with the visual information in the meme, one of the most stable elements of image macros concerns microtypography: the text is typically presented in the font "Impact" (see Figure 3). The font, nearly always used in uppercase, is known for its white letters with a black contour. Brideau and Berret (2014) describe how both technical and functional reasons contributed to the choice for Impact in the initial rise of image macros, and discuss the crucial role played by online meme generators in the further standardization of Impact as "the meme-font".

The second crucial element of an image macro is the image. Although it goes without saying that there would be no image macro without an image, the type of image used in image macros shows variation. Figure 5 and Figure 6 for instance both contain stock characters: the chicken in Figure 5 is an example of image macro series relying on pictures of animals, and the young man in Figure 6 shows how several image macros include pictures of random people, who sometimes over time reach world-wide celebrity status because of their initially incidental appearance in memes. Another important source for images concern "actual" celebrities or mass media figures, such as the Lord of the Rings character Boromir (Figure 7), Fry from the animation sitcom *Futurama*, or Leonardo di Caprio (and see Figure 12 below for a Kanye West meme). To process such image macro, recipients must be familiar not only with the celebrities themselves, but also with the precise context in which they appear in the image macro. For Figure 7, for instance, the context concerns the Lord of the Rings scene where the Council of Elrond reveals that an evil ring must be thrown into the fires of Mount Doom to destroy it. According to Boromir, this is near impossible task, which he shares through the famous words: "One does not simply walk into Mordor."

Fig. 5: Anti-Joke Chicken

Fig. 6: Sudden Clarity Clarence

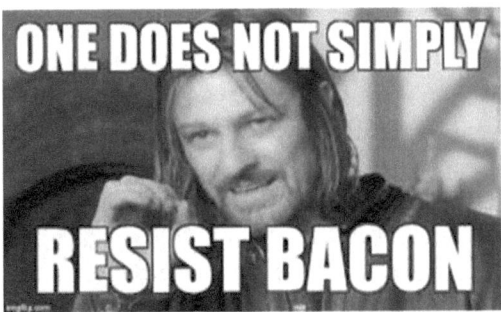

Fig. 7: One does not simply walk into Mordor

As Figure 5 and Figure 6 reveal, some of these image macros only truly make sense – or at least receive an additional layer of interpretation – when the recipient is aware of the name of the meme – or perhaps more accurately, the overall meaning of the meme that is captured by the name. 'Sudden Clarity Clarence', for instance, expresses the fact that any instance of the meme in question needs to be read in terms of an unexpected (though not necessarily deep or crucial) insight. In the theoretical framework of Construction Grammar, this links up with the non-compositionality of constructions: their conventional meaning is more than the simple sum of their parts. Image macros are similarly non-compositional in the sense that their conventional overall meaning suggests how the parts should be interpreted (rather than that the combination of the parts simply determines the overall meaning), often with different layers of meaning superimposed on each other. The name is the only part of the image macro construction that is not explicitly visible: usually only users with high "meme proficiency" are aware of these names, which explains their crucial role in giving memes the status of an ingroup code. In Figure 5, for example, being aware of the fact that "Yo momma so fat she has to wear large clothes" is an instance of "Anti-Joke Chicken" helps better understand the point of the meme. The example also reveals how names are typically not given to individual memes, but to series of memes:[4] every image of a chicken combined with a sort of anti-joke is part of the Anti-Joke Chicken series. These image series are themselves sometimes instantiations of more abstract series: one level up in the schematic representation of memes, the Advice Dog presented in Figure 3, Anti-Joke Chicken in Figure 5 and related examples such as Philosoraptor, Bad Advice Mallard and Actual Advice Mallard are

---

[4] Note that this implies that image macros that are not conventionalized often do not have a name – see e.g. Figure 10.

themselves instances of the overarching image macro schema of Advice Animals. Advice Animals are all image macro series that use a stock character of an animal (and following some definitions even humans such as Clarence in Figure 6) as image. Further research is needed to establish how precisely these names are created, established and diffused.

These image macro series and image macro schemas can then also be combined in constructional blends (Fauconnier and Turner 2002; Coulson 2006), as is illustrated by Figures 8a/b and 9a/b. Socially Awkward Penguin is an image macro series that, as the name indicates, portrays socially awkward situations (Figure 8a). About a year after its first appearance, a spin-off series was created on the social networking site Tumblr: Socially Awesome Penguin is quite the opposite of Socially Awkward Penguin, which is visually supported by the horizontal flip in the image of the original penguin (Figure 8b). The coincidence of the two series gave rise to both straightforward and more intricate blends, as is shown in Figure 9a and Figure 9b respectively. This type of creative "constructional play" with different image macros again presupposes a good deal of meme literacy, both on behalf of the sender and of the recipient. An interesting topic for future research here is to connect these different penguin-types with Searle's speech acts (1969), distinguishing between those penguins that give "good" advice (Figure 8a) and the purely narrative macros (Figure 8b).

Fig. 8: Socially Awkward Penguin (a); Socially Awesome Penguin (b)

Fig. 9: Socially Awesome-Awkward Penguin (a); Socially Awkward-Awesome-Awkward-Awesome Penguin (b)

A final building block of the prototypical image macro presented in Figure 4 concerns the verbal elements included in the memes. As concerns macrotypography, a top text and a bottom text are typically present, with a clear juxtaposition between both; where the top text sets the scene, the bottom text functions analogously to the punchline of traditional jokes (see primarily Figure 5, and compare Raskin's 1985 model for "offline" jokes). Another interesting observation is that, within the overarching multimodal construction, several image macros also contain a verbal construction within its textual element. Figure 7 serves as an excellent example: this meme series finds it origin in the Lord of the Rings movie, where the character Boromir utters the words "One does not simply walk into Mordor" to express his scepticism about the feasibility of the task at hand. Subsequently, "One does not simply X" has been recycled for the meme series exemplified in Figure 7 where the top text nearly always reads "One does not simply", and the bottom text reveals an "unstraightforward" task of some sort (see also Dancygier and Vandelanotte 2017 for a more elaborate analysis of "One does not simply X").

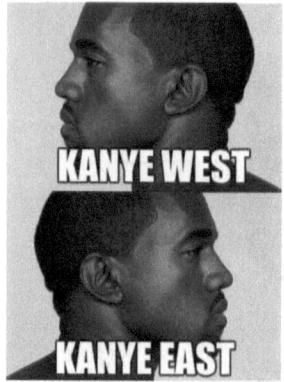
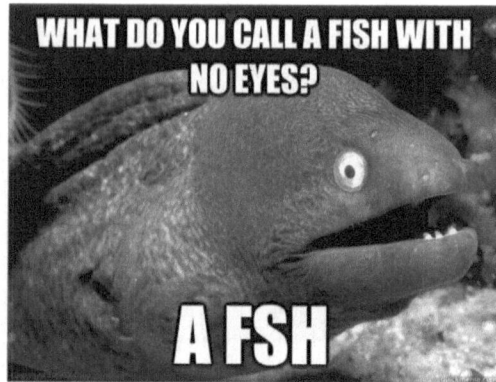

Fig. 10: Kanye West   **Fig. 11:** Bad Joke Eel

Finally, where the visual elements in image macros can give rise to "constructional play" (Figure 9b), the verbal elements often include traditional instances of wordplay (Figure 10–13). Although the focus of this paper is not on types of wordplay, it is interesting to point out that most of the traditional linguistic mechanisms of wordplay are attested in image macros (see Winter-Froemel 2016a), such as homonomy (Figure 10, *West* as a proper name versus *West* as cardinal direction), homophony (Figure 11, the letter 'i' vs. *eye*), paronymy (Figure 12, *don't carrot all* versus *don't care at all*) and variation on the literal and figurative meanings of words (Figure 13).

Below, we will zoom in on the image macros in our database that include such traditional wordplay mechanisms, and we will explore the processing difficulties involved. For now, the main conclusion is that, although the schematic representation in Figure 4 includes the most important elements of macros, variation is in practice attested for each and every single component included in the figure. A task at hand for future research is to investigate how much variation is practiced and tolerated within the genre: what minimal requirements need to be met to consider a digital artefact as an instance of a conventional image macro? And do image macros, given their prototypical structure, undergo semantic change like any other prototype concept (Geeraerts 1997)?

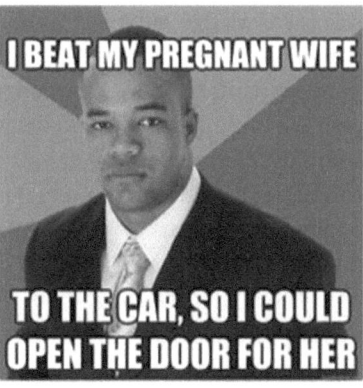

Fig. 12: A random meme

Fig. 13: Politically Correct Black Man

4 Processing wordplay in image macros: Four dimensions

It has repeatedly been argued that the humorous effect of jokes and puns can largely be attributed to (balanced) processing difficulties on the side of the recipient (see Giora 1991; Brône and Feyaerts 2003), who needs to resolve the specific script oppositions that characterize humorous discourse (Attardo 2001). The second goal of our paper is to provide a preliminary inventory of the types of processing difficulties that characterize wordplay in image macros.[5] First, we present four dimensions along which specific image macros can be positioned in terms of processing difficulty after which we discuss a complex example that illustrates the forces of the four dimensions simultaneously.

The first dimension we present focuses on the multimodal nature of image macros, verifying to what extent the visual information provides a contextual cue in the processing of the wordplay. The following three dimensions have to do with the required awareness of the context in which the image macro is produced. Following Winter-Froemel (2013, 2016b) we distinguish between four types of

---

5 Our analysis of processing starts from the assumption that recipients are not only computer literate, but also in a disposition to be entertained, and ready to invest their attention to the decoding of more demanding image macros. Future research could examine whether the decoding of certain complex memes is debated on online platforms, such as Reddit or knowyourmeme.org.

contextual knowledge language users can possess: (i) general linguistic knowledge (mainly grammatical and lexical knowledge); (ii) knowledge of the linguistic context (co-text); (iii) knowledge of the communicative situation; and (iv) general extralinguistic knowledge (encyclopaedic information). The second dimension we present below includes a cline from monolingual to multilingual memes and can as such be linked to the required general linguistic knowledge of the recipient. In its focus on intramedial intertextuality, Dimension 3 presents a combination of the expected knowledge of the co-text and of the communicative situation. The final dimension, then, discusses the encyclopaedic references often included in memes and hence relates to the extralinguistic knowledge needed for successful processing.

Before proceeding, an important note concerns the exploratory nature of the analysis presented here. The four dimensions have been distilled from a careful analysis of the one hundred image macros containing wordplay in our database. To truly assess the way in which memes are processed by recipients, these corpus-based analyses will of course need to be complemented with experimental research (e.g. eye tracking, priming tests, self-paced reading) (see e.g. Vaid et al. 2003).

4.1 Dimension 1: From monomodal to multimodal wordplay

Although one of the prototypical characteristics of the image macro is the fact that it comes with an image, the role the image plays in processing the meme as a whole is highly variable (see also Dancygier and Vandelanotte 2017). Vickery (2014: 313) for example makes the following note on Confession Bear, a meme that combines an image of a sad-looking bear with confessions on behalf of the sender, but where the bear itself contributes little to the meaning of the meme: "the text of Confession Bear memes must be interpreted with limited visual aids. As such, the form of the Confession Bear meme simultaneously enables and constrains the transgressive potential of the meme".

This variable importance of the visual element is also highly relevant for the way in which wordplay is processed in image macros (compare Knospe 2015). We propose a cline that ranges from strictly monomodal wordplay to highly multimodal wordplay. On one side of the continuum we find image macros in which no visual cues are included in the image to help process the wordplay. The other extreme is represented by instances of wordplay that can only be processed when the visual information included in the image is factored in. In between we find cases where sufficient verbal cues are provided in the text of the meme for successful processing, but where – in a metonymical fashion – additional visual anchors help recipients to evoke the right frame for the wordplay. Illustrative examples are provided in Figure 14 to Figure 17.

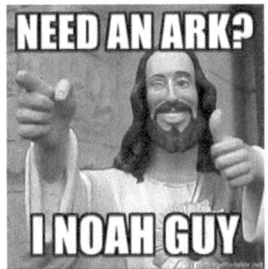

Fig. 14: Linguist Llama   **Fig. 15:** Noah's Ark   **Fig. 16:** Lame Pun Coon[6]

Figure 14 presents an example of Linguist Llama, an animal advice series containing puns tailored to a linguistic audience. Although the image of the llama helps evoke the context of the specific Linguist Llama pun series (see Dimension 3 below), the visual information is irrelevant for the processing of the pun itself.[7] The wordplay is in essence based on the homonymic nature of "tense", "mood" and "irregular", three words which when taken together serve as verbal cues to process the unexpected turn to a grammatical reading in the bottom line of the meme. In Figure 15, we similarly find a verbal cue in the top line ("ark") that helps process the homophonic pun on "know a" and "Noah" in the bottom line. In contrast to Figure 14, the image of Jesus does provide the recipient with an additional visual cue. Although this multimodal cueing might support the processing of the wordplay, it is strictly speaking not necessary, as is made obvious by the fact that the pun also occurs in the image macro series "Lame Pun Coon" (Figure 16), which similar to Linguist Llama simply shows the image of a raccoon complemented with all sorts of lame puns. The lack of the image of Jesus does not seem to prevent a successful processing of the wordplay. Hence, the example can be considered as a moderately multimodal pun.

---

[6] The fact that Figure 16 uses lower-case instead of upper-case might not be purely accidental: it might help processing, in the sense that Noah is more clearly recognizable as proper name.
[7] To some people, the llama might look moody, when seen in the context of this pun. However, Lame Pun Llama is used for a wide range of puns that have nothing to do with moodiness. It thus seem like a far stretch to consider the facial expression of the llama as highly relevant for the processing of this specific pun.

An explicitly multimodal pun, located on the other side of the continuum compared to Figure 14, is found in Figure 17. In this case, the figurative meaning of the expression "to be on a roll" only becomes discongruent and hence humorous against the background of the image of the person literally sitting on a roll. As recipients need to process both the visual and verbal elements, and the opposition between literal and figurative meaning, to understand this pun, we generally expect more processing effort is required in these cases than in the cases located on the more monomodal end of the continuum.

Fig. 17: Random roll meme

4.2 Dimension 2: From monolingual to multilingual wordplay

A second way to increase the processing efforts of the recipient is by including more than one language in the wordplay (see also Winter-Froemel 2016b). Such multilingual puns can only be processed when the recipient is sufficiently proficient in the languages involved (see Stefanowitsch 2002; Knospe 2015; Winter-Froemel 2016b). Three expectations can be derived from this observation in the context of our image macros. First, because multilingual proficiency cannot simply be presupposed in the broad context of the world-wide web, we can expect to find mainly monolingual (English) memes. Second, as Winter-Froemel (2016b) notes, if multilingual punning does occur, it can be expected that "mainly highly frequent and strongly entrenched linguistic items of foreign origin are actualized in multilingual wordplay". Third, if more complex instances of multilingual punning are attested, viz. multilingual puns that require a higher proficiency in the embedded language (Myers-Scotton 2002),[8] a strong linguistic anchor will be present, by which we refer to "a recognizable, entrenched chunk of language serving as a known, easily processed background against which the pun can be perceived" (Stefanowitsch 2002: 69).

Together, these expectations can be translated as a second dimension in the processing of wordplay in image macros, visualizing a cline from monolingual over weakly multilingual to more complex multilingual memes. All examples of image macros that have been presented up to this point serve as examples of purely monolingual cases, which are, as expected, far more frequent than multilingual memes.[9] Figures 18 to 20 serve as illustrations of multilingual memes.

Both Figure 18 and Figure 19 are examples of weakly bilingual wordplay in which linguistic elements are included that are also accessible to minimally proficient bi- or multilinguals. In Figure 18 a highly entrenched loanword is used in an instance of paronymy (*passed away* versus *pasta way*). The paronymy between *I smoke a lot* and *ice mocha lot* in Figure 19 is based on differences between an L1 English accent and a Spanish-English accent. In both memes, the processing is further facilitated by referring to one of the countries where the language is spoken in the top line of the meme ("Italian" in Figure 18, "Mexican" in Figure 19). The example in Figure 20 is more complex in terms of multilingualism, as some basic knowledge of the verbal system in Spanish is required (*soy* being paronymous, referring to the English noun for a specific bean or to the first person singular of the present tense of the Spanish verb *ser*, 'to be'). Again, we find a helpful reference to the Spanish language in the text of the meme, and are further assisted in the processing by the focus on introducing oneself in conversation.

As a side-note, the matrix language (Myers-Scotton 2002) in the multilingual memes in our database is nearly always English, though some rare exceptions can be found: Figure 21 includes a rather intricate English-Spanish pun that additionally also requires some encyclopaedic knowledge of Transformers-toys that transform from for example robots to everyday vehicles (see Dimension 4 below). To summarize, the hypothesis for this dimension holds that the more complex the multilingual pun, the more processing effort is required on behalf of the speaker.

---

[8] "Proficiency" is here used in the broad sense, concerning spelling, pronunciation, the link between both (see Onysko 2007 on the importance of grapheme/phoneme-mapping in lexical borrowing), grammar etc.
[9] Presenting frequency data would be misleading here, as our data collection in part targeted image macros including multilingual wordplay.

Fig. 18: Lame Pun Coon Italian-English

Fig. 19: Mexican Word of the Day Spanish-English

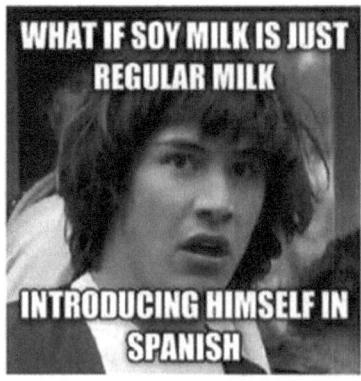 

Fig. 20: Conspiracy Keanu: Spanish-English

Fig. 21: Success Kid: English-Spanish

4.3 Dimension 3: From low to high degrees of intertextuality

Our third dimension deals with the degree of intra-genre intertextuality that is needed when processing the meme. 'Intra-genre' is used here in the sense that we only consider those intertextual references that link to other image macros and series. In such cases of intra-genre intertextuality the recipient first and foremost needs knowledge of the communicative situation and/or of a specific communicative genre/tradition: the correct intertext can only be evoked when the recipient is aware of the fact that he is dealing with the conventionalized genre of Internet memes. Applied to Figure 8, for example, it helps to know that this type of figure presents an image macro. Such knowledge of the general communicative situation sometimes needs to be complemented with more specific knowledge of the co-text: full processing of the wordplay in image macros sometimes hinges on an awareness of specific image macros in particular.

Fig. 22: Otter Animal Pun **Fig. 23:** Puma Animal Pun

Whereas many of the examples that we have presented above do not include such intertextual references to other image macros, the pun presented in Figure 22 does. In this case, a rather explicit reference is made to the series the image macro is itself part of. Animal Puns is an image macro series that combines an image of an animal with a verbal pun based on the name of that animal. Figure 23 provides an example of such an "animal pun", including an instance of paronymy between *puma* and *poo my*. In Figure 22, then, an explicit reference to these animal puns is made in the top line, with a negative appraisal following in the bottom line. What is striking here is that this comment on the shamefully low quality of the puns found in animal pun series is made within an animal pun image macro that itself includes such a cheesy pun, which of course adds irony to the statement. This irony is partly lost to recipients who are not aware of the broader intragenre context of Figure 22. Generally, even for readers who are literate in the meme genre, the processing efforts of intertextual memes are presumably higher than in memes without such intertextual references.

4.4 Dimension 4: From low to high levels of external referencing

For the final dimension, we turn to allusions made to the general extralinguistic context of the meme: "the successful processing of the intended meaning [of puns] heavily depends on the activation of experiential (cultural, social, embodied...) knowledge shared by both speaker and hearer in the current discourse space" (Brône, Feyaerts, and Veale 2006: 215 discussing Langacker 2001; and see Winter-Froemel 2016b).

Fig. 24: Putin

Fig. 25: Who let the dogs out?

A first example of an image macro including wordplay that draws heavily on world knowledge is presented in Figure 24. The example includes three different cases of paronymy that all play on proper names: *seriously* vs. *Syria-sly*; *putting* vs. *Putin*; *aside* vs. *Assad*. These three puns function as verbal cues for each other, and additionally the image of Putin provides the reader with a (not as such essential) visual cue to help process the meme. However, if the recipient is not aware of the socio-political context of the Syrian civil war, it is hard to fully graps the intended effects of the image macro.

Other image macros contain more than one reference to the outside world. To understand the meme in Figure 25, the recipient needs to recognize the person on the image as Ramsey Bolton (one of the characters of Game of Thrones) and further needs to be aware of the fact that, in the series, he has a tendency to send out his dogs on people but eventually gets killed by his own dogs. On top of that, understanding the additional cultural reference to the Grammy Award-winning song "Who let the dogs out?" from the Baha Men adds yet another layer to this complex wordplay. Examples such as these illustrate our hypothesis that the more types of external knowledge need to be invoked in processing the meme, the more difficult the processing will be.

4.5 Combining the dimensions: Multimodal constructional play

Above, we presented four dimensions of processing difficulties for wordplay in image macros. In reality, these dimensions interact and present themselves simultaneously. One prime example of such multimodal constructional play is presented in Figure 26. In the figure, we see what look like the backs of three Hawaiian hula girls, who are wearing colorful straw skirts while dancing. The top text reads "much ass", the bottom text reads "grassy ass". Together, these lines form a pun on the Spanish politeness marker "muchas gracias", with *muchas* being reparsed as "much ass" (cued visually in the fact that we see the girls from the back, waving their hips) and *gracias* being reparsed as "grassy ass" (cued visually in the colorful straw skirts).

Fig. 26: Muchas gracias

This way, complex processing is presented in three of the four dimensions discussed above. First, as the wordplay in Figure 26 cannot be processed without the visual cues presented through the image, this example serves as an instance of multimodal punning and scores quite high on Dimension 1 (multimodality). Second, as the basis for the pun lies in paronymy between Spanish and English forms, the example also scores quite high on Dimension 2 (multilingualism). Finally, Dimension 4 (external referencing) is also important in the processing of this meme, as the recipient needs to be aware of the fact that the typical Hawaiian skirts worn by hula girls are made of grass-like material. To our knowledge, Dimension 3 (intramodel intertextuality) is not relevant for this meme: no clear references to other image macros or image macro series are included in Figure 26.

Although many similar examples can be analyzed, Figure 26 for now suffices to illustrate the ways in which our four dimensions can be combined.

5 Conclusion: From interpretations to remaining questions

To round off, let us summarize the two main points made in this paper. First, in terms of their communicative genre, the image macros analyzed in this paper can be seen as *combining features of jokes and wordplay*. On the one hand, we can consider them as jokes, not only because of their humorous character, but specifically also because the phatic and social meaning of the reproduction process is an essential function of the form: just like the social bonding effect of telling a joke is an essential part of the pragmatic meaning of jokes, strengthening a digital communicative network by reproducing a meme is part of the latter's function: 'sharing' is the basic digital act, i.e. the mimesis is the message. On the other hand, because the joke-like reproduction necessarily takes the form of variation within the image macro, we see similarities with wordplay. In contrast with jokes, humorous variation on the template provided by the image macro and its existing instances is a crucial feature of image macro usage. As with wordplay, a display of creativity is an integral part of the social(izing) message conveyed by the use of image macros: successful image macro usage requires a funny, witty, surprising variation on the existing pattern and its instantiations. Not surprisingly, then, verbal wordplay in the strict sense plays an important role in the make-up of image macros, and we have shown how instances of the various mechanisms of wordplay can be easily identified in a corpus of image macros.

Second, in terms of their linguistic and semiotic status, image macros can be insightfully described with the conceptual inventory of Cognitive Linguistics. Specifically, they may be categorized as *prototypically structured multimodal constructions*. Whereas their multimodal nature consists of an obligatory combination of visual and verbal elements, their constructional character takes the form of a non-compositional combination of elements with varying degrees of fixedness and schematicity. The prototype nature of image macros as categories, finally, derives directly from the crucial role of variability for image macro usage:

their inherent flexibility is structured in the form of more or less typical instances of use. Zooming in on image macros that include traditional instances of wordplay, we analyzed these in terms of four dimensions, indicating how the image macros vary along a typicality cline with regard to the degree of multimodality, multilingualism, intra-genre intertextuality and external referencing included in the construction. Future research can zoom in on each these dimensions, further studying the specific mechanisms at play in the production and processing of the memes. For now, we hope to have drawn attention to the research potential of this often banalized, but highly popular subgenre of Internet memes.

Acknowledgement: We would like to thank Esme Winter-Froemel and two anonymous reviewers for reading through our text so carefully and for their helpful suggestions to an earlier draft of this paper. Needless to say, all remaining errors are our own.

6 References

Attardo, Salvatore. 2001. *Humorous Texts: A Semantic and Pragmatic Analysis*. Berlin & New York: De Gruyter Mouton.

Bauckhage, Christian. 2011. Insights into Internet Memes. *Proceedings of the Fifth International AAAI Conference on Weblogs and Social Media. Barcelona, Catalonia, Spain, July 17–21, 2011*, 42–49. Published by The AAAI Press, Menlo Park, California.

Blackmore, Susan. 1999. *The Meme Machine*. Oxford: Oxford University Press.

Bjarnekans, Henrik, Bjarne Grønnevik & Anders Sandberg. 1999. *The lifecycle of memes*. http://www.aleph.se/Trans/Cultural/Memetics/memecycle.htm (accessed 5 July 2017).

Brideau, Kate & Charles Berret. 2014. A brief introduction to Impact: 'The Meme Font'. *Journal of Visual Culture* 13(3). 307–313.

Brône, Geert & Kurt Feyaerts. 2003. *The Cognitive Linguistics of Incongruity Resolution: Marked Reference-Point Structures in Humor*. University of Leuven, Department of Linguistics preprint no. 205.

Brône, Geert, Kurt Feyaerts & Tony Veale. 2006. Introduction: Cognitive linguistic approaches to humor. *Humor: International Journal of Humor Research* 19(3). 203–228. https://doi.org/10.1515/HUMOR.2006.012.

Cappelle, Bert. 2014. Conventional combinations in pockets of productivity: English resultatives and Dutch ditransitives expressing excess. In Ronny Boogaart, Timothy Colleman & Gijsbert Rutten (eds.), *The Extending Scope of Construction Grammar*, 251–282. Berlin: De Gruyter Mouton.

Coulson, Seana. 2006. *Semantic Leaps. Frame-shifting and conceptual blending in meaning construction*. Cambridge: Cambridge University Press.

Croft, William. 2001. *Radical Construction Grammar: Syntactic theory in typological perspective*. Oxford: Oxford University Press.

Dagsson Moskopp, Nils (erlehmann) & Christian Heller (plomplomplom). 2013. *Internet-MEME. Kurz & geek*. Köln: O'Reilly Verlag.

Dancygier, Barbara & Lieven Vandelanotte. 2017. Internet memes as multimodal constructions. *Cognitive Linguistics* 28(3). 565–598.

Davies, Catherine E. 1984. Joint joking. Improvisational humorous episodes in conversation. In Claudia Brugman, Monica Macaulay, Amy Dahlstrom, Michele Emanatian, Birch Moonwomon, Catherine O'Connor (eds.), *Proceedings of the 10th Annual Meeting of the Berkeley Linguistics Society*, 360–371. Berkeley: University of Berkeley Press.

Davison, Patrick. 2012. The language of internet memes. In Michael Mandiberg (ed.), *The social media reader*. 120–136. New York: New York University Press.

Dawkins, Richard. 1976. *The Selfish Gene*. Oxford: Oxford University Press.

Douglas, Nick. 2014. It's supposed to look like shit: The Internet Ugly aesthetic. *Journal of Visual Culture* 13(3). 314–339.

Fauconnier, Gilles & Mark Turner. 2002. *The Way We Think: Conceptual Blending and the Mind's Hidden Complexities*. New York: Basic Books.

Geeraerts, Dirk, Stefan Grondelaers & Peter Bakema. 1994. *The structure of lexical variation. Meaning, naming and context*. Berlin & New York: De Gruyter Mouton.

Geeraerts, Dirk. 1997. *Diachronic Prototype Semantics*. Oxford: The Clarendon Press.

Giora, Rachel. 1991. On the cognitive aspects of the joke. *Journal of Pragmatics* 16(5). 465–485.

Goldberg, Adèle E. 1995. *Constructions: A Construction Grammar Approach to Argument Structure*. Chicago: Chicago University Press.

Huntington, Heidi. 2016. Pepper Spray Cop and the American Dream: Using Synecdoche and Metaphor to Unlock Internet Memes' Visual Political Rhetoric. *Communication Studies* 67(1). 77–93.

Jenkins, Eric S. 2014. The Modes of Visual Rhetoric: Circulating Memes as Expressions. *Quarterly Journal of Speech* 100(4). 442–466.

Knospe, Sebastian. 2015. A Cognitive Model for Bilingual Puns. In Angelika Zirker & Esme Winter-Froemel (eds.), *Wordplay and Metalinguistic/Metadiscursive Reflection. Authors, Contexts, Techniques, and Meta-Reflection* (The Dynamics of Wordplay 1), 161–194. Berlin & Boston: De Gruyter.

Langacker, Ronald W. 1987. *Foundations of Cognitive Grammar*. Volume I: *Theoretical prerequisites*. Stanford: Stanford University Press.

Langacker, Ronald W. 2001. Discourse in cognitive grammar. *Cognitive Linguistics* 12(2). 143–188.

Leskovec, Jure, Lars Backstrom & John Kleinberg. 2009. *Meme-tracking and the dynamics of the news cycle. KDD '09 Proceedings of the 15th ACM SIGKDD international conference on Knowledge discovery and data mining*, 497–506.

Lou, Adrian. 2017. Multimodal simile: The "when" meme in social media discourse. *English Text Construction* 10(1). 106–131.

Milner, Ryan M. 2013. Pop Polyvocality: Internet Memes, Public Participation, and the Occupy Wall Street Movement. *International Journal of Communication* 7, 2357–2390.

Milner, Ryan M. 2016. *The World-Made Meme*. Cambridge: MIT Press.

Myers-Scotton, Carol. 2002. *Contact linguistics: Bilingual encounters and grammatical outcomes*. Oxford: Oxford University Press.

Nakamura, Lisa. 2014. 'I WILL DO EVERYthing That Am Asked': Scambaiting, digital showspace, and the racial violence of social media. *Journal of Visual Culture* 13(3). 257–274.

Nooney, Laine & Laura Portwood-Stacer. 2014. One does not simply: An introduction to the special issue on Internet Memes. *Journal of Visual Culture* 13(3). 248–252.
Onysko, Alexander. 2007. *Anglicisms in German. Borrowing, lexical productivity and written codeswitching*. Berlin: De Gruyter.
Paradowski, Michał B. & Łukasz Jonak. 2012. Diffusion of linguistic innovation as social coordination. *Psychology of Language and Communication* 16(2). 53–64.
Raskin, Victor. 1985. *Semantic Mechanisms of Humor*. Dordrecht, Boston & Lancaster: Reidel.
Schmid, Hans-Jörg. 2007. "Entrenchment, salience and basic levels". In Dirk Geeraerts & Hubert Cuyckens (eds.), *The Oxford Handbook of Cognitive Linguistics*, 117-138. Oxford: Oxford University Press.
Searle, John. 1969. *Speech Acts*. Cambridge: Cambridge University Press.
Shifman, Limor. 2014. *Memes in Digital Culture*. Cambridge): MIT Press.
Stefanowitsch, Anatol. 2002. Nice to Miet You: Bilingual Puns and the Status of English in Germany. *Intercultural Communication Studies* 11(4). 67–84.
Stroupe, Craige. 2004. "The Rhetoric of Irritation: Inappropriateness as Visual/Literate Practice." In Marguerite Helmers & Charles Hill (eds.), *Defining Visual Rhetorics*, 243–258. Mahwah: Lawrence Erlbaum Publishers.
Vaid, Jyotsna, Rachel Hull, Roberto Heredia, David Gerkens, and Francisco Martinez 2003. Getting a joke: The time course of meaning activation in verbal humor. *Journal of Pragmatics 35*. 1431–1449.
Vickery, Jacqueline Ryan. 2014. The curious case of Confession Bear: the reappropriation of online macro-image memes. *Information, Communication & Society* 17(3): 301–325, DOI: 10.1080/1369118X.2013.871056.
Winter-Froemel, Esme. 2013. Ambiguität im Sprachgebrauch und im Sprachwandel: Parameter der Analyse diskurs- und systembezogener Fakten. *Zeitschrift für französische Sprache und Literatur* 123(2). 130–170.
Winter-Froemel, Esme. 2016a. The Semiotics of Multilingual Wordplay in Linguistic Landscapes: Communicative Settings, the Hearer-Origo, and Contextual Knowledge. In Sebastian Knospe, Alexander Onysko & Maik Goth (eds.), *Crossing Languages to Play with Words. Multidisciplinary Perspectives* (The Dynamics of Wordplay 3), 157–193. Berlin & Boston: De Gruyter.
Winter-Froemel, Esme. 2016b. Multilingual wordplay in Linguistic Landscapes: Communicative settings, the addressee-origo, and boundedness to various types of contextual knowledge. In: Sebastian Knospe, Alexander Onysko & Maik Goth (eds.), *Crossing Languages to Play with Words. Multidisciplinary Perspectives* (The Dynamics of Wordplay 3), 157–193. Berlin & Boston: De Gruyter.
Woerndl, Maria, Savvas Papagiannidis, Michael Bourlakis & Feng Li. 2008. Internet-induced marketing techniques: critical factors in viral marketing campaigns. *International Journal of Business Science and Applied Management* 3(1), 33–45.
Zirker, Angelika & Esme Winter-Froemel. 2015. Wordplay and Its Interfaces in Speaker-Hearer Interaction: An Introduction. In Angelika Zirker & Esme Winter-Froemel (eds.), *Wordplay and Metalinguistic/Metadiscursive Reflection. Authors, Contexts, Techniques, and Meta-Reflection* (The Dynamics of Wordplay 1), 1–24. Berlin & Boston: De Gruyter.

Gesa Schole
Wordplay as a means of post-colonial resistance

Abstract: In post-colonial Mozambique, writers aim to develop a literary tradition of their own, separate from that inherited from its former mother country Portugal. One means of achieving this goal is through the language that the writers use in their works. Living in a linguistically hybrid context, they have the freedom of choice between several languages or varieties. The main research question at hand is by what linguistic means the Mozambican writer Mia Couto supports the new, post-colonial identity of the Mozambican people – an aim that he has set himself. The basis for this analysis is the language that he applies in his novel *A varanda do frangipani* ('Under the frangipani') and which is representative of his style. His literary language reflects colloquial Mozambican Portuguese, which deviates from European Portuguese in some respects. In his works, he functionalizes these deviations and thereby creates wordplays in the broader sense. This act represents a form of linguistic self-mimicry and is the opposite of earlier colonial mimicry. The positions of colonized and colonizer are reversed, the influence of the indigenous people is accentuated and dignified. In this way, wordplay acts as a means of post-colonial resistance supporting the ex-colonies' true independence and their own specific identity. Apart from that, wordplays in the narrow sense in the form of lexical blends as Couto uses them may be taken as metaphors for the hybrid character of post-colonial spaces, and some may even represent the Mozambicans' new hybrid identity. Thus, the research question involves the subcategorization of wordplay phenomena and its linkage to post-colonial concepts. In general, the wordplays that Couto creates are predominantly wordplays *in absentia* whose playfulness is increased by their formal complexity (medial overlapping and contour blends), structural transgression (illicit ways of compounding and violation of linear ordering rules), and the absence of a naming function as there are conventional ways of encoding the same thing.

Keywords: affixation, blend, colonial mimicry, composition, derivation, hybridity, identity, idiom, literature, ludic deformation, Mozambique, portmanteau, Portuguese, post-colonialism, wordplay definition

1 Introduction

Post-colonial spaces are hybrid due to the influence that the colonizer and the colonized exerted in the past (Young 1995: 20). This hybridity is reflected in the language that the people in former colonies predominantly use to communicate with each other. In many former colonies, there is a creolized variety which has emerged over the generations (Young 1995: 5). However, in Mozambique, there is a non-creolized, colloquial variety close to European Portuguese (Perl 1994: 122–123) which reflects the Mozambicans' ludic attitude towards language and their tendency to use ad-hoc creations, a feature that they share with other formerly colonized peoples. The deviations of this variety from European Portuguese are unstable and not consistent among its speakers (Perl 1994: 123).[1] The Mozambican author Mia Couto functionalizes some characteristics of this hybrid language in his literary works. The paper at hand analyzes wordplays and deviations in his novel *A varanda do frangipani* ('Under the frangipani') ([1996] 2003). The aim is to show that these deviations frequently represent wordplays in the broader sense and complement wordplays in the narrow sense. In addition, the case of Mozambique allows us to illustrate how wordplays may be functionalized in order to support a post-colonial, linguistic resistance in favor of the (linguistic) independence of the Mozambican people.

Mia Couto is one of Mozambique's most famous writers and in 1998 was elected to the *Academia Brasileira de Letras*, the Brazilian authors' association, becoming its first African member. It should be pointed out that Mia Couto is a man and not a woman: António Emílio Leite Couto nicknamed himself Mia because of his affection for cats when he was a child (Laban 1998: 1033). As a writer, he aims to break with the literary traditions that Mozambique inherited from Portugal and to support a Mozambican identity so that true independence may be achieved (Matusse 1998: 76). Couto is a descendant of Portuguese immigrants and enjoyed the advantages such as schooling and higher education that his background offered him over the Bantu population. Nevertheless, perhaps because of his anti-racist and Christian upbringing, he solidarized with his Bantu neighbors (Chabal 1994: 275; Laban 1998: 1010). In the preface to the novel, Henning Mankell describes him as a "white body" with a "black soul" (Couto 2001: vii). Indeed, as a journalist when the war of independence broke out in

---

[1] Instead, the degree of deviation corresponds to the speakers' level of education (Enders 1997; Kuder 1997).

1964, he supported the liberation movement *Frente para a Libertação de Moçambique* (FRELIMO) (Mattoso 1994a: 540; Laban 1998: 1009, 1031; Chabal 1994: 281). Ten years later, the war ended with the Lusaka Accord, and Mozambique's return to independence was scheduled for 25th June 1975, the founding date of the FRELIMO (Mattoso 1994b: 66–67). During the subsequent civil war, Couto travelled all over the country and gathered Bantu myths that he incorporates into his literary works (Schönberger 2002: 190; cf. Gebert 1991).

In the following, I show how Couto's drive for a new Mozambican identity is embedded within post-colonial concepts. I point out how wordplays can serve to highlight the hybrid nature of post-colonial spaces and be implemented as a means of resistance. For this purpose, I introduce the post-colonial terms *hybridisation* and *mimicry* and link them to the field of wordplay.

2 Linguistic hybridisation and colonial mimicry

As a post-colonial space, Mozambique is a multilingual country. The most widely spread languages of the Mozambican indigenous people are Ronga, Makhuwa, Changana, Chisena, Tsonga, Malawi, Shona, and Yao. European Portuguese has become the official language of this former colony and allows the speakers of the many indigenous languages to communicate in a language that is common to all of them. As such, the Portuguese language is extremely important. However, the Mozambican variety of Portuguese as it is spoken nowadays reflects some systematic deviations from the European norm. They emerged and became manifest because of the previous high rate of illiteracy among the indigenous population of Mozambique and through the general ludic attitude towards language that the Mozambican people share with other former colonies (cf. Enders 1997; Kuder 1997). These deviations have already been described in detail in lusophone research and primarily involve lexical borrowings from Bantu languages and phonological and grammatical changes (cf. Hundt 1989; Leiste 1991; Perl and Schönberger 1991; Perl 1994; Wodtke 2003; Gonçalves 2005; Mendes 2008).

Borrowing from Bantu languages is common to all Portuguese-speaking countries in Africa (*Países Africanos de Língua Oficial Portuguesa*, PALOP) (Wodtke 2003: 301). The predominant Bantu languages that serve borrowing in Mozambique are Ronga and Changana (Mendes 2008: 242). In his literary work, Couto mainly adopts Bantu words for the domains of flora (*nkakana* 'a specific herb'), fauna (*matumanas* 'caterpillars') and indigenous natural religions (*ntumbuluku* 'the time when the first people came into the world'). The primary reason may be lexical gaps as the borrowed lexemes are naturally, culturally or spiritually bound. With regard to general word formation patterns, Mozambican Portuguese makes frequent use of derivation and composition (Leiste 1991: 42), including the substitution of normative affixes by alternative ones and changes of word class. In the grammatical domain, case and verb government changes, e.g. intransitive verbs are transformed into transitive verbs, and the gerund has been taken over from Brazil (Gonçalves 2005: 191). In relative clauses, the prepositions governed by the respective verbs disappear or are used in the subordinate clause instead of in the main clause, e.g. *a pessoa que viajei com ela* ('the person who I travelled with her') (Gonçalves 2005: 191). A more comprehensive list of differences is provided by Perl (1994: 123–139).

The influence of the Bantu languages on Portuguese suggests that the Mozambican colloquial variety can be seen as a linguistic hybrid. The term *hybrid* has been applied to pidgins and creolized languages because of their fusion of, crudely, the colonizer's vocabulary with the grammar of the colonized (Young 1995: 5). Although the Mozambican variety that I deal with here is not creolized but simply colloquial, it still complies with the defining criteria of hybrids which represent *crosses* between (two) different languages (Young 1995: 8, own emphasis). Bakhtin (1981: 358) defines the term *hybridisation* as "a mixture of two social languages within the limits of a single utterance, an encounter, within the arena of an utterance, between two different linguistic consciousnesses, separated from one another by an epoch, by social differentiation, or by some other factor" (cf. Young 1995: 20). Accordingly, the Mozambican variety of Portuguese is a hybrid between Portuguese as it is spoken in Portugal and the diverse languages of the Bantu peoples living in Mozambique. In contrast to Bakhtin's definition, it is a mixture of more than two languages (which are reflected in the variety to differing degrees) and of more than two different linguistic consciousnesses which are separated from one another by social, cultural and political differentiation.

From an evolutionary perspective, the Mozambican variety emerged as an *organic* hybrid under the dominance of the Portuguese colonial power: "unintentional, unconscious hybridization is one of the most important modes in the historical life and evolution of all languages" (Bakhtin 1981: 358). The mixture of the respective languages aimed at fusion, not at divergence, but at the same time it has the potential to express different world views such as those connected to the source languages (Bakhtin 1981: 360).

Organic hybrids differ from intentional hybrids in their unconscious application. *Intentional* hybrids "enable a contestatory activity, a politicized setting of cultural differences against each other dialogically" (Young 1995: 20). They have been interpreted by Bhabha (1991: 57–58) as "an active moment of challenge and resistance to a dominant cultural power" (Young 1995: 21). The colonizer's language was the language of authority, and authority aims to be single-voiced by definition (Young 1995: 22). However, the linguistic traces of the indigenous people within the hybrid turn the variety into a double-voiced medium by "enter[ing] upon the dominant discourse and estrang[ing] the basis of its authority" (Bhabha 2003: 114). When speaking the emerging variety, the colonizers adapted to the colonized just as the colonized adapted to the colonizers. Thus, the fusion of different languages can serve to unmask both the colonized and the colonizers (Young 1995: 22–23). Each party concedes to the other party to some extent. The linguistic traces of the indigenous, however, undermine the colonizers' authority because the traces are proof of the incompleteness of their (linguistic) power over the new territories (cf. Bakhtin 1981: 344).

Couto functionalizes the deviations from the norm that colloquial Mozambican Portuguese reveals in his works. Thereby, the variety becomes an intentional hybrid within his literary work. He emphasizes the position of the formerly colonized people and strengthens their independence from the former mother country: "The display of hybridity – its peculiar 'replication' – terrorizes authority with the ruse of recognition, its mimicry, its mockery" (Bhabha 2003: 115).

Mimicry is the result of hybridity and refers to the simultaneous appropriation of features of the colonizers by the colonized and their resistance to the colonial authority with the consequence that neither their appropriation nor their resistance is complete but yields a mixture of the two (Bhabha 2003: 120): "colonial mimicry is the desire for a reformed, recognizable Other, *as a subject of a difference that is almost the same, but not quite*" (Bhabha 2003: 86, original emphasis). In Lacan's words, the effect of mimicry is not "harmonizing with the background but, against a mottled background, of becoming mottled" (1977: 99). This mottled nature does not represent the colonized in part but as a whole: the mottled, mixed reality becomes their separate identity (Bhabha 2003: 89). This concept is reversed in Couto's literary language: it is not the colonizer's input that is imitated but the input of the colonized. Couto aims "to play in Portuguese, the language [...] that makes us Mozambicans more Mozambique [sic!]" (Cunha and Cintra 2001: VII, translation into English GS). That is, he does not adopt a form of linguistic mimicry but rather a kind of linguistic *self*-mimicry when he opts for the hybrid and functionalizes its indigenous features rather than choosing the country's official and normative language. In this vein, post-colonial mimicry can possibly be understood as the desire for a recognizable Self, one that promotes the integration of indigenous characteristics into the emerged Other.

On a more global level, this linguistic self-mimicry is a form used to build "a new hybrid identity that reflect[s] [its peoples'] new existence as a new nation state" (Anchimbe 2007: 9). The position of the ex-colonized people experiences strengthening in this new hybrid identity through the linguistic means that Couto applies in his works. In the following, I show that wordplay can function as self-mimicry and that it is one of Couto's means of highlighting the hybridity of colloquial Mozambican Portuguese.

3 Wordplay in Couto's work

The category of wordplay can be subcategorized into the three main groups of wordplay in a narrow sense, wordplay in a broader sense, and wordplay in the broadest sense. These subcategories may undergo further differentiations on the basis of the techniques that are applied to generate a particular wordplay. After defining wordplay from a static point of view and as a dynamic approach, I provide examples of wordplays in the narrow sense and in the broader sense from Couto's ([1996] 2003) novel *A varanda do frangipani* ('Under the frangipani') and describe their relation to the post-colonial concepts mentioned above.

3.1 Wordplay from a static and a dynamic point of view

In a narrow sense, wordplay is the juxtaposition, manipulation, or combination of linguistic items that are identical or very similar in form but different in meaning (Winter-Froemel 2009: 1429; Winter-Froemel 2016: 23; Thaler 2016: 49). The defining criteria for wordplay in general involve its producer (or receiver) being aware of the juxtaposition that he or she actualizes, and that the wordplay is actualized in order to create a humorous effect.[2] The playful character of wordplays is primary and is achieved by introducing an unexpected meaning into the communicative act (Winter-Froemel 2009: 1429). Secondary functions of wordplay involve, among many other potential functions, displaying one's linguistic competence and inviting metalinguistic reflection (cf. Thaler 2016: 51–52). The playfulness of wordplays, especially blends, may be increased through

---

[2] Whether serious wordplay exists, is open to debate (Winter-Froemel 2016: 14).

- formal complexity: the overlapping of segments, e.g. overlapping at the inner edges (medial overlapping) or the absorption of one source word (contour blend),
- structural transgression: the violation of structural well-formedness rules, e.g. combining lexical categories that are usually illicit in compounding or violating linear ordering rules,
- graphic play on words: the phonetic overlap of the target word with one source word by means of the alternation of capital and lower-case letters, the use of parentheses or symbols,
- semantic play on words: the substitution of one meaningful segment by its antonym,
- and functional ludicity: the presence of the primary function of ludicity and the consequent absence or weakness of the opposing functions of naming and condensing information.
(Renner 2015: 124–130)

A wordplay may be compressed into one element so that the two or more linguistic items superpose each other. In this case, Hausmann (1974) speaks of vertical wordplays (or wordplays *in absentia*). If all the linguistic elements that make up the wordplay appear in the communicative act, the dimension is horizontal (or *in praesentia*). These two dimensions are considered to be major subcategories of wordplay in a narrow sense (Winter-Froemel 2016: 38). They are intertwined with homonymy (1) and polysemy (2) which reveal identical forms and distinct meanings.

(1) G. *Kater* 'tomcat' / 'hangover'

(2) E. *green* 'fresh' / 'young and inexperienced'

Homonymy denotes the phenomenon whereby two or more lexical items share orthography and / or phonology, but have distinct meanings (Blank 2001: 103–117). A polysemous item is a lexical item that has two or more distinct but related meanings. For example, the relation may stem from a metaphorical extension as in (2). As homonyms and polysemous items are identical in (at least one) form, they are likely to be frequently actualized as wordplays *in absentia*. In contrast, paronymy (3) which represents another phenomenon of wordplay in the narrow sense and is based on formal similarity, is more likely to occur in horizontal wordplays. In example (3), paronymy plays on the phonetic similarity between *bottle in front of me* and *frontal lobotomy*.

(3) E. *I'd rather have a full bottle in front of me than a full frontal lobotomy.* (Chiaro 1992: 19, cited from Thaler 2016: 56)

The techniques that serve to create wordplay are usually extra-grammatical. To a much lesser extent, grammatical techniques may, however, also be employed (Sablayrolles 2015: 198–200, 204–205; and Sablayrolles in The Dynamics of Wordplay 7). The techniques involve the manipulation of letters, sounds, syllables, morphemes, and lexemes. One may manipulate the order in which letters, sounds, or syllables are presented, two or more morphemes (4) or lexemes may be combined via general word formation patterns such as derivation (5) and composition (6), sometimes involving clipping and/or overlapping as in portmanteau words (7) (Thaler 2016: 57–58; Renner 2015: 119). On the lexical level, the phenomena comprise play on semantic opposition (8) and phraseological elements (9) (cf. Jaki 2015; Thaler 2016). The level on which particular wordplays operate can serve to categorize the phenomena (Lecolle 2016: 63–68).

(4) E. *(Flirtation is)*
All attention
But no intention
(Alexander 1997: 35, cited from Thaler 2016: 58)

(5) F. *Avec Carrefour, je positive.* 'With Carrefour, I'm positive' (Advertising slogan of the French supermarket chain Carrefour, 2003, cited from Thaler 2016: 58)

(6) G. *Drahtesel* 'wire donkey' for bicycle (cf. Duden, cited from Winter-Froemel 2016: 26)

(7) E. *Spork* 'utensil that can be used both as a spoon and a fork' (Renner 2015: 124)

(8) F. *Les présents du passé.* 'Presents from the past'
(poster in an antique shop, cited from Lecolle 2016: 68)

(9) L./E. *Cogito ergo boum.* (Sontag 1969, cited from Winter-Froemel 2009: 1431)

Example (4) plays on the words attention and intention and juxtaposes the morphemes *at* and *in*. In example (5), the adjective *positif* ('positive') is transformed into the verb *positiver*. Example (6) represents a compound of the two German words *Draht* ('wire') and *Esel* ('donkey') and denotes a bicycle. This compound does not involve clipping or overlapping, unlike the portmanteau in (7): the two source words *spoon* and *fork* overlap at the inner edge and form the name of a utensil that has a spoon and a fork at either end. Example (8) opposes the meanings of *présent* ('presence'/'present') and *passé* ('past'), and in example (9), Descartes' famous phrase *Cogito ergo sum* is played with by substituting the homoephonic segments of *sum* and *boum* in order to refer to self-destructive behaviour.

As long as the techniques lead to the manipulation of two or more meanings and of two or more forms, we are dealing with wordplay in the narrow sense. The same techniques, however, may also serve to produce wordplays in the broader sense. These are defined as the juxtaposition, manipulation, or combination of formally identical or very similar linguistic items with the difference that a manipulation of meaning is not essential (Winter-Froemel 2016: 37). Wordplay in a broader sense involves palindromes (10) and lipograms, for example. A palindrome reads the same backward as forward and so juxtaposes the letters that are involved in the sentence. The meaning remains the same so that there is no manipulation on the semantic level.

(10) E. *Was it a car or a cat I saw?* (English palindrome)

Wordplay in the broadest sense refers to variations of linguistic items in general, rendering the requirements of formal similarity and semantic juxtaposition unnecessary (Thaler 2016: 50). Phenomena that belong to this category are pangrams (11) and play on punctuation, among other things. Pangrams are sentences that use each letter of the alphabet at least once.

(11) E. The quick brown fox jumps over the lazy dog. (Thaler 2016: 50)

The question of where to draw the line between wordplay and non-wordplay is crucial and has been discussed thoroughly (Knospe 2016: 82). The classification of a particular phenomenon into one specific wordplay category or as non-wordplay may depend on the perspective from which a particular instance of wordplay is analyzed. The difference between ludic deformations and ludic innovations helps understand where wordplay is considered to end. Ludic deformations are wordplays in the broader sense: a sublexical element is substituted for another sublexical element with the same or a very similar function (Winter-Froemel 2016: 38–39). The neologism which evolves reveals a (near-to-)equivalent meaning and juxtaposes the new and the original form with the objective of drawing attention to the arbitrariness of language. In contrast, ludic innovations are "based on establishing new semantic/conceptual relations" (Winter-Froemel 2016: 39). In other words, the evolving neologism does not juxtapose two meanings, but creates a new one; and the linguistic items that are involved in its creation may be combined, but they are not juxtaposed. Another reason why ludic innovations are not wordplays is that "the strength of the ludic effect seems generally weaker or more unstable for forms which designate new concepts than for forms which introduce a (near-)synonym for a conventional expression" (Winter-Froemel 2016: 26). The reason is that the naming function is primary in innovations but insignificant in deformations because the semantic or conceptual relation that deformations denote is already named by the source word (cf. Renner 2015: 129–130). Additionally, the opposing ludic function is primary in deformations because there is no necessity to create them, and playfulness is guaranteed by the receiver's confrontation with an expected meaning in the disguise of an unexpected form. Ludic deformations play an important role in Couto's imitations of colloquial Mozambican Portuguese (see section 3.2).

The three categories of wordplay in the narrow sense, wordplay in the broader sense, and wordplay in the broadest sense are often perceived as discrete (Thaler 2016: 50). In contrast, Delabastita (2011: 141, see also the contribution by Delabastita, this volume) proposes a gradual approach to wordplay which he defines as "the various discursive phenomena in which certain features inherent in the structure of the language(s) used are mobilized to produce a communicatively significant, (near-) simultaneous confrontation of at least two linguistic units with more or less dissimilar meanings and more or less similar forms". This view allows us to see wordplay as a radial category with prototypical instances situated in the center and peripheral cases at its fuzzy boundaries (cf. Brugman 1983; Lakoff 1987; Brugman and Lakoff 1988). The defining features comprise (a) two or more linguistic structures, degrees of (b) their formal similarity and (c) their semantic dissimilarity, and (d) the communicative significance of the emerging linguistic unit (cf. Delabastita 1996: 128). This dynamic view relates to the category of wordplays in the narrow sense. Correspondingly, we may define the category of wordplay in the broader sense as the various discursive phenomena in which certain features inherent in the structure of the language(s) used are mobilized to produce a communicatively significant, (near-) simultaneous confrontation of at least two linguistic units with more or less similar forms. And wordplays in the broadest sense comprise those discursive phenomena which manipulate certain features inherent in the structure of the language(s) in order to produce a communicatively significant, (near-) simultaneous confrontation of at least two linguistic units. These distinct categories of wordplay overlap at their fuzzy boundaries, i.e. where the meanings of two linguistic structures are (almost) identical (wordplays in the broader sense) and where their forms are (almost) completely dissimilar (wordplays in the broadest sense). Adopting a dynamic view on wordplay categories is a natural consequence of the possibility of increasing their playfulness via formal complexity, structural transgression, graphic and semantic play on words, and functional ludicity because they show that the same techniques and the same phenomena may generate and represent more or less prototypical instances of wordplay.

The requirement of a minimum of two linguistic structures should not be understood in terms of wordplays *in praesentia* – the case of idiom transformations which are only interpretable when the transformation is mapped onto the original idiom, shows that only one of the manipulated forms needs to be present given that the other form is part of the common ground (Sablayrolles 2015: 196–197).

A rather recent development in the analysis of wordplay is the inclusion of the receiver's position (*discursive phenomenon*) (cf. Delabastita 1996). A wordplay may be actualized by a receiver who detects a wordplay potential in the producer's contribution which the latter did not notice or intend to convey (cf. also Gibbs, this volume; for further examples, see also the contribution by Sablayrolles in The Dynamics of Wordplay 7). Accordingly, Nemo (2016) stresses that one generating characteristic of wordplay is the moment in which the first observed meaning is cancelled in favor of the detection of a second linguistic influence. These points meet the demands of a recent extension of the analytic tools to the communicative setting: wordplay occurs in any kind of communication (e.g. literature) and between any kind of producer and receiver (e.g. writer and reader) to varying degrees of directedness (e.g. addressees and bystanders), involvement and comprehension (e.g. in-group vs. out-group humor) (cf. Winter-Froemel 2016: 12–14). It is possible to differentiate even more, e.g. between the intradiegetic and the extradiegetic level in literary pieces (cf. Oster 2015; Véron 2015). The communicative significance of a wordplay is the sum of the particular communicative context, situation, and interaction, its historicity, primary function and potential secondary functions. In the case of Mia Couto's works, the wordplays are produced and received on the level of writer and readership. The characters in his works do not react to the instances; it seems as if the literary language does not appear unusual to the characters.

3.2 Wordplay in Couto's novel *A varanda do frangipani* ('Under the frangipani')

In the novel *A varanda do frangipani* ('Under the frangipani'), written by Mia Couto ([1996] 2003) and translated into English by David Brookshaw (Couto 2001), an inspector is called to a remote retirement home to investigate a murder. During the investigation, he immerses himself in the mythical and spiritual stories of the retired people.

The literary language involves wordplays in the narrow sense and in the broad sense. Wordplay in the narrow sense comprises lexical blends and idiom transformations. Wordplay in the broad sense is represented by ludic deformations. All the following examples are in Portuguese and taken from Cavacas' (1999) analysis of Couto's literary language. The translations into English are taken from the official English translation *Under the frangipani* by David Brookshaw (see Couto 2001). The English translation often focuses on the semantic content; Couto's ludic attitude and the imitation of colloquialism are lost in the translations.[3]

3.2.1 Lexical blends and portmanteau words

Lexical blends and portmanteau words are considered wordplays in the narrow sense. A lexical blend is the result of "coalescing several words into one after an act of clipping [...], of overlapping [...], or of both clipping and overlapping" (Renner 2015: 121). A portmanteau word evolves from an act of lexical blending that involves overlapping of a shared homophonic segment (Sablayrolles 2015: 191). Sometimes, clipping is taken as a defining feature for portmanteaus as well (cf. Fromkin, Rodman, and Hyams 2008: 354). The definitions for both lexical blends and portmanteau words vary so that they sometimes denote the same phenomenon, and sometimes portmanteaus are considered a subtype of lexical blends. The lexical blends in the novel at hand share homophonic or homoephonic segments, or are created on the basis of semantic opposition.

Blends that share a homophonic segment involve phonetically, and frequently also graphemically, identical elements and are associated with the different meanings of the original lexemes (cf. Thaler 2016: 52). Example (12) plays on the homophony of the syllable *palha* and amalgates the meanings of *atrapalhado* ('confused') and *palhaço* ('clown'). In combination, the two words underline how short-changed the protagonist feels. The portmanteau visualizes his mixed reaction. Its playfulness is increased by formal complexity (contour blend), structural transgression (violation of linear ordering rules) and functional ludicity.

(12) *Quando percebi, até fiquei atrapalhaço.* (14)
 'When I realized what was happening, I didn't know what to do.' (4)
 > *atrapalhado* + *palhaço* 'confused' + 'clown'

---

[3] The pages where the examples can be found in the original novel and the translation respectively are given in brackets.

(13) *O polícia estava todo desalinhavado.* (144)
 'The policeman was losing his coordination.' (143)
 > *desalinho* + *alinhavado* 'misalignment' + 'tacked'

(14) *Ergueu-se sobre as patas traseiras, nesse jeito de gente que tremexia comigo.* (15)
 'It drew itself up on its hind legs, like a real person trying to rouse my interest.' (6)
 > *tremer* + *mexer* 'shiver' + 'shake'

In example (13), the homophonic element *alinh* is shared between *desalinho* ('misalignment') and *alinhavado* ('tacked'). The playfulness is increased by formal complexity (medial overlapping) and functional ludicity. The verbs *tremer* ('shiver') and *mexer* ('shake') in example (14) share the segment *me*. The playfulness of this blend is increased by medial overlapping, structural transgression (verb-verb combination), and functional ludicity. The three portmanteau words share a homophonic segment that is graphemically identical and which enables overlapping. All the examples furthermore involve a minimal degree of clipping. The meanings of the source words are related by association in (12) and (14) and opposite in (13).

The portmanteau words invite metalinguistic reflection on the arbitrariness of language through the combination of items that are in part identical but are at the same time associated with more or less different meanings. The frequent use of such amalgamation in Couto's novel highlights his ludic attitude towards language. Furthermore, the fusion of two individual items into a single new form resembles the hybridized status of post-colonial spaces so that these blends can be considered metaphors for Mozambique's hybridity. As hybrids, they enable a dialogue between the meanings of the respective forms and primarily stress the arbitrariness of the colonizers' language. As replications of hybridity, they underline the linguistic independence from the former mother country. These functions are supplemented by a further layer in the following examples.

Sometimes, lexical blends are created on the basis of a homoephonic segment, i.e. a segment that is pronounced in a similar but not identical way (cf. Thaler 2016: 53). In example (15), the play is based on the phonetic similarity of the syllables *cum* and *con* and blends the prefix *circum* ('circum') with the lexeme *consequente* ('consequent') by fusing the two similar syllables into the new syllable *cun*. The evolving meaning stresses the roundness of a woman's body as a consequence of her pregnancy. Its playfulness is increased by medial overlapping and the ludic function.

(15) *Também o ventre de Ernestina inchou, circunsequente.* (136)
 'Ernestina's belly also began to swell and curve.' (133)
 > *circum* + *consequente* 'circum' + 'consequent'

(16) *Fiquei surpreso, inesparado: o sacana nos deixava, assim?* (52)
　　'I was surprised, taken aback: the scoundrel was leaving us just like that.' (47)
　　> *inesperado* + *parado* 'surprised' / 'ecstatic' + 'paralyzed'

(17) *Vasto, surumático, aguardava o primeiro helicóptero.* (136–137)
　　'Vastsome gloomily waited for the first available helicopter.' (133)
　　> *suruma* + *sorumbático* 'melancholy' + 'gloomy'

Example (16) plays on the similar pronunciation of the syllables *per* and *par*. It amalgamates the adjectives *inesperado* ('surprised') and *parado* ('paralyzed'). In example (17), the source words *suruma* ('melancholy') and *sorumbático* ('gloomy') are fused on the basis of the homoephony of *suruma* and *sorumbá*. The playfulness of all the examples is increased by – apart from the slight phonetic dissimilarity – retaining the complete source words (cf. Renner 2015: 129). The latter two examples represent contour blends.

As before, these blends prompt reflection on the arbitrariness of language and underline the writer's linguistic ludicity. Moreover, it is not just the two source words that mirror the hybrid character of Mozambique: the homoephonic segments themselves also do so in their hybridized form. That is, blends based on homoephonic segments are hybrids on both a lexical and a sublexical level, and as such are double-layer hybrids. Thereby, the homoephonic segments yield a mixture on the sublexical level, the homoephonically based amalgam, which resembles the mottled background of mimicry: it is almost the same but not quite. In this way, the mottled segment can be regarded as a metaphor for the new hybrid identity of the formerly colonized people.

Lexical blending may also proceed on the basis of semantic opposition, also referred to as lexical sets (cf. Thaler 2016: 57). In example (18), the relation between the underlying adjective *forte* ('strong') and *fraco* ('weak') is antonymic, which increases its playfulness (semantic play on words). Its ludic character is further supported by the absence of a naming function and its formal complexity (contour blend). Wordplays based on semantic opposition are often wordplays *in praesentia* while their relation remains *in absentia* (Lecolle 2016: 67–68).

(18) *Visto do alto, a fortaleza é, antes, uma fraqueleza.* (22)
　　'Seen from up here, the fort is anything but a stronghold.' (14)
　　> *fraqueza* + *fortaleza* 'weakness' + 'fortress'

Again, as a consequence of the antonymic relation, this blend invites metalinguistic reflection and underlines the writer's linguistic ludicity. In contrast to the blends above, it does not represent any post-colonial concept.

3.2.2 Idiom transformations

Phraseological elements can be played on by contrasting a segment of the original phrase with a phonetically or semantically similar or opposed one (Winter-Froemel 2009: 1431; Thaler 2016: 56). Mainly, Couto transforms idioms by transposing single elements and by substituting homoephonic segments. In example (19), the element *salteado* ('attacked', 'browsing') is substituted by the phonetically similar unit *sal tirado* ('salt taken'). The evolving literal meaning changes from 'to know by heart and attacked / browsing' to 'to know by heart and taken salt'. The English translator opts for a combination of the idioms 'to know by heart' and 'to know back to front'.

(19) *Palavra de pangolim, já eu há muito a sabia de cor e sal tirado.* (124)
 'As for the anteater's argument, I had known it by heart and back to front for a long time.' (121)
 > *saber de cor e salteado* 'to know by heart'

The transformed idiom activates the conventionalized form from common ground. Together, the present unconventional form and the absent conventional form represent two linguistic structures that are juxtaposed *in absentia*. The playfulness of the idiom transformation in (19) is increased by its formal complexity and ludic function as a nonsense contour blend. It points out the arbitrariness of particular idioms through the phonetic similarity between the original, meaningful idiom and its derived, meaningless transformation.

3.2.3 Ludic deformations

As stated above, the Mozambican variety of Portuguese is particularly prone to derivations and compositions (cf. Perl 1994: 128ff). In more detail, prefixion often serves to reverse the meaning of the source word, and suffixation frequently involves the substitution of an original affix by an alternative but semantically (near-to-)identical one.

Mainly, prefixion in Mozambique is resolved with *des-* ('separation', 'opposite')[4], *im/in-* ('negation', 'absence'), *não-* ('negation'), and *auto-* ('self') (Leiste 1991: 42, cf. Cunha and Cintra 2005: 87–89). Couto frequently makes use of the prefixes *des-* ('separation', 'opposite') and *im/in-* ('negation', 'absence').

---

[4] The quotation marks contain the meanings of the Portuguese morphemes since there are no true English equivalents.

In example (20), the glorification that the protagonist achieved during his earthly life is lost because of the way that he was buried after he died: his funeral was inappropriate with respect to his tribe's customs. The verb *glorificar* ('glorify') is prefixed with *des-* ('separation', 'opposite'). In example (21), the noun *cambalhota* ('somersault'), used here as a verb, evokes positive associations that are negated and intensified by the prefix *des-* ('separation', 'opposite'). Example (22) plays on the idiom *sem pestanejar* ('without batting an eyelid'): the prefixation of the verb *pestanejar* ('twinkle') with *im-* (here: 'negation') forms a semantically identical but formally distinct neologism. In all three examples the evolving meaning of the neologism can be calculated from the combination of prefix and lexeme. In this respect, the neologisms would usually not be regarded as word-plays. However, they play on the existence *in absentia* of conventional ways of expressing the same thing, i.e. the simple negation (*não* 'not') of the lexeme that is prefixed, or an alternative paraphrase. The actualization of the conventional form through the unconventional form of expressing the same thing results in the juxtaposition of two linguistic structures. The semantic identity of source and target draws attention to the arbitrariness of language. The absence of the naming function increases their playfulness. In sum, the examples fulfill the requirements of wordplay in the broader sense.

(20) *Se vivi com direiteza, desglorifiquei-me foi no falecimento.* (11)
   'Though I was an upright citizen while alive, my death was inglorious.' (1)
   > *des-* + *glorificar alg/a.c.*
   > prefix ('separation', 'opposite') + 'glorify so/sth.'

(21) *Mas um xipoco que reocupa o seu antigo corpo arrisca perigos muito mortais: tocar ou ser tocado basta para descambalhotar corações e semear fatalidades.* (15)
   'But a spirit that reoccupies its former body risks mortal dangers: when it touches or is touched, it's enough to send hearts thumping backwards and sow fatal consequences.' (5)
   > *des-* + *cambalhota* + *-ar*
   > prefix ('separation', 'opposite') + 'somersault' + verbalisation

(22) *Aguentei, impestanejável.* (53)
   'I put up with it all, without batting an eyelid.' (47)
   > *im-* + *pestanejar* + *-ável*
   > prefix ('negation', 'absence') + 'twinkle' + suffix ('capable of', 'worthy of')

The latter two examples further prove that wordplays can involve several techniques simultaneously such as the change of word class (noun/verb (21), verb/adjective (22)) in addition to prefixion. In the novel, the function of these wordplays is to reflect on the arbitrariness of language and to highlight the writer's linguistic ludicity. Furthermore, these deformations mirror the Mozambicans' ludic attitude towards language and are representative of colloquial Mozambican Portuguese. They embody the hybridity of this language variety and emphasize the writer's choice of the influence of the ex-colonized to the disadvantage of the (single-voiced) language of the ex-colonizers, i.e. they serve to imitate the Self instead of the Other and thus represent a form of linguistic self-mimicry.

Another kind of deformation in Mozambican Portuguese is suffixation which is applied in a ludic way whenever an existing suffix is substituted by an alternative suffix with a similar or identical meaning. Couto uses suffix substitution with nouns and adjectives. Example (23) plays on the meanings of the nominal suffixes *-ice* ('quality', 'possession', 'condition', 'state') and *-aria* ('collective concept') (cf. Cunha and Cintra 2005: 96f). The substitution of the suffix slightly intensifies the noun's meaning, pointing to the totality of the character's crazy actions. Based on the presence of dissimilar meanings, one might argue that example (23) is a peripheral member of the category of wordplay in the narrow sense. Its playfulness, though, is low (functional ludicity).

(23) *Você fala de Nãozinha, suas malucarias.* (70)
 'You talk about Little Miss No and her crankiness.' (64)
 > *maluquice* + *-aria*
 > 'madness' + suffix ('collective concept')

(24) *Colava-se nas minhas costas, eu sentia suas redonduras se colando em mim.* (122)
 'It squeezed against my back, I could feel its roundness nestling up against me.' (119)
 > *redondeza* + *-ura*
 > 'roundness' + suffix ('quality', 'possession', 'condition', 'state')

(25) *Se vivi com direiteza, desglorifiquei-me foi no falecimento.* (11)
 'Though I was an upright citizen while alive, my death was inglorious.' (1)
 > *direitura* + *-eza*
 > 'righteousness' + suffix ('quality', 'possession', 'condition', 'state')

The examples (24) and (25) (which is given above as example (20)) play on the identical semantics of the suffixes *-eza* and *-ura* ('quality', 'possession', 'condition', 'state'; Cunha and Cintra 2005: 97). Interestingly, the substitution of the two suffixes occurs in both directions, i.e. *direitura* ('righteousness') is transformed into *direiteza*, and *redondeza* ('roundness') into *redondura*. Their playfulness is based on the presence of the ludic function only. Still, the substitution invites metalinguistic reflection about arbitrariness. Additionally, example (25) shows that a single utterance or sentence may involve several instances of wordplay simultaneously (see the discussion of example (20) above). Again, these deformations reflect colloquial Mozambican Portuguese and incorporate a kind of linguistic self-mimicry as they imitate the language of the ex-colonized instead of that of the ex-colonizers.

Adjectives may be formed with the suffixes *-oso, -ado, -udo* ('full of'), *-ável* ('capable of'), and *-eiro* ('relating to', 'possession', 'origin'; Cunha and Cintra 2005: 100). Example (26) plays on the noun *escavadeira* ('digger') by utilizing an almost identical adjective that is made up of the verb *escavar* ('dig', 'burrow') and the suffix *-eiro*.[5] The evolved adjective refers to the act of burrowing. The respective nominal phrase as a whole describes a mole.

(26) *Mas não era o bicho escavadeiro.* (13)
 'But it wasn't that burrowing creature.' (4)
 > *escavar* + *-(d)eiro*
 > 'burrow' + suffix ('relating to', 'possession', 'origin')

(27) Veio o poente. Veio a assombrável sombra: a noite. (84)
 'The sun set. The frightful shadow of night fell.' (33)
 > *assombrar* + *-ável* 'astonish' + suffix ('capable of', 'worthy of')

Example (27) plays on the existing adjective *assombroso* ('astonishing'). The target adjective *assombrável* is formed from the source verb *assombrar* ('astonish') and the suffix *-ável* ('capable of', 'worthy of'). The evolved meaning is associated with darkness, shade, suddenness, and even fright. Aside from stressing the arbitrariness of language and the writer's ludicity, the suffixation of adjectives serves to imitate how Portuguese is spoken in contemporary Mozambique and to accentuate both its double-voicedness as a hybrid and, above all, the influence of the Mozambican people.

All the instances of ludic deformations given here represent wordplays *in absentia* and actualize the source word from linguistic common ground. The (almost) identical meanings of source and target word stress the arbitrariness of language and thereby create a comic effect. They represent wordplays in the broader sense because of their very similar meanings and are rather typical members of this category as the juxtaposed forms are also quite similar. Their playfulness is based on the ludic function only, but it is emphasized by the reference to the arbitrariness of language. In the novel, they serve to mimic the linguistic influence of the ex-colonized on contemporary spoken Mozambican Portuguese and thus function as a form of linguistic self-mimicry by highlighting

---

[5] The suffixation requires the consonant *d* between the verb and the suffix because of the Latin participle (Cunha and Cintra 2005: 99).

the Self in contrast to the Other in order to emphasize the country's linguistic independence from its former colonizer.

4 Conclusion

Colloquial Mozambican Portuguese is an organic hybridisation of European Portuguese and Bantu languages. It is characterized by lexical borrowings from the many Bantu languages and grammatical (and phonological) peculiarities that probably have their source in the Bantu languages, as well. The writer Mia Couto functionalizes the specificities of this variety in his literary works and so transforms the hybrid which has grown organically into an intentional hybrid. Hereby, the deformations work as a kind of linguistic self-mimicry: the appropriation does not relate to the Other but to the Self, i.e. the linguistic features of the hybrid which has grown organically are repeated. The hybrid experiences strengthening in relation to other varieties that persist in the post-colonial space. This fosters the linguistic resistance to influences from outside and supports the development of a specifically Mozambican identity.

In Couto's works, the intentional deformations primarily fulfill a ludic function and invite metalinguistic reflection about the arbitrariness of language. They represent wordplays in the broader sense as the receiver maps the deformed target onto its conventional source which makes up part of the linguistic common ground. These forms are fairly similar, but their meanings are almost or completely identical. In addition, Couto uses wordplays in the narrow sense in the form of blends in general, in particular portmanteau words and idiom transformations. Most likely, these are not imitations of colloquial Mozambican Portuguese but part of Couto's literary style. Their playfulness is mainly increased by formal complexity, structural transgression, and their ludic function. Apart from that, we may interpret the presence and nature of blends as a metaphor for the mixed character of the hybrid space in post-colonial Mozambique. Blends are crosses of at least two sources which result in an amalgamated offspring. Their composition reflects the linguistic, social, cultural, and political hybridity of former colonies. Moreover, blends that are based on the amalgamation of homoephonic segments can be interpreted as metaphors for the mottled background of colonial mimicry. In this way, they are representative of the identity of the formerly colonized people and strengthen their position in the post-colonial hybrid space of Mozambique. In sum, Mia Couto supports the development of a new hybrid identity of the Mozambican people through the creation of wordplays in the narrow sense and wordplays in the broader sense alongside the use of Bantu vocabulary and Bantu myths in his works.

Acknowledgement: I would like to thank the participants of the wordplay conference for sharing their expertise, and two anonymous reviewers for their helpful comments on earlier versions of this paper. The topic is partially based on my diploma thesis (Schole 2010).

5 References

Alexander, Richard J. 1997. *Aspects of verbal humour in English*. Tübingen: Narr.
Anchimbe, Eric A. 2007. Introduction. Multilingualism, postcolonialism and linguistic identity: Towards a new vision of postcolonial spaces. In: Eric A. Anchimbe (ed.), *Linguistic identity in postcolonial multilingual spaces*. Newcastle, UK: Cambridge Scholars. 1–22.
Bakhtin, Mikhail M. 1981. *The dialogic imagination: Four essays*. Austin: University of Texas Press.
Bhabha, Homi K. 1991. The postcolonial critic. *Arena* 96. 47–63.
Bhabha, Homi K. 2003. *The location of culture*. London: Routledge.
Blank, Andreas. 2001. *Einführung in die lexikalische Semantik für Romanisten*. Tübingen: Niemeyer.
Brugman, Claudia M. 1983. *Story of Over*. Indiana: Indiana University Linguistics Club.
Brugman, Claudia M. & George Lakoff. 1988. Cognitive topology and lexical networks. In Steven L. Small, Garrison W. Cottrell & Michael K. Tanenhaus (eds.), *Lexical ambiguity resolution: Perspectives from psycholinguistics, neuropsychology, and artificial intelligence*, 477–508. San Mateo, CA: Morgan Kaufman.
Cavacas, Fernanda. 1999. *Mia Couto: Brincriação vocabular*. Lisbon: Mar Além.
Chabal, Patrick. 1994. *Vozes moçambicanas: Literatura e nacionalidade*. Lisbon: Vega.
Chiaro, Delia. 1992. *The language of jokes: Analysing verbal play*. London & New York: Routledge.
Couto, Mia. [1996] 2003. *A varanda do frangipani*. Lisbon: Caminho.
Couto, Mia. 2001. *Under the frangipani*. English translation by David Brookshaw. London: Serpent's Tail.
Cunha, Celso & Luís F. Lindley Cintra. 2005. *Nova gramática do português contemporâneo*. Lisbon: João Sá da Costa.
Delabastita, Dirk. 1996. Introduction. In Dirk Delabastita (ed.), *Wordplay and translation*. Manchester, UK: St. Jerome Pub, 127–139.
Delabastita, Dirk. 2011. Wholes and holes in the study of Shakespeare's wordplay. In Jonathan Culpeper & Mireille Ravassat (eds.), *Stylistics and Shakespeare's language: Transdisciplinary approaches*, 139–164. London: Continuum.
Enders, Armelle. 1997. *História da África lusófona*. Mem Martins: Inquérito.
Fromkin, Victoria, Robert Rodman & Nina M. Hyams. 2008. *An introduction to language*. Boston, MA: Wadsworth / Cengage Learning.

Gebert, Heike. 1991. Aspekte dramatischer Literatur aus den ‚Países Africanos de Língua Oficial Portuguesa' (PALOP). In Luciano Caetano da Rosa & Axel Schönberger (eds.), *Studien zur lusographen Literatur in Afrika: Akten des 1. Gemeinsamen Kolloquiums der Deutschsprachigen Lusitanistik und Katalanistik (Berlin, 20.–23. September 1990). Lusitanistischer Teil*. Vol. 5, 9–19. Frankfurt a. M.: TFM, DEE.
Gonçalves, Perpétua. 2005. O português de Moçambique: problemas e limites da padronização de uma variedade não-nativa. In Carsten Sinner (ed.), *Norm und Normkonflikte in der Romania*, 184–196. München: Gärtig.
Hausmann, Franz Josef. 1974. *Studien zu einer Linguistik des Wortspiels. Das Wortspiel im ‹Canard enchaîné›*. Tübingen: Niemeyer.
Hundt, Christine. 1989. Vergleichende Untersuchungen zur Phraseologie des europäischen und moçambikanischen Portugiesisch. In Matthias Perl (ed.), *Beiträge zur Afrolusitanistik und Kreolistik*, 125–134. Bochum: Brockmeyer.
Jaki, Sylvia. 2015. Détournement phraséologique et jeu de mots: le cas des substitutions lexicales dans la presse écrite. In Esme Winter-Froemel & Angelika Zirker (eds.), *Enjeux du jeu de mots: Perspectives linguistiques et littéraires* (The Dynamics of Wordplay 2), 245–272. Berlin & Boston: De Gruyter.
Knospe, Sebastian. 2016. Discursive dimensions of wordplay. In Sebastian Knospe, Alexander Onysko & Maik Goth (eds.), *Crossing Languages to Play with Words: Multidisciplinary Perspectives* (The Dynamics of Wordplay 3), 79–94. Berlin & Boston: De Gruyter.
Kuder, Manfred. 1997. *Die Gemeinschaft der Staaten Portugiesischer Sprache: Ziele, Strukturen und die sieben Mitgliedsländer*. Bonn: DASP-Institut für Brasilien – Afrika – Portugal.
Laban, Michel. 1998. *Moçambique – Encontro com escritores*. Porto: Fundação Eng. António de Almeida.
Lacan, Jacques. 1977. *The four fundamental concepts of psycho-analysis*. London: The Hogarth Press.
Lakoff, George. 1987. *Women, fire and dangerous things: What categories reveal about the mind*. Chicago: University of Chicago Press.
Lecolle, Michelle. 2016. Some specific insights into wordplay form: sublexical vs. lexical level. In Sebastian Knospe, Alexander Onysko & Maik Goth (eds.), *Crossing Languages to Play with Words: Multidisciplinary Perspectives* (The Dynamics of Wordplay 3), 63–70. Berlin & Boston: De Gruyter.
Leiste, Doris. 1991. Aspekte der lexikalischen Entwicklung des Portugiesischen in Mosambik. In Matthias Perl & Axel Schönberger (eds.), *Studien zum Portugiesischen in Afrika und Asien: Akten des 1. Gemeinsamen Kolloquiums der Deutschsprachigen Lusitanistik und Katalanistik (Berlin, 20.–23. September 1990). Lusitanistischer Teil*. Vol. 6, 39–48. Frankfurt a. M.: TFM, DEE.
Mattoso, José (Ed.). 1994a. *História de Portugal*. Vol. VII: *O Estado Novo 1926–1974*. Lisbon: Estampa.
Mattoso, José (Ed.). 1994b. *História de Portugal*. Vol. VIII: *Portugal em transe 1974–1985*. Lisbon: Estampa.
Matusse, Gilberto. 1998. *A construção da imagem de moçambicanidade em José Craveirinha, Mia Couto e Ungulani Ba Ka Khosa*. Maputo: Universidade Eduardo Mondlane.
Mendes, Marília. 2008. Português de Moçambique na Literatura: Formas de Resistência Cultural. In Hans-Jörg Döhla, Raquel Montero Muñóz & Francisco Báez de Aguilar González (eds.), *Lenguas en diálogo: El iberorromance y su diversidad lingüística y literaria. Ensayos en homenaje a Georg Bossong*, 239–255. Madrid: Iberoamericana.

Nemo, François. 2016. *Wordplay, plurisemy, wit: Overturning the interpretation of what is said*. Talk at the International Conference "The dynamics of wordplay – Interdisciplinary Perspectives". Trier University, 29.09.–01.10.2016.

Oster, Patricia. 2015. "Ne nous tutoyons plus, je t'en prie". Jeux de mots et enjeu du langage dans le théâtre de Marivaux. In Esme Winter-Froemel & Angelika Zirker (eds.), *Enjeux du jeu de mots: Perspectives linguistiques et littéraires* (The Dynamics of Wordplay 2), 81–92. Berlin & Boston: De Gruyter.

Perl, Matthias & Axel Schönberger (eds.). 1991. *Studien zum Portugiesischen in Afrika und Asien: Akten des 1. Gemeinsamen Kolloquiums der Deutschsprachigen Lusitanistik und Katalanistik (Berlin, 20.–23. September 1990). Lusitanistischer Teil*. Vol. 6. Frankfurt a. M.: TFM, DEE.

Perl, Matthias. 1994. *Portugiesisch und Crioulo in Afrika: Geschichte – Grammatik – Lexik – Sprachentwicklung*. Bochum: Brockmeyer.

Renner, Vincent. 2015. Lexical Blending as Wordplay. In Angelika Zirker & Esme Winter-Froemel (eds.), *Wordplay and Metalinguistic / Metadiscursive Reflection: Authors, Contexts, Techniques, and Meta-Reflection* (The Dynamics of Wordplay 1), 119–133. Berlin & Boston: De Gruyter.

Sablayrolles, Jean-François. 2015. Néologismes ludiques: études morphologique et énonciativo-pragmatique. In Esme Winter-Froemel & Angelika Zirker (eds.), *Enjeux du jeu de mots: Perspectives linguistiques et littéraires* (The Dynamics of Wordplay 2), 189–216. Berlin & Boston: De Gruyter.

Sablayrolles, Jean-François. 2018. Des innovations lexicales ludiques dans des situations d'énonciation marginales ou spécifiques. In Esme Winter-Froemel & Alex Demeulenaere (eds.), *Jeux de mots, textes et contextes* (The Dynamics of Wordplay 7), 77–94. Berlin & Boston: De Gruyter.

Schönberger, Gerhard. 2002. *Mosambikanische Literatur portugiesischer Sprache: Entstehung und Probleme einer Nationalliteratur*. Frankfurt a. M.: DEE.

Sontag, Susan. 1969. *Styles of radical will*. London: Secker & Warburg.

Thaler, Verena. 2016. Varieties of wordplay. In Sebastian Knospe, Alexander Onysko & Maik Goth (eds.), *Crossing Languages to Play with Words: Multidisciplinary Perspectives* (The Dynamics of Wordplay 3), 47–62. Berlin & Boston: De Gruyter.

Véron, Laélia. 2015. Jeu de mots et double communication dans l'œuvre littéraire: l'exemple de la *Comédie humaine* de Balzac. In Esme Winter-Froemel & Angelika Zirker (eds.), *Enjeux du jeu de mots: Perspectives linguistiques et littéraires* (The Dynamics of Wordplay 2), 93–111. Berlin & Boston: De Gruyter

Winter-Froemel, Esme. 2009. Wortspiel. In Gert Ueding (ed.), *Historisches Wörterbuch der Rhetorik*, Vol. 9, 1429–1443. Tübingen: Niemeyer.

Winter-Froemel, Esme. 2016. Approaching wordplay. In Sebastian Knospe, Alexander Onysko & Maik Goth (eds.), *Crossing Languages to Play with Words: Multidisciplinary Perspectives* (The Dynamics of Wordplay 3), 11–46. Berlin & Boston: De Gruyter.

Wodtke, Angela. 2003. Varianten des mosambikanischen Portugiesisch in der postkolonialen Literatur: Suleiman Cassamo und Ungulani Ba Ka Khosa. In Dietrich Briesemeister & Axel Schönberger (eds.), *Imperium Minervae: Studien zur brasilianischen, iberischen und mosambikanischen Literatur*, 297–314. Frankfurt. a. M.: DEE.

Young, Robert J. C. 1995. *Colonial desire: Hybridity in theory, culture and race*. New York: Routledge.

Monika Schmitz-Emans
Examples and poetics of wordplay in Han Shaogong's language-reflective novel *A Dictionary of Maqiao*

Abstract: As a literary format, the dictionary of words and verbal phrases provides an important reflection model that points to an evidently self-referential interest on the part of literary authors in the elements and uses of language. With his lexicographic novel *A Dictionary of Maqiao* (originally Chinese 1996), the Chinese author Han Shaogong continues a Western literary tradition of writing alphabetically structured text sequences which are presented as a dictionary or lexicon. Wordplay here becomes an important medium of reflection, concerned with language and culture, and in this context even an indirectly used device for political criticism.

Keywords: alphabet, Chinese history, Cultural Revolution, dictionary, language reflection, lexicographic novel, lexicon, local dialect, names, satire, vocabulary

1 Literary dictionaries

For centuries the text form of the dictionary has been used as a model for literary writing (cf. Corbin and Guillerm, eds., 1995: 345–355). One might already regard artificial word lists, as compiled by Rabelais and by mannerist writers, as a kind of dictionary, a form which is here placed in a broader context. Literary dictionaries in a stricter sense emerge in the eighteenth century, when language, words and the usage of words become the focus of criticism. Since the Age of Enlightenment, language reflective writers and satirical critics of culture have adapted the dictionary form for literary projects. The German satirist Gottlieb Wilhelm Rabener ([1746] 1751) conceived of a satirical German dictionary (*Deutsches Wörterbuch*) whose entries would be dedicated to selected words, and he wrote a few entries as model texts.[1] In these entries, Rabener does not actually explain the conventional meanings of the selected terms, but criticises forms of human behaviour linked to the (mostly euphemistic) misuse of words – as for instance when they are applied by hypocrites in order to conceal their vanity and selfish

---

[1] Cf. Jung (1974: 37–46).

interests. Thus, the entries in the dictionary cast light on strategies of social behaviour and their verbal expression. Publishing only a few articles himself, Rabener suggested that this project should be extended and become a collective enterprise. Georg Christoph Lichtenberg took up this idea and wrote a number of new articles for "Rabeners Wörterbuch", following, however, different satirical writing principles (Schmitz-Emans 1993: 141–167).

Rabener's, Lichtenberg's, and other satirical "dictionaries" focus on the use of words as a process of labelling ideas, objects, attitudes, modes of behaviour, characters etc. According to the implications of their model of language use, these labels can either be used 'appropriately' or 'inappropriately' – i.e. either in a way that transparently provides information about the respective signifieds (ideas, objects, attitudes, modes of behaviour, characters etc.) – or otherwise in a way that renders the signifieds opaque or misinterprets them. The language concept implied here is closely linked to the ideal of clarity, precision and transparency in speaking and writing, but also to the ethical requirement of truthfulness, honesty and sincerity. Berkeley's and Locke's critical reflections on the misuse of words probably paved the way for Enlightenment satirical dictionaries. As they suggest, there may be two possible reasons for the misuse of words that obscures facts rather than conveying reliable information: on the one hand the speakers' incompetence, their stupidity or one-sidedness, on the other hand their conscious and intentional abuse of words in order to conceal the truth or themselves. Hypocrisy, pretence, bluff, allusion and misleading euphemisms form a complex of dominant issues in satirical literary dictionaries.

In spite of their serious thematic interest, the satirical dictionaries of rationalist writers are playful pieces of literature. According to their basic model of labelling words or expressions and labelled items – that is, of an arbitrary relation between signs and signifieds – their play is mainly concerned with these relations: it is a play with 'false' or misleadingly used labels – and it usually suggests at the same time that there are rules for the language game that ensure 'correct' and 'appropriate' ways of labelling. In this context, correct and appropriate usually means that the labelling process both documents and catalyses knowledge and insight. In a way, the rule for the game newly established by the satirical dictionary writer superimposes the conventional rules of language: it is a rule of systematic and transparent violation of the rules of 'proper' labelling. The basic rhetorical device of satirical dictionaries is irony, more precisely irony with regard to the individual explanations and comments on certain words' meanings – and with regard to the apparent intention and function of the dictionary as a whole. Dictionaries written as satirical devices are fundamentally ironical; and their irony also affects the dictionary as a text form and its particular writing styles. The probably best known satirical dictionary based on the idea of 'false labelling' is Ambrose Bierce's compendium of words, which was first published as *The Cynic's Word Book* and later on as *The Devil's Dictionary*. Bierce ([1911] 1993) has had many successors, and dictionaries similar to his prototype are still published by contemporary writers. Following Bierce's model, many comparable satirical projects were dedicated to the criticism of language, although they sometimes operate according to new rules and focus on new subjects.[2] As a device complementary to cynical, 'diabolical' or (sometimes) just fuzzy and weird vocabulary, the idea of an honest and transparent use of words provides the frame of reference.

Motivated by a generally strong tendency to reflect on language and language use, the dictionary format was sometimes also used as a means of direct, non-ironical criticism in twentieth-century literature in referring to 'false', hypocritical, illusionary, mendacious or stupid ways of speaking. The "Dictionarist" Ewald Gerhard Seeliger (who playfully called himself "Ewger Seliger") combines indirect ironical writing strategies with open criticism; frequently he replaces neutral or euphemistic expressions for evil and dangerous things with clearly negative and pessimistic terms, thus revealing what, in his opinion, is the true nature of things. In his *Wörterbuch des Schwindels* ("Dictionary of Fraud" but also "of Dizziness" as "Schwindel" means both) of 1922, Seeliger eloquently articulates his protest against obscure and dangerous political ideas and practices, forms of violence and stupidity, intolerance and uniformity, social injustice and the abuse of power, and he emphatically proclaims the freedom, the rights and the importance of the arts.[3]

A new chapter in the history of literary dictionaries begins when surrealist writers start exploring this text format.[4] Several surrealist dictionaries have been produced by either collectives or individuals. In some cases, there is a strong focus on explaining or at least naming things, persons, art works, art styles and projects, institutions and so on – rather than on the headwords as such. The surrealists' dictionaries are usually written in conventional language. Most of the

---

[2] Cf. for example Bowler (1979); Finkielkraut (1981); Adams and Lloyd (1990, 1992); Drews (1990).
[3] Cf. for example his dictionary entry about "Kunst" (art): "KUNST. Die Arbeit an der Erde bezweckt die gegenwärtige, die K.[unst] die künftige Lebenssicherung. Eine Menschenmenge ohne K. ist kein Volk, denn sie hat keine Zukunft. [...] Nur der völlig freie Mensch vermag ein richtiger Künstler zu sein. Der allerfreieste Künstler aber ist der Dichter [...], da er zu seiner K. keines Erdenstoffes bedarf. Er schafft durch sein richtiges Denken und Vorausdichten die ewige selige Menschheit." (Seeliger [1922] 1986: 132–133).
[4] Cf. Breton and Éluard ([1938] 2005).

entries do not create a tension between 'appropriate' and 'inappropriate', literal and ironical, conventional and unconventional ways of naming things, although at least some of René Magritte's paintings focus on the way signifieds are 'labelled' by ostentatiously using , 'false labels' (as, for instance, in *Le clef de songes*). Such new constellations of words and images seem to allude to unfamiliar, often dreamlike dimensions of the world – and to hidden meanings of everyday and seemingly familiar words. Several surrealist dictionaries are collective projects and invite their readers to continue the game: to create new constellations of words, meanings and things, to modify the familiar rules of verbal expression, to create textual alienation effects in order to stimulate new ways of thinking and imagining.

Generally, in the broad aesthetic context of a poetics of defamiliarization (and especially under the influence of avantgardist practices), the literary dictionary was sometimes used quite inventively as a device, a kind of starting platform for creative language use. Neologisms, elements of 'alternative' languages, practices of defamiliarization on different levels formed different types of 'poetic dictionaries'. Often the main focus lies on subversive attitudes towards conventions of speaking and thinking. Likewise, as is often the case, the dictionaries are aimed at discovering hidden meaning potentials of words and verbal expressions. Against the background of a poetics which is mainly focused on language, the 'alternative dictionary' may even be regarded as the very metonymy of poetic writing itself. Under various preconditions and with different emphases, authors such as Michel Leiris, Francis Ponge and Michel Tournier explore the existing dictionaries, but also the dictionary form as such as devices for poetic writing. Ernst Jandl (1985: 562–564) in his essay "Das Gedicht zwischen Sprachnorm und Autonomie" programmatically distinguishes between different types of dictionaries: normative, descriptive and 'projective' ones.[5]

---

5 "[...] es gibt solche [Wörterbücher], die sagen, welche Wörter es geben soll, was sie bedeuten sollen und wie sie gebraucht werden sollen, und es gibt Wörterbücher, die sagen, welche Wörter es tatsächlich gibt, was sie tatsächlich bedeuten, nämlich tatsächlich alles bedeuten können, und wie sie tatsächlich gebraucht werden, nämlich alle die verschiedenen Arten wie jedes einzelne tatsächlich gebraucht wird und gebraucht worden ist, egal wie viele es tun oder getan haben und egal ob es irgendwer tun soll oder nicht." (Jandl 1985: 562) „Um aber endlich zur gemeinten Art von Autonomie zu gelangen [...], bedarf es [...] einer dritten Art von Wörterbuch, eines 'projektiven' Wörterbuchs, die alles an Sprache enthalten, was es daran und darin noch nicht gibt. [...] ein vorauseilendes Wörterbuch, nicht von Sprachen, die es als ganzes noch nicht gibt, einer künftigen Kunstsprache etwa, wie Esperanto es war, ehe es da war, sondern von allem, was es in und an einer Sprache, die es gibt, geben wird, das heißt jetzt noch nicht gibt. [...] ebenso [wie eine entsprechende projektive Grammatik] haben wir uns ein projektives Wör-

Around 1970, the lexicographic novel emerges as a specific novel genre, inspired by and derived from a number of different impulses: first of all, obviously, from literary dictionaries, which had explored strategies, conventions and concepts of lexicographic writing by using the dictionary form. Secondly, lexicographic novels present themselves as programmatic examples of 'open artworks': structured as a series of relatively independent articles which are ordered alphabetically and thus arbitrarily, they encourage the reader to explore them in a nonlinear way. Reading thus becomes a combinatorial game with multiple possible results – similar to the combining of playing cards and other playing devices. In fact, although the alphabetical order of the articles may render their sequence arbitrary, it does not however necessarily do so. In certain cases, there may be a hidden meaning in the way individual articles follow each other – although the lexicographic order suggests that they just follow each other by chance.

Richard Horn (1969) and Andreas Okopenko ([1970] 1983) use the form of dictionary entries to distinguish elements of fictitious worlds. In Okopenko's novel *Lexikon Roman* the text elements, presented as articles of different lengths, resemble children's building blocks from which the reader himself can build a world, exploring possible combinations. In Okopenko's and in Horn's novel the articles form a complex network referring to different fictitious characters and to fictitious events, but also to elements of the factual world and its history, including historical figures and other realities. In Okopenko's second lexicon novel *Meteoriten* the experiment of the "Lexikon Roman" is continued. Here the concept of textual "building blocks" is varied and even stressed. Several lexicon novels following the prototypes of Horn and Okopenko use the text format in order to reflect on the distinction between fiction and historical fact, and to develop their respective narrative strategies. The probably best known example internationally is Milorad Pavic's *Hasarski recnik* [The dictionary of the Chasars], originally written in Serbian and published in 1984, later on translated into various other languages.[6]

Comparable to novels which are written entirely as lexicographic texts are novels using the lexicographic format in certain parts – as building blocks consisting of smaller building blocks. In Milan Kundera's novel *Nesnesitelná Lehkost Byti* (1984) [L'insoutenable légèreté de l'être; The Unbearable Lightness of Being], a dictionary is inserted into the main narrative. It consists of different sections,

---

terbuch des Deutschen zu denken, das alle Wörter enthält, die es geben wird, aber bisher nicht gibt, und alle Wörter, die es anders geben wird, als es sie bisher gibt" (Jandl 1985: 563).

6 Cf. also Sebestyén (1999); Marlowe (2000); Zilahy ([1998] 2008).

all belonging to the third part of the novel, entitled "words that were not understood" or "incomprehensible words" ("Unverstandene Wörter").

Why is the dictionary format so attractive for critical, avantgardist, experimental and language reflective writers? With regard to the wide range of historical examples, a number of different reasons must be taken into account.

(a) They refer to and eventually stress tensions between the familiar and the unfamiliar. Dictionaries in the ordinary sense help their readers to use their respective language's vocabulary resources according to their individual purposes. However, it may occur that the established dictionary fails, that 'proper' terms are missing and new, unfamiliar terms must be found. Literary dictionaries often contain unfamiliar words or diverging explanations; and both strategies stimulate reflection on language itself, its functions and its uses for interpreting and 'ordering' the world – and sometimes also reflections on the tension between the comprehensible and the incomprehensible. In a way, dictionaries of completely invented languages can be regarded as the extreme form of representing an 'unfamiliar' language.

(b) In literary dictionaries, language use becomes self-referential. The pattern of the dictionary automatically steers attention to words 'as words', to language 'as language'. And it raises – among other things – the question of what kind of linguistic knowledge is transmitted here. Is it conventional and codified knowledge framed in an unconventional way by the literary context? Is it 'another' kind of knowledge about words, differing from the subjects of academic linguistics? What kind of alternative knowledge might be transmitted? And what functions does the dictionary pattern have as a framework? As many examples especially from the new avant-gardes confirm, there is a strong affinity between lexicographical literary writing and the poetics of defamiliarization. Literary dictionaries appear to invite their writers to explore alienation effects with regard to their vocabulary, their subjects – and the order in which the subjects appear.

(c) As 'iconotexts', literary dictionaries increase attention for the structural and visual dimensions of texts, for semantic distinctions and hierarchies created by structural and visual means, by typography, layout, page and book design. A structural characteristic of dictionaries is the list-form. The words or phrases themselves are listed, and within the individual entries there are also lists of possible meanings. One typical structural element of dictionary entries is the typographical highlighting of headwords. Vocabularies are often presented in two columns, one consisting of the items which are explained, the other of the explanations (or translations).

(d) Dictionary formats stimulate reflections on bi- and multilingualism, on the identity and distinctiveness of languages, translation and the untranslatable. Literary dictionaries may even raise the question whether the difference between monolingualism and bilingualism is an absolute one. According to the linguist Mario Wandruszka (*Interlinguistik*), we are multilingual within the realms of our own language, using different languages corresponding to diverse practical contexts of living. Languages are not monosystems, and thus there is only a relative difference between the command of the different idioms any language consists of and real multilingualism. Moreover, we never master our native language perfectly; it remains, at least partially, a foreign language for us. Examples of experimental poetic writing have been interpreted as intralingual translation projects pointing to the relativity of this difference and revealing strange and unexplored dimensions within the seemingly familiar everyday language.

Wir sprechen mehrere Sprachen, Teilsprachen, schon in unserer Muttersprache. Wir lernen im Laufe unseres Lebens Regionalsprachen, Sozialsprachen, Kultursprachen, Fachsprachen, Gruppensprachen [...]. Wir ‚übersetzen' immer wieder von einer Teilsprache in eine übergreifende Gemeinsprache oder in eine andere Sprache. [...] wer Ohren hat, zu hören [...], weiß aus alltäglicher Erfahrung, daß eine Sprache eigentlich ein Konglomerat von Sprachen ist. (Wandruszka 1982: 127)
[We speak several languages, language subsets, even in our mother tongue. Throughout our lives we learn dialects, sociolects, languages of specific cultures, languages of different disciplines, languages of different groups [...]. We regularly 'translate' from one language subset into a general common language or into another language. [...] Anyone who has ears to hear [...], knows from everyday experience that a language is a conglomerate of languages; translation by Martina Bross]

With special reference to the French poet Michel Leiris, but also to Edmond Jabès and Georges Perec, the writer and literary critic Felix Philipp Ingold has stressed the significance of what he (also) calls intra-lingual translation as a basic poetic strategy (cf. Ingold 1991: 112–115). Intralingual translation, in Ingold's opinion, dominates large, though peripheral areas of poetry, including phenomena such as anagrammatical texts, palindromes, phonetic readings and other kinds of experiments based on the language- and letter-"material".

As one might summarise, literary texts structured according to dictionary models reveal both the borderline between different 'languages' and the borderline between 'language' and 'non-language' – but at the same time suggest that these borders might be relative and open, even if ambiguity and confusion are the results. However, complementary to this relatively optimistic idea, dictionaries in literature and art may also suggest that on the other side of the borderline – and even on EITHER side of it – there might be something which cannot be explained or translated at all.

2 A Dictionary of Maqiao

Han Shaogong has provided a Chinese translation of Kundera's aforementioned novel *L'insoutenable légèreté de l'être*, which contains lexicographic passages about "incomprehensible words". Adapting the Western genre of lexicographic fiction and literary essayism, and thus contributing to a modern, culturally hybrid form of contemporary Chinese literature, Han followed in the footsteps of Kundera, and also of Okopenko, Horn and Pavic, and explored the options of lexicographic writing for a project of his own that also includes many autofictitious elements. The Chinese writer's book *A Dictionary of Maqiao* (Han [1996] 2003) is an entirely lexicographic novel.[7]

It was first published in Chinese in 1996 and translated into English in 2003. (I will refer to the English translation by Julia Lovell, authorised by the writer himself.[8]) The whole text is composed of entries; the titles of the entries appear as keywords or headwords as with dictionary entries. The entries are arranged as they would be in a dictionary – originally in (Chinese) alphabetical order; the translation is re-structured according to the Latin alphabet and to English vocabulary. It is framed by a preface and a number of paratextual elements. The preface, written by Han himself, who is, however, speaking about himself from the perspective of an anonymous editor, suggests that Han Shaogong has compiled this dictionary of a village himself (Han, *A Dictionary of Maqiao*, p. XV), although as a writer of fiction and essays he possesses no lexicographic skills. By alluding to a fictitious process of research-based compilation, the framing text turns into a piece of fiction itself, and thus from the very beginning, Han's "Dictionary" may be read as a self-referential and autoreflective piece of literature.

---

[7] Cf. Iovene (2002: 197–218); Lee (2002: 145–177); Leenhouts (2002: 168–185); Choy (2008); Lin (2005).

[8] In her "Note on the Translation", translator Julia Lovell explains that in agreement with Han she left out five entries of the original Chinese text and shortened one – in order to avoid "extensive and distracting explanations" which would have been necessary with regard to the relevant parts of the novel. These entries concern special verbal expressions and examples of Chinese script and refer in part to the fact that in Chinese writing homophonous words are sometimes written in different, distinct characters.

With regard to Han's limits as a lexicographer, as the "Preface" also explains, his entries were accepted just as they were written, although they are mainly narrative texts, unlike conventional dictionary entries. (Obviously, this is another auto-referential remark indicating that Han's "Dictionary" is a piece of literature.) The novel is based on notes the author himself actually collected during the years he spent in the Southern Chinese province of Hunan. Mainly based on personal observations, his book portrays the concrete reality of a historical world, but also includes references to objects of popular religious belief, myth, legends and superstition. A list of entries at the beginning of the novel functions as a table of contents, and the keywords listed form the titles of the chapters. Within the chapters, the predominantly narrative texts are combined with elements of historiographic information and more general remarks and reflection on a number of different subjects. Sometimes the articles are divided into different parts in order to give space to more extended narratives.

In its more than 100 entries Han's "Dictionary" describes the fictitious Southern Chinese village of Maqiao, its history and its inhabitants, its customs, habits and especially its communication practices. It tells numerous stories about people of different decades, forming a complex network and covering several generations. Most of the stories are situated within the historical framework of Chinese history during and after the Cultural Revolution.

The narrator – a kind of literary alter ego of the author as a youth – named "Han", is one of the village's inhabitants, but at the same time a stranger. Coming from a city, he is a member of the so-called educated youth, who, during the Cultural Revolution, were sent to the country after leaving school so that they should become integrated into rural society by becoming accustomed to physical work. Generally, the young man accepts resettlement; his story is not a story of homesickness, isolation and lost roots, but about curiosity, new experiences and sympathy with several village inhabitants. According to the narrative framework, the dictionary is based on this 'educated youth's' observations in the village, combined with information concerning the past in the form of second-hand information provided by other characters who tell him their stories or the stories of other persons. This second- or sometimes third-hand information includes stories from previous decades and centuries, always from the same region.

As the title "A Dictionary of Maqiao" already indicates, language, vocabulary and the use of language are central issues of the novel. The major focus lies on idiomatic peculiarities of the local dialect, which differs from the official Mandarin Chinese regarding both vocabulary and pronunciation. Maqiao is a fictitious place, but its dialect as depicted in the novel is based on the actual Hunan dialect. (According to the author's explanation, he invented some phrases but generally used his factual knowledge.) By explaining typical Maqiao words, expressions and phrases and their respective histories, Han's narrator depicts a whole world with its social structures and cultural habits. There is an implicitly political accent on the difference between the regulated and standardised official language of politics and bureaucracy on the one hand, and the lively and in some respects irregular Maqiao way of speaking on the other. The inhabitants of Maqiao are no less shaped by their language than those who use the official language, but they differ remarkably in how they express themselves and interpret the world. The novel's main story complex takes place in the era of the Cultural Revolution. The particular language of Maqiao differs from the languages of cultural revolutionary bureaucracy – as well as from later, post-revolutionary language use.

In Maqiao, common words are often used in a way that differs remarkably from their official meanings and functions. As a consequence, seemingly self-evident truths, seemingly self-evident concepts and conventionalised major differences concerning knowledge and ethics are questioned, either implicitly or explicitly. For instance, in the Maqiao language the word "scientific" has negative connotations referring to something removed from everyday practice, something complicated, even absurd. So the lazybones who refuse to participate in the villagers' collective work are contemptuously characterised as "scientific". With this example (and others) the reader is invited to reflect on the relationship between public order and individual deviance, on ideology and life, abstract theories and concrete ways of life. The narrator explicitly states that the meanings of words depend on the spaces of everyday experience in which they are used – and that these contexts can differ significantly with regard to different collectives and different individuals.

> [...] the process behind understanding a word is not just an intellectual process, it's also a process of perception, inseparable from the surroundings in which the word is used and the actual events, environment, facts relating to it. Such factors often largely determine the direction in which understanding of this word proceeds. (Han, *A Dictionary of Maqiao*, 45)

Due to the local history of semantics, the word "awakened" in the Maqiao language also expresses something different from the usual meanings: for the villagers, "awakened" people are "odd", "crazy" or "stupid". As the narrator explains, more than 2,000 years ago, rebels against the established order of things, who paid for this rejection with their lives, were characterised as "awakened" – with reference to their claimed deeper insights. In Maqiao, the "awakened" are those who are too sensitive not to get upset about life's deficiencies, unable to cope with reality as a consequence of their 'awakedness' – whereas those who sleep are regarded as clever.

> Directly opposed to normal understanding in standardised Chinese thinking, this pair of antonyms exchanged places when their meanings were extended in Maqiao: as Maqiao people see it, regaining consciousness is stupid, while sleeping is in fact clever. (Han, *A Dictionary of Maqiao*, 49)

There is a strong thematic emphasis on the distinction between the general and the specific, the official and the private, general regulations and specific cases, common ideology and concrete experience. Several special terms are used in Maqiao to refer to people who refuse to participate in social life and collective work. The 'lazybones' Ma Ming is one of the most interesting characters in the novel. Is he 'awakened' in a positive or a negative sense? The narrator's dictionary does not suggest proper terms, but it sensitises the reader for the inconsistencies of language – as for instance for antonyms that sometimes even exchange their meanings. The narrator comments:

> Every pair of antonyms is in fact the fusing of different understandings, the intersection of different lives and paths of practice, leading in turn to two paradoxical extremes. This type of intersection is concealed in a secret language which often gives those traveling abroad pause for thought. (Han, *A Dictionary of Maqiao*, 50)

Several typically Maqian expressions are ambivalent with regard to the facts they indicate; this kind of "double-talk" is called "jasmine-not-jasmine": it is "ambiguous, vague, slippery, vacillating" (Han, *A Dictionary of Maqiao*, 352). Other expressions are used in an confusingly euphemistic way, as for instance the term "Reincarnation" (Han, *A Dictionary of Maqiao*, 350–352), which refers to the slaughtering of animals – which as a consequence of being killed can 'reincarnate' more quickly compared to other animals. The narrator points to the performative effects of such modifications in the semantics of words.

> Language can change the way people feel: altering a word can mitigate, even erase, the pity that scenes at a slaughterhouse evoke [...]. (Han, *A Dictionary of Maqiao*, 351)

Playing with words is displayed as one linguistic practice among others – however, as a programmatical one. In the context of the novel it occasionally characterises either the characters themselves (as, for instance, in the case of a Daoist outsider, who refuses to adapt to communist ideology and to integrate into the village workers' community and who, although he appears to be poor, turns out to be a cultured man with a literary education) or it characterises the reality to which the wordplay implicitly refers (as, for instance, the practices of ideological cadre talk according to established speaking rules and based on a codified vocabulary).

With regard to Han's novel, no clear distinction can be made between intentional examples of individual wordplay on the one hand and conventionalised expressions that are based on collectively adapted wordplays on the other. Sometimes individual characters consciously play with words, expressions, and phrases, but often their inventions then become part of the *Dictionary of Maqiao* – and unless the narrator explains the stories behind such expressions, their playful character may even be forgotten or neglected. One might argue that conventionalised modes of ambiguous and allusive speaking – for example using 'talking' names or ambiguous expressions – are not 'word-plays' in a stricter sense, as there is nobody intentionally 'playing' in such cases. But actually an important point in Han's entire novel may well be to portray everyday language itself (so to say) as the instance which plays by inspiring people to become inventive and to transgress linguistic norms and conventions. Everyday spoken language as such appears as a driving force that stimulates its users to modify and expand its vocabulary – and to give familiar words an unfamiliar meaning.

Acts of naming people (especially of giving them by-names) more than once appear as inventive plays with the names' meanings. After a time, however, the villagers become accustomed to these names, and only the narrator reveals the complex meanings and the almost forgotten stories behind them. But in his role as the village's annalist, he also adds his own inventions and names his characters according to his personal perspective.

Maqiao is a relatively remote place where the culturally dominant Mandarin Chinese and in particular the official language of the Cultural Revolution is losing its formative influence on collective life (or never gained such an influence to the officially required degree). From this point of view, the provincial space might be regarded as an enclave resisting centralist authorities, unification tendencies and the extinction of regional traditions. But Maqiao and its language are not idealised, as the entry on "Little big brother (etc.)" illustrates (Han, *A Dictionary of Maqiao*, 31–33): in the Maqiao language there is no specific word for sisters or for other female relatives. Women do not even have proper names – or at least they are not usually called these names. On the contrary, they are designated by combining the terms for the respective male relatives with the adjective "little": "little big brother" is the term for older sisters; younger sisters are called "little little brother". Thus, as the narrator explains, women are not only deprived of their identification as something special which would be more than just a derivation of the male – their linguistic 'derivation' is also associated with diminution, with a secondary existence, with social inferiority.

> Language, it seems, is never absolutely objective or neutral. A linguistic space will always be distorted under the influence of a particular set of beliefs. Bearing in mind the namelessness of females, it's easy to draw further conclusions about their social status around here; it's easy to understand why they always bound their chests flat, [...] harboring a deep-felt fear and shame that sprang from their status as females.
> To be given a name is a right of life, the product of love and respect. People always give names to pampered pets, like 'Kitty' or 'Lulu'. It's only the names of criminals that are usually ignored and replaced by numbers [...]. Those we deem nameless vermin are those whose names have no function in public life or are used with such infrequency that they become erased. (Han, *A Dictionary of Maqiao*, 31)

Complementary to the lack of a 'female' vocabulary – a lack that indicates disregard for women and ignorance of female identity – there are playful modifications of language that create new 'realities', such as, for instance, the names for various kinds of imaginary illness. As we learn, the word "streetsickness" alludes to and fosters a local belief: the idea that staying in towns and especially in larger cities is doing people harm.

> Although standard Mandarin has words like 'seasick', 'carsick', and 'airsick', it doesn't have Maqiao's 'streetsick'. Streetsickness was an illness with symptoms similar to seasickness, but which struck sufferers instead on city streets, causing greenness of face, blurred eyesight and hearing, loss of appetite, insomnia, absent-mindedness, apathy, weakness, shortness of breath, fever, irregular pulse, sickness and diarrhea, and so on [...]. A whole swath of quacks in Maqiao had special decoction prescriptions for curing streetsickness [...]. (Han, *A Dictionary of Maqiao*, 166)

Streetsickness is an imaginary disease to which village people, unaccustomed to streets, fall victim during the time they spend in the unfamiliar city space. But the term "streetsickness", invented as an analogy to "seasickness" or "carsickness" is not just a label for an uneasy feeling: it literally creates this feeling, as it suggests the existence of such a malady (Art. Streetsickness, Han, *A Dictionary of Maqiao*, 166–172):

> Dogs have no language, and so dogs are never streetsick. Once humans become linguistic beings, they attain possibilities that other animals lack completely – they can harness the magical powers of language; language becomes prophecy, a mass hysteria that confuses true and false, and that establishes fictions, manufacturing one factual miracle after another. (Han, *A Dictionary of Maqiao*, 167)

Examples like this highlight the power of language to modify the ways in which speakers explore the world. Playing with words (as, for instance, inventing new expressions in analogy to already existing ones) means playing with the world experienced and the self experienced – including his or her somatic experiences.

> [...] language isn't something to be sneezed at, it's a dangerous thing we need to defend ourselves against and handle with respect. Language is a kind of incantation, a dictionary is a kind of Pandora's Box capable of releasing a hundred thousand spirits and demons [...]. (Han, *A Dictionary of Maqiao*, 168)

And in this very context of reflections on a word referring to sickness, the narrator asks himself what kind of impact words like "revolution", "knowledge", "home town" have had on his country and his fellow-citizens (Han, *A Dictionary of Maqiao*, 168).

The deeper 'truths' of wordplay are revealed in the case of homophonic expressions, as the article about "Gruel" illustrates. Gruel is a kind of porridge, a typical poor people's dish. Its Chinese name is pronounced "gang" in Maqiao, in Mandarin, however, 'jiang'. The young people who have come to Maqiao as 'Educated Youths' initially misunderstand local conversations about "eating gang (gruel)" because the name sounds so different from what they are accustomed to. And they take it for an expression for "eating gang (dry grain)". This stirs certain reflections on the role liquids play in Maqiao cuisine. Due to their poverty, in certain seasons Maquian dishes are prepared with so much water that compared to these meals normal porridge resembles dry grain.

> In fact, the people around here always replaced the j sound with a hard g sound: the word for 'river' (jiang), for example, was also pronounced 'gang'. So 'eating gruel' sometimes sounded like 'eating river.' [...] When the harvest was late and the pot in every household held nothing but water thickened with only a sprinkling of grain, this phrase fit perfectly well. (Han, *A Dictionary of Maqiao*, 144)

As a means of pointing to hidden relations and analogies, homophonic wordplay is an important playful device for the lexicologist and narrator. Sometimes homophones refer to concealed experiences – as for instance in the article about "Bramble Gourd". In 1948, there had been a terrible massacre here: a group of counter-revolutionaries, called 'bandits', were shot in an ambush. Older people who still remember this event consider the place to be haunted, as strange and mysterious things have happened here ever since. A wordplay coined by the local Feng Shui master suggests a connection between political terror and spooky places.

> Mr Fengshui [...] bubbled something about these being 'guan' ('Government') ghosts, ghosts connected to catastrophes in government, 'guan' being homophonic with the word for 'coffin', which referred to souls which hadn't scattered after death [...]. (Han, *A Dictionary of Maqiao*, 127)

The function of wordplay as a medium of political criticism is highlighted even more clearly by the article about the "House of Immortals (and Lazybones)". The "House of Immortals" is an old and somewhat spooky building, the home of the so-called lazybones who refuse to participate in the villagers' collective work and choose isolation instead. Ironically, the village people call them "Immortals" because they are old and appear even older than they are. One day, the narrator is sent out to write Cultural Revolution slogans on the walls of the village houses – in a simplified version of Chinese script, now the official writing system, invented in order to foster general literacy by facilitating the process of learning to read and write. Not only have many old characters fallen out of use, the new ones are also less complex than their predecessors, for which they are no real equivalents. Writing on the walls of the "House of Immortals", the young man meets old Ma Ming, a neglected, shabby philosopher. As Ma Ming reads the characters the young man has painted on the wall, he reacts with a wordplay referring to the symbol for "time", which has also been changed. Ma Ming analogises the deficits of present life and culture with the deficient new character for "time": "When time is confused, it must be a time of confusion" (Han, *A Dictionary of Maqiao*, 35). Entering into a dialogue with the 'educated youth', the old man stresses that the writing reform has done great damage to the distinctiveness and rich meaning potentials of Chinese script. He points to important relations between the written and the spoken dimensions of traditional language and disapproves of the reformed writing characters because they are confusing: "These simplified characters had no logic at all" (Han, *A Dictionary of Maqiao*, 35). And his visitor now understands why the confusion of the written symbol for "time" refers to a "confused time": "What was introduced as a measure to reduce confusion in fact completely confused the texture of Chinese characters." (Han, *A Dictionary of Maqiao*, 37).

All in all, Han's novel actually provides a kind of catalogue of options for playing with words – pointing out the different functions of wordplay in a spectrum which ranges from humorous ludic invention to encoded expressions of political criticism. Even though it reflects on words from different perspectives, Han's novel generally opts for individuality, plurality and the right to be different – as against generalisation and standardisation both with regard to language as well as in a profoundly political sense. It thus develops a thoroughly affirmative view on strategies of linguistic deviation and inventiveness, as they are exemplarily characteristic of wordplay – especially at the level of the public use of language. Wordplay is significant on at least two levels in the dictionary novel: obviously there is a remarkable number of concrete wordplay examples at the content level. We learn about individual wordplays invented by individual characters as well as about collectively used playful ways of expressing oneself or describing things – wordplays that were established in the course of history as part of the specifically Maqiao way of speaking. As an example of individual, specific wordplay one might refer to the old lazybones Ma Ming's remark about a confused symbol for 'time' reflecting a confused time; discourses on 'streetsickness', on the other hand, are derived from an anonymous and collectively used invention. Moreover, the entire novel presents itself as a wordplay in a more specific sense. By means of its form as a lexicographic novel, it plays with the format of the dictionary in its function as a book about words and consisting of words. Han's narrative playfully uses a text format that conventionally serves to transmit information to construct a fictitious world for his novel. And he integrates empirically based 'dictionary knowledge' (knowledge about words, which is represented by words in a specific style and arrangement) into a work of narrative fiction. Thus, he plays with a verbal form as well as with the verbal units of composition themselves. Related to these two levels of content and composition are the author's free inventions of some elements of the Maqiao dictionary (as, for instance, "streetsickness"). They can be described as links between the meticulously observed and documented world of the Hunan dialect and its respective language culture on the one hand, and the world of literary fiction on the other: a playful bridge between documentary and inventive narrative.

In his "Afterword" (Han, *A Dictionary of Maqiao*, 385–388), the author explicitly stresses the individuality of all language use and the necessity to regard it as individual.

> Strictly speaking, what we might term a 'common language' will forever remain a distant human objective. Providing we don't intend exchange to become a process of mutual neutralization, of mutual attrition, then we must maintain vigilance and resistance toward exchange, preserving in this compromise our own, indomitable forms of expression – this is an essential precondition for any kind of benign exchange. This implies, then, that when people speak, everyone really needs their own, unique dictionary.
> Words have lives of their own. They proliferate densely, endlessly transform, gather and scatter for short bursts, drift along without mooring, shift and intermingle, sicken and live on, have personalities and emotions, flourish, decline, even die out. Depending on specific, actual circumstances, they have long or short life spans. For some time now, a number of such words have been caught and imprisoned in my notebook. Over and over, I've elaborated and guessed, probed and investigated, struggled like a detective to discover the stories hidden behind these words; this book is the result.
> This, of course, is only my own individual dictionary, it possesses no standardizing significance for other people. (Han, *A Dictionary of Maqiao*, 388)

"Languages" are abstractions; "dictionaries" are based on abstractions, and language regulations are a means of exercising political power. Literary storytelling, however, appears as a strategy to subvert abstract authorities and the authority of abstractions. Composed of stories, the *Dictionary of Maqiao* is conceived of as an alternative dictionary, giving room to what Han calls the individual 'lives' of words – and of their individual users. With regard to the author as well as to his characters, the licence to use words in a playful, allusive and ambiguous way appears constitutive – not only of Han's poetics.

3 References

Adams, Douglas & John Lloyd. 1990, 1992. *The Deeper Meaning of Liff: A Dictionary of things that there aren't any words for yet*. Illuminated by Bert Kitchen. London: Pan.
Bierce, Ambrose. [1911] 1993. *The Devil's Dictionary Unabridged*. New York: Dover Publications.
Bowler, Peter. 1979. *The Superior Person's Book of Words*. London: David R. Godine Publisher.
Breton, André & Paul Éluard. [1938] 2005. *Dictionnaire abrégé du surréalisme*. Paris: Galerie Beaux-Arts.
Choy, Howard Yuen Fung. 2008. *Remapping the Past: Fictions of History in Deng's China, 1979–1997*. Leiden & Boston: Brill.
Corbin, Pierre & Jean-Pierre Guillerm (eds.). 1995. *Dictionnaires et littérature: Actes du Colloque international, Dictionnaires et littérature, Littérature et dictionnaires (1880–1990)*. Paris: Presses universitaires du Septentrion.
Drews, Jörg. 1990. *Das endgültige zynische Lexikon. Ein Alphabet harter Wahrheiten zugemutet von Jörg Drews & Co.* Zürich: Haffmans.
Finkielkraut, Alain. 1981. *Petit fictionnaire illustré*. Paris: Éditions du Seuil.
Han, Shaogong. [1996] 2003. *A Dictionary of Maqiao*. Translation by Julia Lovell. New York & Chichester: Columbia University Press.
Horn, Richard. 1969. *Encyclopedia*. New York: Grove Press.
Ingold, Felix Philipp. 1991. 'Übersetzung' als poetisches Verfahren. In Michel Leiris, *Wörter ohne Gedächtnis. Große Schneeflucht*. Translation by Simon Werle and Dietrich Leube. Mit einem Beitrag von Felix Philipp Ingold. Hg. v. Hans-Jürgen Heinrichs, 112–115. Frankfurt am Main: Fischer Taschenbuch Verlag.
Iovene, Paola. 2002. Authenticity, Postmodernity, and Translation: The Debates around Han Shaogong's Dictionary of Maqiao. *Annali dell'Universita degli Studi di Napoli L'Orientale* 62.
Jandl, Ernst. 1985. *Gesammelte Werke*, ed. Klaus Siblewski, vol. 3. Darmstadt & Neuwied: Luchterhand.
Jung, Rudolf. 1974. Wörterbücher in satirischer Absicht von Liscow, Rabener und Lichtenberg. In Karl Dehnert (ed.), *Das 1. Lichtenberg-Gespräch in Ober-Ramstadt 1972*, 37–46. Ober-Ramstadt: Verein für Heimatgeschichte.
Lee, Vivian. 2002. Cultural Lexicology: Maqiao Dictionary by Han Shaogong. *Modern Chinese Literature and Culture* 14(1). 145–177.
Leenhouts, Mark. 2002. Is it a Dictionary or a Novel? On Playfulness in Han Shaogong's Dictionary of Maqiao. In Anders Hansson, Bonnie S. McDougall & Francis Weightman (eds.), *The Chinese at Play. Festivals, Games and Leisure*, 168–185. London: Kegan Paul.

Lin, Qingxin. 2005. *Brushing History Against the Grain: Reading the Chinese New Historical Fiction (1986–1999)*. Hong Kong: Hong Kong University Press.

Marlowe, Ann. 2000. *how to stop time. heroin from A to Z*. New York: Basic Books.

Okopenko, Andreas. [1970] 1983. *Lexikon Roman. Lexikon einer sentimentalen Reise zum Exporteurtreffen in Druden*. 2nd edn. Salzburg: Residenz-Verlag.

Pavić, Milorad. [1984] 1988. *Das chasarische Wörterbuch. Lexikonroman in 100 000 Wörtern. Männliches Exemplar/Weibliches Exemplar*. Aus dem Serbokroatischen von Bärbel Schulte [*Hasarski rečnik*. Belgrad: Zavod za Udžbenike]. München: Carl Hanser Verlag.

Rabener, Gottlieb Wilhelm. [1746] 1751. Versuch eines deutschen Wörterbuchs; Beytrag zum deutschen Wörterbuche. (First published in: *Bremer Beiträge* 1746, Dritter Band, Erstes Stück.) In Gottlieb Wilhelm Rabener, *Sammlung satyrischer Schriften*. Vol. 2, 173–204 and 205–207. Leipzig: Dyck.

Schmitz-Emans, Monika. 1993. Das Wörterbuch als literarisches Spielzeug: Rabeners "Versuch eines deutschen Wörterbuchs" und Lichtenbergs Beitrag dazu. In *Jahrbuch der Lichtenberg-Gesellschaft*, 141–167.

Sebestyén, György. 1999. *Wirths Roman. Lexikon eines Lebens. Ein Fragment*. Ed. Helga Blaschek-Hahn. Graz, Wien & Köln: Styria.

Seeliger, Ewald Gerhard. [1922] 1986. *Handbuch des Schwindels*. Mit einem Vorwort von Jürgen Lodemann und einem Nachwort von Max Heigl. Frankfurt am Main: Insel-Verlag.

Wandruszka, Mario. 1982. *Interlinguistik. Umrisse einer neuen Sprachwissenschaft*. München: Piper.

Zilahy, Péter. [1998] 2008. *Az utolsó ablaksziráf*. Budapest. English version: The Last Window-Giraffe. A Picture Dictionary for the Over Fives. Foreword by Lawrence Norfolk [translation by Tim Wilkinson]. London, New York & Delhi: Anthem Press.

Natalia Filatkina and Claudine Moulin
Wordplay and baroque linguistic ideas

Abstract: The paper tackles the question of what the dynamics of wordplay mean for Early Modern language philosophy and what function wordplay fulfills at a time when linguistic norms and cultural values of a particular language are being sought. In Part 1, the current definition of wordplay suggested in Winter-Froemel (2016) is presented as a theoretical framework for the analysis which follows. In Part 2, we give a brief sketch of the main features of Early Modern linguistic thought with a particular focus on the concepts of *play* and *wordplay*. As one of the language theorists of 17th century Germany, Georg Philipp Harsdörffer (1607–1658) is widely known for the sophisticated integration of these concepts into his "linguistic" œuvre, and this will determine the main focus of the current article. Two of Harsdörffer's works will be the center of attention: the *Frauenzimmer Gesprächspiele (FZG)*, published 1643–1649 in Nuremberg, an eight-volume series of dialogues about social, poetic and scientific matters, which incorporates much of Harsdörffer's thoughts on language and one of the best-sellers of the 17th century, and the *Delitiae Mathematicae et Physicae (DMP)*, a three-volume scientific work, to which Harsdörffer added the last two of the three volumes (1651–1653, Nuremberg). Based on the study of various subtypes of wordplay with letters in Part 3, we shall argue that in the context of baroque linguistic ideas wordplay should be defined in a broader sense. It is deeply rooted in a particular view of language peculiar to European baroque culture that provided a conceptual background not only for language "theories", poetry, education and standards of knowledge but also for the role and functions of wordplay. As Harsdörffer found his inspiration in and was strongly influenced by similar ideas of other scientists, particularly in Italy and France, the results of the analysis of the German baroque sources allow for more general assumptions that are not restricted to one language only.

Keywords: baroque linguistic ideas, discourse traditions, Georg Philipp Harsdörffer, grammatization, letterplay, linguistic norm search, soundplay, vernacular language

1 Theoretical framework: (Current working) definition of wordplay

Play is an essential and fundamental element of culture, a necessary companion of individual development and human civilization in general. According to the Dutch historian and philosopher Johan Huizinga ([1938] 2016), such areas of our culture as poetry, law, science, art, sport and many more would have not appeared, did human beings not have an intrinsic desire to play. In Huizinga's philosophy of culture, the duality "man as a thinker (*homo sapiens*)" vs. "man as a craftsman (*homo faber*)" is complemented by an equal third parameter – "man as a player (*homo ludens*)". Declaring play an inherent epiphenomenon of culture, Huizinga stresses its important role at any time in history, including Antiquity, the Middle Ages, the Baroque, the Renaissance, and Modernity. Many types of play come to life through language or have language as their object. Therefore, playing with words is as fundamental to our culture as play in general.

Being an interface phenomenon, wordplay has a long research tradition in various fields of science and the humanities such as rhetoric and classical philology, philosophy, literature, linguistics, phonetics, anthropology, psychology, theatre, cultural studies etc. But as most recently pointed out in Zirker and Winter-Froemel (2015), Winter-Froemel and Zirker (2015) and Knospe, Onysko, and Goth (2016), many questions remain open despite an interdisciplinary dialogue on the one hand and strong disciplinary research traditions on the other. The open questions still include the core notion of wordplay and its "borders", for example with regard to humor, ambiguity (Bauer et al. 2010) or linguistic creativity, and seem to be linked to the absence of standardized terminology applied to the analysis of wordplay. In the scholarly research, similar phenomena have been also addressed as *verbal humor* (Attardo 1994, 2006), *language play* (Crystal 2001) or *speech play* (Kirshenblatt-Gimblett 1976; Sherzer 2002).

To adopt Huizinga's philosophical view on play for a linguistic study of wordplay would mean considering language use in general as wordplay.[1] However, for linguistics and language history – both interested not only in stating the phenomenon as such but also in analyzing its changing goals, functions and the mechanisms behind it – such a broad notion appears to be hard to operationalize. For the purpose of the following analysis, we therefore use a linguistic definition of wordplay as suggested in Winter-Froemel (2016), although the larger per-

---

[1] Cf. also Wittgenstein's ([1953] 2001) broad notion of *Sprachspiel* as any communicative act (German: *Sprachhandlung*).

spective on play proposed in the philosophy of culture and other disciplines remains incontestable in our view. According to Winter-Froemel:

> Wordplay is a historically determined phenomenon in which a speaker produces an utterance – and is aware of doing so – that juxtaposes or manipulates linguistic items from one or more languages in order to surprise the hearer(s) and obtain a humorous effect on them. (Winter-Froemel 2016: 37)

The suggested definition turns out to be useful for four reasons: Firstly, it recognizes the inherent dynamic nature of wordplay and places its historical and cultural boundedness at its center. As will be shown below, the data from the 17th century clearly confirm that wordplay is by no means restricted to modern times. Its historical nature is outlined by Winter-Froemel (2016: 33–36) not only with regard to the techniques that lead to wordplay but also with regard to the discourse traditions in which wordplay is embedded. The concept of discourse traditions developed by Koch (1997) promotes the central idea of the pivotal role of consistency and innovation in the process of production of written and oral text types / genres and the influence of the latter on linguistic utterances typical of a certain text type. In other words, the way we use language in a certain communication situation very much depends on our knowledge of social, cultural, historical and linguistic conventions and rules around this situation.[2] Koch applies this model both to modern and historical times. As playing with words is part of language use, the way it is embedded in texts also greatly depends on discourse traditions (Kabatek 2015: 215). In Part 2, we will extend Koch's fruitful concept and speak of discourse traditions not in terms of a text genre but in terms of a common European baroque melting pot of thoughts and ideas as it is manifest in early modern "linguistic" literature dedicated to the search for norms and values of emerging vernacular languages.

Secondly, the above-mentioned definition stresses the interactive nature of wordplay. Wordplay occurs between a speaker and a hearer and can be successful only if the encoding techniques used by a speaker or speakers are properly decoded by his / her / their hearer(s). One of the sources we use for our analysis – Harsdörffer's FZG – is a collection of fictitious dialogues on various subjects related to social life. The dialogues take place between six fictitious young men and women and acquire the status of a play. Even though there is no evidence for

---

[2] Cf. not identical but in a few aspects similar concepts of *Sprachgebrauchsmuster* (Busse 2005), *idiomatische Prägung* (Feilke 1994), *kommunikative Praktiken* (Fiehler et al. 2004) have developed in Germanic linguistics, while the notion of *kommunikative Gattung* (Luckmann 1986) originates from sociology.

the dialogues ever having been used in this concrete form in reality, they are embedded in the baroque culture of polite and civilized conversation, the mastery of which was considered a compulsory attribute for 17th century young people belonging to the nobility or bourgeoisie (Krebs 1994; Moulin 2016). Furthermore, being a play in themselves, many dialogues extensively exploit different types of games with all possible elements and levels of the German language, starting with letters/sounds and moving on to include texts. In such interactions, wordplay is in a sense authentic as it gains a new functional dimension and reflects a baroque tradition of searching for linguistic norms.

Thirdly, the definition suggests that from the speakers' point of view wordplay in general is an intended production of linguistic items by means of manipulation and/or violation of conventional language use. If the first two features of wordplay mentioned above (its historical and interactional nature) are applicable to verbal humor or any kind of linguistic creativity as well (see Part 1), the techniques leading to playful manipulations/violations constitute an area where the majority of the work has consisted of attempts to find distinctive border lines. According to Winter-Froemel (2016: 37–42), playing with different senses/meanings of formally similar words (not sublexical items) is a wordplay in a narrow sense. It results from the arbitrariness of lexical items and is based on their polysemy, homophony or paronymy. In contrast to that, formal manipulations, which combine elements of an utterance at the sublexical (graphic or phonic) level are considered to be wordplay in a broader sense. Formal manipulations are based on either the paradigmatic or the functional similarity of sublexical elements, with the former type leading to soundplay or play with letters, and the latter representing the so-called ludic deformations. As already pointed out in Winter-Froemel (2016: 24), in a strict sense these distinctions can be applied only to prototypical "best cases". The complex nature of wordplay seems to allow for fuzzy boundaries and crossovers rather than for clear cuts. To be able to place our data in this typology, we present Winter-Froemel's classification in Table 1. For reasons of space, we restrict ourselves to a shorter version of it.[3]

The parts highlighted in gray in the table indicate the main focus of our analysis: We shall concentrate on one type of play that Harsdörffer himself calls a play with letters. From the point of view of language history, a play with letters can also be a soundplay as a strict distinction between sounds and letters did not exist in the Early Modern Era. As we shall see, letterplays are deeply integrated into other types of play, making sharp distinctions almost impossible. It is pre-

---

[3] For full version see Winter-Froemel (2016: 42).

cisely this broader sense that makes the above-mentioned definition of wordplay applicable to historical times.

Tab. 1: Working definition of wordplay according to Winter-Froemel (2016: 42)

	Verbal humor					
	Wordplay (broad sense)			…?	Ludic innovation	Ludic translation
Subtypes	Wordplay (narrow sense)	Sound-play	Ludic deformation	Ludic reinterpretation		
Basic level	lexical	sublexical	sublexical	lexical	conceptual	textual
Basic procedure	combination / juxtaposition of pre-existing (conventional) items and / or creation of new items	combination of pre-existing (conventional) items	substitution of sublexical elements of conventional items; sublexical innovation	reinterpretation of ambiguous structure by H in a way not intended by S	combination; lexical innovation	substitution
Formal / functional relation between units involved	homonymy / polysemy / paronymy	paradigmatic similarity	functional similarity / equivalence of sublexical units	homonymy / polysemy	conceptual association	textual equivalence
(Implicit) metalinguistic dimension	highlighting arbitrariness of language and / or motivational dimension of language	highlighting formal similarities	highlighting arbitrariness of language / linguistic convention	highlighting arbitrariness of language	highlighting motivational dimension of language	highlighting divergence of languages and varieties

The fact that this definition includes the functional aspect of wordplay explains the fourth reason for using it as a theoretical framework for our analysis. The discussion around whether a wordplay necessarily has to result in a humorous effect has so far been controversial. The definition we refer to strongly suggests these effects to be a primary function. However, Winter-Froemel (2016: 14–16) mentions other major outcomes, among them aesthetic and didactic goals, even in Modernity. Our data will show that although the intent to surprise and entertain holds true for baroque times as well, wordplay is not restricted to these functions. While the techniques outlining wordplay seem to be relatively stable throughout history, the functional domain demonstrates qualitative and quantitative changes.

2 Baroque linguistic ideas as historical discourse traditions for wordplay: Georg Philipp Harsdörffer

To study wordplay in historical times means to take its contextualization within different views of language at these times into account. The end of the Middle Ages (roughly the 1350s) with Latin as a dominant *lingua franca* and vernacular languages receiving little scholarly attention is marked by a remarkable shift in the attitudes towards the latter. The driving forces preceding and/or accompanying this shift are not linguistic in nature. Innovations brought about by the invention of paper (instead of costly parchment) and printing (instead of handwriting), the development and rising importance of cities and a new social class of the bourgeoisie, the intellectual insights of Humanism, the Renaissance and – especially in the German speaking area – of the Reformation period lead to a stronger presence of vernacular languages in daily life (Moulin 2008a: 19). Although Latin maintains its status as the language of written scholarship and international communication well beyond the Middle Ages, vernacular languages slowly start to grow in importance, not only due to the insatiable practical demand in the changing world for people competent in subjects other than Latin, but also simply because vernaculars start to be considered natural mother tongues, qualitatively no different from Latin (Gardt 1994; Hundt 2000; Moulin 2008a: 17–19, 2008b: 1903). The increasing practical need for written communication in vernacular languages caused the language users of those days to become acutely aware of the lack of normative orientation literature (grammar and spelling books, dictionaries etc.) and accelerated the "linguistic" debate described by Hundt (2000) with the term *Spracharbeit*. Therefore, the shift towards vernaculars leads to their grammatization (Auroux 1992), i.e. to the rise of the codifying orthographic, grammatical and lexicographical treatises that in those days could have been both practical and theoretical in nature.[4] These are texts where language users were advised with regard to various aspects of language use and where the debate about linguistic norms was mainly carried out.

The shift towards vernaculars has to be contextualized within the wider scope of another far-reaching transformation of the western European attitude to the outer world. As Vivien Law (2003: 213) puts it:

> Interest shifted from the universal and transcendental to the particular, visible, material phenomena all around us. [...] Previously, convinced that life on Earth was a punishment rather than an opportunity, Europeans had done their best to ignore the most earthy parts of it; but once that attitude changed, they wanted to get to grips with the material in every conceivable way: by sketching and sculpting it, by weighing it and measuring it, by collecting it, by classifying it, by exploring it and manipulating it to suit their needs and desires. You can see the consequences in every area of intellectual, cultural and economic life.

As language is an inherent part of social and cultural life, the consequences are also reflected in the way people thought about language(s). From the 16th century on, faith in observation and experimentation led to many aspects of language developing in parallel with the corresponding aspects of the sciences. Indeed, during that period, the same individuals were involved in developing both "linguistics" and science. Georg Philipp Harsdörffer is one of such universal, all-around savants whose linguistic program is embedded in the encyclopedic framework, largely integrating rearrangements, translations and compilations of other (older and contemporary) sources in his writings. His DMP is ample proof of this approach (Westerhoff 1999; Roßbach 2015: 48–56). In many of his works, Harsdörffer voices the feelings of his generation of grammarians, lexicographers, literary authors and teachers by collecting evidence and making German a suitable vehicle for the discussion of subjects such as theology, philosophy and law – three domains that had previously been the all-but-exclusive preserve of Latin.

The recognition of the prestige of German as a mother tongue, of its richness and its equality with the three holy languages of the Bible – Hebrew, Latin and Greek – starts later than for instance the appreciation of Italian, French, Spanish or Portuguese. In Germany, the "emancipation" process, also so important to

---

4 For German, this process is documented in detail in Jellinek (1913–1914) and Moulin-Fankhänel (1994–1997).

national pride and the growing consciousness of an underlying folk unity, dates back to the 15th century and intensifies tremendously in the 17th (Auroux 1992; Gardt 2008; Moulin-Fankhänel 1994–1997, 2008b, 2011; Padley 1988; von Polenz and Moulin 2013: 119–121). However, the recognition entails argumentation strategies very similar to those used for Italian or French. The ultimate goal consists – as in other countries – in the cultivation of German in order for it to become an elaborated medium of poetry and science with linguistic and aesthetic norms being codified in grammar books and dictionaries as well as with *copia verborum*, 'copiousness of vocabulary, wealth of lexical resources' (Law 2003: 232) or an extensive, rich lexicon. We shall come back to this in Part 3 when we analyze examples from Harsdörffer's work.

Since the mediaeval Seven Liberal Arts, grammar was viewed as the origin and foundation of all the rest. It was often depicted as a female personification (*Grammatica*) leading already alphabetized young children on to higher disciplines.[5] In accordance with the common 17th century view, Harsdörffer also sees language as the vehicle for learning about the world. Hundt (2000: 61) calls this a "knowledge constitutive function which opens up the world" (*erkenntniskonstitutive, welterschließende Funktion*) of the language. For Harsdörffer, this function is manifest not only at the level of sentences and phrases, but already at the lowest level of single signs. This is why his play with letters is so important.

However, Harsdörffer not only argued a case for the potential of German at a theoretical level, he also took practical steps to develop its potential by being a great educator of young people (Knight 1960, 1991). His main addressees are *vorneme Leute*, male and female, of noble or bourgeois birth as it is precisely these groups who carry social prestige and are crucial for the dissemination of educated German. One of the basic ideas here was that cultivation of German, the *Spracharbeit* (Hundt 2000), is similar to a natural first language acquisition process. In the context of the 17th century, this process is automated, active and strongly bound in with the acquisition of moral values, virtues, noble eloquence, polite discourse and courtesy. It is not purely a linguistic matter and also means cultivation of virtuousness, literature and culture in a profound "European" dimension. Being the most prominent *Kulturvermittler* (i.e. cultural mediator) of his times (Hundt 2011), Harsdörffer is a constitutive part of this "Europe"-wide undertaking. He explains this interplay in volume V (p. 66)[6] of the FZG with the

---

5 A systematic study of the text-picture-interplay in German Early Modern grammar books is provided in Moulin (2008a).
6 When referring to Harsdörffer's work, we use the page numbers of the original digitized sources. See the list of references at the end of the article for further details.

help of three circles representing three fundamental preparatory arts that, once mastered, lead to science (*Wissenschaften*), the core of all knowledge and its center: with *Sprachkunst* (grammar) being the first inner circle, *Vernunftkunst* (logic) in the second circle and *Redkunst* (rhetorics) with its two parts (poetry and the art of singing) at the outer edge.

Like learning a mother tongue naturally, the *Spracharbeit* has to be easy and entertaining. To facilitate and accelerate the studies, Harsdörffer draws on the antique tradition of fictive dialogues (Plato), uses numerous registers, marginal notes, illustrations, emblems (Moulin 2008a) and various typographic means. This is why each of his works claims the right to be interpreted as a printed baroque sneak preview of complex virtual hypertexts of the modern digital era impressively simplified by Harsdörffer for didactic purposes.

This is also the area where wordplay comes into force. Harsdörffer's contemporary fellow academicians within the "Fruchtbringende Gesellschaft" gave him the nickname *Der Spielende* (The Player) as he considered different types of plays, also linguistic plays, a major auxiliary to knowledge creation and the education of the young. Particularly FZG are a kind of introduction into entertaining courtesy and pleasant polite conversation basically about any imaginable subject.[7] Though Harsdörffer is not an inventor of "playing with language"[8], he is certainly the best-known propagator and compiler of the genre. In accordance with his time, he explains the need for play with human nature (FZG, IV, 469):

> Er [der Mensch] ift zwar zu der Arbeit geboren / wie der Vogel zum fliegen; jedoch folchergeftalt / daß er die Sorgenftille Nacht wiederům ausruhen / am Tage wieder an feine Arbeit gehen; von dem Lafte feines Berufes zu weilen abfetzen / den befchåfftigten Geift beluftigen und die laffe Hand ausraften laffen folle.

In Harsdörffer's view, people are born to work. Therefore, they have to rest at night and amuse the tired mind with play in order to regain energy for the next working day. His second argument (not mentioned in the cited excerpt but apparent in his work in general) also fits with the context of the 17th century: As Hebrew, Egyptian, Italian and French savants dedicate a substantial amount of their work to wordplay, German scholars should do the same. By virtue of their mother tongue being no less worthy than these languages, it deserves the same treatment. Harsdörffer (FZG, V, fol. 41r) points out that playing with language has noticeable advantages compared to playing cards, board games or any type of physical exercise. He uses this comparison as his third argument in favor of word-

---

7 For the literary and philosophical contextualization of the FZG, see e.g. Bergengruen (2009).
8 See Zeller (1974: 77–93) for historical traditions.

play. The latter leads to love, friendship and joy, sharpens the mind and educates, whereas the former only produce jealousy, competition and animosity.

As mentioned before, in FZG, Harsdörffer puts many of his programmatic thoughts into the mouth(s) of six young people. While conversing with each other, they create approximately 300 plays, which Markus Hundt (2000: 171–172) classifies into eight main types with numerous subtypes. All aspects of theoretical work are reflected in wordplay as wordplays can be conducted at all levels of a language system (phonology, grapheme system, morphology, lexicology, phraseology[9], syntax) and language use (text, oral conversations[10]). They include knowledge structures in general as well.

For Harsdörffer, playing is the most natural way of learning. Guided by the contemporary philosophical background[11], he connects the etymology of the word *play*, *Spiel* in German, with nature (FZG, IV, 467). The following quotation illustrates this very clearly:

> Auſſer allem 3weiffel hat Adam allen Thieren und Geſchöpfen aus ihren Arten und wirklichen Eigenſchaften woldeutende Namen ertheilet: und ſolchergeſtalt iſt das Wort Spiel in der Natur befindlich / und 3u hören von Berg=abflieſſenden Waſſerbåchen / welche 3wiſchen den bunten Kieß daher liſpelen / und ein angenemes Getön unſeren ſonſt müſſigen Ohren gleichſam einſpielen: daher vieleicht entſtanden / daß alle Sachen / ſo ohne Mühe und Arbeit / aus ſonderem Belieben herflieſſen / Spiele und Spielen genennt worden / daher auch das ſpühlen / ausflöſſen / durchliſpelen oder oft durchseyen den Namen haben mag (Harsdörffer, FZG, IV, 467).[12]

In Harsdörffer's view, it is the role of nature that is of primary importance as he assumes that things receive their names through nature rather than through convention. He sees the German language as singularly apt at reflecting this. The language is thus a hypostatized entity, established by God and Nature, which is so well ordered that it designates the innermost reality of things. Like his contemporaries among the language-planners, he sees the ideal, perfect language as a one-to-one correspondence with things in the universe. As language is a natural product, it has a structure and follows rules. Only in this way can it be regarded as a perfect, ideal creation. Consequently, rules are a large and important part of Harsdörffer's definition of wordplay. As we shall see when we look at the examples, the important tradition, if we are to understand the concept of

---

9   For more detail, not only with regard to Harsdörffer, see Filatkina (2009).
10 For wordplay in table talk, see Moulin (2016).
11 See e.g. Bredekamp (1993: 66–67) for a historical embedding.
12 Harsdörffer devotes many parts of his various works to this onomatopoetic nature of German, e.g. the chapter entitled "Von der Teutschen Sprache Vortrefflichkeit" in FZG, III, 288–295.

Harsdörffer's wordplay, is the combinatorial art or *ars combinatoria* (Ernst 1993: 97–98; Hundt 2000: 218–219).

Spielen means having fun but also moving fast, smoothly and lightly, not so much in a physical sense but rather as movement of the *Geist* or mind. The lightness of play is supposed to resemble the easiness of the learning process, the easiness of reasoning and thinking. At the same time, wordplays function as proof of a high degree of linguistic competence and world knowledge based on the idea that one can only play with a language if he/she has full command of it. As children start learning language naturally with letters, playing with letters is considered the lightest of all wordplay. According to Harsdörffer (FZG, I, 136–140), young people have to start their *Spracharbeit* with precisely this type of play and in due course proceed to the more difficult types such as the creation of texts, interpretation of etymology, and the creation of riddles and puns. Let us now have a closer look at this type of play.

3 Wordplay in Harsdörffer's work: Some examples

3.1 Ambiguity and juxtaposition of letters and signs

Many letterplays are created on the basis of the ambiguity and juxtaposition (see basic procedures of wordplay in a narrow sense in Table 1) of letters and involve persons' names. For example, in FZG, I, 141 (Figure 1), Harsdörffer, or more precisely, the young players, take the name *Julia* and interpret each letter differently by virtue of using each letter in a different word, building a completely new and meaningful sentence (*Ja, Viel Loben ist Artig*) and therefore creating a new meaning. The new meaning arises even if the letters of the name are read backwards: *Armut Ist Listig Und Jmmenart*. The underlying concept demonstrates once more the interwovenness of language and the surrounding world: In the view of the 17th century, language and reality are ambiguous in the same way; in the same way as signs and symbols of the real world can be interpreted in many different ways, linguistic signs permit various interpretations. It is precisely this baroque view on language signs (letters) and real world that allows us to describe the underlying mechanism of such letterplays using the term *ambiguity* even though modern approaches to ambiguity might disagree with that (Bauer at al. 2010; Winter-Froemel 2013).

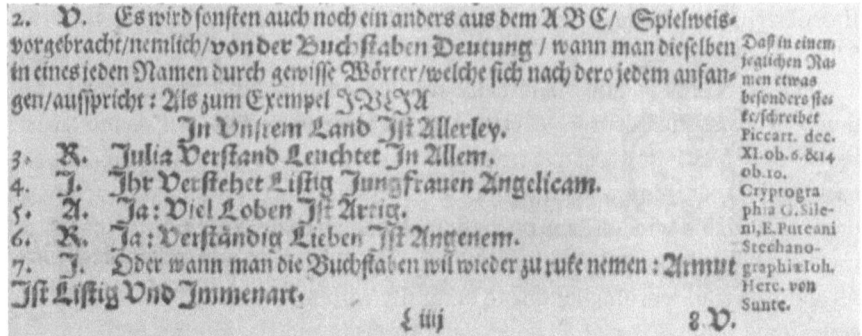

Fig. 1: G. P. Harsdörffer, FZG, I, 141

Though these plays are entertaining in nature, their aim is not necessarily to achieve a humorous effect. The goals are rather manifold: Firstly, the play is thought to demonstrate the powerful ability of the language to create reality such as for instance the name of a person reflecting his/her character. Harsdörffer makes this explicit in the marginal note accompanying the text (*In einem jeglichen Namen stecke etwas Besonderes*).[13] Secondly, it is an entertaining tool to make young people reflect on different moral values while they produce sentences starting with a certain letter. And thirdly, it can be used for the simple purposes of alphabetization. As mentioned before, in the 17th century, learning letters was considered a key step to linguistic competence, just as learning grammar or language was considered a key step to knowledge in general. Harsdörffer was aware of this and dedicated considerable effort to the visualization of letters for language learners. As Figure 2 (FZG, V, 68–69) illustrates, he makes the letter take the shape of an object it denotes.[14] One can find very similar visualization in any modern elementary book for teaching children to read.

---

13 The marginal note also quotes relevant, especially cryptographic literature on the topic. There is a similar play in FZG, VIII, 87–88 where the letters of the name *Cassandra* are reinterpreted with the help of adjectives reflecting human character (*adelig, sittsam, demütig, reich*). The initial letters of the adjectives match the letters of the proper name.

14 This pictographic method stands in a long tradition of alphabetization treatises. Harsdörffer's examples are very close to those given by Tilmann Olearius in "Deutsche Sprachkunst" (1630).

Wordplay and baroque linguistic ideas — 247

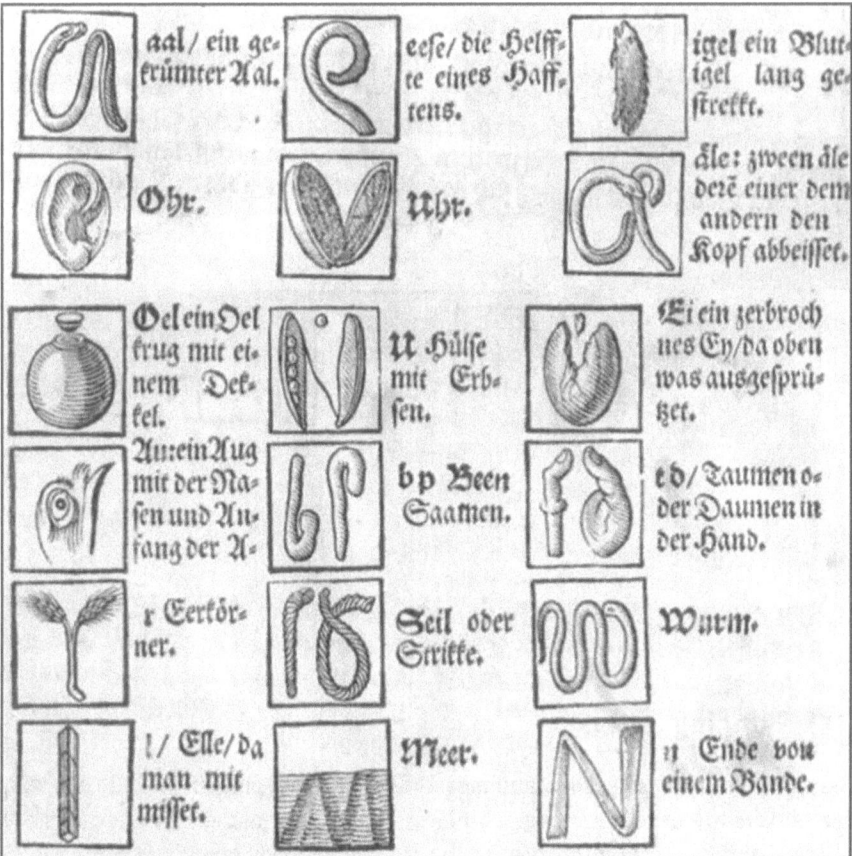

Fig. 2: G. P. Harsdörffer, FZG, V, 68–69

We have mentioned earlier that teaching language or reflecting on it is, in the 17th century, never a purely linguistic issue. This is why teaching letters is also embedded in more complex exercises in creative logical thinking. A good example of this is provided in FZG, VIII, 35 (Figure 3), an example which is also based on ambiguity. Gestures shown in these pictures do not only evoke a symbolic knowledge about their numerical value; they are ambiguous because they are also assigned to letters. Put together, they form the word *fliehe*. The entertaining purpose of the play is explained in the dialog preceding the picture. In addition, the play brings to life the enormous interest in cryptography and stenography typical of baroque times: By means of the gestures in the pictures, secret messages can be transmitted.

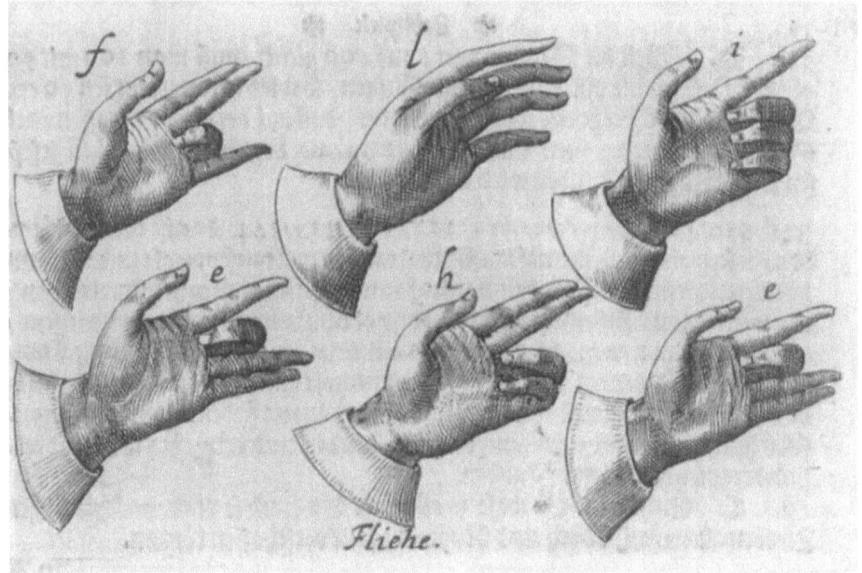

Fig. 3: G. P. Harsdörffer, FZG, VIII, 35

3.2 Skipping letters

Skipping letters is the second and most difficult type of play. In FZG, II, 166–169, the players are asked to create a whole story without using the letter *M*. They succeed and create a one-page long story where a greedy woman is supposed to learn the meaning of the proverb *Three equals one* by virtue of losing all her money when, after her husband dies, she goes against his wishes and sells his cherished horse and dog. In a similar way, other plays suggest omitting only vowels (*Stimmer*)[15] or some specific letters based on a certain rule in riddle form in order for a different word with a different meaning to occur.[16] It is obvious that these plays serve the purpose of entertainment, just as the previous group did.

---

15 Cf. FZG, III, 328–329: The elimination of vowels in the first name *Angelica* can lead to the creation of the noun *Glück* 'happiness' and/or *Unglück* 'unhappiness' by virtue of using the remaining consonants *n*, *g*, *l*, and *c*.

16 Cf. FZG, VII, 426–427: "*Kürbiß* > Nimm das Haupt und Schwanz vom Raben/was verbleibet/ſol uns laben > *Küß*". The wordplay, which does not work in the same way in English, can be paraphrased as '*Kürbis* ('*pumpkin/squash*') – take the head and the tail from the word *Raben* ('raven' = eliminate the first letters of each syllable in the word *Rabe* and do the same with similar letters in the word *Kürbis*), what remains, shall be refreshing for us – *kiss*.'

But this is not their only function: They also transmit moral values (e.g. the play with the letter *M* teaches young people not to be greedy) that at first glance are encoded very implicitly in the body of the play but are almost always the explicit outcome in the discussions following the play. More importantly, to 17th century (and even earlier) eyes, these were the samples of observation predestined to prove how rich German vocabulary was, cf. FZG, VIII, 50: "Unsere Sprache ist so wortreich/daß es wol seyn kann", meaning: 'Our language is so rich in words that it [the creation of a whole story, poem or even sermon without a certain letter, NF & CM] does not require the slightest effort.' Commenting on such plays, Harsdörffer stresses particularly often that German shares the ability to produce text without certain letters with Hebrew. Being on "an equal footing" with Hebrew (as one of the holy languages) is a commonly used argument when we look at the history of baroque linguistic ideas in Germany. It was meant to eliminate any doubts about the age and richness of the vernacular. This aim finds its culmination in our next and last group of examples.

3.3 Regrouping and combining letters, syllables and parts of words

This consists of wordplays that regroup and/or combine letters (*Letterwechselung*), syllables and parts of words. Like no other group, these examples demonstrate the ability of language users to construct reality through language, to use language not as a mirror of the world, but as its fundamental building blocks. Thus, the combination of only 5 letters in the proper name Julia in a different order can be changed 120 times and produce 120 new items (FZG, III, 322–323). The ability of anagrams (*Wortgrifflein* as they are called by Harsdörffer, i.e all those words which are elements of the set of permutations of the first word) to be read in both directions and stay meaningful is interpreted as ample proof of the "kräftige Füglichkeit des Deutschen" ('profound plasticity of German'); "es schärfet das Urtheil, veranlasst zu schönen Gedanken" ('it sharpens judgement, induces beautiful thoughts', cf. the example *Wassermühle – Mühlwasser* in FZG, III, 296). This method can be extended from anagrams based on a single word to the production of anagrams from a sentence or short text. Though anagrams existed long before Harsdörffer, his original contribution is to take these further and integrate them into a ballet, as described in DMP, III, 54–55. The scenario is simple: first, give each dancer a board inscribed with a letter of the alphabet; then watch as new words or phrases emerge from the dance. The very movement of the dancers' bodies will act as a combinatory mechanism from which language springs (Westerhoff 1999: 465). Each of these games uses language not as an abstraction, the purely rational product of the mind, but as quite literally a material object to be manipulated and moved, cut up and combined. By combining the basic concepts one can produce more complex ones and thus gain new knowledge. As Westerhoff explains:

> In this simple mechanization we see how the ideas of the combinatorial nature of the world on the one hand and language on the other hand meet: letters are inscribed onto material elements, so that a permutation of these out of itself generates an anagram without requiring ingenuity. [...] Because language and matter both follow combinatorial principles, it is possible to mechanize the former by inscribing it onto the latter. In the "language machine" the combinatorial features of language and the world which are generally distinct are unified into a single artifact. (Westerhoff 1999: 464–465)

The language "is now no longer a matter for speaker and hearer, but a matter for the eye, so that its users end up by seeing it as something quite independent of speech, with a separate existence of its own" (Padley 1988: 315).

In no mechanism is this belief more evident than in the *Fünffacher Denckring der Teutschen Sprache*, or the *Five-fold Thought-Ring of the German Language* as presented in DMP, II, 516–517 (Figure 4).

The *Denckring* is a visualization of a vast word-formation potential in German. On a practical level, Harsdörffer envisions the *Denckring* as a helpful tool in a poetic process ("hat seinen Gebrauch in der Erfindung der Reimwörter", DMP, II, 518). The *Denckring* is composed of five predicate variables: 48 prefixes in the middle, followed by 60 initial letters, 12 medial letters, 120 final letters and 24 suffixes (Gardt 1994: 208; Hundt 2000: 281–285; Moulin 2008a: 35). Each of these variables is inscribed along the edge of a disc and nested with each of the other discs, forming a simple combinatory mechanism that can generate rhymes, compounds and derivates. Harsdörffer explains:

> Will ich nun alle Stammwörter ordenlich finden/so fange ich bey dem A deß ʒweyten Ringes an/und drehe darʒu das kleine a deß dritten Ringes: dann ſuche ich den vierten Ring Aab/Aabb/Aabd/&c. blinde oder deutunglose Wörter/biß auf das ch/ Aach/*Aquisgranum*, eine benamte Stadt in Niderland/Aal/eines Fiſches und eines Schuſters Werckʒeug Namen/Aas (cadaver)&c. (DMP, II, 516–517)

Fig. 4: G. P. Harsdörffer, DMP, II, 516–517

Gottfried Wilhelm Leibniz ([1666] 1880) calculated that by spinning the discs, the user can generate up to 97,209,600 words (Gardt 1994: 208, different calculations in Hundt 2000: 284–285).¹⁷ Harsdörffer (DMP, II, 519) expresses his hope that not a single word will ever be found that is not depicted on his ring ("wird ſich verhoffentlich kein Wort in unſrer gantzen Sprache finden/welches nicht auf dieſem Ring weiſen ſeyn ſollte"), although in fact the rings are incomplete (Zeller 1974: 167; Hundt 2000: 281–285) and include some letter combinations that the phonetic system of German would not allow. In addition to representing "die gantze Teutsche Sprache auf einem Blätlein" 'the whole German language on one page' (DMP, II, 516), the *Denckring* also forms new words that do not yet exist in German but, because they are formed by combining correct radicals and letters, could exist as legitimate words. The baroque spirit of *inventio* is therefore manifest in Harsdörffer's approach. As in many other parts of his work, Harsdörffer explicitly ties his device to the linguistic theories of Schottelius:

> Iſt also dieses eine unfehlbare Richtigkeit/ein vollſtändiges Teutſches Wortbuch zu verfaſſen/und beharren wir in der Meinung/daß alle ſolche zuſammen geſetzte Wörter/welche ihre Deutung wůrken für gut Teutſch zuläſſig/ſonderlich in den Gedichten/ob ſie gleich ſonſten nicht gebräuchlich/wie hiervon zu leſen der umb unſere Sprache wolverdiente Herr Schottelius in ſeiner Einleitung und in ſeinen Lobreden der Sprachkünſt vorgefüget. (DMP, II, 518)

Because the *Denckring* materializes proper stem words (*Stammwörter*) and mechanizes the proper formula for combining them, any output it produces must also be proper German. In other words, in this view language is fundamentally a material and mechanical phenomenon because it is rooted in monosyllabic stem-words that are in their turn rooted in German letters. By using the *Denckring* and assembling a whole word out of dissembled parts, a poet or any language user can dynamically generate meaning "on the fly". As God assembled the world through combinations of a fixed number of elements, the poet spins the wheel to generate millions of wor(l)ds, many of which exist only as possibilities. In a broader sense, the anagrammatic playful creation of language shows striking parallels with the divine act of creation. But these parallels are not only metaphysical, they are also rational. As Westerhoff (1999: 454) argues, in a similar way to Harsdörffer, Leibniz ([1666] 1880: 89) discusses the parallel between atoms as the primitive particles of matter and letters as the primitive particles of speech: the world is produced in a combinatorial manner from the former and language in the same way from the latter. Linguistic and material combination meet in the mechanized playful production of anagrams – an observation that takes us back

---

17 For comparison, the OED lists 600,000 words; 400,000 words can be found in *Duden Universalwörterbuch*.

to what was said at the beginning about the close connection between linguistic thought and natural science.

4 Conclusions

With regard to poetry, Huizinga ([1938] 2016: 132) notes that to call it "playing with words and language is not metaphor: it is the precise and literal truth". In a similar way, playing with words and language in baroque times is not metaphor: It is a constitutive search path for linguistic norms, knowledge and culture dissemination and the education of the young that is not restricted to German and unites ideas common to emerging early modern vernacular languages (Part 2).

Approaching baroque linguistic theory with modern methods of wordplay analysis provides fruitful insights into both domains. In our paper, we have concentrated on examples drawn from the scholarly work of one of the most influential German authors of the 17th century (Georg Philipp Harsdörffer) and the definition of wordplay developed by Winter-Froemel (2016) primarily for modern languages. As shown in Parts 1 and 3, the definition turns out to be useful from an historical perspective as it includes the dynamic, interactive and functional dimensions of historical wordplay and accounts for the diversity of its subtypes. In accordance with Winter-Froemel's definition (Part 1), for different types of Early Modern play with letters (i.e. at the basic sublexical level), complex creative combinations and juxtapositions of conventional elements appear to be a central procedure. In the majority of the cases, formal similarity of sublexical units and their usage in new contexts lead to the creation of new meaning, i.e. to wordplay in a broader sense.

Harsdörffer's approach to wordplay is multilevel and multimodal. Even plays that he himself considers basic plays with letters and that would therefore at first glance best fit into formal wordplay types in the modern definition of wordplay exceed the level of pure form. They combine different types of letter manipulations, combinations and/or deletion with their symbolic values, visual images and meaning; they shift linguistic skills into the areas of logic, poetic competence or scientific knowledge and examine them within educational paradigms in general.

The chosen methodology thus allows for a more systematic approach to wordplay in a historical context and could be applied to larger corpora and other languages as well.

5 References

Primary sources

Harsdörffer, Georg Philipp. [1643–1649] 1968. *Frauenzimmer Gesprächspiele*. Vol. I–VIII, reprint. Nuremberg and Tübingen: Niemeyer. Digital facsimilies of all original volumes in http://www.die-fruchtbringende-gesellschaft.de/index.php?category_id=6&article_id=18 (accessed 30 March 2017).

Harsdörffer, Georg Philipp & Daniel Schwenter. [1636–1653] 1990–1991. *Deliciae Physico-Mathematicae oder Mathematische und Philosophische Erquickstunden*. Vol. I–III, reprint. Nuremberg and Frankfurt am Main: Keip. Digital fascilimilie of Vol. III in http://diglib.hab.de/drucke/224-3-quod/start.htm (accessed 30 March 2017).

Leibniz, Gottfried Wilhelm. [1666] 1880. Dissertatio de Arte Combinatoria. In Karl Immanuel Gerhardt (ed.), *Die philosophischen Schriften von G. W. Leibniz*. Vol. 4, 27–102. Berlin: Weidmann.

Olearius, Tilman. 1630. *Deutsche Sprachkunst*. Halle an der Saale: Oelschlegel, Melchior / Schmidt, Peter.

Secondary sources

Attardo, Salvatore. 1994. *Linguistic Theories of Humor*. New York: De Gruyter Mouton.

Attardo, Salvatore. 2006. Cognitive Linguistics and Humor. *Humor* 19(3). 341–362.

Auroux, Sylvain. 1992. Introduction. Le processus de grammatisation et ses enjeux. In: Sylvain Auroux (ed.), *Histoire des idées linguistiques*. Vol. 2, 11–64. Liège: Madraga.

Bauer, Matthias, Joachim Knape, Peter Koch & Susanne Winkler. 2010. Dimensionen der Ambiguität. *Zeitschrift für Literaturwissenschaft und Linguistik* 158. 7–75.

Bergengruen, Maximilian. 2009. Die Wahrheit der Illusion. Zur literarischen Mobilisierung von Experienz in Harsdörffers "Erquickstunden" und "Frauenzimmer Gesprächspielen". In Michael Gamper, Martina Wernli & Jörg Zimmer (eds.), *"Es ist nun einmal zum Versuch gekommen". Experiment und Literatur I. 1580–1790*, 196–221. Göttingen: Wallstein.

Bredekamp, Horst. 1993. *Antikensehnsucht und Maschinenglauben: die Geschichte der Kunstkammer und die Zukunft der Kunstgeschichte*. Berlin: Wagenbach.

Busse, Dietrich. 2005. Sprachwissenschaft als Sozialwissenschaft? In Dietrich Busse, Thomas Niehr & Martin Wengeler (eds.), *Brisante Semantik. Neuere Konzepte und Forschungsergebnisse einer kulturwissen-schaftlichen Linguistik*, 21–43. Tübingen: Niemeyer.

Crystal, David. 2001. *Language Play*. Chicago: University of Chicago Press.

Ernst, Ulrich. 1993. *Ars memorativa* und *Ars poetica* in Mittelalter und Früher Neuzeit. Prolegomena zu einer mnemonistischen Dichtungstheorie. In Jörg Jochen Berns & Wolfgang Neuber (eds.), *Ars memorativa. Zur kulturgeschichtlichen Bedeutung der Gedächtniskunst 1400–1750*, 73–100. Tübingen: Niemeyer.

Feilke, Helmuth. 1994. *Common sense-Kompetenz. Überlegungen zu einer Theorie "sympathischen" und "natürlichen" Meinens und Verstehens*. Frankfurt am Main: Suhrkamp.

Fiehler, Reinhard, Birgit Barden, Mechthild Elstermann & Barbara Kraft. 2004. *Eigenschaften gesprochener Sprache*. Tübingen: Niemeyer.

Filatkina, Natalia. 2009. Und es duencket einem noch / wann man euch ansiehet / daß ihr Sand in den Augen habt. Phraseologismen in ausgewählten historischen Grammatiken des Deutschen. In Csaba Földes (ed.), *Phraseologie disziplinär und interdisziplinär*, 15–31. Tübingen: Narr.

Gardt, Andreas. 1994. *Sprachreflexion in Barock und Frühaufklärung. Entwürfe von Böhme bis Leibniz*. Berlin & New York: De Gruyter Mouton.

Gardt, Andreas. [1998] 2008. Die Sprachgesellschaften des 17. und 18. Jahrhunderts. In Werner Besch, Anne Betten, Oskar Reichmann & Stefan Sonderegger (eds.), *Sprachgeschichte. Ein Handbuch zur Geschichte der deutschen Sprache und ihrer Erforschung* (Handbücher zur Sprach- und Kommunikationswissenschaft 2.1), 2nd edn., 332–348. Berlin & New York: De Gruyter Mouton.

Huizinga, Johan. [1938] 2016. *Homo ludens. A Study of the Play-Element in Culture*. Kettering: Angelico Press.

Hundt, Markus. 2000. *"Spracharbeit" im 17. Jahrhundert. Studien zu Georg Philipp Harsdörffer, Justus Georg Schottelius und Christian Gueintz*. Berlin & New York: Mouton de Gruyter.

Hundt, Markus. 2011. Diskursivierung von Wissen durch Sprache – der multimodale Ansatz von Georg Philipp Harsdörffer in den Frauenzimmer Gesprächspielen. In Thorsten Burkard, Markus Hundt, Steffen Martus & Claus-Michael Ort (eds.), *Politik – Ethik – Poetik. Diskurse und Medien frühneuzeitlichen Wissens* (Diskursivierung von Wissen in der Frühen Neuzeit 1), 177–200. Berlin: Akademie.

Jellinek, Max Hermann. 1913–1914. *Geschichte der neuhochdeutschen Grammatik. Von den Anfängen bis Adelung*. Vol. I–II. Heidelberg: Carl Winter.

Kabatek, Johannes. 2015. Wordplay and Discourse Traditions. In Angelika Zirker & Esme Winter-Froemel (eds.), *Wordplay and Metalinguistic / Metadiscursive Reflection. Authors, Contexts, Techniques, and Meta-Reflection* (Dynamics of Wordplay 1), 213–228. Berlin & Boston: De Gruyter.

Kirshenblatt-Gimblett, Barbara (ed.). 1976. *Speech Play. Research and Resources for Studying Linguistic Creativity*. Philadelphia: University of Pennsylvania Press.

Knight, Kenneth G. 1960. G. P. Harsdörffer's "Frauenzimmergesprächspiele". *German Life and Letters* 13. 116–125.

Knight, Kenneth G. 1991. Harsdörffers Gesprächspiele und ihre Nachwirkung. In Italo Michele Battafarano (ed.), *Georg Philipp Harsdörffer. Ein deutscher Dichter und europäischer Gelehrter*, 181–194. Bern: Peter Lang.

Knospe, Sebastian, Alexander Onysko & Maik Goth (eds.). 2016. *Crossing Languages to Play with Words. Multidisciplinary Perspectives* (Dynamics of Wordplay 3). Berlin & Boston: De Gruyter.

Koch, Peter. 1997. Diskurstraditionen: zu ihrem sprachtheoretischen Status und ihrer Dynamik. In Barbara Frank, Thomas Haye & Doris Tophinke (eds.), *Gattungen mittelalterlicher Schriftlichkeit* (ScriptOralia 99), 43–79. Tübingen: Narr.

Krebs, Jean-Daniel. 1994. L'apprentissage de la conversation en Allemagne au XVIIe siècle. In Alain Montandon (ed.), *Pour une histoire des traités de savoir-vivre en Europe*, 215–244. Clermont-Ferrand: Association des Publications de la Faculté des Lettres et Sciences humaines de Clermont-Ferrand.

Law, Vivien. 2003. *The History of Linguistics in Europe: From Plato to 1600*. Cambridge: Cambridge University Press.

Luckmann, Thomas. 1986. Grundformen der gesellschaftlichen Vermittlung des Wissens: Kommunikative Gattungen. *Kölner Zeitschrift für Soziologie und Sozialpsychologie* 27. 191–211.
Moulin, Claudine. 2008a. Grammatik im Bild – Bilder der Grammatik. Räume des sprachlichen Wissens in der Grammatikographie der Frühen Neuzeit. In Katharina Bahlmann, Elisabeth Oy-Marra & Cornelia Schneider (eds.), *Gewusst wo! Wissen schafft Räume: Die Verortung des Denkens im Spiegel der Druckgraphik*, 17–36. Berlin: Akademie.
Moulin, Claudine. [1998] 2008b. Deutsche Grammatikschreibung vom 16. bis 18. Jahrhundert. In Werner Besch, Anne Betten, Oskar Reichmann & Stefan Sonderegger (eds.), *Sprachgeschichte. Ein Handbuch zur Geschichte der deutschen Sprache und ihrer Erforschung* (Handbücher zur Sprach- und Kommunikationswissenschaft 2.2), 2nd edn., 1903–1911. Berlin & New York: De Gruyter Mouton.
Moulin, Claudine. 2011. Grammatische Architekturen. Zur Konstitution von metasprachlichem Wissen in der Frühen Neuzeit. In Sabine Frommel & Gernot Kamecke (eds.), *Les sciences humaines et leurs langages: Artifices et adoptions*, 25–44. Roma: Campisano.
Moulin, Claudine. 2016. "Nach dem die Gäste sind, nach dem ist das Gespräch". Spracharbeit und barocke Tischkultur bei Georg Philipp Harsdörffer. In Simone Schultz-Balluff & Nina Bartsch (eds.), *Perspektiv-Wechsel oder: Die Wiederentdeckung der Philologie*. Vol. II: *Grenzgänge und Grenzüberschreitungen. Zusammenspiele von Sprache und Literatur im Mittelalter und Früher Neuzeit*, 261–287. Berlin: Erich Schmidt.
Moulin-Fankhänel, Claudine. 1994–1997. *Bibliographie der deutschen Grammatiken und Orthographielehren*. Vol. I: *Von den Anfängen der Überlieferung bis zum Ende des 16. Jahrhunderts*. Vol. II: *Das 17. Jahrhundert* (Germanische Bibliothek N.F. 6. Reihe: Bibliographien und Dokumentationen 4–5). Heidelberg: Winter.
OED = *Oxford English Dictionary*. http://www.oed.com/ (accessed 16 July 2018).
Padley, G. Arthur. 1988. *Grammatical Theory in Western Europe 1500–1700*. Vol. I: *The Latin Tradition*. Vol. II: *Trends in Vernacular Grammar II*. Cambridge: Cambridge University Press.
von Polenz, Peter & Claudine Moulin. 2013. *Deutsche Sprachgeschichte vom Spätmittelalter bis zur Gegenwart*. Vol. II: *17.–18. Jahrhundert*. 2nd edition by Claudine Moulin and Dominic Harion. Berlin & Boston: De Gruyter Mouton.
Roßbach, Nikola. 2015. *Lust und Nutz. Historische, geistliche, mathematische und poetische Erquickstunden in der Frühen Neuzeit*. Bielefeld: Aisthesis.
Sherzer, Joel. 2002. *Speech Play and Verbal Art*. Austin: University of Texas Press.
Westerhoff, Jan C. 1999. Poeta Calculans: Harsdörffer, Leibniz, and the "Mathesis Universalis". *Journal of the History of Ideas* 60(3). 449–467. http://www.jstor.org/stable/3654013 (accessed 30 January 2017).
Winter-Froemel, Esme. 2013. Ambiguität im Sprachgebrauch und im Sprachwandel. Parameter der Analyse diskurs- und systembezogener Fakten. *Zeitschrift für französische Sprache und Literatur* 123(2). 130–170.
Winter-Froemel, Esme. 2016. Approaching Wordplay. In Sebastian Knospe, Alexander Onysko & Maik Goth (eds.), *Crossing Languages to Play with Words. Multidisciplinary Perspectives* (Dynamics of Wordplay 3), 11–46. Berlin & Boston: De Gruyter.
Winter-Froemel, Esme & Angelika Zirker (eds.). 2015. *Enjeux du jeu de mots. Perspectives linguistiques et littéraires* (Dynamics of Wordplay 2). Berlin & Boston: De Gruyter.
Wittgenstein, Leo. [1953] 2001. *Philosophische Untersuchungen. Kritisch-genetische Edition*, ed. by Joachim Schulte. Frankfurt: Wissenschaftliche Buchgesellschaft.

Zeller, Rosmarie. 1974. *Spiel und Konversation im Barock. Untersuchungen zu Harsdörffers "Gesprächspielen"*. Berlin & New York: De Gruyter Mouton.

Zirker, Angelika & Esme Winter-Froemel (eds.). (2015). *Wordplay and Metalinguistic / Metadiscursive Reflection. Authors, Contexts, Techniques, and Meta-Reflection* (Dynamics of Wordplay 1). Berlin & Boston: De Gruyter.

Appendix

List of contributions and abstracts

The Dynamics of Wordplay 6 & 7

The following overview contains all the contributions from volumes 6 and 7 of *The Dynamics of Wordplay* and furthermore includes all the abstracts from the French contributions in volume 7.

Karine Abiven: The power of wordplay. Domination by language in contexts of social inequality (Pouvoir du jeu de mots. Dominer par la parole en contexte d'inégalité sociale)

This article examines wordplay, here classically defined as the exploitation of a double meaning, as it is used in repartee, within unequal interactions in the French court society (17th–18th centuries). Exploring a varied corpus of courtesy books, collections of brief forms and memoirs, I would like to demonstrate the role of wordplay as social regulator: in a society of orders where hierarchies render the stances in interaction more or less fixed, but where the intellect is credited with a strong social added value, the wordplay makes it possible to save face, even when the speaker is in a prediscursive situation of inferiority. By adopting a pragmatic perspective, the aim is to examine how this type of use of the wordplay, culturally assimilated to what is then called the "bon mot", constitutes a weapon of defence or domination: it serves to convey implicit content through the use of figures (antithesis, analogy) and metalinguistic detour. Wordplay thus makes it possible to temporarily equalize the relative positions of power, while maintaining the forms of *decorum*: absence of aggressiveness and rudeness, and honesty. Ambiguous as it is, the repartee is difficult to refute; and surprising as it is, it defuses potential replies. The frequency of the intellectual repartees between unequals at the time does not allow us to speculate on any concrete effectiveness of wordplay on the social mobility of the subjects; it does, however, allow us to examine the linguistic imagery of the forms of domination, and the means of circumventing them.

Salvatore Attardo: Universals in puns and humorous wordplay

See this volume.

Angelika Braun and Astrid Schmiedel: The phonetics of ambiguity. A study on verbal irony

See this volume.

Dirk Delabastita: The dynamics of wordplay and the modern novel: A paired case study

See this volume.

Hélène Favreau: "Allumeeez le fun": Wordplay at the intersection of linguistic and sociolinguistic dynamics in advertising discourse ("Allumeeez le fun": le jeu de mots comme lieu de croisement des dynamiques linguistique et sociolinguistique dans le discours publicitaire)

Wordplay is based, at least in advertising, on the speaker's intentional deviation from established linguistic norms, first in order to capture the hearers' attention, then to make them smile or laugh. This phatic function, together with an aesthetically pleasing playfulness, suffices to account for the advertisers' almost systematic use of this linguistic mechanism. Yet it is quite clear that certain issues and challenges underlying this strategy go beyond its strictly communicative goal. To what extent can the extensive use of wordplay in advertising be considered a successful communication approach? This paper analyzes several examples in order to highlight the way French-language advertising successfully takes advantage of its many systemic potentialities as it shakes off a number of linguistic constraints by playing with words on the phonological, lexical and semantic levels. Such infringements reflect the dynamic nature of language. The focus then shifts onto the different dynamics at work when the hearer is supposed to reconstruct the meaning. This process involves and commits the latter to a varying extent, from mere collusion to active participation – even physically in certain cases. The hearer may also have to appeal to a common cultural knowledge so as to decipher the intertextuality or the subtext conveyed by wordplay. Wordplay may lose its frequent hapax status whenever it comes into current use by speakers whose reappropriation of the lexeme can lead, in some cases, to meaningful alterations. Finally, we will examine the sociolinguistic dynamics at work and consider the advertising discourse as both reflecting the natural evolution of French and also instigating new linguistic trends.

Natalia Filatkina and Claudine Moulin: Wordplay and baroque linguistic ideas

See this volume.

Raymond W. Gibbs, Jr.: Words making love together: Dynamics of metaphoric creativity

See this volume.

Peter Handler: Domain names – a new source of linguistic creativity (Les noms de domaine – une nouvelle source de créativité langagière)

Choosing a domain name (or web address) usually means searching for suitable generic terms, exploiting various possibilities of word-formation or drawing from the abundance of phraseology. However, more eye-catching techniques, such as word play in the broader sense, are also utilised and worth consideration. The range of these creations includes, for example: blends, phonetic alienation, paronymy (classic play on resemblance), double meanings, or permutations as in the French "verlan". Language creativity, combined with the constraints of specific technical standardisation, allows play with certain domain name extensions (mostly assigned to countries), which are reinterpreted or integrated into selected terms or phrases. Ideally, striking and meaningful domain names achieve several objectives at once: they draw attention, are easy to memorise and convey a message. This contribution intends to present an overview of the types using proven word play schemes. It also aims to identify and classify those which are intrinsically due to the characteristic conditions and standards of the domain name system (considerably expanded following the introduction of the "New generic Top Level Domains" – NgTLDs).

Joshua T. Katz: Exercises in wile

See this volume.

Catherine Kerbrat-Orecchioni: The fortunes and misfortunes of wordplay (Heurs et malheurs du jeu de mots)

In this article, the lexeme "wordplay" (JDM) is understood in its narrow sense (given that there are other ways to play with words), which includes the levels of signifier and signified simultaneously. More precisely, it includes the conscious and deliberate production of a *double sens*, contrary to normal language use, in which polysemous units become monosemous when they are actualized. When consulting dictionaries, it becomes clear that it is hard to evaluate wordplays, i.e. to say whether a JDM can be classified as "good" or "bad". Which is why this paper addresses the question. In fact, it seems that we as linguists are able to identify a certain number of factors that may be relevant in these evaluative judgements, even if we have to admit that such evaluations are highly subjective. The factors can be divided into three categories. From a formal viewpoint, the quality of a wordplay can be related to its degree of complexity: from this angle, I examine paronomasia *in praesentia*, antanaclasis, paronomasia *in absentia* and syllepsis. From a semantic viewpoint, the JDM may be more or less "motivated" ("pertinent") vs. "unmotivated". Finally, from a pragmatic viewpoint, the principal conditions for the success of a wordplay will be discussed (comprehensibility, acceptability, adaptation to the genre in which the wordplay is embedded). In any case, while the linguistic tools allow us to effectively analyze the mechanisms of a wordplay, its effects remain largely unpredictable.

Michelle Lecolle: Collectivity at play – collective nouns in wordplay (Enjeu du collectif – noms collectifs en jeux)

Starting from the postulate that certain instances of wordplay are based on striking characteristics of language, this article deals with wordplay in which the notions of the collective and plurality are the main features. The utterances examined are taken from French literature, advertising and – mainly – from the French press. They include collective nouns and singular and plural expressions including a definite article; it is on the basis of this linguistic material that wordplay is constructed by exploiting its morphosyntactic (morphological singular), semantic (double level of collective nouns) and interpretative (collective and distributive interpretation) characteristics. Starting from these examples, we discuss the limits of the idea of wordplay and defend the idea that wordplay generates intellectual pleasure without necessarily being conceived or perceived as humorous.

Jiaying Li: Wordplay in the dramaturgy of the avant-garde of the 1950s: The examples of Ionesco and Tardieu (Le jeu de mots dans la dramaturgie d'avant-garde des années 1950: les exemples de Ionesco et de Tardieu)

Wordplay, seen from the broader perspective of the nature of play in general – the creation of a pleasurable and relaxing illusion outside real life –, means a departure from the usual conventions and the utilitarian purpose of language, a refuge, based on *joking* and *entertainment*, from the seriousness and banality of everyday use. As it is used in traditional (Aristotelian) comic drama, wordplay reinforces illusionist effects by emphasizing the comic in an idea, a character or a situation. The avant-garde theatre of the 1950s, freed from the preoccupation with *mimesis*, releases wordplay from its servile attachment to the *verisimilitude* of the illusion and to the dramatic connivance that the author sought from his audience, thus allowing it to attain a degree of purity and freedom – which makes it, at the same time, a catalyst for drama's empowerment. Eugène Ionesco and Jean Tardieu are both jugglers of words in the tradition of Jarry; they share the avant-garde's dream of an abstract drama, while adopting two very different post-war attitudes towards language and dramatic aesthetics – rupture and reconciliation. Ionesco worked on the dysfunction of language and the failure of communication, while Tardieu exploited the comic imagination and the musical potential of language. The wordplays of the former, despising logic and reason, are part of the anarchic spirit which is the basis of *joking* and has a critical function; those of the latter, exploring the ludic and poetic dimensions of words, approach the aesthetic principal of *entertainment* and assume a constructive function. A comparison of these two types of wordplay, on both paradigmatic and discursive levels, will throw light on the important role of wordplay in the renewal of dramatic language and the general view of language at the middle of the last century.

Elena Meteva-Rousseva: Wordplays in Anthony Burgess's *nadsat* – how its French translators took up the challenge (Les jeux de mots dans le *nadsat* d'Anthony Burgess – comment ses traducteurs français ont relevé le défi)

Anthony Burgess' futuristic dystopian novel *A Clockwork Orange*, published in 1962 and ranked among the 100 top novels of the 20th century, owes its fame not only to Stanley Kubrick's film of the same name, but also, to a large extent, to the slang that Burgess invented for his juvenile thugs of the future. He called it *nadsat* (the suffix of Russian numbers from eleven to nineteen). Its vocabulary is a strange mix of Russian and colloquial English, studded with cockney rhyming slang, neologisms, childish English, old English, gypsy, references to various literary works, etc. Our attention will focus on the wordplay with which Burgess's text is laced. We will begin by identifying the issues that wordplays pose in translation as a whole and will sketch the potential ways of solving them. Then we will attempt to reveal the specificity of the wordplays in this novel. Bilingual for the most part, referring to Russian, a language unfamiliar to English speaking people, they represent secret wordplays, as discussed by Matthias Bauer (2015). Thus they seem appropriate in this context, since they are used to coin a type of slang-language, which is meant to help construct a group identity, and to be cryptic and playful. In Burgess's work, the wordplays assume two dominant functions: a referential one and a qualifying one. Examples will be given to illustrate both and to present an idea of how the French translators of the book Georges Belmont and Hortense Chabrier (the translation appeared in 1972 under the title "L'Orange mécanique") proceeded to tackle the challenges of these wordplays, which in addition are for the most part translinguistic.

Cécile Pajona: The dynamics of syllepsis in the novels of Boris Vian (La dynamique de la syllepse dans la construction fictionnelle chez Boris Vian)

This paper is a study of syllepsis – a figure of speech where a part of speech is made to cover two different functions – in the novels of Boris Vian. The main focus is to shed light on the dynamics of syllepsis-based wordplay in his fiction. A detailed study of this particular figure of speech allows an investigation of its literary effect. Starting by exploring the role of syllepsis in wordplay (and putting it into perspective compared to the pun), this paper clarifies the function of wordplay based on syllepsis and the role of this type of wordplay in deidiomatization. It appears that Vian creates a special bond between syllepsis and the deconstruction of linguistic standards. Next, the study focuses on enunciative heterogeneity in syllepsis. Due to the meeting of two isotopies, or of two understandings of a single word, syllepsis is a place where points of view meet, each of them being in charge of one different understanding of the world. Finally, this paper drafts a pragmatics of syllepsis in Vian's novels. This figure of speech, being at the origin of wordplay, takes part in the construction of a particular fictional world. It creates new norms as well as being normalized by the context. In this regard, it allows a negotiation of this new world with the reader. Syllepsis is then a particularly effective fictionalization tool since, as it proposes new norms, it creates a particular bond with the reader in order to make him accept the new rules presented.

Astrid Poier-Bernhard: Wor(l)dplay: Reflections on a writing-experience

See this volume.

Alain Rabatel: Under what circumstances can the *lapsus clavis* be considered puns? (À quelles conditions les *lapsus clavis* sont-ils des jeux de mots?)

This paper analyses the lapsus realized with a computer keyboard within a corpus of e-mails, and argues that some of them, by definition unintentional, can be considered good lapsus and consequently intentional puns. First, the paper reviews different types of lapsus, *calami* and *clavis*, and reexamines the difference between lapsus and typographical error or misprint. The paper then attempts to establish a hierarchy between the morphological, syntactic, semantic and interactional criteria that complement the lapsus as the utterance is produced, in order to explain how more or less successful lapsus can be regarded as puns. A distinction is made between morphological and phonological criteria, which provide clues in the case of a problematic utterance, semantic criteria, which highlight the hypothesis of the lapsus, enunciative and interactional criteria, which confirm the hypothesis and assess the lapsus, and the criterion of relevance/success, which depends on the shareability of the lapsus. The hierarchy of these criteria is not only production-related, but also reception-related, emphasizing the co-construction of the conditions or criteria of success that transform an *a priori* unintentional lapsus into an *a posteriori* intentional creation. Finally, as the lapsus is based on a conceptual conflict, the paper offers a pragmatic and enunciative analysis in order to emphasize the conflict, the phenomena of commitment of cumulative or substitutive points of view, related to the postures of co-, over- and under- enunciation.

Anda Rădulescu: From simple to complex puns in Frédéric Dard's novel *À prendre ou à lécher* (Du calembour simple au calembour complexe dans le roman *À prendre ou à lécher* de Frédéric Dard)

Puns represent one of the most important categories of wordplay and can be seen as "a tribute paid to language by authors who enrich it by using it" (Buffard-Moret 2014: 56, our translation). In literary works, puns are both a source (= a means) of enriching the language through their power to enhance verbal creativity, and a resource (= an aid) for entertaining, defining a character or a situation, or as a disguise for taboos. Frédéric Dard, one of the most famous French writers due to the numerous puns he invented, used them in his novels to relieve tension and to amuse his readers. As scholars have not yet agreed upon a final definition of the word *play* and upon a delineation of its categories, we consider it useful to revisit some of the criteria and classifications of wordplay, and focus on the underlying mechanisms of puns. Typical examples taken from the novel *À prendre ou à lécher* are provided, our aim being to highlight and exemplify the most frequent pun types used by the author, from common to complex ones, based on different mechanisms such as homophony, paronymy, synonymy, antinomy, polysemy, spoonerisms, malapropisms, meaning extension, evolving into cultural allusions, and the defrosting of proverbs, sayings and famous quotes. The result of the author's play with the sounds and meanings of words in French as well as in other languages (English and German in particular) has a comic effect that establishes a connivance between the writer and the reader and a dialogue beyond the written text.

Lisa Roques: *Symposium's* plays: a poet's words vs a strategos's words (Jeux de banquet: mots de poète, mots de stratège)

The story takes place in Chios, a West Aegean island, in the fifth century B.C. The social, political and intellectual elite is meeting for a *symposium* in the house of the Athenian *proxenus* Hermesilaos. After a few glasses of wine, the guests, among them, Sophocles, speak freely and make jokes and puns – what the Greeks call *paidia* – to the amusement of the assembled company. Poet Ion of Chios has preserved the memory of this moment for us in his (now fragmentary) work, the *Epidemiai*. Most often, the wordplays are based on the repetition of someone else's words with a malicious shift of meaning, a humorous syllepsis. Sophocles pretends to understand a word with poetical echoes in a material sense: what could a "ῥοδοδάκτυλος" hand be if not a dyer's hand? He intentionally confuses connotation with denotation to laugh at his adversary. Moreover, he applies the verb denoting glorious military rule "στρατηγεῖν" [to be a strategos] to petty seduction. This syllepsis is obviously an attack on the most famous strategos of the century, Pericles; Sophocles hurls barbs at him. From here on, the tone becomes more political... Of course, these taunts are made to bring a smile to the listeners' faces, but Sophocles uses wordplays here as a weapon in a verbal fight. A battle in which the weapons of the poet are arrayed against those of the strategos. These cutting remarks take on a social significance which cannot be ignored.

Catherine Ruchon: Wordplay in grief discourse: an offensive discursive play (Le jeu de mots dans les discours sur le deuil: un jeu discursif offensif)

Games with the very substance of language play a part in the expression of pain in the context of child mourning. The study of a corpus of some twenty books written by bereaved parents and some fifty names of parents' associations as well as statements taken from their sites show that expressions of grief present an unexpectedly diverse selection of wordplays. This corpus allows us to hypothesize that in a social context of reception not disposed to "dolorism", the bereaved find with wordplays a way to express their pain and to circumvent the taboos on mourning a child. Their formal mechanism is based on various techniques, often related, such as homophony and paronymy (*mourir avant de n'être, impansable*) or homophony and the principle of the paragram (*Sauve qui veut*). They also rely formally on morphology (*AbanDON Adoption, Alter Native*) or semantically on phrasemes (*Nos étoiles ont filé, Un ange est passé*) which belong to the category of "double meaning" (Freud [1905] 2009: 89f.). The analysis is based on the concepts of economy (of words) and condensation (of meaning) that Freud developed about the dream and applied to verbal humour. Wordplays make it possible to associate divergent ideas in a disjunctive synthesis (Deleuze 1969) and play the role of interpellation. This discursive creativity reveals a linguistic insubordination in the face of a doxa that encourages the silence of pain.

Aurélie Rusterholtz and François Chaix: Interview: The ludic dimension of language in the theatre – reflections and experiences (Interview: La dimension ludique du langage au théâtre – réflexions et expériences)

Within the framework of the conference programme of "The Dynamics of Wordplay/La dynamique du jeu de mots" (Trier, 29 September–1st October 2016), Trier theatre staged a reading of Louis Fuzelier's comedy *L'Amour maître de langue* (1718). This contribution presents the actors' reflections on the verbal humour in this comedy and also in their professional lives in general.

Jean-François Sablayrolles: Ludic lexical innovations in marginal or specific contexts of enunciation (Des innovations lexicales ludiques dans des situations d'énonciation marginales ou spécifiques)

This contribution attempts to examine some instances of playful innovations on lexical units in French outside of the mainstream of regular lexical creativity where playfulness plays only a minor role. Some situations of verbal exchange lend themselves to plays on words aimed amongst other things at amusing the interlocutors listening, who appreciate the speakers' efforts and are thus favorably disposed towards them. One of these marginal forms of lexical innovation is the emergence of purposefully incorrect flexional forms (*je téléphonis, frétillone, mon émolument...*). Some creative wits collect fanciful words, portmanteau words (*hebdrolmadaire, zobsédé*), or parody scientific words (*Le pornithorinque est un salopare capillolingualocuteur, capillotétratomie*). Another different aspect is the period when the child, during the process of acquiring the mother tongue, takes pleasure in playing with words, producing such mixtures as *un sardin*, les *clapins sont dans les lapiers* and other paronyms.

Monika Schmitz-Emans: Examples and poetics of wordplay in Han Shaogong's language-reflective novel *A Dictionary of Maqiao*

See this volume.

Gesa Schole: Wordplay as a means of post-colonial resistance

See this volume.

Françoise Sullet-Nylander: Wordplay in headlines of yesterday and today: the dynamics and diversity of a text type (Jeux de mots à la Une d'hier et d'aujourd'hui: dynamique et diversité d'un genre)

In our previous work (Sullet-Nylander 1998, 2005, 2006, 2010, 2012a and b, 2013 and 2014), we analyzed wordplay in the headlines of the French press, particularly in those of *Libération* and *Le Canard enchaîné*. We first studied the headlines as autonomous texts, then through their relationship with the introductory paragraph and the body of the article and through their intertextual or interdiscursive relationship with other circulating utterances. Thus, in a synchronic approach, we studied the processes that trigger the wordplay as well as its semantic effects in relation to the linguistic fixation or cultural fixation it is based on. In the present study, we base our analysis on two catalogues: *Les 100 unes qui ont fait la presse* of Christophe Bourseiller (2013) and *Libé. Les meilleurs titres* of Hervé Marchon (2016). The former brings together 100 front pages from French newspapers, both daily and weekly, ranging from the front page of Theophraste Renaudot's *Gazette* on May 16, 1631 to the front page of *Le Parisien*, December 21, 2012. The second catalogue contains 372 headlines of the French daily newspaper *Libération* covering a period from 1972 to 2015. Using this new material, we investigate the diversity of journalistic wordplay in the daily newspaper over the past four decades. The first part of the study shows that the headlines with wordplay from Bourseiller's catalogue are clearly a minority, which, in our opinion, is due to the fact that the 100 headlines were selected according to historical rather than linguistic criteria. The second part of the study, which deals with Marchon's book, shows that at *Libération* there has over the last 40 years been a strong continuity in the process of creating wordplay. However, this does not minimize the originality and dynamics of wordplay or the significant effects that this newspaper's headlines create in the context of the daily news.

Giovanni Tallarico: Lexical creativity and wordplay in advertising: forms and functions (Créativité lexicale et jeux de mots dans les messages publicitaires: formes et fonctions)

This paper focuses on forms and functions of wordplay in French advertising. The following analysis is based on a corpus of two years' issues of the free Paris weekly *À Nous Paris* (2015–2016). Wordplay is divided up according to the language features involved: wordplay exploiting language itself (alliteration and onomatopoeia); puns based on sound (homophones and paronyms); puns based on meaning (polysemous words and antonyms) and wordplay involving allusion (playful modification of fixed expressions). Although the visual element is increasingly important in advertising today, slogans remain a central feature. It emerges that slogans and wordplay share several key features and functions: concision, originality and efficiency in particular. As far as lexical creativity is concerned, slogans may resort to *lexical blending* and to the pragmatic-semantic matrix which may be glossed as hijacking a fixed expression. Slogans are meant to capture attention. They add a positive gloss, tend to alter canonical expressions and have a phatic, enhancing and mnemonic function. Wordplay too has multiple functions: it hooks readers and involves them in constructing the meaning of the utterance (complicity or "colludic" function); it blurs the commercial ploy by using a playful approach which defunctionalizes language. It emerges from the sample analyzed that wordplay in advertising concerns vocabulary rather than sentences. In addition, neology is quite marginal and takes the form of anomalous collocations. Puns on meaning, especially those playing on the different senses of a word, can be found in half the cases identified: as a consequence, polysemy emerges as the favored strategy for creating wordplay in slogans, since it can be used flexibly and is easy for readers to understand.

Esme Winter-Froemel and Pauline Beaucé: Language contact and verbal humour in French comedy at the turn of the 17th and 18th centuries (Contacts linguistiques et humour verbal dans le théâtre comique français au tournant des XVIIe et XVIIIe siècles)

Plurilingualism can be considered to be an important source of verbal humour in the comedies of the Ancien Régime period (Ciccone 1975, 1980; Garapon 1957; Louvat 2015). This contribution aims to study phenomena of language contact in these comedies from an interdisciplinary angle, bringing together linguistic and literary perspectives. We will analyze plays by Molière and comedies of the *théâtre de la Foire* in order to determine what the languages and idioms are that come into contact, and how these contacts are realized in the plays. We will show that the contacts can be presented in different ways, including code-switching between different characters or within the utterances of individual characters, interference and mixing of elements from different languages, and also creating new languages that parody linguistic stereotypes. In addition, we will investigate the social values attributed to different languages and the dramaturgic use of these languages. We will show that the language contact phenomena are related to certain traditions of verbal humour, but at the same time also partly transgress the linguistic and dramaturgic conventions. The verbal humour based on the plurilingualism of French theatre of the period investigated is thus characterized by a ludic orchestration of linguistic differences and tensions.

Ilias Yocaris: "En trou si beau adultère est béni": The poetics of wordplay in Claude Simon's *Histoire* ("En trou si beau adultère est béni": poétique du jeu de mots dans *Histoire* de Claude Simon)

Claude Simon's predilection for wordplay is widely known, and is prompted first and foremost by compositional considerations. As Simon explains in his Nobel lecture, the stylization displayed in his novels seeks to ensure that the unfolding of the narrative derives not from an extratextual causality, but from an "internal causality" resting on formal properties. By definition, wordplay is precisely the most appropriate stylistic device for creating a textual order which claims to be purely formal. The puns that are foregrounded in *History* (homonymies, paronomasiae, etymological reactivations, syllepses, portmanteau words...) are therefore the fruit of a verbal logic that makes them "textually indispensable": each one of them is part of a complex relational system, with which it interacts in a holistic way. Their use serves three purposes: (a) an organizational purpose (they densify the text by creating a network of multidirectional relations between its different components); (b) a referential purpose (they increase the investigative potential of "ordinary language"); (c) a metadiscursive purpose (they draw the reader's attention to the verbal materiality of the Simonian text, while modelling its structures and its functioning mode).

Eline Zenner and Dirk Geeraerts: One does not simply process memes: Image macros as multimodal constructions

See this volume.

Index

A Concise Chinese-English Dictionary for Lovers See Guo, Xiaolu
affixation 198, 209
alphabet 118, 140, 143ff., 148ff., 155, 159, 203, 221, 224, 249
ambiguity 2, 6, 10, 48, 50, 55, 64, 71, 92f., 97ff., 112f., 223, 227f., 233, 236, 245ff.
articulatory precision 118f.
automatic mental processes 26f., 29f., 36, 40f., 44
automatic writing 30ff.

baroque linguistic ideas 8, 245, 249, 253
Barthes, Roland 5, 77, 80f.
– *jouissance* 5, 77, 80f.
– pleasure of the text 77, 80f.
bilingual pun *See* pun
blend 7, 13, 29, 38, 178, 200f., 206ff., 213
Bök, Christian 140, 144, 148ff., 157, 160

Calvino, Italo 5, 77, 79f.
– exactitude 5, 77, 80
– lightness 5, 77, 79
– multiplicity 5, 77, 80
– rapidity 5, 77, 80
– visibility 5, 77, 80
clang response 101, 104
colonial mimicry 7, 199, 213
communication 1ff., 5, 9, 11, 61, 77, 114, 172, 205, 225, 237, 240
composition 32, 37, 51, 79, 117, 147, 174, 177, 190, 198, 202, 209, 213, 232
conceptual metaphor *See* metaphor
consciousness 26, 30ff., 40, 64, 79, 198, 242
construction 7, 11, 41, 79, 91, 170, 174f., 177, 179, 190
Construction Grammar 172, 175, 177
convention 13, 34, 60, 78, 100, 122, 124, 144, 151, 157, 171, 174, 177, 180, 187, 204, 209f., 213, 217ff., 225f., 228, 232, 237, 244
Cratylism 100, 103, 105
creativity 4, 12, 24, 26, 28f., 33, 35f., 43, 76ff., 80ff., 157f., 171, 174, 190, 236, 238

Cultural Revolution 225f., 228, 231

deliberate metaphor *See* metaphor
derivation 101, 139, 198, 202, 209, 228
dialect 50, 59, 90, 139, 150f., 158, 225, 232
dictionary 6f., 54, 56, 60, 148, 152f., 159, 217ff., 227f., 231, 233, 241
dictionary novel *See* novel
discourse tradition 3, 237
Dylan, Bob 23f., 29, 32

elusiveness 5, 51, 62
emoji 138, 159
emotion 32, 91, 120, 133
exactitude *See* Calvino, Italo

folk linguistics 101f.
formants 119
frequency 113, 115, 123, 125ff., 132, 143, 145, 151f., 154f.

global novel *See* novel
glossolalia 101, 104f.
grammatization 241
Guo, Xiaolu 5, 51ff., 57, 60, 72

Harsdörffer, Georg Philipp 8, 237f., 241ff., 249f., 252f.
humour/humor 2f., 5, 10, 26f., 35, 39f., 53, 66, 81, 89ff., 94, 96, 98ff., 106, 172f., 181, 184, 190, 200, 205, 231, 236
– humour research/humor research 2, 170, 173
– verbal humour/verbal humor 2f., 5f., 10f., 13, 61, 89, 94, 98f., 236, 238
hybridity 196, 199f., 207, 211, 213

iconicity 101, 103, 148, 158, 169
identity 6, 14, 38, 52, 105, 196f., 199f., 208, 210, 213, 223, 229
idiom 26, 55, 60, 62, 205f., 209f., 213, 223, 225
image macro 7, 170ff., 187ff.
intensity 80, 113, 115ff., 121, 123, 127f., 132f.

Internet meme 6f., 168ff., 187, 191
intertextuality 7, 64, 169, 172, 182, 186f., 190f.
irony 2, 6, 68, 111ff., 119f., 132, 171, 187, 218
– kind irony 6, 114, 121, 124ff., 130, 132f.
– sarcasm 6, 121f., 124ff., 128, 130, 132

Jakobson, Roman 48, 79
– poetic function 78
jouissance See Barthes, Roland

kind irony *See* irony

language reflection 217, 222
letterplay 238, 245
lexicographic novel *See* novel
lexicon 6, 104, 152, 155, 159, 242
lightness *See* Calvino, Italo
linguistic norm 11, 14, 228, 238, 241f., 253
lipogram 144, 146f., 149, 203
literature 1, 4, 7, 23, 26, 51, 75f., 79, 89, 92, 103, 113, 115, 138ff., 142, 145, 147, 155, 205, 218f., 223ff., 236f., 240, 242, 246
loudness 116
ludic deformation 203f., 206, 212, 238

malapropism 52, 67ff., 71
marginal phenomena 159
meme *See* Internet meme
metaphor 7, 24ff., 33f., 36ff., 50, 77ff., 112, 169, 207f., 213, 253
– conceptual metaphor 34, 42
– deliberate metaphor 26f., 41
– metaphoric creativity 4f., 31, 33
– mixed metaphor 37, 39f.
mixed metaphor *See* metaphor
modern novel *See* novel
monolingualism 61f., 223
Mozambique 7, 196f., 207ff., 212f.
multilingual literacy 5, 51, 62, 72
multilingualism 7, 62, 185, 189, 191, 223
multimodality 7, 168ff., 172, 174f., 179, 181ff., 189ff.
multiplicity *See* Calvino, Italo
My Sister, My Love See Oates, Joyce Carol

name, proper name 10ff., 52, 54, 61, 64ff., 90f., 100, 102, 112, 145, 148f., 169, 177f., 180, 183, 187f., 202, 228ff., 244ff., 248f.
novel 5ff., 9, 11, 14, 51f., 54f., 57, 59ff., 67ff., 71f., 75f., 90, 140, 147, 149, 154, 157, 196, 200, 205ff., 210, 212, 221f., 224f., 227f., 231f.
– dictionary novel, lexicographic novel 7, 53, 64, 221, 224, 232
– global novel 5, 51, 62f., 72
– modern novel 5, 72
– postmodern novel 64, 72
Nufer, Doug 157f.

Oates, Joyce Carol 5, 51, 62f., 68, 71f.
Oulipo 75f., 140, 142f., 147, 158

paralinguistic cues 132
paretymology 101
pedagogy 138, 150
Perec, Georges 140, 143, 147ff., 159, 223
phonetics 4, 6, 95, 112, 115, 118, 120f., 133, 150f., 155, 201, 206ff., 236
pitch 34, 114ff., 120, 125, 132
playfulness 5, 31, 78, 80, 82f., 218f., 228ff., 232f.
pleasure of the text *See* Barthes, Roland
poetic function *See* Jakobson, Roman
portmanteau 9, 167, 202, 206f., 213
post-colonialism 196f., 200, 207f., 213
postmodern novel *See* novel
proper name *See* name, proper name
prototype 48, 172, 174f., 179f., 182, 190, 204f., 219, 221
pun 2, 5f., 9ff., 14, 27, 48ff., 53ff., 57, 59, 61f., 65, 69f., 77, 80ff., 89, 91ff., 105f., 137, 139, 141, 170, 173, 181, 183ff., 187ff., 245
– bilingual pun 61f., 72

rapidity *See* Calvino, Italo
rhyme 50, 101, 104, 112, 141, 250

sarcasm *See* irony
satire 65, 217ff.
Scrabble 89f., 139ff., 143, 159
semiotics, semiotic 80, 92, 190

Sheen, Charlie 33ff., 40
sincerity 113f., 116ff., 120ff., 126f., 129, 131ff., 218
sound 50, 56, 60, 76f., 79ff., 91ff., 98, 100ff., 117, 120, 139, 141, 143, 149ff., 154, 156, 202, 238
sound symbolism 101ff.
soundplay 238
speaking tempo 117ff.
speech error 101, 105
Stevens, Wallace 28

taboo 10, 101f.
Trump, Donald 37f., 112, 120

verbal humour / verbal humor *See* humour, humor

vernacular language 237, 240, 253
visibility *See* Calvino, Italo
vocabulary 54, 198, 219, 222, 224f., 228f., 242, 249
voice pitch *See* pitch
voice quality 120

word salad 37f., 40, 142
wordplay definition 5, 8, 48f., 62, 140ff., 173, 200, 203f., 237ff., 245, 253
worldplay 5, 76f., 83

Zipf's law 154f.

List of contributors

The Dynamics of Wordplay 6 & 7

Karine Abiven (Sorbonne Université)
Karine Abiven is an assistant professor at Sorbonne University and member of the *Institut Universitaire de France*. She specializes in the French language and literature of the 17th and 18th centuries. She has worked on the short forms of non-fiction writing (*L'Anecdote ou la fabrique du petit fait vrai*, Paris: Classiques Garnier, 2015), and has edited several issues of periodicals on the writing of current events and history (*Littératures classiques* 78 and 94). She now focuses on the digital exploration of the pamphlets on the Fronde ("mazarinades").

Salvatore Attardo (Texas A&M University-Commerce)
Salvatore Attardo, PhD (Purdue, 1991), is professor of Linguistics at Texas A&M University-Commerce. He has authored two monographs (*Linguistic Theories of Humor*, 1994, and *Humorous Texts*, 2001). For ten years, he was editor-in-chief of *HUMOR: International Journal of Humor Research*. He edited the *Encyclopedia of Humor Studies* (Sage, 2014) and the *Handbook of Language and Humor* (Routledge, 2017). He has published over 100 articles on various topics in semantics and pragmatics.

Pauline Beaucé (Université Bordeaux Montaigne)
Pauline Beaucé (b. 1986) has a PhD in French language and literature (2011) and was a post-doctoral researcher in the ERC DramaNet project (FU Berlin, 2013). Since 2015, she has been a lecturer in theater studies at the University of Bordeaux Montaigne. Her research focuses on the history of representations in the 18th and 19th centuries, including the history of dramaturgic forms (parody, musical theatre, pantomime) and entertainment (fairground theatre, circus, *vauxhall*). She has published *Parodies d'opéra au siècle des Lumières* (PUR, 2013), 30 articles and entries in dictionaries as well as academic editions of unpublished dramatic texts. Pauline Beaucé is a member of the Dynamics of Wordplay network and participates in the Ciresfi ANR-project on Italian comedy and fairground theatre in the 18th century (University of Nantes, Françoise Rubellin).

Angelika Braun (Universität Trier)
Angelika Braun studied German linguistics and phonetics at the University of Marburg. She took her Ph. D. in linguistics and phonetics in 1988. From 1986 to 2000, she worked as a full-time forensic phonetician for the German Federal Criminal Bureau (BKA) and the State Forensic Laboratory of North Rhine-Westphalia. In July 2000 she obtained her post-doctoral degree (Habilitation) from the University of Marburg and later that year, she joined the faculty of that university. Since 2009, she has held the post of professor of general and applied phonetics at the University of Trier. Her main research interests include speaker characteristics and speaker variability as well as sociophonetics, specifically speech and emotion, non-actual speech (irony), and phonetic aspects of wordplay. From the beginning of her academic career, she has also maintained an interest in and published on the history of phonetics.

François Chaix (actor / director, Paris)
After attending courses by Anicette Fray and Jean-Laurent Cochet, François Chaix went to drama school in Paris (Classe Supérieure d'Art Dramatique de la Ville de Paris (ESAD)), which he left in 1989. Since 1990 he has worked as a professional actor and has appeared in numerous productions (Molière, Musset, Rostand, Brecht, Feydeau, etc.). For many years he has had a permanent position at the Auguste Théâtre-Cie Gilles Robin. He has also taken part in several performances by Jean-Marie Villégier (*Le Fidèle* by Pierre de Larivey, *La Répétition interrompue* by Charles Favart, etc.) and in 2007 joined Aurélie Rusterholtz for the lecture performances at the Grand T in Nantes, the annual meeting at which rare texts of the 17th and 18th centuries are performed on stage (Fuzelier, Soulas d'Allainval, Gueullette, Regnard, Piron, Boisfranc, Coypel, Autreau). In 2011, he played in *Arlequin Sauvage* by Delisle de la Drevetière (produced by Thierry Pillon) in Quebec. He co-directed and acted in *Spectacle Eclair* in 2015, directed and acted in Satyrics, after Jean-Claude Grumberg, in 2016 and co-directed *Travaux – Les entretiens d'embauche* by Jacques Jouet in 2017 and *Regardez le soleil pour moi... – Paparazzi* by Matéi Visniec. In 2018, he played Capitaine Alpy in *Emmanuel P. fusillé pour l'exemple* by Bernard Briais and directed by Pascale Sueur. He has appeared in films with Michel Béna and Rodolphe Marconi, and in television productions with Christophe Barraud, Jean-Teddy Philippe, Myriam Touzé, Philippe Roussel, Kevin Connor, Roger Young, etc. Recently, he has been much in demand for voice-over work.

Dirk Delabastita (Université de Namur)

Dirk Delabastita teaches English literature and literary theory at the University of Namur and is a Research Fellow at KU Leuven. He has published widely on Shakespeare's wordplay and the problems of translating it. His book-length publications include *There's a Double Tongue* (1993), *European Shakespeares* (co-edited with Lieven D'hulst, 1993), *Traductio. Essays on Punning and Translation* (edited, 1997), *Fictionalizing Translation and Multilingualism* (co-edited with Rainier Grutman, 2005), *Shakespeare and European Politics* (co-edited with Jozef de Vos and Paul Franssen, 2008), *Multilingualism in the Drama of Shakespeare and his Contemporaries* (co-edited with Ton Hoenselaars, 2015), and *"Romeo and Juliet" in European Culture* (co-edited with Juan F. Cerdá and Keith Gregor, 2017). He co-edits the Translation Studies journal *Target* (with Sandra Halverson, 2012–), as well as a comprehensive Dutch-language open-access dictionary of literary terms entitled *Algemeen Letterkundig Lexicon* (http://www.dbnl.org/tekst/dela012alge01_01/index.php).

Alex Demeulenaere (Universität Trier)

Alex Demeulenaere is lecturer ("Akademischer Oberrat") in Romance languages and literatures at Trier University. He has published work on (post)colonial and (post)national literatures in francophone cultures (France, Belgium, Africa, Canada), translation studies, travel narrative and literary theory (Said, de Certeau). In his dissertation (Leuven 2007), he used the framework of discourse analysis and enunciation studies to analyze the narrative ethos and the construction of scientific credibility in French colonial travel narratives. As a member of the IRTG "Diversity", his current research is based on the same framework (i.e. posture) which enables a diachronic case study of national and postnational Quebec literature. He has had considerable teaching experience at the Universities of Leuven and Trier, has also organized multidisciplinary seminars in cooperation with Saarland University and is in charge of a masters seminar on interculturality and literature at the University of Luxembourg.

Hélène Favreau (Université Catholique de l'Ouest, Angers)

Hélène Favreau is a lecturer in Language Sciences at the Faculty of Humanities at the Université Catholique de l'Ouest, Angers. Her PhD in French sociolinguistics mainly dealt with speakers' attitudes towards norms and varieties of French. This research has led to several publications, among them: "Linguistic norms and standards: towards social exclusion" (in *Norms in Educational Linguistics*. Oxford: Peter Lang, 2010); "Speakers' Attitudes to Language: Generators or Mirrors of Sociolinguistic Changes?" (The French Example) (*Forum for Anthropology and Culture* 21. Saint Petersburg: Russian Academy of Sciences, 2014); "'On s'keep in Sosh' ou l'exemple du français libéré dans et par la publicité" (*Voix Plurielles* 12.1, 2015). Her present research areas also include lexicology and more specifically lexical creation, from both morphological and semantic perspectives.

Natalia Filatkina (Universität Trier)
Natalia Filatkina studied linguistics and intercultural communication at the Moscow State Linguistic University and at the Humboldt University of Berlin. She obtained her PhD in Germanic Linguistics from the University of Bamberg. Since 2003, she has been teaching Historical Linguistics of German at Trier University, where she also worked as Principal Investigator of the Research Group "Historical Formulaic Language and Traditions of Communication". In 2017, she gained her habilitation (post-doctoral degree) from this university and is currently an adjunct professor ("außerplanmäßige Professorin") and "Akademieprofessorin" for medieval language and culture at Trier University and the Academy of Sciences and Literature in Mainz. Her main research interests include language change, formulaic and figurative language, standardization and normalization, historical dialogue, text and discourse studies as well as digital humanities. She is also one of the editors of the book series "Formelhafte Sprache / Formulaic language" (De Gruyter).

Dirk Geeraerts (KU Leuven)
Dirk Geeraerts is professor of linguistics at the University of Leuven, where he founded the research unit Quantitative Lexicology and Variational Linguistics. His main research interests involve the overlapping fields of lexical semantics and lexicology, with a specific descriptive interest in social variation, a strong methodological commitment to corpus analysis, and a theoretical background in Cognitive Linguistics. As the founding editor of the journal Cognitive Linguistics, he played a significant role in the international expansion of Cognitive Linguistics. His publications include the following monographs: *Paradigm and Paradox* (1985), *The Structure of Lexical Variation* (1994), *Diachronic Prototype Semantics* (1997), *Words and Other Wonders* (2006), *The Oxford Handbook of Cognitive Linguistics* (2007), and *Theories of Lexical Semantics* (2010).

Raymond W. Gibbs, Jr. (University of California, Santa Cruz)

Raymond W. Gibbs, Jr. is a cognitive scientist and former Distinguished Professor of Psychology at the University of California, Santa Cruz. His research interests focus on embodied cognition, pragmatics and figurative language. He is the author of almost 300 articles and book chapters and has published many books, including *The poetics of mind: Figurative Thought, Language and Understanding* (1994), *Intentions in the Experience of Meaning* (1999), *Embodiment and Cognitive Science* (2006), *Metaphor Wars: Conceptual Metaphor in Human Life* (2017), and (with Herb Colston) *Interpreting Figurative Meaning* (2012), all published by Cambridge University Press. He is also editor of the *Cambridge Handbook of Metaphor and Thought* (2008, CUP), and editor of the journal *Metaphor and Symbol*.

Peter Handler (Wirtschaftsuniversität Wien – WU)

Peter Handler is an assistant professor at the Institute for Romance Languages in the Department of Foreign Language Business Communication of Vienna University of Business and Economics (Wirtschaftsuniversität Wien – WU). His main research fields include stylistics (neology, phraseology, text theory), word-formation, language creativity, languages for specific purposes, software-supported presentations and the new media (linguistic and semiotic phenomena). He teaches courses in business French and business German. His doctoral thesis *Wortbildung und Literatur* gives an analysis of poetological aspects of word-formation. Among his recent publications are the following handbook articles: "Word-formation and literature" in *Word-Formation* (ed. by P. O. Müller, I. Ohnheiser, S. Olsen & F. Rainer, Handbooks of Linguistics and Communication Science 40) and the chapters "Business presentations" and "Company websites" in *Handbook of Business Communication. Linguistic Approaches* (ed. by G. Mautner & F. Rainer, Handbooks of Applied Linguistics 13).

Joshua T. Katz (Princeton University)

Joshua T. Katz is Cotsen Professor in the Humanities, Professor of Classics, and member (and sometime Director) of the Program in Linguistics at Princeton University, where he has been on the faculty since 1998, the year he received his Ph.D. in Linguistics from Harvard. Recent publications have tackled linguistic, literary, and cultural issues in works that range from the 8th- or 7th-century B.C. Greek poetry of Homer and Hesiod to 20th- and 21st-century A.D. experimental fiction in English by Russell Hoban and Paul Kingsnorth. He has a special interest in the history and practice of wordplay.

Catherine Kerbrat-Orecchioni (Université de Lyon 2)
Catherine Kerbrat-Orecchioni is an Honorary Professor at the Université of Lyon 2. She has also been a visiting professor at Columbia University in New York, the University of Geneva and the University of California, Santa Barbara. From 2000 to 2005, she held the chair "Linguistics of Interactions" at the *Institut Universitaire de France*. Her areas of specialization include pragmatics, discourse analysis and conversation analysis. In these areas, she has published numerous articles and books, e.g. *L'énonciation, L'implicite, Les interactions verbales* (3 volumes), *Les actes de langage dans le discours, La conversation, Le discours en interaction* and in 2017 *Les débats de l'entre-deux-tours des élections présidentielles françaises. Constantes et évolutions d'un genre*.

Michelle Lecolle (Université de Lorraine)
Michelle Lecolle is an Associate Professor HDR (with a post-doctoral degree) in linguistics at the University of Lorraine in Metz (Crem / Centre de Recherches sur les médiations). Her main research topics concern nominal semantics within the discourse, collective nouns and proper nouns that designate groups of humans, semantic neology, and "language awareness" (of non-linguist speakers). Selected publications: Dénomination de groupes sociaux: approche sémantique et discursive d'une catégorie de noms propres (in Franck Neveu, Peter Blumenthal, Linda Hriba, Annette Gerstenberg, Judith Meinschaefer & Sophie Prévost, eds., *Quatrième Congrès mondial de linguistique française*, 2265–2281. Berlin: SHS Web of Conferences, 2014); Jeux de mots et motivation: une approche du sentiment linguistique (in Esme Winter-Froemel & Angelika Zirker, eds., *Enjeux du jeu de mots. Perspectives linguistiques et littéraires*, 217–243. Berlin & Boston: De Gruyter, 2015); Some specific insights into wordplay form: sublexical vs lexical level (in Sebastian Knospe, Alexander Onysko & Maik Goth, eds., *Crossing Languages to Play with Words. Multidisciplinary Perspectives*, 63–70. Berlin & Boston: De Gruyter, 2016); Noms collectifs humains en français: enjeux sémantiques, lexicaux et discursifs (submitted).

Jiaying Li (Université Paris Nanterre)
Jiaying Li is a PhD student in drama studies at Paris Nanterre University. Her thesis deals with verbal play in 20th century French theatre (Jarry, Ionesco, Tardieu, Novarina). She has published several articles in China and Europe, particularly on the issue of language play in "non-dramatic" theatre. Among her most recent publications: The *modern* silence in Valère Novarina's 'holed writing' (*Quêtes littéraires* 7, 2017); The issues of Jean Tardieu's radio plays

(*Revue Sciences / Lettres*, 2017); From Novarina's idiolect to linguistic individualism (in Michel Viegnes and Jean Rime, eds., *Représentations de l'individu en Chine et en Europe francophone*, Alphil-Presses universitaires suisses, 2015). She is also the Chinese translator of Madeleine Bertaud's book: *François Cheng. A journey towards the open life* (Hermann, 2011).

Elena Meteva-Rousseva (Sofia University "St. Kl. Ohridski")

Elena Meteva-Rousseva is an Associate Professor at the Department of Romance Studies at Sofia University "St. Kl. Ohridski". Research fields: discourse analysis of the press; reported speech in the press; history of translation, translation studies; translation of humour. Publications: Le comique – défi linguistique et extralinguistique pour le traducteur (in A. Tchaouchev et al., eds., *Traduction et communication interculturelle*, 98–108. Presses universitaires "St. Kl. Ohridski", 2010); Calembours, expressions figées détournées – comment y faire face en traduction (*RumeliDE Journal of language and Literature Studies* 6, April, Special Issue 2, 2016. 33–42); L'humour dans *Les Carnets du major Thompson* de Pierre Daninos et les problèmes que celui-ci soulève en traduction anglaise et bulgare (in Sophie Anquetil et al., eds., *Autour des formes implicites*, 293–304. Presses Universitaires de Rennes, 2017).

Claudine Moulin (Universität Trier)

Claudine Moulin holds the Chair of German Historical Linguistics at Trier University and is the academic director of the Trier Center for Digital Humanities. She studied German and English Philology in Brussels and Bamberg. After her PhD (1990) in the domain of Early New High German orthography, she was a researcher at the University of Bamberg, where she gained her habilitation (post-doctoral degree) in 1999 in the field of German Linguistics and Philology. In 1995 and 1997 she spent several periods of research in Oxford as a Heisenberg Fellow of the German Research Foundation (DFG), working on vernacular paratexts and marginalia in medieval manuscripts, and in 2002 was professor of Linguistics at the University of Luxembourg. She has been a Visiting Professor at the École Pratique des Hautes Études EPHE / Sorbonne in Paris and a Research Fellow at the Institute of Advanced Studies / Institut d'Études Avancées in Paris. Her research covers the fields of historical linguistics and language change, medieval languages and literature, grammaticography, lexicography, graphematics and digital humanities. She is also one of the editors of the journal *Sprachwissenschaft* and the book series *Germanistische Bibliothek* (Winter).

Cécile Pajona (Université Nice Sophia Antipolis)

Cécile Pajona is a PhD student in literature at Bases Corpus Langage (UMR 7320) in Nice. Her thesis, which is conducted under the direction of Geneviève Salvan, studies the process of fictionalizaton in Boris Vian's novels. Through a pragma-enunciative approach of Vian's work, it examines figures of speech as well as their contribution to manufacturing a fictional universe. The corpus is particularly suited to the study of wordplay, humor, as well as their contribution and their pragmatic efficiency. Her papers mainly focus on shedding light on the peculiarity of Boris Vian's stylus.

Astrid Poier-Bernhard (Karl-Franzens-Universität Graz)

Astrid Poier-Bernhard has been a professor of Romance Literature at the Institute for Romance Studies in Graz since her habilitation (post-doctoral degree) in 2010, focusing on contemporary constrained literature in France and Italy. In her doctoral thesis, a second book and numerous articles, she devoted herself to the work of Romain Gary (*Romain Gary – Das brennende Ich. Literaturtheoretische Implikationen eines Pseudonymenspiels*. Tübingen: Niemeyer, 1996; *Romain Gary im Spiegel der Literaturkritik*. Frankfurt am Main & Wien: Lang, 1999). Since 1998 much of her research work has concerned Oulipo and potential literature. This subject is also the main theme of a literary essay in the pastiche genre, *Viel Spaß mit Haas!* (Wien: Sonderzahl, 2003) and the (academic) book *Texte nach Bauplan. Studien zur zeitgenössischen ludisch-methodischen Literatur in Frankreich und Italien* (Heidelberg: Winter, 2012). Astrid Poier-Bernhard is involved in numerous collaborations with cultural institutions and artists. In 2013 she was co-opted by the Oplepo group (Opificio di letteratura potenziale).

Alain Rabatel (Université de Lyon 1)

Alain Rabatel is Professor of Linguistics at the University of Lyon 1 and a member of the UMR ICAR (University of Lyon 2). His areas of specialization include the theory of enunciation, text linguistics and discourse analysis. He is the author of five books and more than 160 articles, and has (co-)edited about twenty books and journal issues. Alain Rabatel first became known for his work on points of view, empathy and polyphony in narration (*Une histoire du point de vue*, CELTED / Klincksieck, 1997; *La construction textuelle du point de vue*, Delachaux and Niestlé, 1998). He then turned to the links between indirect argumentation, enunciative erasure and points of view (*Argumenter en racontant*, Deboeck-Duculot, 2004, *Homo Narrans, Pour une analyse énonciative et inter-*

actionnelle du récit (2 vol.), Lambert-Lucas, 2008). He also works on tropes based on the notion of point of view (*Langue française* 160, *Le Français Moderne* 79(1), *Vox romanica* 71 and 74, *Tranel* 61–62 and two articles in the series DWP 2 and 4). He has also published numerous articles on religious discourse and media discourse, on questions of responsibility and enunciative stance as well as on corpora of oral interaction in didactic contexts identifying different instances of co-, over- and under-enunciation at the intersection of cognitive, enunciative and interactional issues. See also: http://www.icar.cnrs.fr/membres/arabatel.

Anda Rădulescu (Universitatea din Craiova)

Anda Rădulescu is a professor in the Department of French in the Faculty of Letters at the University of Craiova, Romania. She has written three books on translation studies and four on French syntax and has published approximately 100 articles in national and international peer-reviewed journals. She has participated in about 30 international conferences. Since 2013 she has focused on studying various forms of humor and the mechanisms of puns. In 2017 she co-organized an international conference in Craiova on the humor in San-Antonio's novels, in whose work she takes a special interest. She is editor-in-chief of the *Annals of the University of Craiova. Series Romance Languages and Literatures*, a member of the scientific committee of the journals *Translations* (West University of Timișoara), *Colocvium* (Craiova), *Argotica* (University of Craiova) and *Annals of the University of Craiova, Series: Philology, Applied Foreign Languages* (all of them peer-reviewed).

Lisa Roques (Université Bordeaux Montaigne)

Lisa Roques' PhD Thesis (in Ancient History, Languages and Literature) is devoted to the fragmentary works of Ion of Chios, a polymath writer of the 5th century B.C. In this research, historical and political aspects meet literary and stylistic analysis. These different aspects can be seen in two publications (De Cimon à Périclès: un regard insulaire. In *Elite und Krise in antiken Gesellschaften/Élites et crises dans les sociétés antiques*, Collegium Beatus Rhenanus, Vol. 5, 47–57. Stuttgart: Franz Steiner Verlag, 2016; Ion à la table d'Athénée. In S. Trousselard and S. Coin-Longeray (eds.), *Les intentions de la citation. Les Cahiers d'ALLHiS* 4, 2016, 37–58) or in a number of papers (Quelques vers de Chios..., Internationale Konferenz: "Die literarische Form", Westfälische Wilhelms-Universität, Münster, October 2015; L'homme qui ne savait pas jouer de la cithare: rumeur et arborescence d'Ion de Chios à Saint Augustin, Journée d'étude: "Trames arborescentes II", Tours, December 2016). Having obtained her *agrégation* (qualification to teach at upper secondary or university level) in Classical Letters, she has a full-time job in a secondary school in an Educational Priority Area near Paris.

Catherine Ruchon (Université Paul-Valéry–Montpellier III, Membre associé du laboratoire Pléiade)

A doctor in language sciences specializing in discourse analysis, who teaches at Paul-Valéry Montpellier III, Catherine Ruchon studies the expression of suffering, in various fields, mainly that of motherhood, birth, and mourning. The subject of her doctoral thesis was: "On the Analgesic Virtues of Discourse? The expression of Pain and Attachment in the Discourse on Maternity" (2015, directed by Marie-Anne Paveau). More broadly, her current research themes are animal discourse analysis, funeral discourse analysis (about humans and animals), identity discourse, folk linguistics, digital discourse analysis, interactivity and ethics. She has written several articles on these subjects including: Lexique, catégorisation et représentation: les reformulations métalinguistiques dans le discours animaliste (*Les carnets du Cediscor*, numéro spécial, 2018, forthcoming); Une situation d'interlocution spécifique: les discours numériques du parent endeuillé à son enfant décédé (*Semen* 45, 2018, forthcoming); L'être et le nom: éthique de la nomination dans le cadre du deuil perinatal (*Langage & Société* 163, 2018, 101–119); Identité numérique de parents endeuillés. Le pseudonyme comme pratique de deuil (in: Thierry Guilbert and Pascaline Lefort, eds., *Discours et (re)constructions identitaires*, Presses Universitaires du Septentrion, 2017, 133–148).

Aurélie Rusterholtz (actor / director, Paris)

After leaving drama school at the National Theater in Strasbourg (École Nationale d'Art Dramatique du T.N.S.) in 1993, Aurélie Rusterholtz has acted mainly in Ibsen (*Hedda Gabler*, directed by Gloria Paris), Maeterlinck (*Pelléas et Mélisande*, directed by Pierre Guillois), Marivaux (*La Fausse Suivante*, directed by Gloria Paris), Molière (*Les Femmes savantes*, directed by Isabelle Moreau and Gloria Paris), Destouches (*Les Philosophes amoureux*, directed by Jean-Marie Villégier), Emmanuel Bourdieu (*Je crois?*, directed by Denis Podalydès) but has also appeared in works by Seneca, Brecht and many more. Knowing sign language, she acted in *K. Lear*, a special performance in French and sign language which was produced by Marie Montegani and directed by Emmanuelle Laborit in 2007 at the International Visual Theater in Paris and then also toured in

Korea. In 2011, she participated in the re-creation of *Arlequin sauvage* by Delisle de la Drevetière (directed ed by Thierry Pillon) in Quebec. From 2004 to 2012, Aurélie Rusterholtz accepted the annual invitations to the Grand T in Nantes for the lecture performances of rare texts from the 17th and 18th centuries. At first she performed alone, but from 2007, she appeared with François Chaix. She has acted in films by Claudio Descalzi (*Ghost in the Machine*), Luc Besson (*Adèle Blansec*) and Emmanuel Bourdieu (*Edouard Drumont*). In 2014, she founded the LESGENSDU4AVRIL in Paris, a theater with an adjoining drama school, where she co-directed *Spectacle Eclair* in 2015, acted in *Satyrics* after Jean-Claude Grumberg (directed by F. Chaix) in 2016 and co-directed *Travaux* after *Musée haut – musée bas* by Jean Michel Ribes in 2017 and *Regardez le soleil pour moi...* after *La mastication des morts* by Patrick Kermann in 2018.

Jean-François Sablayrolles (Université Paris 13)

After obtaining the *agrégation* (qualification to teach at higher secondary or university level) in grammar, Jean-François Sablayrolles went on to defend a doctoral thesis on the neology of contemporary French (University Paris 8 in 1996). He was appointed to a lectureship at the University of Limoges (1997–2002), then at University Paris 7 (2002–2005). He completed a habilitation (post-doctoral degree) in 2004 and became a full professor at University Paris 13 (Sorbonne Paris Cité). He has been a member of the following research teams: CERES at Limoges, CIEL at Paris 7, LDI UMR 7187 then HTL UMR 7597. His major research interest is the neology of contemporary French, in particular borrowings and their native equivalents. In 2000 he published *La Néologie en français contemporain* (Champion), then *Les néologismes* (with Jean Pruvost, Collection "Que sais-je?", PUF, 2003, 3rd ed. 2016), *L'innovation lexicale* (Champion, 2003, the proceedings of the conference held at Limoges 2001), *La fabrique des mots français* (Lambert Lucas 2016, the proceedings of the conference held at Cerisy 2015, with C. Jacquet-Pfau), *Les néologismes, créer des mots français aujourd'hui* (Garnier/le Monde, 2017). In 2006 he founded the journal *Neologica* (Classiques Garnier), which he co-edits with John Humbley.

Astrid Schmiedel (Sorbisches Institut – Serbski Institut Bautzen)

Astrid Schmiedel studied phonetics and computational linguistics at Trier University, where she obtained her Ph. D. in 2016 with a thesis on the phonetics of ironic speech. From 2010 to 2014 she worked as a research assistant in the phonetics department at this university. After various administrative positions in the civil service, in 2018 she joined the Sorbian Institute – Serbski Institut in

Bautzen. In the domain of scientific data processing she deals with topics related to automatic language processing, digitization processes and corpus linguistics with a special focus on the two minority languages Lower Sorbian and Upper Sorbian.

Monika Schmitz-Emans (Ruhr-Universität Bochum)
Monika Schmitz-Emans holds the chair of General and Comparative Literature Studies at Ruhr-University Bochum. She graduated from the University of Bonn with a degree in German Studies, Philosophy, Italian Studies, and Esthetics. She published her doctoral dissertation *Schnupftuchsknoten oder Sternbild: Jean Pauls Ansätze zu einer Theorie der Sprache* in 1986, which was followed by her habilitation (post-doctoral degree) thesis *Schrift und Abwesenheit: Historische Paradigmen zu einer Poetik der Entzifferung und des Schreibens* in 1995. She has numerous publications on literature from the 18th to the 21st century, on the relation between text and image in literature, on questions concerning literary theory, and on the literary forms of the book. Her latest publications include *Literatur-Comics. Adaptationen und Transformationen der Weltliteratur* (2012); *Komparatistik sprachhomogener Räume. Konzepte, Methoden, Fallstudien* (co-edited with Natalia Bakshi and Dirk Kemper, 2017).

Gesa Schole (Eberhard Karls Universität Tübingen and Universität Trier)
Gesa Schole has a degree in Translation Studies (Portuguese, Spanish, Law) from Ruprecht-Karls-University Heidelberg and a degree in Language Sciences from the University of Bremen. During her studies abroad at Universidade Nova de Lisboa, Portugal, she focused on African and Portuguese Literature. In her diploma thesis, she analyzed the German translation of Mia Couto's romance *A varanda do frangipani*. At the Universities of Tübingen and Trier she taught translation, sociolinguistics, ambiguity and pragmatics, and she is completing a PhD on *Ambiguity at the Semantics-Pragmatics-Interface in Spanish and German Dialogues* within the Research Training Group (GRK 1808) "Ambiguity: Production and Perception" at the University of Tübingen. Her research interests range from cognitive linguistics, spatial cognition and prepositions to pragmatic meaning, the study of dialogues and ambiguity.

Françoise Sullet-Nylander (University of Stockholm)
Françoise Sullet-Nylander is a Professor of French Linguistics and Discourse Analysis at the Department of Romance Studies and Classics at the University of Stockholm. Since her doctoral thesis, she has published a number of scientific

articles focusing on the problems of reported speech, rephrasing and wordplay in journalistic texts. She has also co-edited several books: *Le français parlé des médias* (2007), *La linguistique dans tous les sens* (2011), *Discours rapporté, genre(s) et médias* (2014), *Le discours rapporté: une question de genre?* (2015) and *Political Discourses at the Extremes: Expressions of Populism in Romance Speaking Countries* (Forthcoming). Her recent studies have dealt with journalists' questioning strategies in political debates, terms of address and denominations in French presidential debates, as well as with the phenomena of enunciative heterogeneities in journalistic texts. Since 2014, she conducts an interdisciplinary research project on Political Discourses in Romance Speaking countries (ROMPOL).

Giovanni Tallarico (Università degli studi di Verona)

Giovanni Tallarico is an assistant professor at the University of Verona. His interests and publications are in lexicology (focusing on neologisms and lexical borrowings), bilingual lexicography, sports vocabulary and translation studies. In 2013 he co-edited an issue of *Études de linguistique appliquée* (*Les dictionnaires bilingues et l'interculturel* 170, April–June 2013) and is the author of *La dimension interculturelle du dictionnaire bilingue* (Paris: Champion, 2016). He is a partner in Néoveille, an international project coordinated by Emmanuel Cartier (Université Paris 13 – Sorbonne Paris Cité), a platform designed to identify, analyse and follow up neologisms in seven languages.

Verena Thaler (Universität Mannheim)

Verena Thaler holds a PhD in linguistics from the University of Salzburg and is currently working as a Postdoctoral Research Fellow in Romance Linguistics at the University of Mannheim. Her research interests include pragmatics, linguistic politeness, media communication with a special focus on computer-mediated communication, interactional linguistics, and pragmatic particles. She has published numerous works in these fields, including two books on computer mediated communication (*Chat-Kommunikation im Spannungsfeld zwischen Oralität und Literalität*, 2003; *Sprachliche Höflichkeit in computervermittelter Kommunikation*, 2012) and various papers in international journals. She has also co-edited a book on the onomastics of product names and brand names (*Kontrastive Ergonymie. Romanistische Studien zu Produkt- und Warennamen*, 2013) and another on current developments in media communication (*Medienlinguistik 3.0. Formen und Wirkung von Textsorten im Zeitalter des Social Web*, 2016).

Esme Winter-Froemel (Universität Trier)

Esme Winter-Froemel is Professor of Romance linguistics at Trier University. Her research interests include language change, contact linguistics, lexical semantics and ambiguity (see among others her monograph on lexical borrowing, *Entlehnung in der Kommunikation und im Sprachwandel. Theorie und Analysen zum Französischen*, 2011, and the co-edited volumes *Diskurstraditionelles und Einzelsprachliches im Sprachwandel / Tradicionalidad discursiva e idiomaticidad en los procesos de cambio lingüístico*, 2015, with Araceli López Serena, Álvaro Octavio de Toledo y Huerta and Barbara Frank-Job, and *Cognitive Contact Linguistics*, in press, with Eline Zenner and Ad Backus). In her recent research she focuses on semantic and pragmatic changes in lexical borrowing as well as on the role of ambiguity and discourse traditions in language change. Another main research interest is the domain of wordplay. Since 2013, she has directed the scientific network "The Dynamics of Wordplay: Language Contact, Linguistic Innovation, Speaker-Hearer-Interaction" funded by the German Research Foundation (DFG). In addition, she is a member of the Graduate Research Training Group "Ambiguity – Production and Perception" (Graduiertenkolleg / GRK 1808, Universität Tübingen).

Ilias Yocaris (Université Côte d'Azur)

Born in 1971, Ilias Yocaris is a senior lecturer in French Literature at the UCA (Université Côte d'Azur). His research interests include the French novel of the 19th–21st centuries (Hugo, Zola, Roussel, Proust, Giono, Robbe-Grillet, Simon, Littell), literary semiotics and conceptual foundations of postmodern fictions (literary and cinematic). He has published, among others, *L'Impossible totalité: une étude de la complexité dans l'œuvre de Claude Simon* (Toronto, Paratexte, 2002) and *Style et semiosis littéraire* (Paris, Classiques Garnier, "Investigations stylistiques", 2016).

Eline Zenner (KU Leuven)

Eline Zenner is an assistant professor at KU Leuven (Campus Brussel), where she teaches Dutch proficiency to future interpreters, translators, experts in multilingual communication and journalists. She studied Germanic Languages (Dutch-English) at KU Leuven (MA 2007). In March 2013, she defended her PhD thesis, titled "Cognitive Contact Linguistics. The macro, meso, and micro influence of English on Dutch". Her research interests include the cross-fertilization of usage-based Cognitive Linguistics and contact linguistics, acquisitional perspectives to variation between standard and vernacular language variants and semantic differentiation in lexical variation, which she studies from both fundamental and applied perspectives.

www.ingramcontent.com/pod-product-compliance
Lightning Source LLC
Chambersburg PA
CBHW031800220426
43662CB00007B/472